THE DIARY OF VIKENTY ANGAROV

THE DIARY OF VIKENTY ANGAROV

BY VICTOR MURAVIN

Translated from the Russian
by Alan Thomas

NEWSWEEK BOOKS, New York

Original edition privately published under the title *Aurora Borealis*, copyright © 1975 by Victor Muravin. All rights reserved. No part of this book may be reproduced or utilized in any form or by any means, electronic or mechanical, including photocopying, recording or by an information storage and retrieval system, without permission in writing from the publisher. Inquiries should be addressed to Newsweek Books, 444 Madison Avenue, New York, N.Y. 10022. Published simultaneously in Canada by Prentice-Hall of Canada Ltd., 1870 Birchmount Road, Scarborough, Ontario.

Printed in the United States of America.

First Edition 1978

Library of Congress Catalog in Publication Data

Muravin, Victor
The diary of Vikenty Angarov.

(Newsweek books)
Illustrations by Ernst Niezvestny.
Includes map and glossary.
1. Russia, 1937–1954—Historical Fiction.   I. Title.
PZ4.M97385Di [PG3483.3.U73] 891.7'3'44
ISBN 0-88225-254-2
77-89148

Book Design: Joyce Weston

To Russia

CONTENTS

PART ONE: The Forest

PART TWO: Gold

INTERNATIONAL BOUNDARY
AS OF 1937

BOUNDARY OF AREAS
CLAIMED BY INCORPORATIO[N]
BY U.S.S.R. IN 1939 AND 194[0]

SWEDEN

FINLAND

Helsinki

ESTHONIAN
S.S.R.
Ta[llinn]

LATVIA

Murmansk

BARENTS
SEA

NOVAYA ZEMLYA

Leningrad
Petrozavodsk

KARELO-FINNISH
S.S.R.

Archangel

Smolensk

Vologda

Yaroslavl

MOSCOW

Ivanovo

KOMI A.S.S.R.

Vorkuta

Ryazan

Syktyvkar

R U S S I A N

Gorki

MORDVIN

Tambov

MARI A.S.S.R.

Kirov

Kazan

UDMURT
A.S.S.R.

TATAR
A.S.S.R.

Izhevsk

Molotov

S O V I E T

Saratov

Volga R.

Kuibyshev

BASHKIR

Ufa

Sverdlovsk

KRAS[NOYARSK]

A.S.S.R.

Chelyabinsk

Ob R.

Ural R.

Tobol R.

Irtysh R.

F E D

Guryev

Aktyubinsk

Kustanai

K A Z A K H

Omsk

Ob R.

Yenisei R.

U
KARAKAL
PAK

ARAL
SEA

S

S

R

Akmolinsk

Novosibirsk

Kra[snoyarsk]

Kraslag
Prison Camp

TURKMEN

ASSR

Karaganda

Medvezhie
Village

Yenisei R.

[Ashk]abad

Semipalatinsk

K R A I

Balkhash

Ust Kamenogorsk

TANNU T[UVA]

L. BALKHASH

250   500   750   1000
MILES

⋯·⋯·⋯ BOUNDARY OF UNION
           REPUBLIC (S.S.R.)

──────── BOUNDARY OF AUTONOMOUS
           SOVIET SOCIALIST REPUBLIC

─ ─ ─ ─ BOUNDARY OF KRAI

┼─┼─┼─┼ RAILROAD (SELECTED)

NORTH LAND

L A P T E V
S E A

Pevek

Y A K U T S K

Kolyma R.

Indigirka R.

K R A I

A.

S. S. R.

Kolyma
Gold Fields

Magadan

OYARSK

R A T E D

Lena R.

S O C I A L I S T

Vilyuisk

Yakutsk

Aldan R.

Lena R.

K H A B A R O V S K   R E P U B L I C

Angara R.

Nikolaevsk

B A I K A L

M O N G O L A S S R

Irkutsk

Ulan-Ude

Chita

Sretensk

Amur R.

CHINA

Birobidzhan

Khabarovsk

ME KRAI

CHINA

BURYAT

PREFACE

A striking feature of Victor Muravin's book, *The Diary of Vikenty Angarov,* is that it does not focus on any of the traditional themes dominant in works of fiction. It is not concerned primarily with romantic love, generational conflict, adventure, or mores. Nor does it touch upon other themes that Soviet writers might be expected to find intriguing, such as the impact upon the population of rapid industrialization or the horrors of the Second World War. Like so much of the prose written by Russians during the past decade and a half, the plot of the book turns on arbitrary arrest, exile, slave labor camps, the will to survive in the face of incredible adversity. Significantly, the agonies of the main character, Vikenty, result neither from accidental events nor the ill will of isolated individuals, but rather from the very nature of the Soviet government, which for the last five decades has held the entire population, now numbering some 240 million, in a state of subjugation.

Actually, Muravin's book cannot be characterized simply as fiction, although it is partly that. It also contains elements of both biography and history. According to the author, every major event is based on incidents that actually occurred in Russia in the years from 1937 to 1954, though no one character participated in all of them. Essentially, the book constitutes a synthesis of the experiences of a large number of people. The single most important source was a captain in the merchant marine, the hero of the book, whom Muravin named Vikenty Angarov. Angarov wrote autobiographical sketches which, for reasons of security, he hid in

11

jars in a cowshed. Muravin, a close friend of the captain, read these sketches, and often talked with him about his experiences.

The picture the author draws of official arbitrariness, human misery, sadism on the part of officials, and occasional acts of kindness by officers in the labor camps rings true. There is nothing in the many eye-witness accounts and historical studies already published—Solzhenitsyn's is only the most famous—that would lead one to question the essential authenticity of Muravin's portrayal. But the reading of *The Diary of Vikenty Angarov* is made particularly poignant by the fact that it dwells on the suffering of a single person. Of course, it is impossible to understand Stalinism without descriptions of the Soviet system of government and statistical information on how many perished from its excesses; but ultimately, numbers and analyses of political structures are too impersonal to convey fully the extent of the human suffering caused by Stalin. Most of us find it easier to identify with the anguish of one man than to sympathize with the plight of millions.

Captain Angarov's experiences stagger the imagination. Arrested in 1936 on trumped-up charges of spying for Japan, he was sent to a slave labor camp. At the same time the police arrested his wife for being married to an "enemy of the people" and sent her to another camp, where she soon died from brucellosis. Their young son was sent to a children's home. An incredibly strong person, physically as well as spiritually, Angarov adjusted to camp life and rose to the position of "technical chief," which meant that he administered the internal affairs of the camp. He fell in love with a sensitive young woman inmate and, despite the horrible conditions, they developed a touching and tender relationship.

Except for a single year of freedom, Angarov spent seventeen years as a captive of the Soviet system.

In itself, Muravin's account of human torment cannot fail to move the reader, but appreciation of *The Diary of Vikenty Angarov* will be heightened by the realization that the incidents related in the book were not occasional or accidental occurrences. There were, indeed, millions who endured fates similar to that of the hero of Muravin's book.

When the Bolsheviks (soon to be known as Communists) under Lenin took power in 1917, the expectation was widespread that the Russian people would at last be freed from the political oppression and poverty that had been their lot for centuries. But optimism quickly gave way to disappointment. The Bolsheviks, representing a small minority of the population and facing strong opposition to their socialist policies, proceeded to establish a one-party state. By 1921 all non-Communist parties were outlawed and many critics of the regime were either exiled or imprisoned. Still, although the Russian people endured many hardships, most citizens not directly involved in politics remained unmolested.

The critical change took place in 1928, when Stalin emerged as victor from the four-year struggle for power that had erupted after Lenin's unexpected death. Unlike the other men at the helm of the Communist party, Stalin was neither an original thinker nor a gifted orator. He was a plodder. But he possessed other qualities that can be decisive in furthering a politician's career. He was crafty, opportunistic, highly intelligent, and an outstanding administrator. Readily accessible to party officials in the lower ranks and eager to help them, Stalin put many of these bureaucrats in his debt. This was crucial in the intraparty struggle and enabled him to defeat his more renowned rivals.

Once in power, Stalin did not take long to set his own course. In 1928 he began to advocate a Five Year Plan designed to bring about rapid industrialization of Russia. What has come to be known as Soviet totalitarianism was in large measure an outgrowth of Stalin's decision to transform Russia into a powerful industrial country in which all the means of production would be owned by the state and the entire labor force would be employed by the state.

Fanatically committed to the creation of a new society, Stalin resorted to a maximum use of force to secure obedience to his orders. Peasants who resisted collectivization of their lands were sent to remote areas of the country or surrounded by troops and shot. Many peasants, realizing that they could not prevent collectivization, vented their anger by destroying crops, smashing tools, and slaughtering their cattle. Better to enjoy a few good meals than hand the animals over to the state. Stalin himself admitted that within four years Russia lost over half its cattle and horses and two-thirds of its sheep and goats. In addition, large tracts of land remained untilled. The upshot was that in 1932-33 Russia suffered a terrible famine. It has been estimated that collectivization and the famine caused the deaths of at least five million people.

In urban centers draconian measures of a different sort were introduced to goad laborers into more disciplined work habits. Any laborer who missed a day's work without a legitimate excuse was to be fired and ejected from his lodgings, a punishment that often meant starvation. After 1931 the authorities assumed the power to assign a worker to a job anywhere in the country, and a passport system was established to regulate the movement of citizens from one city to another. The state now also dominated all institutions: labor unions, the church, schools, the press, radio, to mention but a few. But the most distinctive feature of Soviet totalitarianism was the state's systematic use of terror against its own population.

To safeguard his position of leadership, Stalin began rooting out all potential opposition. The "war against the nation" now moved into high gear. Many revered leaders of the Communist party were brought to trial for alleged crimes: plotting with foreign powers to overthrow Stalin and restore capitalism, conspiring to dismember Russia by promising to cede large areas to Germany and Japan. Several of the accused confessed and were shot. Others were executed even without benefit of a show trial. Hundreds of thousands of rank and file Communists and millions of non-Communists were sent to slave labor camps.

In order to cloak the terror with an aura of legitimacy, the government urged citizens to denounce anyone who strayed in the slightest from the official line on issues or made an even remotely critical comment about Stalin. People would denounce colleagues, friends, wives, parents, in part because they believed that this was one way of protecting themselves against arrest. Some no doubt did so from a sense of duty. We know of one Communist who denounced no less than 230 people. Thus, many ordinary citizens became accomplices in the vast campaign of terror. Moreover, the average Russian, fearful that the expression of an opinion might lead to arrest, became distrustful of all acquaintances, friends, and even closest relatives. The result was the atomization of society, a condition under which the individual felt that he could confide in no one and that he must render total loyalty to Stalin, and only to him.

For most of those placed under arrest, the trial, if they had one at all, was a mockery of judicial procedure. One survivor of a labor camp revealed that she was declared guilty after a trial of seven minutes. It took the court two minutes to deliberate before pronouncing judgment, although twenty minutes were needed to type up the long list of charges. Alexander Solzhenitsyn relates an incident that occurred in 1945 at the Novosibirsk Transit Prison, which sheds further light on the Stalinist judicial system. The chief of the convoy guards was interested in a particular prisoner who had been sentenced to a twenty-five year term in a labor camp. "What did you get it for?" he asked. "For nothing at all." "You're lying. *The sentence for nothing at all is ten years.*"

The terror struck citizens in every walk of life, but those who occupied high positions in Soviet institutions were in the greatest jeopardy. A few statistics will tell the tale: 98 of the 139 members and candidates elected to the Central Committee of the Communist Party at the 17th Party Congress in 1934 were shot within four years; 90 per cent of all generals and 80 per cent of all colonels were liquidated. Probably more than one-half of the entire officer corps of 35,000 was arrested.

The accuracy of these statistics has been officially confirmed by the Soviet government. We do not have such reliable information on how the terror affected the population at large. But scholars estimate that in the years from 1936 to 1950 the slave labor camps had an average population of eight million. In the course of those fourteen years twelve million people probably died as a result of the harsh climate, totally inadequate diet, long hours of hard, physical labor, and primitive medical services. During the same period about one million Russians were summarily executed. If we add to these figures the five million who perished because of collectivization and famine, we find that Stalin's policies caused the loss of life of eighteen million Russians. This is in every respect a conservative figure.

The following statistic affords yet another insight into the reach of Stalin's terror: by late 1938 no less than five per cent of the population had been arrested at one time or another. This means that on the average a member of one-half of the country's families had been imprisoned. It therefore seems inconceivable that anyone could have remained unaffected by the terror, though probably few understood the full extent of its sweep.

What possessed Stalin? Why did he wage such a ruthless war against his own people? Such western leaders as Winston Churchill and Franklin Roosevelt, who met the Soviet dictator several times, never thought him so irrational as to classify him as insane. On the contrary, they found him well-informed, shrewd, and an able defender of Soviet interests.

Stalin was clearly a fanatic, convinced that he alone possessed the truth about Russia's needs and that anyone who opposed him must be perverse. That he was also touched by megalomania is borne out by his insistence that he be regarded as the fountainhead of all creative achievements. Furthermore, he was deeply distrustful of his colleagues in the Communist party, many of whom considered him a usurper and believed that the hardships caused by his policies could not but engender grumbling among many sectors of the population. "Everywhere and in everything he saw 'enemies,' 'two-facers' and 'spies,'" said Khrushchev. Khrushchev also quoted a comment made to him in 1937-38 by Nikolai Bulganin, then prime minister of the Russian Federated Republic: "It has happened sometimes that a man goes to Stalin on his invitation as a friend. And, when he sits with Stalin, he does not know where he will be sent next—home or to jail."

But Stalin may also have been moved to launch the terror by a cold, rational calculation. He probably realized that under a totalitarian system of rule, in which the state attempts to control the citizen's thoughts and actions in every sphere of endeavor, everyone is potentially disloyal. By and large, people are simply not prepared or able to subordinate themselves totally to the state. Under the circumstances, the only way the regime could feel completely secure was to so terrorize the population that no one would dare consciously to defy the will of the dictator.

Victor Muravin belongs to the first generation of Russians to have been brought up entirely under Stalinism. Born in 1929 in Vladivostok, in the Soviet Far East, he spent his youth in the country as an agricultural laborer and horse wrangler. A member of the Pioneers and the Komsomol, the Communist youth organizations, he had grown up an ardent follower of the regime and of Stalin. But his father, an agronomist on a state farm, was imprisoned in 1937 as a German spy and although his father survived the purge and was later released, young Muravin no longer enjoyed the regime's political trust. As a result, when he joined the merchant marine in 1945, "straight from the saddle," he was denied the freedom to sail abroad. He spent nine years in the Soviet Pacific and Arctic as a deck boy, sailor, and radio officer, but was repeatedly dismissed from ships bound for foreign ports.

There followed hard years "on shore," when Muravin was either unemployed or worked as a stevedore. Meanwhile, he studied. Having attended two merchant marine colleges, he began furthering his education on his own, learning English, attending a teacher's training college, and eventually finding work as an English teacher, translator, and lecturer in American and English studies. He became associate professor and head of his department at a college and wrote two text books of English that were used at about three hundred colleges throughout the Soviet Union.

Still, Muravin's relations with the regime remained strained. In the late 1960's he moved to Moscow to arrange a trip to the United States for his ailing mother, who had sought a visa for over twenty years to visit a brother she had not seen for half a century. As Muravin tells it, the Russian secret police, "sensing a possible scandal," at last permitted her to leave. But shortly after his mother's departure, the KGB "secretly" declared Muravin an "enemy of Soviet power" and ordered his confinement in a lunatic asylum, a frequent punishment meted out to citizens suspected of disloyalty. "I didn't want to spend my days saying 'cock-a-doodle-do,'" says Muravin, "so I procured a cyanide pill and was ready to die if I was arrested." Fortunately, friends in Moscow intervened on his behalf and persuaded the KGB to revoke the sentence.

But by this time, says Muravin, "all my patience and possibilities had been exhausted." He began to think of emigrating. He requested political asylum from two foreign embassies, but was refused. For this indiscretion he was interrogated for five days by the KGB. Muravin persisted by petitioning the Presidium of the Supreme Soviet of the USSR for an exit visa to the United States or any other country where he would be able to join the merchant marine.

"I did not want to emigrate," he says. "I loved Russia. It is my land. I tilled it, suffered with it. It saved me twice from starvation. I left my sweat in it. But on this land I lived my life in poverty and serfdom. I decided to emigrate in order to go back to sea and regain my personal freedom. For this I gave up everything that was dear to me. I lost my friends, my adopted son, my wife, my land, my forty-two years of life. I had to begin again from zero."

It took the authorities a year to decide on Muravin's request. While he waited he earned his living as a private tutor and worked on the manuscripts he had started when he first arrived in Moscow. He completed a nine-hundred-page typescript on the "ordinary Soviet citizen" and the first two volumes of a trilogy on the life of Captain Angarov. The first volume of the trilogy deals with the period from 1914 to 1937 and the third, which he wrote in the West, covers the years from 1955 to the death of Angarov in 1970. *The Diary of Vikenty Angarov*, the second volume in the series, is so far the only volume to have been translated. Muravin took extraordinary precautions to prevent the KGB from seeing his writings. He buried the manuscript on the Soviet citizen in a park near his home. By the time he wrote the present volume he was so closely watched by the police that burial seemed too risky. He would write during the day and burn his work at night, having committed the text to memory. He left the USSR in 1972. On the part of the authorities his emigration was a form of political exile. Unable to return to sea for health reasons, he concentrated instead on his writing. His "pent-up hatred for the Communist system," he has said, "needed release."

Muravin lived in Europe for a year before moving to the United States, where he was finally able to clear his head of the ideas that had been drummed into him during the first forty-odd years of his life: "My head was full of isms: Marxism, Stalinism, Socialism, Communism, Collectivism. I simply could not live under that burden."

Muravin now lives in New York City. While waiting for his health to improve so that he can return to sea he has been working as a translator and studying for a doctorate in political science.

In an understandable reaction against his Soviet experience, Muravin now strives to be apolitical. Indeed, he insists that he "does not consider his books anti-Soviet or anti-Communist." He writes "simply for history, so that posterity may know at what cost the Soviet system was built." In a few decades it may be possible to read *The Diary of Vikenty Angarov* with the dispassion the author favors. But Muravin may be asking too much of the contemporary reader, who is aware that even now the Soviet system, despite the liberalization it has undergone during the past twenty years, still has little respect for human rights.

We cannot escape the fact that the awesome presence of Stalin is still very much a part of our collective memory, and Muravin's treatment of the dictator is bound to stir up that memory. Like other Soviet writers—most notably Solzhenitsyn—he feels obliged to probe Stalin's psychology in depth. Somehow he must try to understand how it all could have happened. In the book too, Vikenty is obsessed by his hatred of the dead leader. After gaining his freedom, he is overcome with a desire to spit on Stalin's body in the Lenin mausoleum. What occurs when Vikenty finally reaches the mausoleum is rather interesting, but I will leave it to the reader to find this out for himself.

Even though *The Diary of Vikenty Angarov* can probably not be read with detached curiosity, the book does suggest that the Stalinist system was less effective than is often assumed in crushing the sensibilities of the Russian people. Despite the ghastliness of life in the labor camps, some inmates and even a few guards retained a basic decency. Many officials sought to mitigate the suffering of the prisoners, and many inmates tried to make the best of things in the hope of a better future. They would help each other in times of special crisis and sometimes fell in love. In short, they did not give in to despair. Even at its worst, Stalinism did not fully succeed in breaking the human spirit. This may not deter future tyrants from attempting to create a totalitarian system, but it should give heart to those who are determined to resist.

Abraham Ascher

Chevy Chase, Maryland
August 1977

Abraham Ascher, Professor of History at Brooklyn College of the City University of New York, specializes in modern Russian history. He is currently director of the Division of Education Programs of the National Endowment for the Humanities.

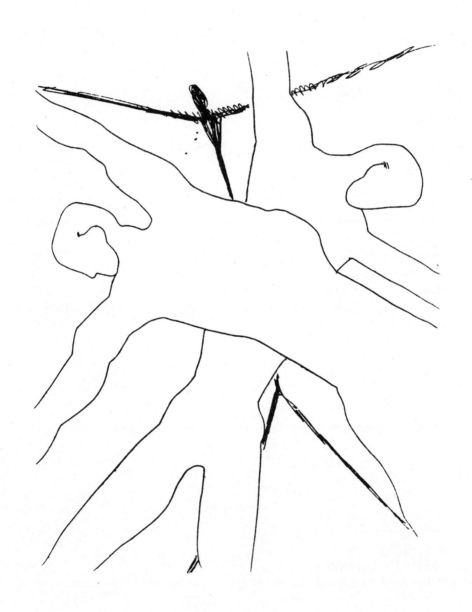

PART ONE: THE FOREST

1

IN THE TAIGA

For hundreds of years, Siberia has served as an unfenced prison. Thousands of exiles in chains have clanked their way here along a six-foot-wide strip of flat stones, called the Great–Siberian Road, which began near Moscow and ran eastward through Europe and on into the depths of Asian Siberia. From this road a whole country stretched for thousands of kilometers in all directions: countless fir and spruce, under whose dense cover lay an eternal gloom and dampness. This impenetrable taiga began ten meters from the road. No inexperienced traveler could find a way along its paths: paths made by wild beasts and choked with branches blown down by the wind or blocked by the half-rotted trunks of fallen trees. He would die of hunger or cold, or be torn to pieces by a predator. The wild boar, the wolf, and the lynx shared this kingdom of silence and peace, yielding only to the bear—the lord of the taiga—or to some hunter in search of pelts.

The crystal waters of mountain streams flowed down the hillsides and gradually merged into powerful rivers feeding the great Yenisei and Angara rivers and Lake Baikal. Scattered along their banks were taiga villages, consisting of a score or so of cabins built of thick logs and inhabited by either Russian or local hunters, the latter the descendants of once-powerful Mongol tribes. In summer they fished the rivers and in winter went into the taiga to trap for pelts, which they sold at their taverns to traveling merchants who passed them along to auctions in St. Petersburg, London, and Paris.

The first locomotive of the Great Siberian Railroad broke the age-old silence of the taiga at the turn of the century, pulling toward the rising sun a string of rickety passenger and freight cars—heralds of the abrupt changes that were to take place in the decades to come. The taiga would receive thousands of new exiles and settlers. Like mushrooms after rain, hundreds of strange new settlements sprang up.

The saws buzzed, the axes rang out, and with a sound like a deep sigh the giants of the forest crashed to the ground and were dispatched west as logs for the great construction sites of communism. Barely discernible dirt roads stretched like thin threads from the camps to the felling areas in the depths of the taiga. Once used, the roads quickly faded and a new growth sprang up in place of the felled trees, as if eager to cover up the traces of the activity of man, the unwelcome visitor.

In winter, cold reigns. The frost cracks the bark on the trees; the hare runs his loops, leaving an intricate pattern understood only by the fox and the wolf; the squirrel springs from branch to branch, showering the ground with snow and the shells of nuts; the bear sleeps in his warm lair, his paw in his mouth, waiting for the spring and new life.

But now the winter is over. The hot Siberian summer has set in and the taiga heat is intense. The sun blazes down mercilessly, as if seeking revenge for the long months of freezing autumn and ferocious winter.

At the tops of the hills the forest gives way to rock. Directly to the south there are other hills, then others, smaller and more distant: the foothills of the Sayan Mountains, stretching away to the horizon like innumerable green dunes. The light-blue sky is cloudless, filled with sun.

Upon the slopes of the hills mighty cedars and pines climb to the summits in even ranks like ancient warriors. A thick layer of half-rotted leaves and pine needles and cones covers the ground beneath the trees. The beasts of the forest move noiselessly across it, the hunter sleeps on it, in no danger of getting wet, for the rainwater immediately filters through, leaving the soft upper layer always slightly damp, but warm. Here in the half-light it is cool. Small glades and clearings among the trees are covered with tall grass, up to a yard high. Briars and woody nightshade, cloudberry and the ancient fern, feathergrass, daisies and bright-red poppies, and hundreds of other flowers grow together in harmony, stretching thirstily upward to the sun to drink in its life-giving rays, filling the air with a stupefying fragrance. It is the hot summer of 1937.

Vikenty was lying in the grass near the top of a hill, exposed to the sun, with only his head in the shade of a cedar. Below him the other zeks were also sunning themselves on the grass. They had removed their dark-gray jackets and were lying in baggy prison trousers, which were made of a kind of material that could go for several years without washing. A lieutenant and four soldiers with dogs were positioned on a flat rock on the summit of the hill, from which they had an excellent view of the hillside as it sloped into a hollow. The guards were also taking a rest. The dogs were breathing heavily as they slept, their red tongues hanging out with the heat. The soldiers had stripped to the waist and were sunning themselves as they smoked hand-rolled cigarettes and talked.

Vikenty plucked a blade of grass. A caterpillar was crawling up a green stalk. Where was it going? Did it have a goal and a direction? He nudged it gently. The caterpillar froze, merging completely with the stalk. He picked it off with difficulty and ran the blade of grass along its green, ridged back. The caterpillar did not move. It wanted to live.

He regarded it with a smile. A little to the right he noticed a spider. It busied itself for a long time right underneath the head of a flower, attaching something, then it sprang boldly down like a mountaineer and hung on the thread, as if undecided what to do. Then it moved on down, swaying slightly, and disappeared in the grass. It reappeared a moment later, ran up the same thread like an acrobat, and then rushed down again.

Vikenty lost count of the number of times he saw the spider run up and down. A few minutes later it was running across the web it had spun, which was surprisingly like the sail of a schooner. A fly flew past, buzzing sleepily; it brushed the web with its wing and darted aside, dragging with it the whole web and the spider too, which had been resting on top of its construction in expectation of a catch.

The web withstood the shock. The architectural calculations had been exact. Covered with a thin layer of gum, the web held out against the desperately buzzing fly while the builder hurried down to its victim. The spider stopped an inch from its catch, for some reason unable to make up its mind to go up close. It circled around the fly, mending the broken threads. When the fly had become still, the spider pressed up against it and was also still.

Leaning on his elbows, Vikenty had followed the little drama. He could not make out how the spider was holding the fly, but he could see that the fly was shriveling up. It soon appeared no bigger than the spider.

It had been sucked dry. The thought stunned him. For did not he in a way resemble a fly, whose juices, blood, and life were being sucked out of him in a different and enormous web?

Vikenty lay for a long time trying to shake off the unpleasant feeling. When the spider had finished sucking the fly's blood, it had run upward again and hidden itself. Vikenty wanted to crush that loathsome nimble insect that lived on the blood of other creatures. But an inner voice stayed his hand. "Live, damn you!" he swore viciously.

Perhaps it had to be that way. Surely Nature had known what she was about when she had created the world, separating the bloodsuckers from those who had their blood sucked out.

He had no watch but, being an experienced navigator, could tell by the sun that it was already three o'clock. The heat would soon grow less intense, and they would go back to work, sawing at the thick trunks with handsaws until the giants crashed to the ground. Then they would finish them off with axes. After sunset they would make the journey back along the road that had been laid through the taiga by a skidding-tractor. Every day for the last four months the zeks had marched the five kilometers from the camp into the taiga and the five kilometers back to the camp.

He lay there trying not to think about the people around him. He remembered his past, his life at sea. It was like a fairy tale about people from another planet.

For a while the majestic taiga around him filled his heart with peace and tranquility. "What is man?" he wanted to ask someone invisible, omnipotent. "Who is he? Why is he in the world? What is such a vile creature doing amidst this beauty? Can man too be part of nature?"

He started and his hand moved instinctively to the axe lying beside him. He had the feeling that someone was watching him. He lay motionless, every muscle tensed. Perhaps it was just his nerves playing tricks. His fingers curled gently around the axe handle. He was almost unable to look round, feeling almost as though that gaze was pressing against the back of his head. Three yards behind him, just beyond the cedar, was a solid wall of undergrowth.

Obeying his instinct for self-preservation, he suddenly turned, gripping the axe, and crouched ready to leap aside. A huge brown bear was standing in the half-light beyond the cedar. It was holding the branches aside with one paw, while the other, with its big claws that looked like fingers, hung down over its belly in a comical way. It was standing upright

26

and staring hard at the man. They looked at each other for a few seconds. Then the bear blinked and shook its head to free itself from the piercing gaze of the strange half-clothed animal. It had had enough to eat, it was hot and wanted to sleep. It had already been circling the hill for several hours, drawn by the noise and the odor of people. Finally, like an experienced hunter, it had approached from the northern side, downwind, moved by an insuperable curiosity. Now it stood up to the full extent of its great height, not caring either to attack or to retreat.

Those few seconds seemed like an eternity to Vikenty. Should he get out from under the cedar? Shout? The others would be there in a flash. They would kill the bear with their axes, tear it to pieces and eat it raw. You rarely saw meat when you were on camp rations. Vikenty was not afraid. He had known the habits of the lord of the forest since childhood in his native village, some fifty kilometers to the south. He knew that bears always had enough to eat in summer and usually would not attack unless provoked.

He swallowed his saliva. He desperately wanted to eat. But that would mean killing the strong but defenseless beast and skinning it. Then it would no longer walk through its taiga but would be left as a pile of bones, which the wolves would gnaw bare that night.

"Live, bear," he said gently. "Live! There are people here. Do you know what people are? Run away into your taiga. Don't look back and don't return."

The bear did not respond to the strange unthreatening sounds. It continued to gaze at the man with its big brown eyes.

"Well, are you going to stand there forever?" Vikenty stood up, stepped toward the bear and waved his axe. . . . The leafy branches of the cedar continued to sway for a long time in the place where the bear had been standing. The giant of the forest had vanished without a sound.

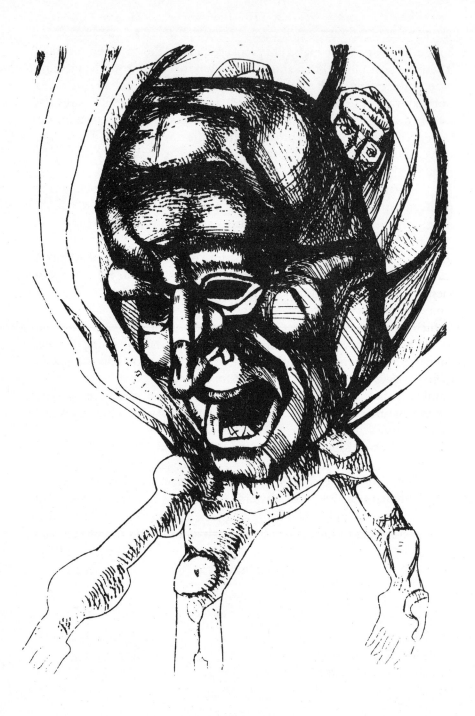

2

LIEUTENANT MUKHIN

Lieutenant Mukhin looked at his watch. It would soon be time to rouse these sleeping pigs. The zeks, who had obeyed his order not to form groups of more than two, were lying like dark stains all over the hillside, resting after their lunch of wild berries and ice-cold spring water.

Lieutenant Mukhin liked his work. He was responsible for the discipline of the soldiers and for the whole detachment of zeks, who had to fulfill the daily norm for the cutting of timber. In his native village in the Tambov region, Vanka Mukhin had completed, not without difficulty, the fourth grade of the elementary school. He had then joined the local Komsomol cell. He could never understand what the Komsomol was or why it had been established. But, just as his grandfathers had obeyed their leaders, he was absolutely certain that the chairman of the kolkhoz and all the other district officials were more clever and knowledgeable than he. That was why they were always entitled to instruct him in all things and to punish him if he did wrong. In part, these simple truths had been transmitted to him in his genes and with his mother's milk; in part, they had been acquired as a result of the careful attention that the local leaders gave to the correct upbringing of young people.

Mukhin's simplicity of soul, his assiduity, and the almost canine expression of his eyes did not go unnoticed by the officials. He was sent to town and eventually found himself in an NKVD school, from which he graduated with the rank of sublieutenant. As a result of the almost daily political studies in the NKVD school, he acquired a firm grasp of the fact that there was no better country than his Russia, the Soviet Union, the center of which was Moscow, followed by Tambov. He knew that his

29

country was surrounded on all sides by enemies—the imperialist countries, in which the world bourgeoisie had long been preparing to attack and crush the Soviet Republic and deprive its people of their freedom and, most importantly, to kill Comrade Stalin, the people's beloved leader, and his colleagues.

The world bourgeoisie was not only building up its forces to attack, it was also developing enemies of the people within the country. That was why the people, the Party, and he, Mukhin, must be on guard and keep watch on every person, including their own wives and children. "The class enemy is experienced, dangerous, and unscrupulous," the political commissar used to tell him in the NKVD school. "He recruits into his ranks the sort of people you would never think of as being enemies."

A world-wide conflict between labor and capital was in progress. It was a fight to the finish. Things were difficult for the Party and Comrade Stalin. We must be prepared for an external attack and at the same time we must isolate from the people a whole army of internal enemies. They must be rendered harmless and made to expiate their guilt through honest work.

"Damn traitors!" He spat in the direction of the hated zeks. But why was it forbidden to kill them? What generosity the Party and Comrade Stalin displayed toward these vipers who had dared to go against their own people!

Lieutenant Mukhin was currently studying for admission to the Bolshevik Party, which had the difficult title of All-Union Communist Party of Bolsheviks (he had mastered the title, but the meaning of the individual words constantly escaped him). He recalled his conversation a month ago with Colonel Degtev, who had summoned him to the Kraslag headquarters to discuss the question of his joining the Party.

Mukhin had learned the charter of the All-Union Communist Party of Bolsheviks by rote, and he saw to it that the discipline and work of his subordinates and the zeks were above reproach: for hours on end he would keep watch on one of them, then on another; he would memorize their features and their walks in an effort to understand what it took to make a spy, a traitor, an enemy of the people and of Comrade Stalin. When a prisoner felt Mukhin's gaze upon him, he would lower his head and go on working with his eyes averted.

Mukhin stood up, pulled on his jacket, buckled his belt, and jumped down from the rock. The soldiers followed him in silence. They were more afraid of him than they were of the camp commandant, Colonel Orlov. They knew that under the unwritten law of the camps an officer could shoot a soldier for failing to carry out an order, or for any other misdemeanor that could be put down as disobedience.

The prisoners dispersed to their work areas in silence. Once more the taiga was filled with the sound of axes punctuated by the crash of falling trees. Mukhin made a round of each pair of sawmen. He would stand looking at their sweating bodies and listening to them breathing heavily as they worked. They always worked as hard as they could when he was watching, for his frail figure had a cold and sinister effect on each of them. They tried not to see his narrow foxlike face with its tiny deep-set eyes.

He had almost finished his round when he stopped dead, unable to believe his eyes. Two strapping prisoners stopped working and came to attention.

"You, pig face!" Mukhin poked red-bearded Vikenty in the chest with his switch. "What's that drawing on your chest?"

"A tattoo, Citizen Lieutenant."

"But what's it supposed to be?"

Vikenty squinted sideways. The soldiers had come up and were standing nearby, restraining the dogs. The zeks had stopped work and were listening.

"It's a lighthouse, Citizen Lieutenant. A lighthouse—to guide ships at sea."

"Who gave you permission?" Mukhin frowned.

"I'm sorry, Citizen Lieutenant, but it was done a long time ago, fifteen years ago, when I was a seaman."

"You were a seaman?" Mukhin repeated automatically. "Do you see what he's got on his arm?"

"Who?" Vikenty did not understand.

"Him!" Mukhin nodded toward the prisoner with whom Vikenty had been working for the past two weeks. He was a tall man with coarse features and a tangled, gray-streaked beard. He looked at Mukhin in silence. "What's wrong, can't you see anything?" The Lieutenant laughed ominously.

"Yes, they're portraits of Lenin and Stalin."

"Where'd you get those drawings, pig?" Mukhin squinted at the zek. "Were you a sailor too?"

31

"No, Citizen Lieutenant," the man answered in a deep voice, his eyes fixed above Mukhin's head, "I was a colonel in the NKVD."

"You're a traitor, you scum!" Mukhin slashed him across the face with the switch. "And you've got the gall to wear a portrait of the leader on your filthy hide? Get rid of it!"

"What!"

"I said get that portrait of Comrade Stalin off your hide. Unless you want to be buried with it."

"But . . . how can I?" The former NKVD colonel was stripped to the waist. He stood in his baggy convict's trousers staring at the small man standing in front of him. He had turned pale, sensing serious trouble. "I'm sorry, Citizen Lieutenant, but I had these portraits done when I was a boy, in the Komsomol."

"You were in the Komsomol too?" Mukhin stepped back in amazement. "You kontra! You had them put on, you can get them off! You can't defile the portrait of the leader. Well, get on with it!"

A lanky soldier stepped forward. "But Comrade Lieutenant, it's against the regulations to . . ."

"What's wrong with you, sergeant?" Mukhin turned abruptly toward him and took out his revolver. "Are you in with them, with the enemies of the people? I'll whip you like a dog—and I won't have to answer for it. Get back to your place. Move! Three days in the guardhouse!"

Sergeant Gusev froze for a moment, then stepped back and turned away. The other three guards said nothing and held their rifles at the ready. The prisoners stood motionless, listening. There was no point in running away. There was nowhere to run to, and they would not get far anyway. The life of every one of them depended on this man's will. It was unusual for anyone to be punished for killing a zek. They all knew that. And they all wanted to live.

"Here, scum!" Mukhin pulled a small knife from the top of his boot and tossed it on the ground. "Well, pick it up!"

The man bent down and picked up the knife.

"What are you waiting for? Cut them off!"

"Cut them off?" The zek looked at the officer with hatred, and at the knife in his hand. Then he slashed himself firmly across the left arm, across both portraits. The bright-red blood streamed down his arm and dripped onto the ground. The portraits were covered by the blood, but part of the tattoo was still visible to the left, high up on his arm. The ex-

32

colonel turned white and stood swaying, the knife in his hand dripping blood.

"Cut off the rest of it!" Mukhin shouted, glaring at the man with mad eyes.

"I can't!" He shook his head. "I'd rather die. I can't do it again."

The revolver jerked in Mukhin's hand and a shot rang out. The bullet tore across the arm just below the shoulder, ripping off the rest of the tattooed skin and throwing up a spray of blood. The man fell to the ground unconscious, his blood staining the green grass.

Vikenty had been standing all this time as if in a trance, oblivious of where he was or what was happening around him. Now he stepped forward, and as he had often done as a young man during brawls in seamen's bars, he kicked Mukhin in the stomach. The lieutenant collapsed in a heap.

Holding back the furiously barking dogs, the soldiers looked in alarm to Gusev, whose confused gaze moved from the collapsed figure of Mukhin to the wounded zek lying near him, then to Vikenty and the motionless circle of zeks.

At last he pulled himself together. "Don't shoot, men!" he shouted. "Don't shoot! The colonel will have to deal with this." He turned to the zeks. "Here, three of you, quick! Bandage that arm and get some water for the lieutenant. Tie this one up!" He nodded toward Vikenty, who was still standing between the two men sprawled on the grass.

A half hour later Vikenty was standing in front of a revived Mukhin with his hands tied behind his back. He was prepared to die and felt complete indifference toward this man whose hate-filled eyes were fixed upon him. He did not look at the soldiers or at his fellow prisoners. He knew that no one would risk helping him and he did not blame them for it. The odious square face of the investigator Bydlin flashed across his mind: Bydlin who had interrogated him for five days after his arrest in Archangel. He remembered Bydlin's frightened look and the seven shots he had fired into the wall around his head. Vikenty had won that battle for survival because he had been stronger and bolder than his executioner. But this time?

When he had regained consciousness after the terrible kick, Mukhin had sat on the grass for a long time, gazing dully at the men standing around him awaiting his orders. The blow had been so powerful that it had knocked all the spirit out of him as well as the wind. Nothing like it had ever happened to him before. The thirst for revenge possessed him so powerfully that he had to push the revolver deeper into his pocket to suppress the impulse to shoot the pig at once. He began searching his mind for some special punishment, but nothing suitable occurred to him.

He got to his feet in front of the red-bearded man, but this time kept his distance. He examined him for several minutes as if he were a wild animal in a zoo. "What are you looking at, you idiot?" Vikenty said quietly. He knew instinctively that only a miracle could save his life and that in this situation any ordinary words or actions would lead to death.

"Calling me an idiot?" Mukhin looked at him with genuine amazement. The soldiers smiled. Sergeant Gusev gave the zek an approving glance. He regretted that in a few minutes time this handsome man would be lying under the tree with six bullet holes in his body. Mukhin liked that number for some reason.

"You know that I'm going to shoot you?"

"Yes, so what are you waiting for, you bastard?" Vikenty swayed forward, and Mukhin recoiled, pulling the revolver from his trouser pocket. "If you've got a mirror," Vikenty continued, enjoying the unexpected role of condemned man and the freedom it gave him, "take a look at yourself. Were you really born of a woman? What a disgusting snout! And not a single gray cell! Stalin can't expect any good of his henchmen when they look like you!"

"What!" Mukhin lost his self-control at the mention of Stalin's name. He jerked up the revolver and several shots rang out. Twigs broken off by the bullets showered down on Vikenty. Mukhin stood leaning forward, his face contorted.

Vikenty swallowed and shifted his weight from one foot to the other. "You know why you didn't kill me?" he said softly. "You didn't miss, you were just afraid. You're afraid that the colonel will get rid of you for killing me."

"You think you're so important to him?" Mukhin waved the revolver under Vikenty's nose. "No, I don't care about the colonel, understand? I can knock you off now and tomorrow they'll thank me. I'll go on leave, home, to my mother who gave me birth. But you're not going anywhere, kontra, you're going to rot here in the taiga. I don't want to waste a bullet on you." He smiled almost happily. "I've thought of something for you. You're going to be strung up here until morning so that you can think about what our Soviet motherland means and how you should behave toward Comrade Stalin and me, your superiors. I don't want you to die too quickly. I want to see what shape you're in tomorrow morning. You took an interest in me, and now I'm taking an interest in you. It's mutual, see? Ha, ha, ha!"

His laughter rang out in the silent glade.

Vikenty said nothing and lay down on his back on the ground. He watched as the soldiers sullenly tied ropes to his arms and legs.

When they had finished their work, Mukhin gave the order and they released the four birch branches to which Vikenty had been tied. The branches whipped up, hoisting him six feet into the air.

He looked down at his fellow prisoners, but they kept their eyes lowered. He heard Gusev say, "But, Comrade Lieutenant, he's too low. The wolves'll get him. He won't live till morning. I'm reporting it to the colonel!"

"To hell with you, Gusev," Mukhin answered affably as he admired his handiwork. "Pull him up a bit higher then. I'll settle with you later."

"Fall in!" The lieutenant's sharp order sounded. The zeks glanced somberly at their spread-eagled comrade as they moved off into the forest along the narrow road. The soldiers marched along in silence, avoiding one another's eyes. Only the wounded zek looked back at the solitary figure suspended between sky and earth.

"Halt!" Mukhin shouted abruptly, struck by a sudden thought. He ran back and untied the ropes from two of the birches, lowering his victim almost to the ground. He cut off all his clothes with a knife and then hoisted him up again. He glanced with satisfaction at the naked body showing up white against the blue sky, then strode back to the column.

Vikenty had been hanging in the air for half an hour. His eyes were closed and he did not have the strength to think about anything. The ropes gradually cut deeper into his flesh. Far above him the blue sky began to grow dark as the sun set beyond the forest, its last rays falling on the tops of the cedars. The owls began to hoot, and it grew colder. Vikenty squinted down—seven feet, at least. Would he live till morning? It would have been better if the swine had shot him.

He closed his eyes again. His powerful body fought for life. He used his straining muscles to take the weight off each of his arms and legs in turn, which were beginning to grow numb where the ropes bit into them. He filled his lungs with the fresh forest air. What would they be doing in the camp just now? Supper would be over and they would have gone to their beds. They would be lying and thinking, thinking about him. Of course by now the whole camp knew that he, Vikenty Angarov, once a navigation officer and captain, was hanging here in his native taiga, waiting for death.

He had ten years to serve. What of his wife, Katya? The poor thing. Arrested of course. His son, Valery, would be living in some miserable children's home.

A bird with the hooked beak of a predator was hovering above him. It hung in the air above this strange white creature, not sure whether to swoop down. It squinted at him with puzzled beady eyes, then flapped its wings and vanished.

It was growing dark more quickly now, and the waves of warm air from the ground suddenly changed into a cool stream that seemed to wrap his body in a cold wet sheet. He lacked the strength to control his shivering. His body was seized with a violent shuddering that shook the branches of the birches.

Then it all vanished. He was in the warm south again, wearing his white naval uniform with the rings on the sleeves. In his mind's eye flashed momentary images of Cape Town, Madagascar, Singapore, Sydney, Seattle, and all the countless ports and bars and pretty girls. A warm sea breeze was blowing, the beer foamed in the glasses, the wind was in the rigging again, forcing the masts of the schooner down toward the water. . . . He remembered only events that had taken place before his return to Shanghai, before the moment when he had taken that fateful step and set out on the road that had brought him to this end. His mind would not accept anything that had happened after that moment, even the memory of Katya and his son. It rejected them and hid them away in dark remote corners. Now while his big strong body was slowly dying, his mind was striving to brighten these last hours by bringing out from their hiding places only memories that would not hurt him. His internal world was struggling for survival against the external world that was carrying him to his death.

Later he saw other images. Blyukher, the Red Army commander, with his vodka-red face, slicing the fat red salmon with a penknife as he explained to him, the young navigation officer, the essence of the world proletarian revolution. Investigator Pogodin, who had saved his life at the end of his five-day interrogation last winter. Then the general, Gugo Udras, to whom they had given permission to take one last bath in the prison bathhouse, before they shot him. And other people, good and bad, who had shared that stormy era with him, all locked in a desperate struggle for survival.

A whole eternity seemed to have passed when his dimming eyes lighted upon an area of black starry sky that stirred another memory in his brain. Yes, it was by these constellations that were now watching his slow death that he had been able to fix the position of the schooner in the ocean and set a course for the shore and safety. . . . Was this now the end? How many times he had avoided death already! He had twice fled from Russia, from war. He had sailed through terrible typhoons. He had defeated his interrogator and had survived. He used to dream sometimes of spitting on Stalin's grave. Damn dwarf! And now it was the end? Perhaps it had been pointless to kick that animal? No, he hadn't done it for himself, but for them all. In that feeble lieutenant he sensed the very same evil strength that had torn him and all the others away from their lives and tossed them aside, here, into this world separated from the real world by a barbed-wire fence.

A high-pitched buzzing in his ears finally roused him from his reverie. A bear powerless against a mosquito, he stared into darkness, trying to pick up the outline of the tiny enemy circling around him. The high-pitched tone would sound right in his ears, only to die away again. Then it stopped. "Now its giving the anesthetic!" he thought gloomily, sensing that this tiny creature with the long proboscis adapted for bloodsucking had already landed somewhere on his body. He felt a lump swelling up around the bite. He twitched convulsively, then threw back his head and stared at the sky. Morbid fear showed now in his eyes.

After a few moments the buzzing resumed, louder this time. His back began to itch, then his legs and chest. . . . Several mosquitoes settled on his face. He twisted his head frenziedly, jerking his whole body and shaking the four birches gleaming white in the darkness. Vikenty felt as if his whole body was swelling up and turning to lead. His lips burned and his eyes swam. Through the narrow slits of his puffy lids he saw a great cloud of mosquitoes descending on him out of the darkness.

Breathing hoarsely, he watched as they covered his body with what looked like a black layer of soot. He suddenly felt hot. He closed his eyes and felt the mosquitoes go to work on his lids, filling his eyes with pain.

His heart was now pounding loudly in his chest and echoing in his temples. His body was on fire. And suddenly his whole being shuddered at a terrible thought. They were going to suck his blood! Just as the spider had sucked the blood out of the fly that morning. "I'm melting! Ma-a-a-a!" A terrible wail burst from his chest and rang out across the dark taiga. "A-a-a-a!"; a second later the echo returned from the taiga.

For a moment he lost his reason. He opened wide his terrified eyes and concentrated all his strength and his will to survive into a single terrible convulsion. The two branches tied to his legs snapped and he crashed feet first to the ground, still suspended by his arms. He gave another mighty jerk and tore the two branches from the tree. He threw himself face down in the grass, clawing at his body and smearing it with the blood of the crushed mosquitoes.

Trembling, he tried to untie the ropes from his wrists and ankles, but he could hardly move his numbed fingers. He was too weak to drag the four large branches behind him. They were full of sap and he could not break off the bigger twigs. He loaded his birch fetters onto his back and set off, almost at a run, through the taiga toward the camp, where there were people. The branches kept catching in the trees, jerking him to the ground. But he climbed back to his feet and set off running again, his white body flashing through the dark forest.

3

COLONEL ORLOV

It is night over the taiga. The silence is absolute and the huts stand buried in darknesss. The prisoners are sleeping, tired after a day of heavy labor. They sleep and dream their dreams.

The doors of the huts are wide open—it is hot even at night. Two guards stand on each of the four watchtowers at the corners of the rectangle of the camp, leaning against the wooden railings, chattering about their own affairs, about anything, only not about the people crammed into the wooden sheds, sleeping. The searchlights along the low barbed-wire fence are switched off—it's a pity to waste electricity. If a prisoner escapes, or even several of them together, the officers don't make much of a fuss—let them escape, they won't get far. The taiga is the best fence. It's easy to walk into it, but almost impossible to get out. It doesn't matter if a man reaches another camp or village; they'll catch him straightaway and give him another term for escaping. Let them work for nothing for the rest of their lives!

The guards gaze calmly into the forest—there's never any need to expect attack from that direction. It's good to serve in these remote normal-regime camps in the taiga. That's why the guards feel well disposed toward the world and, despite the ranting of Lieutenant Mukhin, it's rare for the guards to show excessive cruelty toward the prisoners. Even though they're enemies of the people and have been convicted of crimes against the motherland and Comrade Stalin, they're still human beings, and you feel sorry as hell for them, these zeks, especially the women and younger girls.

The orders are to shoot without warning if anyone tries to escape.

But the soldiers usually pretend not to notice some doomed wretch, crawling away flat on his belly like a lizard. He crawls, then stops, then crawls a bit farther through the yellow leaves into the darkness of the forest. A soldier might fire a shot over the fellow's head so that he'll be able to tell the officer he did something. But that's all.

And in two weeks' time the fugitive will be sawing trees again, serving fifteen years instead of ten—four months for every day of "freedom." But sometimes he doesn't come back. Then, if you go through the taiga a month later, you may find his gnawed bones in some remote bear's den.

The soldiers stand there making their simple talk. Petro is thinking about his Marusya, back on the Red Lighthouse kolkhoz in the Moscow region; she promised to wait on the farm and not go with the other lads, to wait until her Petka came back from his term of service in the Red Army, somewhere in the Far East. It's impossible to write her the truth. He's ashamed to have to stand here with his rifle in his hand guarding women and girls, instead of doing a real soldier's job. His best friend, Ivan, from a small Siberian village in the Omsk region, doesn't write the truth to his Katyusha, either. He tells her that he's doing a hard job guarding the frontiers of the motherland in the Far East. Colonel Orlov told him to say that. "You men," he said, "are the same as frontier guards, only they are guarding the motherland against external enemies, and you against internal ones." Ivan felt bad standing there all day with his rifle, watching the women and girls dragging logs, straining their female insides. Sometimes they look sad, as if they aren't enemies at all. But who can tell? The officers know best!

But there are pigs in the guard, too. A month ago one of them was hit, apparently accidentally, by a stray bullet. There are still two left, and the lieutenant. The men have been wondering whether to let him have a bullet in the back. The taiga will take care of everything! This stringing-up business had spoiled it all. The whole camp had been buzzing with the story—a man had been left in the forest, strung up naked in the trees. The zeks stood around for a long time by the huts, muttering among themselves, but no one had gone to the commandant—they were too afraid. Mukhin had been ranting about going to get the zek in the morning, but would he still be hanging there in the morning? The taiga isn't the Moscow woods!

"Who goes there? Halt, or I'll shoot!" Petro raised his rifle.

Down below, the white shape froze. Ivan tumbled down the steep staircase and shouted, "Petro, here, quick!" Grasping their rifles, they stood silent and afraid, staring at the tall white ape. It had reddish-black stripes all over its body, which was enmeshed in a tangle of birch branches and ropes. Human eyes flashed from the thick beard which covered the entire face.

"Don't move, and keep quiet!" Ivan waved his bayonet at the ape.

"I'll keep quiet," the ape answered softly in a human voice, "but don't take me to Mukhin. I'd rather you shot me right here. Take me to the camp commandant."

"Wait!" Petro vanished into the darkness.

"You're sure you didn't dream all this?" Orlov said as he followed the soldier. "You'd better be careful or you'll find yourself in trouble. Where is he? I can't see anyone."

Ivan loomed up out of the darkness. "Here he is, Comrade Colonel, here, he fell over when Petro went to get you."

For a few moments Orlov stood over the semicorpse, which was hardly visible in the long grass. Then he said softly, "Cut him free, men. Wrap him in an overcoat and get him to the sickbay. And don't let anyone see him, or I'll have your hides. You'll be shot if a single soul finds out he's here. Is that clear? Then tell Gusev to come to my office, and at two o' clock, Mukhin. Let him sleep for the moment. Do you understand?"

"Yes, Comrade Colonel, all understood!" The two friends came to attention in front of their commandant, then Petro ran up into the watchtower to get a coat.

Orlov made a round of the camp. It was quiet. He returned to the duty office, a small whitewashed room in the administration hut. The single window was covered on the inside with a thick iron grill.

Gusev's and Mukhin's dossiers were already lying on the table, but Orlov knew their histories by heart anyway. He went over to the iron washstand in the corner and rinsed his face in cold water. The towel was old and almost in shreds. He regarded the still-young face in the mirror: a handsome face, almost sleek, the lower half somewhat elongated, ending in a pointed beard. The nose above the sharp line of the mouth was straight. He gave himself a satisfied glance, then sat down. He smiled when he saw his own dossier: Regimental Commander A. A. Orlov.

41

He knew this was only a copy, and that the original was kept some-where in the labyrinth of the NKVD in Moscow, in the Holy of Holies, as the archive was secretly called. Regimental Commander Aleksandr An-dreyevich Orlov was the scion of an ancient Russian noble family. He was not certain that his ancestors had been directly linked by birth with Count Orlov, Catherine the Great's favorite, but he knew that his line was quite distinguished, although impoverished. "The remnants of such noble stock, downtrodden by an upstart heel, rejected by capricious fate." He recalled Lermontov's lines. How well the poet had put it! Almost three generations of Orlovs had served in the guards. They had not made great careers at court but were of good standing among the nobility.

At the time of the February Revolution, Lieutenant-Colonel Orlov had been at the western front. As the deputy commander of a division in the czarist army, Orlov was occupying a post inconsistent with his noble rank. His "liberalism" with his subordinates had gone against him among the general staff, where his promotion was constantly blocked. And so he finished the First World War without making the rank of colonel. Never-theless, his authority had been absolute among the soldiers and younger officers. For this reason the divisional commander, General Batov, had asked him to be his deputy. Batov had made the right choice. After the disastrous June advance, the mutinous soldiers turned for home. They settled scores with certain officers on the way, but Orlov had personally conducted General Batov safely to his car. Batov was grateful.

Orlov did not understand the revolution, yet he could not imagine living anywhere except Russia. So he yielded to the decision of the sol-diers and young officers who made up the divisional committee: he took command of the remnants of the division. Hordes of leaderless soldiers were traveling from the front to the interior and their homes. Only a few battle-fit formations remained in the front line, Orlov's among them. At first it was repugnant for him to think that he had to carry out the orders of the rank and file. Then they began to receive the decrees of Lenin and the Soviet government, in which Orlov sensed the strength inherent in all the earlier Russian governments, the strength that the government of the czar had so lacked in recent years.

Orlov had been carried along by the tide of events. When the army was disbanded, he found himself in Moscow at the staff headquarters of the Red Army. He felt ashamed when he saw generals and other officers he knew from before the war wearing the new uniform with the red tabs.

He felt sick at the thought that he would have to devote his knowledge to the struggle against the White armies, in which the largest and best part of the Russian officer class was fighting. But Aleksandr Orlov was not merely an expert in military matters, he was also familiar with history and politics. He understood that the Bolsheviks controlled the manpower and material resources of Central Russia and had a better chance of winning the Civil War. Besides, he was tired of the disorder that had reigned in the army and in the country in recent years. Although in his heart Orlov nurtured mistrust and scorn for this power that had driven his former colleagues from the country and him into service, he never revealed what he thought. Somehow he must make an accomodation, so as not to be crushed by events. He did not aim too high, having no inclination for the senior administrative posts. Being regimental commander was a world away from being an army commander. And this very prudence had turned out to be his saving grace, especially after the purges began in all sections of the state and the army.

When, in the 1930's, the government began to expand the network of corrective-labor camps, which could not cope with the flood of new inmates, the chief of the general staff summoned Orlov and read him the order for his transfer to the internal security forces. The former lieutenant-colonel in the czarist army, Comrade Regimental Commander Orlov, heard the order in silence. He pondered the situation in a moment, and saluted. "Yes, Comrade Chief of the General Staff!"

That same evening, in the People's Commissariat for Internal Affairs, his chief of staff spread out before Orlov a map of the USSR, across which existing camps and those under construction were scattered like islands in a huge archipelago. The head of the Central Camps' Authority was sitting in a chair gazing searchingly at the former czarist officer: he was expecting a difficult interview with this son of the old Russian nobility, whom he would have shot during the Civil War but whose hand he now had to shake.

"Comrade Colonel!" This head of the Gulag offered his hand across the desk and motioned Orlov to a chair. "How do you like your new appointment?"

"Fine, thank you, Comrade Deputy People's Commissar," Orlov answered firmly, noticing the grateful light that flashed in the commissar's eyes. All the others addressed him as "Comrade Chief of the Gulag" and this "Deputy People's Commissar" sounded as sweet music to his ears. He looked with unaccustomed tenderness at the commander. A clever man!

"Nevertheless . . ." The Deputy People's Commissar decided to state the basic point. "Nevertheless, it's not the same as serving in the army, even less on the general staff. To be frank, it's more a question of guarding people. Do you think you'll like that kind of work?"

"I serve Russia, the Party, and Comrade Stalin. It doesn't matter to me where I serve. I will go wherever my superiors find it necessary to send me."

"Well said, very well said, Comrade Orlov!" The Deputy People's Commissar had adopted a more intimate tone. "You don't want to join the investigation section? They have to interrogate people there . . ."

"Thank you for your confidence in me, Comrade Deputy People's Commissar. I will accept any appointment, but . . ."

"But what?" He looked at Orlov with a wry smile.

"But, if I have the choice, I would prefer Siberia."

"What!" The Deputy People's Commissar was so astonished that he sat bolt upright in his chair.

"Yes, Siberia! Some camp in the taiga, far from the noise of the town."

"Are you serious or joking, Comrade Orlov?" He could not conceal his amazement.

"Quite serious. People are needed there too. I want to spend a few years in the forest, in the fresh air, and chop some wood. To tell you the truth, I'm a bit tired of being here in the center of things. My health's not too good. And of course my wife won't object."

"Really, comrade, this is the first time in my experience that an officer has requested a transfer from the capital to the back of beyond, to the taiga. You won't change your mind?"

"No, Comrade Deputy People's Commissar," Orlov answered firmly. "That's my decision and my request. I shall be very grateful if you can see your way . . ."

When he had sent Orlov off with his new assignment, the Deputy People's Commissar stayed in his office, puzzling over Orlov's strange request. It was not until several years later, in Beria's time, when he was sitting in a lonely cell in the Lubyanka, awaiting interrogation and, clearly, a firing squad, that he understood Colonel Orlov. How important it is to be able to foresee events.

Orlov knew that the hundreds of zeks living in the gloomy huts depended on his will, but also that his own career, indeed his life, depended on theirs. People will maintain discipline as long as they have a hold on life, as long as a spark of hope burns in each doomed heart. But when that spark dies, then a man will stop at nothing, even death, and he becomes a deadly threat. It is a mistake to drive people to that fatal point beyond which an explosion is inevitable. The consequence? Unthinkable. The least disorder in the camp spelled death for the camp commandant. The Kraslag officials would invent whatever story was necessary to justify themselves to the higher authorities, making sure that suitable punishment—even death—was meted out to negligent camp commandants. And then there was that bastard Colonel Degtev, head of the administrative section of the Authority. Degtev was his immediate superior—and the only enemy he had had throughout his career. When this former workman from the Donbass coal-mining region had arrived on the scene, he had taken a violent dislike to Orlov, the former aristocrat, nicknaming him "the Liberal." Degtev was envious of the success of Orlov's camp, where the norm for the dispatch of timber was always exceeded by a wide margin, much wider than in any other camp. Orlov was constantly hearing rumors about Degtev's attempts to get him thrown out of the army, but he pretended to know nothing and always smiled politely when they met.

At conferences with the Deputy People's Commissar in Moscow, Degtev would put in a word about Orlov: "A liberal blue-blood should be appointed as interrogator, for re-education!" But in vain. The men around the table said nothing, and the answer of the Deputy People's Commissar was short and to the point: "Orlov knows how to fulfill the plan; the country needs timber, and torturing people—that's your work, Comrade Degtev!" After this hint Degtev calmed down, but his hatred was greater than ever and he was just waiting for his chance. Orlov knew it and knew he had to act carefully. He knew, too, that the only thing that had prevented an explosion today was the age-old habit of the Russian people of tolerating everything the ruling class thought up.

"Yes!" he called in response to a knock at the door. "Come in, Gusev. What have you got to say?"

"Well, Comrade Colonel . . ." The lanky Gusev lowered his head awkwardly so as to seem shorter in the tiny room. "Well, what happened was the lieutenant, that is, the comrade lieutenant, I mean, he hit . . ."

"Sit down, Gusev, and calm yourself. You have nothing to fear. Talk sense."

Gusev sat down on a chair in the middle of the room.

"There was this tattoo, on his arm, I mean . . . ."

"On Mukhin's arm?"

"No, not his arm, the zek, on the zek's arm. And the comrade lieutenant, he says, 'Cut it off!' And he gives him a knife . . . ."

"Do you like the lieutenant, Gusev?" Orlov asked after he had heard Gusev's story.

"Yes, well I mean, I'm not overly fond of him, Comrade Colonel. None of the men is."

"He's a strict officer of course. He does his duty."

"Sure, Comrade Colonel, and we do our duty. But you shouldn't break the regulations. They don't say anything about making fun of a fellow, even if he's a zek, as long as he does his work."

"All right, Gusev. How long will it take you to forget all about our talk?"

"How long?" Gusev stood up in amazement. "No time at all. I've already forgotten it. But look, Comrade Colonel, it'd be better if Lieutenant Mukhin went away, otherwise . . . you can never tell . . . things can happen in the taiga. It's risky to fool around with the men. There's two or three of us and a couple of hundred zeks, and they've all got axes . . . ."

"Thank you, Sergeant, you may go. Tell the soldier on duty to bring Mukhin here at two. And forget all about this . . . What if Mukhin doesn't go away?"

"It won't work, Comrade Colonel. He has threatened to settle with me, but the men won't let him. If he stays, you'll have to change the whole guard."

For the next half an hour Orlov paced somberly around the office. He regretted that Nadya was not there. She was at the apartment in Krasnoyarsk, where he would go on Saturday. There was comfort there, and peace. But out here you never knew what might happen. Here, in the wilds of Siberia! But what was happening now in Moscow? How much worse it must be there! He shuddered at the thought. How difficult it was to survive in these times.

"Ah, Comrade Lieutenant!" Orlov went to meet Mukhin and shook his hand. He motioned him to a chair by the table. "Well, what's new with the guards?"

"New?" Mukhin felt a stab of anxiety, but a glance at the colonel's affable expression reassured him. "Everything's normal, Comrade Colonel. We're guarding the enemies. . ."

Orlov interrupted. "You've been serving in the NKVD force for three years now, since you finished military school?"

"Yes, three . . . what of it?"

"Nothing. I was just wondering what to do with you." Orlov answered sharply, his expression altered.

"What to do? With me!" He stood up in astonishment. "But I'm serving . . ."

"Whom are you serving?" Orlov regarded him coldly across the table.

"Who? The Soviet Union!"

"So it was for the Soviet Union that you strung up a man in the forest?"

"But he's a criminal two times over. He tried to kill me. I had a right to kill him, you know that." Mukhin was growing bold.

"How many soldiers were with you?"

"Four."

"What if the prisoners had mutinied and killed you? There were two hundred of them. Did you think of that?"

"Mutinied? Impossible! How could they mutiny?" he muttered confusedly, feeling his palms breaking out in a cold sweat.

"Comrade Lieutenant, all mutinies are caused by careless officers like yourself. You exceeded your authority, do you understand?" Orlov stood up from behind the table, his face finally showing his rage. "You've brought the whole camp to the brink of mutiny and you will be court-martialed. Your action can only be interpreted as incitement to mutiny. Did you think of that? What did you achieve, may I ask, by stringing a zek up in the forest?" Orlov had begun to lose his self-control.

Mukhin turned white, "I . . . I don't . . . know," he stammered. "I didn't know it was incitement . . . I wanted to punish him so he'd know who's boss."

"Are you an officer, or a hooligan from the streets? Only the Party and the State give orders here. You are obliged to do what is required of you, and only what is required, nothing more. Is that clear, Comrade ex-lieutenant?"

"What do you mean 'ex'?" Mukhin took a step forward, gulping for air.

"I am compelled to strip you of your rank in order to prevent trouble in the camp. If I submit your case to the court, you will be shot. For inciting the prisoners to mutiny by exceeding your authority and using unauthorized methods in your dealings with them. Are you aware that almost all the guards will give evidence against you? You're a fool, an idiot! How have you manged to survive in the NKVD up to now? It's your good fortune that you're serving under me."

"Comrade Orlov!" The lieutenant fell to his knees. His lower lip was trembling and his face was smeared with tears. "Don't destroy me. I'm just a simple man, from the country. I've served Comrade Stalin faithfully. I hate these enemies—why do they go against him?"

"You did all this out of love for Comrade Stalin?" Mukhin did not catch the irony in the colonel's astonished exclamation.

"Yes, yes!" he shouted sincerely. "Surely you can see what they're like inside? I see through them. I'd have them all shot!"

"Get up, Comrade Mukhin." Orlov took him by the shoulders in a conciliatory manner and sat him on the chair. "Your sincerity makes a big difference. Your sincere love for Comrade Stalin does you credit. You could even say that it has saved you. I've decided against submitting this case to the court. I will hush it up, in the hope that you will think over all that has happened and draw the necessary conclusions. Remember, Comrade Stalin does not permit his subordinates to exceed their authority. His command is the law for all of us, but today you broke it."

"I broke Comrade Stalin's law?" Mukhin asked dazedly.

"Yes, we've already discussed that, Comrade Mukhin. Now you must choose: either you will make out a report addressed to me and then go away to study in some staff college, or I will submit the case to the court. Decide now, before you leave this room. You must be off the camp by morning."

"Yes, yes!" he nodded joyfully. "But where can I go to study? I've only been through NKVD school. I haven't got much learning. But I agree, I agree, thank you very much . . . I'll make out the report right away, only first, with your permission, I'll run down into the forest and get that zek. Perhaps he's still alive."

"He is. He managed to get back here from the forest with your ropes still on him," Orlov said viciously, his eyes boring into Mukhin. "And you're lucky that he was strong enough to break the branches and make it here through the forest. Anyone weaker would have died. Then you would certainly have been shot. Not for killing a zek but for incitement to mutiny, you damned idiot. Take this paper and write the report as I dictate it. Write: 'To the commandant of corrective-labor camp No. 8 of the Kraslag system, Comrade Colonel A.A. Orlov, from the officer commanding the camp guard, Lieutenant I.N. Mukhin. Report: I urgently request one month's leave in order to obtain admission to officer's training school. I also request the Authority to assist me to gain admission, as my general education is weak. I undertake to make up the lost ground during my studies and justify the trust of the Party and of Comrade Stalin. Lieutenant Mukhin.'

"Good. Sign it and give it to me." Orlov took the paper and scrawled his signature on it. "Remember one more thing, Comrade Lieutenant. I know that you are on good terms with Colonel Degtev. That's your personal affair. I just want to remind you that if he had been in my position he wouldn't have taken all this trouble. It would have been a court-martial and firing squad for you! Just remember that. I've shown you mercy because you really are a simple fellow, you've not had much education, and you love Comrade Stalin sincerely. You may go. Study hard. Study to be a true servant of the Party, to help and not to hinder it. When will you leave for the station?"

"Right away, with your permission!"

"Fifty kilometers? While it's still dark?"

"It doesn't matter, I'm not scared. I can hitch a ride."

"All right! Hand over your gun. Good." He took the revolver from the lieutenant and held out his hand. "Let's forget this incident. You've learned your lesson. Keep your nose clean in the future. These things often end badly. I hope you enjoy your studies!"

"Thank you!" Mukhin took Orlov's hand in both his own. "Thank you, Comrade Colonel. I'll never forget this. God grant you health!"

"Health!" Orlov thought as he watched the door close behind Mukhin. "He wants to live, the bastard. Well, so what? Now he'll spend the rest of his life praising me, in any court in the land. How he wants to live, the slob! They're all the same. Those who care nothing for other people's lives tremble like pigs when they're put up against the wall themselves. Mukhin! He turned up here by chance. But what goes on in Moscow? The Mukhins are the masters there!"

49

He took an opened bottle of vodka from a drawer, poured himself half a glass and drank it off. He chewed a piece of black bread as he brooded. He had never had occasion to crush someone morally, the way he had that fool. But what else could he have done? Any repetition of such barbaric behavior would jeopardize the whole camp and his own future. People had been killing other people for hundreds of years in interrogation rooms and torture chambers, but they didn't do it in front of the prisoners. You had to take people's psychology into account. The idiot! How good it was here in the wilds of Siberia! Who could tell how things would have turned out if he had remained in Moscow. The Siberian taiga might not be Paris, but it wasn't bad—when you thought of the scale and the horror of what was happening in the rest of the country.

Did he regret not having emigrated after the revolution? Yes, deep in his heart there burned a spark of self-pity mixed with loathing for everything that he had to see and in which he had taken part—even an indirect part. He was witnessing a power struggle that no one would have dreamed of under the Czar. So much for your workers and peasants. Let them have power! What was there in the history of mankind to compare with the deeds of Soso Dzhugashvili, the former seminarist from Gori? Oh, he was well acquainted with the whole life story of Stalin—"Cast upon us by a whim of fate, as he sought his fame and fortune."* Well put! Russians were killing Russians, persecuting, torturing, starving, humiliating, enslaving each other. They had trained a whole army of cutthroats like Mukhin—"simple folk." An Oprichnina! A Bironovshchina! When would it end? Not until changes occurred at the top. What had Marx been aiming at? This? Philosophers! They should come and spend a week here.

Orlov went to the window and gazed out at the first paleness of dawn. Well, anyway, it was an ill wind . . . If he had emigrated, some Mukhin would be standing here as camp commandant, and that would be very bad for the prisoners, those people in the huts, snubbed by fate and by history. In the morning he would have to visit this "hanging man." The fellow must have something to have kicked Mukhin in the stomach in front of a squad of soldiers. He obviously wasn't afraid to die. If he should regain consciousness, it might be possible to use him. Strong men were needed.

---

*From Lermontov's verse, "On the Death of the Poet."

4

THE PIRATE

Lieutenant Mukhin took his small suitcase and departed from the camp in the predawn twilight. He did not wish to meet either the zeks or the guards, who only the previous evening had been under his command. The soldier at the gates came to attention and saluted. "Good morning, Comrade Lieutenant. Where are you off to this early?"

"I'm leaving you," Mukhin answered confusedly as he stood, suitcase in hand. "I'm going to college. Carry out your duties faithfully, Comrade Corporal."

"Yes, Comrade Lieutenant, I will. Good-bye!"

Biting his lip, Mukhin waved genially and strode away. But once he was beyond the bend in the road, he turned and shook his fist in the direction of the camp.

When the zeks heard what had happened they were stunned. They whispered among themselves in the huts but went out to work as usual. The meager breakfast was over by seven o'clock, and the columns of gray uniformed men were disappearing into the forest soon after.

Vikenty remained behind, in the sickbay. A room fifteen feet by twelve, it had whitewashed walls and two tiny windows. Four wooden cots stood along the walls. He opened his eyes. There was a roaring in his head, as if he had been drinking heavily. His wrists and ankles ached where they had been rubbed raw by Mukhin's ropes. It was almost dark in the room. The gray light of dawn filtered through the windows. He could make out the figure of a woman sitting on a creaking stool near his bed. He tried to distinguish her face, but it was in darkness.

The woman stood up and pulled the blanket from him in silence. He felt awkward lying before her in his shorts, but she laid her gentle hands on his chest and said almost inaudibly, "Lie still. I'll put some more ointment on the bites."

She smeared some kind of sharp-smelling cream on her palm and rubbed it onto his neck, chest, and legs. Then she made him turn over onto his stromach and rubbed his back. He felt quietly happy at the firm but gentle touch of her hands. He said nothing, and flexed his muscles under her fingers, hoping that she would not stop.

"Lie on your back." She put her arms gently around his neck and helped him up. Then she went back to the stool and sat watching him.

She was of medium height and had a shapely figure. The big gray eyes in the rather oblong face with the dimpled chin reminded him partly of Florence, long ago in Seattle, partly of his wife, Katya. Even Svetlana's face appeared in his mind's eye, like a snapshot from his high-school years. He liked this gray-eyed woman.

Noticing that he was looking at her, she smiled kindly and simply. She stood up and placed a chair by the head of the bed. Then she opened a cupboard and placed a piece of black bread, a fork, and a bowl of meat stew on the chair. "This is for you."

Vikenty felt sick at the sight of food and his mouth filled with saliva. But he controlled himself and asked, "What is it? Who sent it? It's not from Mukhin, is it? Let him choke on it himself!"

"No,no." She leaned over him. "I heard that Mukhin's leaving, on the colonel's orders."

"Thank God!" He almost spat the words out. "Otherwise it would have been him or me . . ."

"Don't excite yourself." She placed her hand on his. "They have the power. You must wait."

"Yes." He looked at her with interest. "But who sent the food?"

"Gusev brought it last night, on the colonel's orders."

He picked up the fork and began to eat. He could hardly stop himself from swallowing the bread and the stew straight down without chewing it. She moved away and stood at the window while he ate.

"What's your name?" He placed the fork on the chair and lay back on the pillow.

"Lida."

"Come here."

"Why?"

"Please."

"You're a nuisance, dear patient." She came and sat on the chair.

"Patient? You sound like a doctor."

"I am a doctor, really. I was in my last year at medical school."

"The last year?" he repeated mechanically. "Why didn't you finish?"

He stopped short, seeing her gray eyes suddenly fill with tears.

"We'd better not talk about that." She hung her head. "Someone's coming. I'll leave you . . ."

Vikenty looked in annoyance at the uniformed figure standing in the doorway through which Lida had disappeared.

Orlov sat down on the same chair near the bed. They stared each other in the eye for several seconds without speaking.

Orlov's chair creaked. "Well, what have you got to say?"

Vikenty said nothing.

"Don't be afraid. There are no microphones here."

"It's too late for me to be afraid," Vikenty answered in a soft resentful voice. "My life's worthless. Mukhin could have killed me yesterday, and tomorrow somebody else . . ."

Orlov nodded. "Yes, he could have killed you. You understand of course that the way he treated you was the normal, accepted thing, and my attitude is the exception to the rule."

"Yes, I understand. What can I do for you?"

"You sound as if I'm here to ask a favor." Orlov smiled wryly. "It's the officer coming out in you. I've read your dossier."

"Of course."

"There's one thing I don't understand. Why was it that when you were deputy head of a steam navigation authority, doing the work of an admiral, you remained a captain, second rank?"

"It's simple. There wasn't time for them to complete the formalities for my promotion or to process my Party membership."

"They made time in my case. And do you know why? I understand the spirit of the times. You missed your chance at some point. I'm an aristocrat of course, like Molotov and many others . . . Our leaders use all this talk about 'proletarian origins' simply as a tactical convenience. But you're not a peasant either, it seems."

"No, I'm working class. My father was a railroad engineer."

"Yes, but your grandfather was an aristocrat."

"Well, what's the point of all this?" He looked up questioningly at the well-nourished face with the pointed beard.

"You're a strong and intelligent man. I'm sure you would never let me down . . ."

"Of course not." Vikenty nodded.

"Well, judging by what's going on in the world just now, there's going to be a war."

Vikenty sat up higher in the bed. "What do you mean? I don't believe in fairy tales."

"You're simply not up with things." The colonel stood up and moved away. He lit a cigarette and turned to Vikenty with a serious expression. "I'm an old military expert, and I know something about politics. You apparently realize that I feel the same as you about Comrade Stalin?"

"Are you trying to blackmail me?" Vikenty paled slightly. "I'll report it!"

"No." Orlov smiled gently. "You won't report it. Not even a sparrow can get out of the camp without my knowing, let alone a message. I'm not Lieutenant Mukhin! I never harm anyone unless he tries to interfere with me. But if anyone does interfere, I'll shoot him myself, with my own hands, and without any philosophizing. But I'm sure I won't have to kill you. I'm seeking an alliance with you, just as the strong seek the strong in any social upheaval. Now, about the war. I don't like this system, and Comrade Stalin, and his brainless butchers, the Lieutenant Mukhins. I hate Marx and his insidious doctrine. The criminal experiment going on just now isn't the fault of Stalin alone. He is merely putting into practice what had been prepared before by those who had an influence on Russian history during the past hundred years. The blame, Captain, rests primarily with our aristocratic class, which failed to do two simple things: eliminate Lenin and all the other revolutionaries and carry out some long-overdue economic and political reforms. That would have cut the ground from under the Bolsheviks once and for all. We didn't do these things. And the results? The Czar was murdered. The majority of my aristocratic comrades left the country with the White Army, some of them were shot, or imprisoned like you, and only a few survived, like me, by lying low and serving Soviet power faithfully and then, just as faithfully, serving Stalin, who is destroying that same Soviet power. Few people understand what's happening, but it's not just people like you and me who hate and fear Stalin. They're afraid of him abroad, too. In fact, they're afraid of everything that smells of Red politics. Hitler would never have come to power in Germany if the West had not feared communism as it does. But now that Hitler has the power, he'll go further, and his route will lie to the east, toward us."

He paused and crushed the cigarette under his foot. He took out another one and struck a match.

"I'm speaking to you frankly because I feel I know you. When you kicked Mukhin in the stomach you confirmed what's written in your dossier. I need you. You want to survive. So do I . . . I'll help you and you'll help me. I don't need to explain to you what is meant by 'the selection of personnel.' For me it's the most important question. I'm a great diplomat, but even I have enemies, and serious ones. I want you to understand that my enemies are your enemies. If they manage to get rid of me on some pretext, then this Mukhin business will come out and you'll be shot. Do you see my reasoning?"

Vikenty nodded.

"There are cases being tried in Moscow right now, hundreds of cases. On Stalin's orders the NKVD is destroying the whole of the upper layer of society, the pride of Lenin's Party. You can hear the shots twenty-four hours a day in the cellars of the Lubyanka. The executions go on all the time. Instead of the old revolutionary Cheka we now have the NKVD.

"Our Russia drew the short straw once again. The destruction of the cream of society is merely the beginning. It will be followed by the annihilation of many more. We aristocrats are part of the Russian people, and we will pay a hundredfold for our political blindness, for our thoughtlessness, for everything that leads to the downfall of a ruling class."

"You make it sound as if there's no hope," Vikenty said quietly.

"You and I are direct participants in this tragedy and this crime," Orlov answered stiffly, staring at the man lying on the bed. "We were lucky—we're among the strong. That's why we're still alive. I'm on top, and you're underneath, but we're alive. It's natural—a necessity—that I should have survived in the ruling class. Stalin is just a favorite of history. Everything he's creating will collapse immediately after his death. That's the way it was with Tamerlane, Alexander, all the great tyrants. That's the way it will be with him too. But Russia will remain. Russia will be wiser after this bloodbath. You and I will survive, and many others. Officers like me are awaiting their hour. When Stalin dies, they will shoot the men who are now sitting at the top issuing their criminal orders.

"But for me to survive the next ten years, two things are necessary: the camp must fulfill the plan for the shipment of timber and there must be no disturbances. For nonfulfillment of the plan they can remove me from my post, and you, whom I have today appointed camp technical chief, you they can shoot. And if there's the slightest disturbance in the camp, we will both be shot."

He went to the window and turned to face the bed: "I need a man who's had experience as a leader, who understands how people think, especially political prisoners and criminals, and who knows the laws of economics, about incentives. A man who will be able to control these fifteen hundred zeks, organize their daily lives, and brighten up their existence a little. He must insure that the timber is cut and discipline maintained. I've chosen you and I ask you not to object. You will have a room in the guard quarters, additional rations, and a pass to travel to Krasnoyarsk on camp business . . . Is there anything you don't like about it?"

"Only one thing." He sat up, gripping the bedstead. "That's being shot for something that might be outside my control. There was a time in the Arctic, when the screw snapped off in the ice. It was something beyond my control—a natural element. It's the same here—such things could happen. But I agree. Otherwise I won't last out ten years here."

Orlov smiled. "You're a clever man. You can think straight. If you remain an ordinary zek your chances of surviving are almost nil. But as technical chief you'll have every chance. But no one can guarantee that there won't be accidents, so there's no sense in thinking about it. Have you any specific suggestions about reorganizing the living conditions and work in the camp, Vikenty Filippovich? Yes, Vikenty Filippovich! But only between ourselves, otherwise it's Citizen Technical Chief and Comrade Camp Commandant—don't ever get it wrong. Mukhin's departure and your appointment are a turning point in the life of the camp. It's a minor revolution you might say. What do you think?"

Vikenty lowered his feet to the floor and wrapped himself in a blanket. He looked at Orlov, who was standing at the window. "First, organization. It'll be better for all the work to be done by mixed gangs of politicals and criminals, not more than twenty men in each. That will teach the criminals to work harder and it will show up in the plan. And if we keep gangs comparatively small, it will avoid the possibility of a large-scale escape or a clash with the guards. Two soldiers for every twenty prisoners will be quite enough. If they decide to escape into the forest, they'll take both soldiers without any trouble, but we'll only lose two soldiers and twenty prisoners."

"Agreed!" Orlov said approvingly.

"Second, living conditions. We must draw up a schedule for the kitchen workers. It'll be best to appoint a permanent head cook. The kitchen needs better handling—they use only the weak and the sick and women there. We must also appoint a permanent bootmaker and a tailor. And a cooper—we'll need barrels. We'll draw up a special schedule for picking mushrooms and berries. Then we must clear the forest around the camp so that potatoes and vegetables can be planted in the spring—we're not here just for a year, but for many years . . ."

"Third, production. The felling gangs must be permanent: two sawmen and two auxiliaries—weaker men. There must be plenty of soup and the bread should be issued according to the work—the maximum to the sawmen and a third less to the others. For any overfulfillment of the norms the bread rations must be increased accordingly."

Orlov listened in silence.

"Then we must pick a team of machine operators to work with the tractor and deliver the logs to the railroad station. Then organize a special group of politicals and criminals who agree to cooperate, for the maintenance of discipline, and allow them to carry knives."

Orlov pulled a long face. "Won't that be risky, Vikenty Filippovich?"

"No. They have weapons anyway. They make them out of any old piece of iron. They're experts. Also, I'll have informers."

"All right!"

"Next, warn them all that they'll be shot without trial if they commit bodily harm or murder. If the people are scared of the criminals you won't get much work done. So we must keep the thieves under our thumb."

"Yes! That's my thinking too."

"Next, set up a reading room somewhere. And we can organize our own little theater. Perhaps we'll be able to go to other camps and give performances. It'll help the people to endure, and they'll work better for it.

"Another thing. For good work and overfulfillment of the plan, apart from the usual rewards, a few people should be released each year before their time's up. That's a big incentive. They'll try hard, and the plan will always be overfulfilled."

"I agree to everything, Vikenty Filippovich." Orlov leaned toward him. "It's not within my power to authorize you to carry a revolver, but a knife by all means."

"Thank you." Vikenty shook his head. "I don't need a knife. I have my own methods. And knives won't save you anyway. You have to control the men's feelings. There's no other way."

"Yes, you're right of course. The whole guard is at your disposal. Sergeant Gusev's in charge for the time being, until a replacement arrives for Mukhin." Orlov grew serious. "But now I have some bad news. I didn't want to upset you, but you and I are men. It's better for you to know the whole truth. It's about your wife."

Vikenty turned cold inside. He understood what it was. He compressed his lips and frowned at the colonel. "My Katya's dead?"

"Yes." Orlov turned away and took another cigarette from his case. "I knew about it a month ago, but I didn't want to poison your life with the news. Are you . . . do you regret bringing her from China?"

Vikenty stared at the floor in silence for a long while. Then he slowly raised his eyes to Orlov. "Yes, I regret it. I stand guilty before her, before her memory . . . How did she die?"

"Brucellosis. She was a bookkeeper in a camp near Kustanai. When you're released, you'll be able to go there and take a look . . . They gave them milk contaminated with brucellosis. It was impossible to cure them . . . You must accept it and go on living. Think about the future. She wasn't the only one who died. Thousands die every day."

"You don't know anything about my son?" He looked at Orlov with the eyes of a trapped wolf in which there burned a spark of hope.

Orlov shrugged. "Not for the moment. But I promise to keep you informed and if necessary try to do something for him."

"Thank you. When can I start work?"

"Today if you like." Orlov went to the door, and looked back. "Work and life are waiting for you. I've bet a lot on this card, entrusting the whole camp to you. Don't make any mistakes."

Vikenty gazed at the closed door a long time. Then he lay down, pulled the blanket over his head and buried his face in the pillow. "Forgive me, Katya, forgive me," was all he could whisper as he tried to dispel the image of the brown-haired girl with the snub nose and shapely figure whom he had met long ago in Shanghai.

Technical Chief Vikenty Angarov drew from the store a decent gray suit (from someone else's back), a pair of boots (from someone else's feet), socks, underwear, a hat, knee boots, a gray rubberized raincoat, and a quilted jacket. He arranged all this in the wooden cupboard in his room, which now contained an iron bedstead with a regulation mattress, two patched but clean sheets, a straw pillow, a table made out of three rough-hewn boards, and a chair.

Cleaning this room became an additional duty for Lida, the medical orderly. She tried to come when the new technical chief was not in, and he avoided meeting her, deliberately going off into the taiga for the whole day when he knew she had no patients. That short meeting in the sickbay had alarmed them both. They both knew that their first meeting would not be the last.

Angarov would spend the day walking about the camp and inspecting the felling areas in the taiga. Or he would travel around the neighboring state farms to get potatoes, and milk for the sick. Once he acquired three piglets and brought them back in a sack. They ran freely about the camp by day but spent the night in a pigsty built for them outside the fence. Even the old recidivists had to smile at them.

Angarov knew the taiga and he knew the possibilities of this area, which was where he had been born and had spent his childhood. He wanted to help these people who wanted so much to live. They did not know how to survive, but he knew. Life depended on many factors: the organization of the work, mutual relations, careful economy in the camp, the percentages by which the plan was overfulfilled. Life was the bread ration, a bowl of soup, a piece of sugar once a month, a warm stove during the fierce cold, a pair of boots mended in time.

Skillfully and gradually Vikenty laid the material and moral foundation of a tolerable life for the people who would occupy the huts for the next ten years. The political prisoners had received the news of his appointment with scarcely concealed jubilation. The criminals' hut greeted him with silence. Hundreds of pairs of eyes watched him warily, or with curiosity or hostility. One day he went into the criminals' hut alone, without any guards, although he knew that there were plenty of knives there. He walked between the bunks to the middle of the hut, sat down at the long rough-hewn table and gazed around at the silent faces.

"Citizens, will the gang foremen please come to the table, and the rest of you listen from your places. We're going to talk about matters of life and death."

The men smiled. They understood that kind of talk.

About twenty men came sauntering up, one at a time, and sat at the table. Among them was Scarface, whom he had met on the train but who now tried to avoid Vikenty's eye. Since their meeting in the prison train, Scarface had acquired a certain respect for "the Pirate," as Vikenty was called because of his red beard and naval background.

"So, gentlemen," Vikenty began, as if he were sitting at a diplomatic reception rather than among a band of cutthroats. "I have been appointed technical chief for the camp."

"The bastard's sold himself to 'em!" Scarface muttered between his teeth. The scar on his forehead turned livid.

"You're all under me," Vikenty continued, taking no apparent notice of Scarface. "Even the guard. You've struck lucky, believe me," he added, to approving laughter.

"Here's a question for the citizen chief," Scarface said, and continued without waiting for a reaction, "I'd like to know why we're all so damn happy about this. That's the first thing, and second, why you, Pirate, aren't afraid to come into our territory without any red tabs? That isn't accepted in our circles. It's bad form. Or are you tired of living?"

"That's enough, Scarface," Vikenty said in a soft but firm voice, staring hard at him. "I came here precisely because I do want to live. The reason why we're behind the wire is each man's personal affair. We've all got different sentences. We're not people, we're zeks. They can kill any one of us without trial any time they like. We're outside the law. As they say in Odessa, we have only two choices: to live or to die. It's possible to survive, if you use your head. There's a difficult time ahead. I want to be released and returned to life. I know what has to be done to achieve that. Anyone who doesn't want to live, let him say so, right now. There's no sense in dragging fools along with us. Let them go out and try to escape. The guard will open fire. Well, who's first?"

Total silence.

"So you don't want to die? You want to live! Two things are necessary to live: work and discipline. Work means rations, and discipline protects you from the firing squad. I warn you all once more—anyone who doesn't want to live, let him make up his mind right now. The politicals want to live. They'll do everything without arguing. You too. There's no other choice. If I find out that you're starting to separate into thieves, pigs, and muzhiks, as they do in other camps, where the muzhiks do the work while the thieves lie in their bunks, I'll shoot you myself. Get it into your heads, gentlemen, that here the difference between life and death is very small. I want to survive. I'll kill anyone who tries to prevent me.

"Another thing. Anyone who's thinking of running off into the taiga should bear in mind that there are no people anywhere near here. There are a few state fur-farms about fifty kilometers away. They're guarded by special units with orders to shoot fugitives on sight. In the taiga there's only wolves and bears. Also, anyone who plans to escape had better make sure I don't know about it. Otherwise I'll call out the guard and shoot him on the spot. For you I now represent Soviet power, the law, and your hope of survival. You'd be worse off with a different technical chief. I don't intend to sell you out.

"And another thing. If anyone plans to escape, don't touch the guards, don't kill them. That way, if you're caught, they'll only increase your sentence. If you kill a soldier, you're finished . . . Choose a hut leader from among yourselves. And obey him without question. Are there any nominations?"

Silence. They all stared at their feet. In this hut you could be killed "accidentally" for one careless word.

"Okay. I'll help you. I propose Scarface. Anyone object?"

"Agreed! Give us Scarface!" they shouted from all sides.

"But have you asked me, you sonovabitch?" Scarface said calmly, tapping his fingers on the table.

"You were fishing for the job yourself, Scarface," Vikenty answered just as calmly. "So don't get smart. Your insults don't bother me. Wasn't it you who led the action against the politicals in the train? You took charge there, so you can take charge here too. I'm not authorizing you to kill. If you do, you'll go before the court. Any serious quarrels must be settled through me."

"But I can work 'em over?" Scarface looked cheerfully at the technical chief.

The men around him laughed.

"It's settled then. You and the foremen will be entirely responsible for running the hut. Every evening you will report on the day's work. I warn you all, play cards only for what you'll have on the outside, don't gamble for things in the camp. If you gamble for people's lives or even for bread, there'll be trouble. I ask you, men, take part in the whole life of the camp. Forget that you were once thieves. You're the same camp garbage as the rest of us."

"Really?" The thin squeaky voice made them all start. A lean man with a thin, sensitive face emerged from the thicket of zeks. The gray uniform fitted him like a skin, and a long fringe hung down over his high forehead. "It's odd, but you seem to have quite forgotten about me." He looked around, completely relaxed.

Scarface gave a wheeze and stared at the table. The others also avoided the man's eyes.

"You're the Pirate, and I'm the Intellectual." He stood with his legs apart, holding one hand to the pocket of his trousers. "Why don't you share your power with me? This distinguished meeting of zeks will give me a full vote of confidence. Isn't that right, men?" The zeks remained silent. They all knew what it meant to tangle with the Intellectual. It was difficult to get the better of him or his razor.

But now, under the Pirate . . . something had to change. Vikenty understood this.

He stood up, face to face with the Intellectual, his beard almost touching the Intellectual's own sparse whiskers. "Let's say you were vice regent enjoying full favor with the monarch. Then the monarch died. A different king came to the throne and appointed a new vice regent to take your place, but decided not to hang you for the moment. Have you studied history? It always happened that way. Accept it, for the present, just as the smarter courtiers did. The ones who weren't satisfied to sit in the shit but had to bellyache as well, they lost their heads. What do you think of my history lesson, gentlemen?"

The hundreds of faces smiled. The Intellectual sensed that he had lost the duel of words. The instinct of a thief who had spent his whole life in a deadly struggle for power prompted him to take the only way out: to join in the game.

"Your Majesty!" He bowed to the Pirate. "I accept my retirement. I will hand everything over to your new favorite, Scarface, and I will await your merest attention in the future."

The whole hut sighed with relief. The crisis had passed.

"Good man!" Vikenty said curtly and left.

There was a silence in the hut after the Pirate had gone. A criminals' collective is a very complex social organism, more complex than any state structure. Scarface understood that very well. He had begun his career at ten, as lookout for a gang; he had worked as a pickpocket and as a safe-cracker. He knew the criminal code as well as any professor of law and he understood the minds of individuals and the collective psychology of the whole hut. But he had not expected this appointment.

"Now, look, you men," his voice finally rang out. "I didn't ask to be a boss. I've always been a thief and I'll stay a thief. We'll get by. Maybe lady luck'll smile on us and we'll make it to the outside. If anyone's against me, say so, and I'll go and tell 'em it's all off.

"Nothing to say? Okay. If anyone turns on me, I'll do for him straight off." He pulled a dagger out from under his jacket. The long blade gleamed. "You don't need no speeches from me. That all clear? Let's go. It's grub time. Then we'll go down to the woods and earn our bread."

A hubbub arose from the gray crowd of prisoners. They poured into the yard where the long narrow wooden tables stood under a wooden awning. They lined up at the copper pot of steaming soup, rattling their aluminum mess tins.

The next morning the men went readily off into the forest, away from the huts and the barbed wire that surrounded the camp, the administration hut, and the watchtowers. The natural beauty of the grass, the trees, and the sun in the blue sky lifted their spirits and gave them room to forget that they were zeks, not men, that they had no families or girls, nothing, except a place on a bunk, a soldier with a rifle beside them, and a dream of freedom waiting there ahead, many years away.

They felled the trees with handsaws, choosing the thinner, straighter ones. Then they trimmed off the branches and trussed up the trunks behind the tractor in huge bundles of ten or fifteen. During their breaks they munched cloudberries and strawberries and any other berries they could find. This allayed their hunger a little. They worked steadily, trying to overfulfill the already demanding norm. If they did, there would be a celebration in the evening—an extra two hundred grams of black bread, made out of bran and potatoes. The daily ration of six hundred grams was not enough for anyone. They all tried to eat as much potato soup as they could at dinner, when it was permitted to ask for more.

Each gang of twenty men was guarded by two soldiers with the red epaulets that designated the troops of the People's Commissariat for Internal Affairs. The zeks would light a fire when they sat down to rest, and the soldiers would hang their rifles on a branch and join them. No one tried to escape. The zeks were more afraid of the gloomy taiga, six feet away, than they were of the camp, where a bed and a piece of bread welcomed them, and even newspapers and radio. Only death awaited them in the taiga.

Vikenty was gradually going through the zeks' dossiers, which were piled on the floor in his room. He already knew the criminals quite well, but the political prisoners presented a more complex problem. They included people of from eighteen to seventy, people of various occupations and views and with different histories. Almost every one of them had left at home a wife, children, or a girl, parents, and friends, as well as a normal life with its beliefs and habits. They brought to the camp only their battered souls and the poignant question "Why?"

There were former students, workmen, peasants, officers, soldiers, engineers, office workers, teachers, physicians, doctors of science, chairmen of town councils, directors of major industries, Party and Soviet workers, old Bolsheviks, former partisans . . . Each had only his number on his jacket, but the dossiers gave the name that the prisoner had once carried through life.

Gradually they forgot about their past. Some adapted themselves to camp life and patiently counted the days, weeks, months. Others, weaker in body or spirit, quickly succumbed to malnutrition or disease. There were hardly any medical supplies. The best treatment was the fresh taiga air, filled with the aroma of forest and flowers, but this treatment depended upon the vitality and recuperative powers of the men themselves. The weaker men were gradually sifted out. If a stay in the sickbay produced no results, the patient was transferred to another room, something between a morgue and a cemetery, where he simply lay and waited to die, eating rations brought to him by his comrades. Patients were not taken to the town, even for appendectomies. Lida performed such operations herself. The more serious cases turned out badly.

Vikenty took special interest in the men whom he judged to be more valuable than the others. If they were ill, he kept them in the sickbay and unobtrusively increased their rations. He saved a number of men this way. It was thus that a former Chairman of the Council of Ministers of the Turkmen SSR and a former head of the Moscow taxi fleet avoided death. When such zeks fell ill, they received extra rations secretly, on the orders of the technical chief, and they ate them in secret, under the blan-

64

ket or in the lavatory; they always looked gratefully on the technical chief. Trying to salve his conscience for the death of Kondratyuk, his chief in Shanghai, whose sentence he had once signed, Vikenty pulled selected prisoners back from the edge of the grave. Many years later, after the death of Stalin, when all the people Vikenty had saved had been released by Khrushchev and had resumed their lives, he received a number of letters: some were short, some long; some were simple, some written in style; but they all mentioned the bread.

The sun rose above the tops of the cedars and firs and irradiated the camp, sparkling on the puddles of rainwater and warming the cool early morning air. A babel of birdsong rose on all sides. The wonderful aroma of the taiga in summer filled Vikenty's lungs.

It was warm now, and the day would be hot. In a few days it would be fall, and the rains would begin. Then frost would come down from the north and freeze the earth solid, covering it with a blanket of snow. Blizzards would rage during the long months. Spring would follow with the sun. What is there more powerful than the sun? It dissipates and destroys the epicenters of hurricanes, drives away the clouds, and pours down onto the earth, where the life it created has been flourishing for millions of years. While the sun exists, life will not be extinguished.

"Ah, Katya, Katyusha!" Vikenty stood in the forest, leaning against the trunk of a cedar and covering his eyes to blot out the majestic beauty of nature that surrounded him. Tears welled up in his eyes. "Katya, my love! Dear Florence and Yuko! You're lucky. You live your lives and know nothing. Your troubles are nothing compared with our grief. My Katya lost. She looked for happiness, but now she's lying in her grave. They killed her." And he was to blame for her death. He clenched his fists in impotent rage . . . His little son was still alive, somewhere. He must survive, and see him.

To survive, he had to keep the criminals under better control. At their work alongside the political prisoners, they kept within the limits of the regulations; but in the huts, among themselves, they immediately lapsed into their habitual mood of violence. He had bribed a few zeks with bread and they told him everything. The Intellectual had resumed his position as uncrowned king. He rarely went to work, but lay on his bed at one end of the hut surrounded by a group of cutthroat intimates. Another group of thieves had emerged, headed by a man who was called

Horse, on account of his long, equine face. This group occupied the other end of the hut. Between them, the central area of beds was occupied by Scarface and his followers, whom the hut already looked upon as "pigs" because they worked honestly. These three groups of thieves and pigs accounted for no more than fifty men. The majority were the "muzhiks," who lived in constant fear of the thieves. The muzhiks rendered what service they could in the hope of patronage and protection, or simply indifference.

Some were gambling for their lives. In the weeks that had passed since Angarov's appointment, a dozen bodies had been dragged out of the hut at night and buried in the taiga without the knowledge of the officers. Vikenty knew all this. He understood Scarface's difficult position and he did not want to precipitate events. It was necessary to wait a few more months. But it was also necessary, indeed essential, to break the hut.

Standing there under the cedar, Vikenty had an unpleasant feeling that someone was watching him, nearby but out of sight. Another bear? He stood motionless and examined through half-open eyes the leafy forest that surrounded him. There was no one there. A few moments later the branches on his right trembled slightly. He kept his head still, but his keen sailor's eye caught an almost imperceptible shadow. His heart turned to ice. It was Olya! Images from the past flashed through his mind: the barge sailing up the Yenisei from Krasnoyarsk the night before they arrived; the Intellectual, surrounded by his cronies, raping sixteen-year-old Olya and her mother. That was when the girl lost her reason.

In the camp the mother, gray-haired but still young, lived quietly. She never spoke. She would lie at night caressing her daughter, soaking the mattress with her tears and dreaming of an early death, for herself and the child. Olya never cried. She even tried to help tidy up the hut. But they did not allow her to work. The women were afraid of the misty, languishing stare of her blue eyes. She would wander silently through the camp in her gray jacket and trousers and cast-off men's boots, her hair hanging down almost to her waist. Then she would disappear into the forest and would circle the camp all day, gathering berries and mumbling something to herself as she watched the birds. Sometimes she would stand for hours by a tree, looking up and smiling at something. People would turn aside if they met her. It was difficult to look into those eyes. The motionless figure, the fixed gaze, and the waist-long hair filled even the thieves with fear.

The branches parted. Olya advanced slowly and stopped fifteen feet away from him, holding her head on one side, her eyes boring into his face. With a sinking heart he smiled at her. He did not know what to say. She took another step and stopped, her serious eyes watching him unblinkingly, then another step.

"What is it, Olya?" Vikenty asked softly, surprised at the sound of his own voice.

"Did you see the thrush?" She stopped just in front of him and stared into his face with her unfathomable, misty eyes. "It taps with its beak," she said quietly, and held out her hand to him.

"I did see the thrush, Olya." He took her hand and squeezed it softly in his hardened palm.

"You did?" A joyful expression flitted across her face. "It taps, taps all the time. I've been listening for a long time. Why does it tap? Do you know? At home I . . . " She glanced around uneasily, as if trying to remember something. "At home . . . I had a home . . . there was a thrush there . . . above my window . . . but no, that was a woodpecker . . . it's the woodpecker that taps, and the thrush . . . what does the thrush do?"

Vikenty stood as if bewitched, saying nothing and squeezing her tiny hand.

"What a strong hand you have!" She smiled and opened her misty eyes. "Why don't you pull me onto the ground? He pulled me onto the ground. Did you see?"

"Yes, Olya, I saw it all."

"You saw?" she repeated. "But where's my daddy? I don't recognize you. How you've changed! What a funny beard you have!" She stretched out her hand and stroked his beard a few times. Her fingers hesitated at his lips, then brushed across his eyes. She stepped closer, almost pressing against him. Some inner anxiety showed in her face. "You're a nice man, aren't you? I sometimes see the one who pulled me onto the ground. Why doesn't he come to me any more?"

She pressed her whole body up against him, buried her face in his chest, and was still. Almost crying, Vikenty squeezed her gently against his body and stroked her long mermaid's hair. He was torn by conflicting feelings. He felt a momentary desire to draw her down to the ground in the thick grass. But the desire vanished as soon as he remembered her eyes. The strength of his pity for her and his hatred for the Intellectual took his breath away. He hugged her fiercely, then held her away from himself. "Go back to the camp, Olya, and tell them in the kitchen that I want them to feed you. Are you hungry?"

"Yes, I'm always hungry." She stepped back, and her face grew serious. "I'll go home later. I want to be in the forest just now. It's nice in the forest. Aren't you afraid of me?"

"No, Olya, I'm not afraid of you."

"The others are. I know. They all run away from me in the forest, but you didn't run away. Are you brave? Will you help me if someone else tries to pull me onto the ground . . . I want to go home!"

"You will go home, Olya, I promise." He stepped toward her, took her by the shoulders, and gazed into her eyes. She stood looking up at him, just like a child, with her parted childlike lips and her big eyes, which were not at all childlike, reflecting her devastated inner world. "No one will ever hurt you again. Try to remember the way you were before, at home. You can remember it all. Go and walk. I have to go to work."

"To work!" She stood like a statue, gazing after him. "I had a home."

Vikenty looked back. The small gray figure was still standing motionless among the trees. He set off along a familiar path to the nearest work site.

Hidden by the trees, he circled around a few groups of working zeks. He could not see the Intellectual. That meant he had cut work again. And he had not been in the hut that morning. Where was he? That man kept the whole hut in a nervous state that hindered the work. Something had to be done. It was as if the meeting with Olya had reminded Vikenty that the Intellectual's time had run out.

Vikenty searched through the forest for an hour, outflanking the gangs of workers. Surely the Intellectual hadn't risked going off into the taiga? Then he emerged from a thicket into a small clearing and saw the man sitting under a tree with his legs stretched out and his face turned to the sun.

They regarded each other in silence for a minute. Each of them was thinking hard, weighing up his chances. The Intellectual stood slowly. Smiling his usual malevolent smile, he walked forward jauntily to the center of the clearing, his right hand pressed against his breast pocket.

"Take them off!" The Intellectual said, pointing at Vikenty's boots. Seeing the Pirate's puzzlement, he added, "It'll be easier for you to run. You'll never get away from me in boots."

"Wrong again," Vikenty said, shifting his weight from one foot to the other. "I was looking for you. There's no sense in my running away."

"Isn't it more sensible for you to live?" His right eyebrow and his fringe rose in surprise.

"You mean you're going to kill me?" Vikenty was genuinely amazed.

"God, that's sharp of you, Pirate!" The Intellectual looked at him almost with approval. "You're not as stupid as I thought. You're educated too."

"I'm educated too? And you . . . are you an educated man?"

"What do you think? Do you think I was simply born a thief? You must still be wet behind the ears. No, I've done the same as the rest of them in my time . . . I was in the Pioneers, and the Komsomol, and I studied all the social sciences."

"Why did you find it so easy to rape that girl?"

"Really, Citizen Chief!" the Intellectual exclaimed with astonishment. "What are you saying? You're almost a statesman here but you don't understand these simple things. Well, what does that girl matter? I didn't kill her, after all. I simply gave her and myself a little pleasure."

He stepped to the side. Vikenty did not move.

"I wouldn't have expected such a lack of sophistication in you, Pirate," the Intellectual continued. "Here in our beautiful sunny country we have indiscriminate violence under the leadership of our communist comrades. They had no compunction about raping me, you, and all the others. If someone stronger than me can rape me, why can't I rape someone weaker than myself? Why should I have pity for people when no one has pity for me? It's a free-for-all. Look at Lieutenant Mukhin—he didn't take pity on you when he strung you up in our wonderful forest. It was no trouble at all. And here you are spouting about morality! You tracked me down to kill me, but you can't kill me!"

"Why not?"

"Because I know just as many tricks as you do."

"Ah!"

"I'll give you 'Ah!' As we say in Tambov, 'You're still sipping your shchi out of your boot.'"

"You're just playing for time."

"What's the hurry?" The Intellectual took another step to the right. Vikenty shifted his weight . . . and almost fell down as he barely managed to dodge the knife that whistled past his ear.

Now they stood crouched, like two animals, poised to pounce.

"I understand your theory," Vikenty said, looking him in the eye.

"And I understand yours," the Intellectual answered, reddening slightly. He leaned forward with his arms held out as if he was about to embrace someone. "I've studied history, but I couldn't get on with this worker-peasant power. I finally found my vocation." He laughed wryly, watching Pirate closely. "And I'm a big success. They're scared of me and they obey me; I'm for them what your Central Committee is for you. Only on a smaller scale. Yes, Pirate, and you won't get in my way. I give you permission to depart, but only if you take your boots off."

"Take your time. I have something else to say to you. I don't know why you ended up in this particular camp, under a liberal like Orlov. In any other camp they would have settled with you long ago, if not the guards, then your own zeks. You've been a parasite here for months now. Some historian you are! You don't understand the simplest things. I saw what you did to that wretched girl. You disciple of the devil! Are the people suffering so little that you need to trample them into the ground? The politicians will be removed and so will their criminal accomplices. And you're going to be the first to go!"

He had scarcely finished speaking when the Intellectual made a dive for his legs. Springing forward, Vikenty threw himself over the other man. They got to their feet, breathing heavily. Two attempts had failed, and Vikenty could see that the Intellectual was beginning to lose his nerve. His face had suddenly darkened and he was no longer looking the Pirate in the eye—but was circling him like a bird of prey, his wings spread to attack.

"You've been in my way for too long," continued Vikenty, for whom the moral annihilation of this subhuman creature had now become more important than the physical. "You're a walking, breathing parasite, you scum!" Vikenty kept turning on the spot, his eyes fixed on the Intellectual's face. "You're like a poisonous insect sucking the blood from an animal that is being made to work before it's driven to the slaughterhouse. The forest is thick here . . . "

"The forest? What of it?"

"Go on, you can still escape." Vikenty almost shouted. He sensed that the game was coming to an end; his hatred was beginning to blur his eyes. "But don't ever show your face in the camp again."

"You shit! You bastard! You think you can threaten me?" The Intellectual's face twisted with rage. With a sharp explosion of breath he lunged forward and kicked Vikenty in the ribs. It was a powerful blow, but Vikenty kept his feet and caught hold of the thief's heel in mid-air. He twisted the leg close to his body. The Intellectual nose dived to the ground only to jump up again, spitting out dirt. He hurled himself at the Pirate and seized his beard. Vikenty saw the knee coming and managed to tense his neck and pull his head back, but he did not break the full force of the blow against his chin. Through the ringing in his ears he could hear the Intellectual's hoarse breathing.

Vikenty aimed a rabbit punch at the Intellectual's neck, but only knocked him sideways to the ground where, once again, he leaped to his feet. "You . . . I'll fuck your mouth!" he wheezed, still circling. "I'm not Scarface and I'm going to fix you, now!"

From some hidden place in his baggy trousers he produced a slender steel spike. It hissed through the air. Vikenty caught the spike in his left hand and felt the crunch as a bone in his palm snapped. Blood splattered onto the bright-green grass. He hurled away the spike and made a fist to stem the flow of blood. He went straight for the Intellectual . . . Taking several blows without feeling them, he kicked the Intellectual and flailed at him with his right arm. The Intellectual was knocked repeatedly to the ground and kept coming back to the attack. But his blows were growing weaker.

"You pig!" Vikenty whispered through his teeth as he felt the Intellectual's ribs crack under the toe of his boot. "You shit! So you want my life!" He hurled the Intellectual to the ground and crashed down on top of him, delighting in the sound of his weary foe's labored breathing. He seized him by the throat in an iron grip. "Don't you want to escape?"

"N-n-n-no!" the Intellectual croaked, clawing at the Pirate's hand with both his own as he tried to release his throat. A bloody foam was bubbling from his mouth.

"Don't you want to, pig?" The Pirate was panting wildly into the face of his enemy as they lay on the ground. "Yes, you do, or you will soon!" He hit the Intellectual in the face with his left hand and flooded his eyes with the blood from his wounded palm.

"A-a-a-a!" The Intellectual wheezed, choking from the pressure on his windpipe. He clawed at the Pirate's right hand and tried to wipe the blood from his eyes and face with his elbow.

"Well, take a breath!" Vikenty released his grip on the Intellectual's throat, jumped up, and kicked him in the ribs. Now he could easily finish off the man, but he was taking a visceral pleasure in beating the gray body lying in the dust and blood. He kicked the Intellectual in the stomach and chest, feeling something crack and gurgle.

"Are you going to escape into the forest, pig?" Vikenty knelt on the Intellectual's chest and squeezed his throat, pulling toward him the wispy beard under which he could see the pale unwashed skin. He wanted to end the whole performance by striking this skin with the edge of his hand, but something held him back. He wanted to hit him again, hear one more croak. He wanted to prolong indefinitely this confrontation that had aroused his whole being and which was giving him such ineffable pleasure.

He stood up, dragging the body with him. The mouth was dribbling a bloody foam, but still the Intellectual's eyes glared at Vikenty with all the ineradicable hatred of a wounded predator.

Standing with his feet apart and with the Intellectual almost dangling from his fist, like a hare, he beat him with his bloody left hand, in the face, the chest, the stomach, until the man hung limp and unconscious. He threw the body onto the ground and turned it over with his toe, then smashed his heel once more into the chin.

Bloody teeth sprayed onto the grass. The skin on the neck split and steam rose from the wound, followed by the death rattle. The popping eyes caught a last glimpse of the blue sky overhead.

"Are you going into the forest, pig?" His whole frame trembled from the release of fury as he stood over the lifeless body. He regretted that the fight had ended so quickly. The Intellectual did not reply. His already glassy eyes stared up at the sky.

Vikenty turned him over once more, then again and again. The one-time terror of the criminals' hut wobbled and rolled along at his prods, like a dead jellyfish, leaving a bloody trail in the grass.

Vikenty went to the edge of the clearing and lay down in the shade under a tree. He buried his face in the scented green grass and lay motionless, his mind blank.

He opened his eyes when he felt a breath of cold air. It was evening. The sun was sinking fast beyond the treetops, its last rays falling on the man beneath the tree and the body lying tranquilly in the middle of the clearing.

He circled the corpse for a long time, still flooded with rage. Even now the Intellectual was fearsome to Vikenty, fearsome in his blind belief in the inevitable rape of the weak by the strong. He had never had such an enemy and had never killed anyone in that way.

He picked up the spike and the knife and set off toward the camp. The peaceful evening forest cooled his burning face, calmed him and changed his mood. Before his eyes hovered the Intellectual's thin face, with the lofty thinker's forehead under the long fringe.

He washed off the blood in a pool near the camp and bandaged his injured palm with his handkerchief. It was growing dark. Just before he reached his room he saw a zek coming toward him, one of his informers. The zek walked past him unconcernedly but contrived to whisper, "Look out, Pirate, Scarface lost you in a card game!"

Vikenty went on into his room without stopping. He came out immediately and looked around. No one. Just before he reached the criminals' hut he noticed the lanky Sergeant Gusev following him in the darkness, alarm showing in his face.

"Don't, Gusev!" He halted him firmly with his arm. "There's no need. This is my affair. My accounts! Wait here."

He went into the hut. Home-made cigarettes were burning in various parts of the gloomy shed. The one kerosene lamp stood on the central table. Hundreds of indistinct faces turned toward the door. Silence fell.

Vikenty made his way toward the upper bunk where Scarface was sitting, surrounded by his friends. As the Pirate approached they all scattered to their own beds. Scarface lay down.

"Get down here!" He stopped by Scarface's bed and laid his hand on the wooden frame.

"What you want?" Scarface's anxious voice came from the upper bunk. He lay motionless. The hut watched in silence.

"Get down! And be quick about it!"

"Pirate, you pig, what's up? What are you after? Buzz off, and leave me be . . . "

"Come on down!" Vikenty said. He took hold of Scarface's foot and twisted it sideways. "Oi!" Scarface howled and jumped down to the floor.

"Oof!" He collapsed in an unconscious heap from the vicious kick in the groin. No one moved.

"I killed the Intellectual today!" Vikenty moved away from the bed into the middle of the hut. "I killed him in a fair fight, man to man. The bastard! He'll never eat your bread again. You have enough parasites as it is. You'll get by without him. I didn't want to kill him. He refused to escape into the taiga. Bury him tomorrow, in the clearing where he died.

"I haven't killed Scarface. He'll never have any kids, but he'll survive. He'll come round by morning. I told you, you damn rabble, not to gamble for people's lives. Scarface disobeyed my order. Do you know how the zeks live in the other camps? If you can't understand kindness, I'll use force. If I ever hear of any more trouble in this hut, I'll bring the soldiers and I'll have the troublemakers taken out into the open and shot. That's all. Good night!"

He left, accompanied by silence.

"You've ruined Scarface's prospects!" Orlov said to Angarov that evening. They were sitting in Orlov's room over a bottle of vodka.

Vikenty drank his vodka straight down and drew hungrily on the Kazbek he was smoking. "I should have killed him. I saved him for the sake of the hut. He's a leader. His marriage prospects don't matter. There are plenty of others to produce offspring. Anyhow, he may recover. I aimed off center."

"You've hardened, Captain." Orlov shook his head and watched Angarov through the cloud of tobacco smoke.

"Apparently it's impossible to behave any other way in these times . . . What's happening in the women's hut?"

"The three who are about to give birth have been taken to the district hospital. The other pregnant ones have been put onto light duties, and their rations have been increased—a little more potato."

"More potato!" Orlov repeated himself. "Mother Russia in the glorious thirties of the twentieth century. God help the women! It's bad enough for the men to be cut off from women, but it's worse for them, all alone, with no family—and especially if they're in for life. A woman's time for love and children is short. What barbarity!"

He went to the window and turned his back. Vikenty was also silent. The women's hut was a source of much concern for both of them. The women sawed the timber on a par with the men, but they were not strong enough to drag the logs to the tractor trailer. Many of them broke down during their imprisonment and died. Many were constantly sick. The women did almost all the domestic work, the washing and mending for the whole camp.

Prisoners were not allowed to marry, but it was impossible to prevent love affairs or meetings in the forest. The presence of the women eliminated homosexuality in the men's huts and introduced an element of normal life into the camp existence, all of which had a good influence on labor productivity. This was Orlov's main concern, and so he insisted to the authorities that the men and women should not be segregated, and he tolerated the few inconveniences connected with the ancient instinct to reproduce.

Every three months, General Bukin, the head of the Kraslag, sent a summary of the overfulfillment of the plan to Moscow. Colonel Orlov's camp always took first place in the list. Accordingly, the general winked his eye at this "experiment."

The women all wore the regulation gray uniform in summer and the quilted jacket and trousers in winter. It was cleaner and cozier in their hut, but Vikenty did not like to go there. It reminded him too much of his own home, and Katya and his little boy, Valerka.

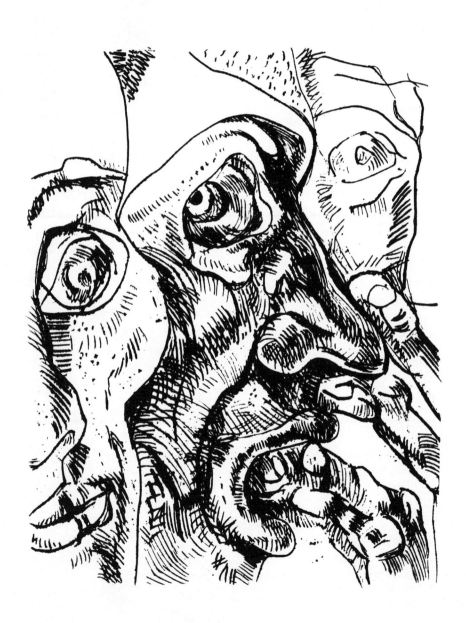

5

THE UPRISING

Four years passed. Lieutenant Mukhin had been permanently replaced by Gusev. Many people had died and many newcomers had arrived; and Lida, the camp medical orderly, still avoided Vikenty. Everyone lived by his own hopes, but time passed at the same speed for them all.

Vikenty had long enjoyed the right to carry a hunting knife and the privilege of going into Krasnoyarsk once a week on camp business. He rode in an ancient one-and-a-half-ton truck as far as Rodnikovo, then by bus. Every time he went to Krasnoyarsk, he thought of his village, Medvezhie, which lay only a hundred kilometers to the south.

In Krasnoyarsk he stayed at the Yenisei Hotel, presenting his temporary NKVD pass instead of a passport. He would complete all the business involving camp supplies as well as Orlov's personal errands in good time, and then he would go to wander in the town. He even found his way to the birthplace-museum of the painter Surikov. He stood in the yard of the green, two-story house in silent wonder at the fact that such a talented man could have been born and could have lived in such a hovel.

Once, farther beyond the station, he was astonished to come upon a plaque fixed above the door of a four-story, red, wooden house, which faced onto the town and the Yenisei River. It read: "Here in the house of a merchant . . . the great founder of the Party and the Soviet state, Vladimir Ilich Ulyanov-Lenin, worked and wrote during his exile." He spat viciously and then he examined the strange house in which the unknown merchant had once lived: "And why did this merchant take Lenin in, and why as an honored guest? The liberals went a bit too far that time!"

Toward evening he would make his way to the restaurant in the Yenisei Hotel and sit down at an empty table in a secluded corner from which he could see the room and the other diners. He would order vodka, herring with potatoes, and a steak, and would sit for hours, slightly drunk, dreaming about his past—free and rich, as in a fairy tale. He never got into conversation with anyone. He was not allowed to tell the truth about himself and he did not want to lie. If some stranger sat at the table and proved too talkative and intrusive, he would answer curtly, "I'm a riverboat captain." Vikenty knew that the NKVD agents, who kept watch in the restaurant from opening to closing time, would report on him— where he had been, what he had done, whom he had spoken with, and about what.

These trips lasted one or two days. During this time he managed to get everything done and to rest and buy a present for Lida. He knew that she would accept the present with a grateful light in her eyes.

Before returning to the camp he would often go down to the Yenisei, past the two-story wooden houses. He would stand for long periods on the steep bank, gazing with pleasure at the mighty river carrying its icy waters from the Tien Shan Mountains northward to Port Dikson, where five years ago he had captained the icebreaker *Arktika*.

Now he had nowhere to hurry to. Behind him lay his youth, his devastated family, the camp. Ahead, over five more years in the camp, five long years. But it was easier for him now. The memory of Katya was no longer tormenting him. Life in the camp was bearable. Lida was working and living nearby—young, beautiful, clever, tactful Lida. She stubbornly avoided any intimacy with him. This caused him both pleasure and pain, and filled his heart with hope. This time he was taking her a special present—a set of medical books. He knew that she would be delighted. And he wanted to look into her eyes, at last. Not because he wanted her as a woman—there were many women in the camp, and quite a few of them would have agreed to become his mistress. It was simply that this young girl, without asking his consent, had made her way into his heart and lived there always, smiling within him with her big gray eyes. The situation was pleasant and painful, but it could not go on forever.

On June 22, 1941, the whole camp rose as usual at 6 A.M. But the silence in the camp was unusual. After breakfast the men went off into the forest to the felling areas and speculated on why the radio loudspeaker, which was usually declaiming vigorously from the roof of the administration building, was not spewing out its broadcasts from Moscow: the continual reports on the Soviet people's heroic efforts to build a communist society. The broadcasts were usually accompanied by patriotic Soviet songs and Russian folk songs.

Vikenty was puzzled by the radio's silence. When he went out onto the road, his vague feeling of alarm grew stronger: a cloud of dust was moving swiftly toward the camp, and he was not expecting anyone that day. A car drove up and braked sharply. A somber Orlov jumped out and went into the administration building without greeting him. Vikenty and Gusev exchanged glances and went in after him. In the office the colonel asked them both to sit down and said quietly, "It's war, Comrades." Vikenty and Gusev said nothing.

"The Germans have attacked, just as I thought they would. This morning. They bombed Leningrad, Odessa, Kiev, and Sebastopol, and they've launched an offensive along the whole front, from the Barents to the Black Sea."

He paused, lit a cigarette, and turned to Vikenty. "Citizen Technical Chief. This is a difficult time. The Authority is about to review passholders for their reliability. Do you want to remain in your present post? Can I recommend you again? Under the wartime regulations, which have already begun to come into force, if there's the slightest trouble in the camp you will be shot, even if it's not your fault."

"That's all right by me." Vikenty stood up decisively. "There can't be any trouble in the camp."

"Very well." Orlov nodded and looked at them both. "Not a word to the prisoners about the war, for the time being. You'll answer to me for that with your lives. Nobody must know before we receive a specific ruling. The rations are to remain unchanged, but the Authority will give us only bread and salt. We must obtain the vegetables and meat ourselves. We'll announce the truth in a few days' time, when our leaders have recovered from the shock . . . Volunteers will be needed for the front."

"Perhaps they would send me to the front?" Angarov looked at Orlov without much hope.

"No, you're doing the work of a lieutenant-colonel in our system as it is, and you run just as great a risk here as you would at the front. In other words, the camp is also a front. Timber will be needed at any cost."

"You, Gusev!" The sergeant jumped to his feet, but Orlov gestured him to sit down. "Part of your guard, about thirty men, will be transferred to the front or to guard duties at other sites. You'll be left with seventy. It's not many, but two machine guns will arrive in a few days. They've promised some submachine guns for later. To begin with, everything will go to the front. It's going badly there . . . That's all for now. You may both go." When they had left, Orlov went and stood at the window. His lips moved in silent curses as he went over the recent events and thought about what to do. Tukhachevsky! Blyukher! Yakir! Put to death by Stalin! How could a war be won without such officers? He swore viciously at the portrait of his moustached master hanging on the wall. The army had no brains. All that was left was moustaches. Hundreds of officers had been shot without trial, by decision of the "troikas," on the basis of fabricated denunciations; countless thousands were languishing in camps. The army had been decapitated, and what use were blockheads like Colonel Degtev against German technology and military skill? The army had no weapons. The cavalry? Budenny moustaches! There were few submachine guns and not enough rifles. The army would soon be retreating eastward, thousands of kilometers, strewing Russian soil with Russian corpses. The latest massacre of the Russian nation had begun.

He strode up and down the room, smoking one cigarette after another. His heart, which had given no trouble for a long time, had begun to pain him again. He drank a glass of water, sat down on a bench, and buried his face in his hands. They had gotten him out of bed at home in the early morning. He had scarcely had time to say goodbye to his wife. Poor Nadezhda! They rarely saw each other.

His thoughts moved again to Moscow, that strange and beautiful city. What would happen now? How much more would Russia have to pay for this experiment with communism?

And what would these cavalrymen do on the German front? Budenny, Voroshilov, Timoshenko? Good lord! The real generals were dead. It was simply a continuation of the tragedy that had taken place after the October Revolution. How could they have let it all happen? Now Russia would have to pay again, and with its blood, again. Would the nation be able to withstand the German onslaught after the colossal defeat in the rear brought about by the purges? Having lost millions of people in the camps, the Russian people could lose tens of millions more in a cruel struggle with the nazism-drugged Germans. Who would win?

But now he had to think of other things. The location of the camp was a source of anxiety. The border with China was not far away.

A few weeks later, when the two machine guns had been installed in the towers and a new security system had been devised, Orlov received the order to inform the camp about the war. Fifteen hundred gray figures filled the square, waiting to hear what he had to say.

Scarface stood among the listeners. He had survived the kick in the groin. Though he harbored a fierce hatred for the Pirate, he had decided not to settle with him until they were released from camp. He knew that the Pirate had been right in taking his route to freedom. But what was more to the point, Scarface's own position in the camp had grown more complicated. Horse, the recidivist, had taken the Intellectual's place in the thieves' hierarchy. He did not demand the same tokens of respect as had the Intellectual, he did not put on airs, and he went to work along with the others. But he managed to do less and receive more, and he kept almost half the camp's zeks in a state of fear and tacit obedience. Scarface had a gang of about thirty men who wanted to be released one day and so had decided to work along with the noncriminals. The hut was divided into two groups led by Horse and Scarface; Horse's group considered Scarface's group to be "pigs," or traitors to the thieves' tradition.

Everyone knew that this division could not last long, and Scarface and Horse knew it best of all. Scarface did not report the situation to the officers because he realized that the Pirate knew all about it anyway. He simply waited, as he did now, for Orlov to speak.

"Citizens!" Orlov's voice sounded unusually loud in the early morning silence. "I have news for you. Fascist Germany has invaded our motherland, the Soviet Union. Today, right now, anyone who still has two years to serve—if any of you have forgotten how long you've got left, there's a list over there on the wall—can enlist in the army as a volunteer in the punitive battalions. After your first battle your convictions will be expunged from the record.

"Camp rations will remain unchanged. Martial law has been introduced. You will be shot for the slightest violation of discipline.

"After the recruitment of these volunteers, we will decide individually about anyone else who wants to expiate his guilt before the motherland and Comrade Stalin with his own blood. But this is also the front. All sentences will be remitted for good work. Dismissed!"

All that day the camp buzzed like a hive. The war had aroused the hopes of many of the prisoners: "The Germans are coming—they'll set us free!" But the more cautious ones understood that even if the Germans penetrated into that wilderness, the communists had set aside enough cartridges to shoot all the prisoners. With that weighty conclusion everyone eventually agreed.

Four army trucks arrived toward evening, old creaking one-and-a-half-tonners, with two soldiers in each of them. The volunteers, about seventy men and thirty women, climbed into the trucks. The other fourteen hundred stood around the trucks, watching the departure of their comrades in captivity. The women in the trucks were weeping openly: behind them lay the camp, captivity; ahead, death . . . or perhaps freedom.

"Masha, Mashenka! My dear, my girl!" sobbed one of those who was staying behind. She embraced the tear-stained face of her friend, who leaned down from the truck. "You're so brave, and I envy you! God keep you safe! But be careful, don't take risks . . . Remember what we said, if we survive we'll meet at my place, in Taganka."

"Yes, yes!" Masha kissed her friend hurriedly, hanging half over the side of the truck. "It'll all be just like we said, Lyuska, you poor thing . . . But don't you be sad, live out your term . . . Don't be sad about me."

"Kolya, Kolinka!" a young woman whispered in the ear of a stocky middle-aged man who had jumped down from the truck. He hugged her gloomily, oblivious to the people around them, and stroked her hair with his dirty hand.

"You'll see, Kolinka," she whispered, gazing avidly into his eyes. "How lucky you are—you're going to war! You're free again. May my love keep you safe from the bullets! I've still got years in here but I'll wait for you, Kolya, and you'll think about me, won't you?"

"Yes, Tanya, course I will," he answered bleakly, trying not to cry. The noise of voices, shouts, weeping, rose up around them in a solid wall. "Perhaps I'll be lucky and get out alive. I'll come to get you wherever you are. You look after yourself and remember me."

"I will, I will! Only write, darling, even if it's only two words."

"Citizens!" One of the soldiers climbed up onto a truck and shouted to the whole camp, cupping his hands to his mouth. "It's time to go, otherwise we'll miss the train. All aboard! Take your seats!"

The trucks rumbled toward the gates, accompanied by a crowd of sobbing women. The men remained where they were, hanging their heads. They said nothing and tried not to catch one another's eyes.

The whole camp stood for a long time in the clearing outside the gates, watching the cloud of dust on the forest road, which linked their small world with the world outside. When the trucks had disappeared from sight, the crowd began to disperse slowly. "Hell!" someone said aloud. "At least they'll get enough to eat and they'll go free. And a bullet's nothing to be afraid of—you can get one here just as easy."

The loudspeaker on the roof was still silent. Orders forbade letting the prisoners know about what was happening at the front—not a word about the destruction of whole armies and the capture of two million officers and men, nothing about the powerful German military machine that was moving eastward, breaking the heroic resistance of individual Soviet units.

Once a day a news summary did arrive from the political department of the Kraslag; it was to be read out to the soldiers only. These reports were specially prepared by experts, who spoke about heavy German losses and the heroism and self-sacrifices of the Russian soldiers. They contained no mention of the rapid advance of the panzer armies into the heart of Russia.

But once unrest began to affect the camp it spread spontaneously to more and more people. Weary of the long years of penal servitude, they dreamed of returning to life, by any means. In the huts the criminals and political prisoners set up their own central committees, not so much to ensure a better distribution of the bread ration but to follow developments and make the necessary decisions during the stormy times that were imminent. No one doubted that a storm were brewing.

On a fine morning in early fall, Vikenty was invited to a conference in a small clearing. Present were Scarface and Horse and four more from their hut, plus six of the political prisoners. The soldier on watch was far away, beyond some trees. It was possible to talk freely.

They placed a tree stump in the middle of the clearing for Vikenty. He was to be chairman. He looked at the zeks sitting on fallen trunks in complete silence and had to make an effort to open his dry lips. "I declare the meeting open. It has been convened at the request of hut number three. There is only one item on the agenda. We're about to discover what it is." He turned to the ringleaders.

"Well, it's like this, see," Scarface said. "First, we want guarantees that everything that's said here is just between us and no one's going to be put up against the wall. You, Pirate, and the pols, we're asking you as brothers if you'll guarantee to keep it quiet? It's a serious business."

"What do you say?" Vikenty turned to the political prisoners.

"We're all zeks here," one of them answered, a heavily built man with bald patches above his high forehead. He had a piercing gaze and in the gray uniform he looked as though he had just returned from an important meeting of a town committee and had put on his work clothes in order to do some digging in his garden.

"I agree," Vikenty said. "I won't turn you in. Have I ever deceived you these past four years?"

A murmur of approval, and then silence again.

"That's settled, then," Scarface continued. "We're here to parley-voo about the war. This here power, this Soviet power, it's got us by the short and curlies. But we weren't born zeks. Some smart bastard up at the top fixed it so's we'd spend the best part of our life behind the wire. Well now we've got a good chance to get free. The Krauts are on their way to Moscow. Our dear leaders don't tell us so, but we've guessed it. The communists are almost done for. If we hit 'em from here, in the rear, it'll finish 'em." He gave his audience a happy smile, sensing their approval, then continued.

"There's a lot of camps around here. We think we'll get fifty thousand men. Here we'll take our guards easy and we won't kill no one. That means two machine guns and seventy rifles. And we'll take the other camps right away. We'll bust up the whole rear for 'em, then we'll move south. China's not far away. And the Japs are there. Freedom, brothers!"

He gave the others an imploring look.

"What do you say, Horse?" Vikenty asked quietly.

"Scarface's said it all," he answered somberly. "We've nothing to lose except our chains."

"Comrades!" One of the political prisoners raised his hand. "It's not a bad idea. What we've got isn't Soviet power. It's an abomination, a plague, the pox!" He covered his face with his hands and began to sob. "I don't care if it's Germans, locusts, bandits, pirates—anything, as long as it's not these pseudo-communists! I've given this revolution thirty years of my life, I've grown old and sick. I've got practically no hope of being released. I'm ready to take the risk, but I don't want to force anyone else. Each group has six men in the committee. That makes thirteen with the technical chief. Let's take a majority decision binding on us all."

"Agreed! Go on!" Horse roared.

"I'm in full agreement with this plan," the speaker continued. "I see no alternative. And I hope we help to bring down this regime. Please, comrades, let us unite."

"But how will we take the guards?" one of the other politicals asked.

"We've thought it all out." Horse raised his palm edgewise. "Our special group will disarm the soldiers. They've all served in the army before, so they know their business. It'll be over in a minute. Our snipers will have to pick off the machine gunners right away. We'll try not to kill them, but it can't be helped if we do. Otherwise the two machine guns will cut us all down. We can't take the risk."

"And the other camps? Will they join us? How can we be sure?"

"We've planned all the routes—here's the map." Horse held out a page torn from an exercise book. "All the camps within a radius of one hundred kilometers will be ours in one day. There's hardly more than three thousand men in the Krasnoyarsk garrison, but we'll be nearly fifty thousand. While they're bringing up troops from the Far East we'll arrange one hell of a reception for them and we'll manage to get away. Well, we zeks are agreed. What about you?"

The men looked expectantly at the technical chief.

Scarface gestured. "Go on, Pirate, tell us what you honestly think."

He said nothing, giving himself and the others time to think it over a little longer. When he had had to make a similar decision during his Arctic voyage, it had been simpler because he had been dealing with the elements. People and politics were something else. But he weighed it all up and solved it on the principle of the lesser of two evils. He squinted at the rising sun. Its gentle rays had already touched the dew-damp grass. The air was crystal clear and smelled of pine needles, cedar cones, and birch sap, which filled his heart with the joy of living. The others too were well aware of the dichotomy between the bloody plot that fate compelled them to consider and the primeval sense of peace that emanated from the taiga around them.

"Friends!" Vikenty began, his voice hoarse with emotion. He leaned forward, resting his hands on his knees, and looked from one tense face to the next. "Friends, this meeting is perfectly natural—it would have been surprising if it hadn't taken place. All of us, the criminals and the politicals, we all want our freedom. Without his freedom a man's just a sparrow in a cage. I hate Soviet power more than you do. I served it honestly and it killed my wife, took away my son, and robbed me of my life. And all by order of Dzhugashvili. I dream of outliving him. And I will outlive him!

"Now about this business. I'm ready to support any plan as long as I get my freedom. This plan, of course, is a very intelligent one in the present situation. But it will bring us freedom for a week at most."

"What do you mean, Pirate? Are you kidding us?" The criminals were alarmed. "Get to the point!"

"I'll explain. Suppose we manage to deal with our area and even with Krasnoyarsk. I just want to remind you that it would be five hours by truck from here to the border on a good paved road. There are such roads between Krasnoyarsk and the frontier. I know. This is my region. I was born and grew up here. The telephones are working too. Within an hour of our uprising they will order military units up from there. They're not expecting an attack on the border, at the moment. So those units will be here in a few hours. They're special frontier units and every man in them's a Stalinist. A battle will begin between our army and the frontier troops. Scarface, Horse, tell me, how will it end? How many frontier troops will it take to kill every last one of us? At least half our men don't even know how to shoot." He paused.

"Yeah, Pirate." Scarface nodded gloomily. "There's something in that. We didn't think of that. Well, at least we'll die fighting, like men!"

"No, Scarface! It won't be a fight, it'll simply be a firing squad . . . Don't think I'm against you, men. It's just that I've had more experience than you and can think better. It's a game of chess that we're playing here. And we're playing for our lives. Look, judge for yourselves. You, Horse, see what happens when you work it out more accurately." He took from his pocket a pencil stub and an old exercise book. There were still a few dirty pages left between the blue covers, which carried portraits of Lenin and Stalin on the front and the multiplication tables on the back. He started to write. "There are at most seventy rifles in our camp. That means we've got to take ten camps like ours in order to collect seven hundred rifles. So, roughly speaking, we won't be able to arm more than a thousand men. Is that an army? And what about the rest? Machine-gun fodder? It's certain death. Suicide!

"And another thing. It's true that our Russian people are living under the yoke of these pseudo-communists. For many centuries our people have suffered under different forms of oppression, but they have never been brought to their knees by foreign conquerors. And whether or not Stalin and all his gang are replaced, history will never forgive us for stabbing Russia in the back. I may be wrong. I don't want to impose my opinion on anyone. In other words, it's for the conscience of each of us. If we leave philosophy and history aside, we can say that we're outcasts of society and therefore we have the right to look out for our own interests, and let society look after itself!"

"That's more like it, now you're talking!" Even Horse showed his two rows of big yellow teeth in a smile. "That's better than what you were saying before, about a knife in the back."

Vikenty nodded. "Yes, it's better. So I'll go back to my first objection, which is that the plan is unrealistic. We could attempt it if there were only ten of us, but not with a whole army. We would be doomed before we began. It would be the same as taking those fifty thousand and shooting them ourselves. There would be no chance of success. But I understand how you feel . . . "

He paused and listened to the heavy silence.

" . . . and I'm prepared to risk my neck. I'll tell you what to do: anyone who wants to chance his luck, alone or with a small group, should go off into the taiga, straight from the job. If you get to the border, that's your good luck. I won't be responsible for the escape and I'll say I heard nothing about it. That's my last word. Think about it. I wish you luck! There's no sense in voting." He stood up and strode off, without looking back, toward the small clearing where some of the gangs were working. The men dispersed in different directions. Only the two half-rotted tree trunks remained in the thick grass, the sole witnesses to the meeting.

During the next few days eighteen men escaped, singly or in groups. Three of them reappeared in the camp a week after their escape, half-dead. They were sent to their hut, without punishment. Some of the escapees were caught by the guards of nearby state fur-farms. The rest disappeared in the taiga, forever.

None of Horse's men had gone into the taiga and that disturbed Vikenty. His fears were justified. One evening Lida placed a note on his table. It was scratched in pencil in Scarface's hand: "Pirate, Horse hasn't given way. It looks bad. Call me in to see you."

Late that evening, after the planning meeting, Orlov, Vikenty, and Scarface stayed behind in the duty office.

"Well?" Vikenty looked inquiringly at Scarface.

Scarface nodded. "Yeah, Horse's made up his mind to go. My group isn't going. At least here in the camp there's some hope of getting free one day, but if we go with Horse it's certain death. He's out of his mind, he's old. Won't listen to no one. There's about thirty men with him."

"What's the plan?" Orlov asked.

"Disarm the guards, take the machine guns and the other guns, and head south to the border. They're gonna fight their way across if they run into any guards."

"So there's no hope that they'll just leave without a clash with our guards and without arms?" Orlov continued, still not believing what was happening.

Scarface shook his head. "No, they've fixed their plan. I don't know when it's gonna be—they're keeping that quiet. If they do it, what's gonna happen to those who stay behind?" He stood up facing Orlov.

"What will happen to you?" Orlov turned away from the window, took a cigarette from a pack with deliberate slowness, and lit it. "The same as what the technical chief and I can expect—a firing squad. Only they'll shoot us individually, with all the honors, so to speak, but they'll simply surround you and cut you down with the machine guns. They're not likely to leave anyone alive. It's a very serious business. Stalin and the Camps Authority won't have mercy on anyone now. The Germans are advancing on Moscow, and everything's collapsing. The troops are fleeing from the front, and the fate of this state is hanging by a thread. Horse is a political illiterate. Otherwise he would simply have left, like the others before him. It's one thing when a man runs away. When he organizes others to go with him, it becomes a joint escape, and if on top of that he kills the guards and takes their arms, that, in the present situation, is a first-degree crime and leaves him no chance of getting off alive . . . I want to assure you both that in our region, beyond Krasnoyarsk and near the border, there are enough NKVD troops to destroy any uprising, to the last man, in a single day . . . The state cannot take any chances in the rear . . . And the NKVD thought of the possibility of your planning a mass escape to the Chinese border years ago. You mustn't think that they're all murderers and fools. The system operated by the Central Camps Authority has been thought out to the last detail.

"I feel sorry for Horse and his men." Orlov looked pointedly at Scarface. "I must tell you, Citizen Technical Chief and you, Scarface, that

I've known all about this for some days now. I have my sources . . . It's a good thing you came to me. I don't see it as a betrayal of Horse on your part. It's more a question of Horse's group betraying your entire hut. They don't give a damn about you or whether you live or die. They're desperate men and must be destroyed. I don't know how long I have to live or how and where I'll die, but I don't want to die from an NKVD bullet—it's impossible to imagine anything more stupid. What does the hut think about your coming here?"

"It's okay. I come to the planning meeting once a week. It's just like normal." Scarface stood up.

"Sit down!" Orlov gestured impatiently. "Stop jumping up and down. You're getting on my nerves. Stay here if you're afraid to go back to the hut, or I could transfer you to a different camp. You may be a criminal but you do have a little sense. I'll call out the special unit from headquarters. They'll be here in an hour. If Horse and his men won't surrender, we'll have to storm the hut. They'll all be killed. I see no alternative . . . "

"No," Vikenty interrupted. He had not said a word so far. "That's not necessary. I'll try to get into the hut and have a talk with Horse."

"You've already had a talk with him, at the meeting in the forest—I know about it!" Orlov snapped. "And the only reason I haven't taken any action against you for keeping it from me is that I understand that in your position there was nothing else you could have done. Especially since I know everything, every word that's been said inside and outside the camp. You're a brave man, you get along with me and with the men, but now I forbid you to go to that hut. You're still necessary, for me, for the camp, and for our survival. It will soon be dark. It must all be finished by morning. There are times when violence and death are the only means of settling a dispute."

"Citizen Commandant!" Scarface stood up again, his scar standing out like a bright red stripe on his ashen face. "We've been chewing this over among ourselves too. Okay—what you said's quite right. But there's no call to get the specials out here. The whole hut's keeping its mouth shut. The men are scared but they don't wanna die and they won't go along with Horse. They'd go, they'd go with anyone, if there was some hope, but there isn't. The citizen technical chief told us it straight, he didn't lie . . . So, Citizen Commandant, if you wanna take the risk, that is . . . "

89

"Go on!" Orlov almost shouted.

"My men want to deal with Horse's gang themselves. They've got ten knives, we've only got three. There's no other weapons in the rest of the hut. Give us weapons, soldiers' broad swords. We're used to this kind of job. We'll finish 'em all off inside ten minutes. It'll be best for you and for us, and four hundred zeks'll still be alive . . . If you say no and send in the specials, then I'm going back to the hut and die with my brothers."

"Broad swords!" Orlov stared at him in amazement for a moment, then turned to look at Vikenty. "Such a thing has never been heard of in the whole history of the Gulag." He went over to the window again. "Yes . . . what do you think, Citizen Technical Chief? Shall we risk it?"

"When you're at sea, to take a risk is the honorable thing to do," Vikenty answered quietly. "We'd be running a bigger risk by calling out the special unit. Whatever happens, this business is going to have unpleasant consequences. I don't know what will happen to you, but I'm going to be in trouble, even if Horse and the whole hut are wiped out. Anyway, it's better to save the men's lives. The other way they'll all be killed. The special unit won't bother to pick out the guilty ones. They'll set up the machine guns and mow them all down."

"I see," Orlov said. "Well, what do you propose? You understand the responsibility we're assuming if we hand out weapons to the prisoners without permission from headquarters?"

"Yes, I do, Citizen Colonel." Vikenty sat with his shoulders hunched up. His voice was calm, and only the sparkle of his eyes hinted at his intense mental activity, as he tried to make up his mind. "We have no alternative. We won't be putting the camp in any danger if we issue weapons to Scarface's group. We'll have to bring all the guards up to the hut, and the machine guns too. That won't take more than an hour or so. Of course you know that under wartime regulations they often punish you not for what you do but for not doing something that you could have done . . . On the other hand, order will be restored in the camp for many years to come. Horse should have been transferred to another camp long ago. We missed our chance."

Orlov nodded. "Yes, it's too late now. In view of the exceptional circumstances, I accept your decision. I'm making you responsible for the outcome of the operation. But I'll have to answer to Krasnoyarsk . . . You realize that we won't be able to hush up something like this—the liquidation of Horse's group on the spot. It'll all come out, whatever happens. It's not as if two men had run away."

"I'll call Gusev right away." He turned to Scarface. "You'll get thirty broad swords. Arrange with Gusev how they're to be handed over to you and your group. Don't make any mistakes. Horse may suspect you."

"I know," Scarface answered viciously. "I think they're gonna start it tonight. If you give us the swords, it'll be over in a minute. It's not the first time . . . They'll start with us, so we've gotta get in first."

"Agreed! You may go. Wait for Gusev in the passage. One more thing, Citizen Technical Chief. I'll tell Gusev to position the machine guns opposite the doors of the hut."

Vikenty nodded in silence.

"Do you need any help?" Orlov asked Scarface. "Perhaps we should send some of the politicals?"

"No, thanks!" The scarred face twisted in a derisive smile. "Like I said, we're old hands at this. We'll start after midnight. Don't put out the light, it'll be easier with it on." He turned and went out without looking back. Vikenty hesitated for a moment in the doorway. He turned around. Orlov's uneasy gaze was fixed upon him.

Shortly before midnight, Orlov and Vikenty made a round of the camp. Sixty of the guards were covering the windows of the hut, which were lit with the dim glow of a single kerosene lamp. The glow grew brighter. They had switched on the lighting from the emergency generator. The hut was now lit by two electric lamps, suspended just below the ceiling. A soldier was moving away from a corner of the hut. He was carrying an empty sack—the broad swords had been handed over.

Nobody knew anything in the other huts. About fifty yards away, Vikenty, Orlov, and Gusev stood smoking.

It was midnight when the door of the hut opened and a man came out. He recoiled when he saw the machine gun standing ten yards away. Then he began to walk slowly in the direction of the guardroom.

"Scarface!" Orlov called, barely audibly.

He stopped in front of them. Blood was dripping from the sword in his hand. "It's finished!" he answered hoarsely. "Go and take over."

"Have you any casualties?" Vikenty asked.

"Yeah. One killed, five wounded. Horse and all his men are dead."

"Drop the sword!" Vikenty touched him on the shoulder. Scarface's fingers relaxed, and the blade thudded to the ground.

Orlov nodded to Gusev. "Get a truck and take the wounded out of camp to headquarters right away. Let Lida go with them." Gusev saluted and vanished into the darkness.

"Scarface, get some men from the hut and have them load your wounded on the truck. Angarov, give Lida instructions to dress their wounds and to go with them to the clinic in Rodnikovo. Have the dead man buried tomorrow. Scarface, have your men lay out the bodies near the hut right now. When you've finished, go to the bathhouse and then come to the guardroom. They'll set the table and you'll get a glass of liquor."

Scarface said nothing and walked off toward the hut.

Shadows moved silently to and fro in the darkness. The soldiers had pushed up a one-and-a-half-tonner without starting the motor and were loading the wounded into it.

Scarface came up and stood next to them. "It's all cleaned up, Citizen Commandant. What are we gonna do with the bodies? Yeah, and all the men are scared to death. A lot of 'em are crying—we scared shit out of 'em. They're not all like me, or Horse, God rest his soul. Maybe you can rustle up something for 'em, nothing much, just something to eat and a drink."

Orlov nodded in reply to Vikenty's inquiring glance. Ten minutes later four men carried a few sacks of bread and buckets of herring and a cask of liquor from the storehouse into the hut.

The truck carrying the wounded had been pushed for some distance beyond the gates, and the sound of its motor had died away in the distance.

"What shall we do with the bodies?" Vikenty asked.

"Have them buried in the forest, away from the camp. See to it yourself. I'm going to my room . . . my heart doesn't feel too good." He turned sharply away and set off toward the guardroom, taking each step with unnatural care.

"What's up with him?" Scarface asked anxiously.

"It's his heart," Vikenty answered thoughtfully. "If anything happens to him, we'll be in trouble. If anyone else had been our commandant, there'd be four hundred corpses here now, instead of twenty-five."

"And that's the truth!" Scarface muttered. "I'm going back to my men. I'm dead beat."

The truck returned from Rodnikovo. Its next journey lasted an hour—to a common grave, ten kilometers from the camp. The soldiers dug a pit in a remote ravine. In pitch darkness they laid the bodies in the pit, filled it in with fresh sticky clay, then spread branches, leaves, and grass over the top of it.

Vikenty dismissed the soldiers at dawn and went into hut No. 3. Scarface and his men were sleeping the sleep of the dead. A few zeks, with buckets and cloths, were cleaning the blood from the plank beds, carrying out the blood-stained mattresses and washing the wooden floor. Hundreds of pale faces turned toward the technical chief when he entered. Vikenty stopped in the middle of the hut, near the table. "Be grateful to Scarface and his men," he said. "If it hadn't been for them, we would have had to shoot every last one of you. If anything like this happens again, you'll all die. I advise you not to try. Your terms are gradually getting shorter. Each of you has at least some small hope of getting out of here. I still think I'll see a lot of you become free men." He could see from the men's eyes as they watched him that they had not yet recovered from the shock of what they had witnessed a few hours before.

At ten minutes to midnight, Scarface had gone up to the bed where Horse lay, pulled a sword from his baggy prison pants and struck off Horse's head with a single swipe. Then Scarface jumped away and took on his blade two other men who rushed at him . . . For several minutes only groans, harsh breathing, and curses were heard from the knot of men fighting for their lives. A full half of the prisoners had fled to the other end of the hut.

Scarface's men rushed in from all sides. Horse's comrades had not expected the attack and fell one after the other under the swords. The rest of the convicts, petrified with fear, watched the swirling tangle of bodies. Ten minutes later everything was quiet again. A few men had broken away and rushed for the door, but Scarface's men had overtaken them and stabbed them in the back, finishing them off with a thrust to the heart—it was quicker and kinder that way.

It was about fifty kilometers from Krasnoyarsk to Colonel Orlov's camp. The narrow taiga road, hemmed in on both sides by a solid wall of trees, wound around the hills, avoiding any steep climbs or descents. There had been no rain for a week and the road was covered with a thin layer of dust. Here and there were visible the tracks of wild beasts that had crossed the road at night. Nadezhda Alekseyevna Orlova did not notice the tracks. She was sitting in the rear seat of the old M-1 automobile that Orlov had the use of but never took to camp, fearing that it might fall apart on the road.

She sat huddled in the corner, resting her temple against the black velvet that lined the inside of the car and staring at the back of the head of Vasya, her husband's personal driver, as if trying to implant in it the thought that he should drive a little faster. Vasya drove with great skill, turning the wheel ceaselessly, avoiding every big hummock and pothole. Sometimes the blonde woman would fix the absent gaze of her beautiful black-lashed, blue-gray eyes on the nearby taiga. The long green pine needles and the branches of the cedars stretched out toward the car, sometimes scratching against the windows.

From time to time Vasya managed to steal a glance at the old, cracked mirror above the windshield. He could see the woman's shapely figure in the simple gray suit with the short golden hair curling over her extraordinarily pale face. Vasya refrained from making the usual traveler's talk; it was not a day for conversation. When he had heard the rumor of disturbances at Orlov's camp, he had prepared the car without waiting for orders and had sat for three hours in the garage in Krasnoyarsk until he saw Nadezhda Alekseyevna hurrying toward him.

Neither Vasya nor the forest could distract Nadezhda Alekseyevna from her anxious thoughts about the future. She was some twenty-five years younger than her husband. She loved him, was proud of him, and she took a great interest in his affairs and career. She was well enough acquainted with both the whirlpools and quiet backwaters of the new Soviet elite to be apprehensive. Her father was the son of a country teacher and had taught mathematics himself. He had come out of the First World War with the rank of lieutenant-colonel in the artillery and found himself in Moscow at the outset of the Civil War with no idea to which side he should attach himself. Help was at hand. The Bolsheviks mobilized him, making him deputy head of a special section responsible for equipping the army with new types of artillery. In that modest post he survived that stormy period. For a long time he did not join the Party, and he held the rank of colonel when the majority of his colleagues, with lesser qualifications, had long been occupying higher posts. In the small circle of senior army men he was known as "Modesty." Fortunately Stalin's mass repressions passed him by and he survived. Eventually, he did become a general and Nadya began being invited to receptions and banquets, visiting with important military and civil leaders who had either survived or owed their advancement to the purges of the thirties. She was a graceful girl and dressed with taste. She knew how to flirt, and she could talk naturally about everything and nothing. She was attractive to men but kept the proper distance, waiting for the, as yet unknown, tall, strong, and intelligent man whom she believed she was bound to meet in this intricate, dangerous, and beautiful world.

Once her father had taken her to a graduation ball at the academy where prospective members of the People's Commissariat for Internal Affairs obtained their training. She received constant invitations to dance, and in the intervals between waltzes she would go over to an open window from which there was a view of Moscow—the river and almost the whole city sparkling in the night with a million lights.

"Whose daughter are you?" a gutteral voice asked from behind her. It had an unfamiliar accent.

She turned suddenly to face a man standing near her. "I'm General Sazonov's daughter." The man was wearing a black suit. His swarthy face was without a moustache and his sparse black hair was combed straight back. His narrow eyes sparkled with interest behind a pince-nez.

He took a glass of champagne from a tray and offered it to her. "But where is your father stationed?" he asked with a frown. "I don't think I know him."

"But he's my little general!" She dropped a comical curtsy, took the glass, and sipped the champagne. "He works in the scientific section at staff headquarters."

"Little general, you say?" The man smiled calmly. "Did you think up that name yourself or did he teach it to you?"

"They call him 'Modesty,' and he's a good man. Do you want me to introduce you?"

"Oh, 'Modesty'! No, there's no need, I'll introduce myself to him later. But now we must arrange to meet. Would you like me to help you? I can get you anything you want. Where are you studying?"

"I'm studying biology. I'm going to be a teacher."

"Well, that's not enough for a girl like you. I'll have you appointed . . ."

"Oh, no!" She seized his hand. "Let's stop this boring conversation. Today's a day for dancing!" She pulled him away from the window. The man released her hand in confusion. He stood holding an unfinished glass of champagne.

"I'm still a girl. Give me time to grow up!" she called to him affectionately. She saw his thick black brows shoot up in amazement as she disappeared into the crowd.

"You're a clever girl. I'll remember this evening. We'll meet again!" He managed to call after her, but he did not move from the spot. He could not dance and did not wish to.

Soon afterward Nadya had met Orlov, a tall colonel with graying temples. She had swum down into his deep blue intelligent eyes . . . and never resurfaced. They married, and a few months later they left for his post in Siberia. There she became acquainted with the character, career, connections, and potentialities of every member of the Kraslag Authority. And she also kept up her own connections in Moscow, especially with the wives of important officials. A year after their departure from Moscow she knew all the details of what Lavrenty Pavlovich Beria, the new favorite and powerful head of the NKVD, had said about her after she had snubbed him so girlishly at the graduation ball.

Beria had been going through dossiers in his office and he had examined the photograph of Orlov's wife for some time. He turned to the aide standing behind his chair.

"Do you see this photo?" Beria tapped it with his finger. "This girl turned me down once. I still blush when I think about it. Not bad, eh?"

"Not bad at all!" said the aide, a colonel with crimson epaulets. "Shall I bring her in?"

"This one?" He removed his pince-nez thoughtfully. "No, not this one. I know Orlov. He does his job. But it's a pity, she's a beauty. We'll leave them alone . . . I'll come back to this dossier later."

Along mysterious channels, known only to those on the highest levels, all such conversations seeped through from deep inside the nerve center of the enormous NKVD machine and flowed out by way of the apartments of senior officials . . . a whisper in an ear . . . and reached their destination. Sometimes they even returned to their source, to the office where they had first taken place. Everybody, including Nadya, knew that young girls were a favorite diversion of Lavrenty Pavlovich. Driving through the streets of Moscow in his closed, black, armor-plated limousine, he would point out to his aide this and that shapely girl as she went about her business through the crowd, hurrying to a store or an institute, or even to school.

Another car would drive up to her, and she would be asked, politely, to get into the rear seat. Then she would be driven away. In an old mansion not far from the Sadovoye ring road there was a quiet, simply furnished room where this all-powerful man would already be waiting for the latest chosen one. He would be wearing a golden Persian robe and sitting at a table that would have been envied by the chef of the best restaurant in Paris. They would chat during the delicious meal and then would make love, with or without kisses.

If the latest girl knew where she had been taken, she would usually obey the officer's instructions as how best to prepare herself for the man waiting upstairs. This submissiveness stemmed from the people's innate or instilled fear of their rulers and from the inevitability of obedience. Sometimes considerations of material advantage influenced the decision, since in those hard times many a Moscow girl would be happy to become the secret mistress of some "big" patron who would pay for her favors with money, protection, or presents. Only in very rare cases would a victim refuse, tearfully and with pleas to be allowed "to go home to mama." Beria's men would then release her in some quiet street, and she would hurry home trembling, without even knowing where she had been, and afraid of telling anyone about it. But most of them agreed.

Beria never got around to Nadezhda Orlova—he was too busy. And anyway it wouldn't really be convenient to bring her here from Siberia. And Orlov had quite a few connections, especially in the army. If he took a risk, it might reach the master's ears. The little man with the moustache was the only man on earth whom Lavrenty Pavlovich Beria feared. It was a kind of bestial fear that froze his blood when he thought that some day he might fall out of favor and go the same way as the scores he had killed himself and the hundreds of thousands destroyed by the machine of which he was the head.

"Foo!" Nadezhda Alekseyevna shook her head in an effort to drive away the memory, which she had never revealed to anyone, even her husband. What would she do if anything should happen to Orlov? Beria! That was a strong card! But to be played only if that cretin Degtev managed to slander Orlov somehow and bring about his retirement or arrest. "I'm the commander of your rear!" She often played that role, with inspiration, delighted that fate had sent her such a man, such a life.

She started at the piercing sound of a horn. Vasya pulled sharply to the left. A car overtook them on the right, enveloping the old M-1 in dust. In the rear seat she glimpsed the square red face of Colonel Degtev.

"He's on his way, the bastard, and in a hurry." Her face turned to stone at the thought. Everyone in the Authority knew that "Thick-Skull" Degtev hated Orlov, for no apparent reason, but feared his wife, the strawberry blonde Nadezhda Alekseyevna. "Our looks are our weapon," her mother had always told her. So far, she had used her weapon with the utmost skill.

"Step on it!" Degtev tapped the army driver on the shoulder with his finger. The driver twitched as if he had been bitten by a snake and stepped sharply on the accelerator. The car leaped forward, and Degtev banged his head painfully on the window frame. He glared furiously at the back of the driver's head but checked himself—his order had been carried out to the letter. He liked to give orders and he liked them to be carried out exactly, promptly, and without question.

Now Colonel Degtev sat with his feet propped against the back of the front seat for stability. He clung onto the metal door handle and thought. One moment his thoughts would flock together like stray goats, the next they would fly apart like clouds driven by the wind. He tried to compose these thoughts into some kind of decision. And this was very difficult work for Degtev.

Unlike Lieutenant Mukhin, who had started life as a peasant, Degtev prided himself on his working-class origins. True, his father had been the foreman in a coal pit and had not taken part in the revolution. There the young Degtev had worked in the pit in the town of Lugansk in the Ukraine for a year as a pony man, carting coal below ground with a sickly pony and a little wagon. He had time to foster his working-class pride, and with it his hatred of the czarist autocracy and his love for the revolution. He had received little education and after the revolution found himself at loose ends, watching longingly as the best positions in the new society were allocated to other, more efficient people. At last, fortune smiled on him—he was noticed and given a job in the local Cheka. The move was a success. He worked avidly, but, since the Cheka officials knew very well that Degtev was not especially intelligent, they gave him the dirtiest work. He made arrests and extracted the necessary confessions and signatures from persons under interrogation. Gradually he became irreplaceable in this work. He was promoted and graduated as a secret policeman from the GPU's school at Kharkov. Then he was transferred to Moscow, to the Central Authority.

He could have risen to great heights in those stormy days when all the prisons were packed with enemies of the people waiting for him to crack them so that they would reveal their secrets. But an unhappy incident spoiled his prospects. The section chief instructed him to interrogate once more a certain elderly professor who had a thorough knowledge of aviation but who was quite unwilling to admit that for many years he had been selling his ideas, by word of mouth and on paper, to enemy intelligence services. "Take it easy with that effete old fool," the chief warned Degtev. "We don't want him to go and die on us." And Degtev did try to prevent him from dying. But it turned out badly. The hatred burned in Degtev's heart, and the old man just breathed hoarsely into his face, his goatee turned up toward the sky, and said nothing . . . nothing. And he would not sign. "All the others signed and you'll sign too, you snake!" Degtev turned the professor in his hairy paws. But the professor had fallen completely silent. He was dead. Degtev could not believe it at first, then he broke out in a cold sweat. What could he do? How could he bring this dead cabbage back to life?

"You tried too hard, you bear!" the chief told him reproachfully that evening in his office. "Couldn't you have been easier on him? He was an educated professor, you know. Even if he hadn't confessed, we could have used him on technical work in prison."

"I'm sorry, Comrade Section Chief," Degtev muttered as he stood there on the carpet, facing his superior. He hung his head and gazed almost with hatred at the long powerful arms dangling beside his own body. "I lost my temper, I forgot he might die . . . he wouldn't say anything, the dog, anything at all."

"None of them say anything at first." The chief nodded sympathetically. "You've been doing good work, Degtev, and so the organization heads have decided not to bring you before the court."

"What's going to happen to me?" Degtev asked, cheering up and looking his chief in the eye affectionately.

The man sitting behind the desk was wearing a dark-blue uniform and had several tabs on his collar. "We will help you to become a man!" he said. "The Party and Comrade Stalin need trustworthy people. You've been an underdog too long. You will go to Siberia, to Krasnoyarsk, where you'll work for Bukin, the chief of the Kraslag, as head of the administrative section. All the camps will come under you. You'll be responsible for discipline. How does that suit you? And we'll give you the rank of regimental commander so that you'll carry enough weight." The chief had pushed a sheet of paper toward him.

"Thank you, Comrade Section Chief, and I thank dear Comrade Stalin," Degtev breathed quietly, almost choking with joy.

"Off you go, then. Work hard!" The man came out from behind the desk and gave him a patronizing pat on the shoulder.

Degtev had never properly gotten over the old man's death and the deadly threat that had hung over him. He was dimly aware of his helplessness in the whirlwind of events, the essence of which he had never been able to understand. He tried to ingratiate himself with everyone; he knew instinctively that he was surrounded by people who were just as strong and just as trusting of the Party and Comrade Stalin but who were more intelligent. Accordingly, he expected mischief, intrigue, and treachery from everyone. Naturally, he hated Orlov and even Orlov's superior, General Bukin, but he held his ground in the Authority thanks to his connections in Moscow. It gave him pleasure to think how much he was hated by Orlov and Bukin and many of the others occupying these cozy seats, far from the center of events.

A few years earlier he had listened, like father to son, to the confession of Lieutenant Mukhin. He had advised him not to tangle with Orlov and had helped him to gain admission to the special school as a student. But he remembered very well the lesson that Orlov had given Mukhin. He felt as if it had not been Mukhin but he, Degtev, who had gone down on his knees to Orlov.

And now an uprising in Orlov's camp! If Moscow got wind of it, it would be the end for Orlov, and he might well get it in the neck himself. There was a war on! Mocking, superior, blue-blooded Orlov had had the sense, of course, to call the Authority himself. Cunning rogue! Bukin was away. He, Colonel Degtev, was now performing the duties of chief of the entire Kraslag. He gripped the metal handle furiously. Angarov, Orlov's favorite! Birds of a feather certainly did flock together! They had found each other, the former aristocrats. Never mind. All that filth must be swept away with a firm hand now, before the whole camp collapsed. He nearly stood up in his seat when he caught sight of the gates of the camp.

Familiar with his chief's liking for strong effects, the driver braked sharply in front of the administration building. The car stopped dead, raising a cloud of dust. Degtev climbed out and waited, seeing Orlov approaching. Orlov came to attention, out of habit, and saluted. "Comrade Deputy Commander of the Kraslag, I have to report . . ."

"That'll do!" Degtev snapped, without greeting Orlov or shaking hands. "Get the prisoners out here and have them fall in," he added, squinting at Angarov, Gusev, and a few guards who were standing away. Farther off he could see the crowd of people in gray uniforms who were uncertain whether to come nearer.

Orlov's face was white. He gave the necessary orders and stood to one side, alone, pressing his left hand against the place in his chest where his heart was. When he was nervous, it began to ache, begging for rest and peace; but there was no peace, there was only war, going on all around, concealed or open, honorable or base, an elemental, irreversible struggle for power, for life.

For a few minutes Degtev stared in silence at the huge gray square of people that filled the camp yard. He gathered his thoughts, although he was sure that in the present instance no particular thoughts were needed—everything was clear.

"Now you listen to me!" He cleared his throat and tried to inject assurance into a voice that sounded husky with emotion and with the anger he felt toward all and everything. "The fact that you turned up here alive means that the motherland and Comrade Stalin let you off and gave you a chance, you scum, to expiate your guilt. So what are you up to here, eh? You eat the people's bread and yet you want to sit here, a burden on the people and on all of us. Is that it, eh?" He leaned forward, his right fist clenched. "You want to betray the motherland, eh? We didn't give you a good enough thrashing, that's clear. So you're rebelling? Traitors, eh? Have the liberals corrupted you here?" He glanced at Orlov. "Your technical chief spoiled you, so you're all working together against our Soviet power, and working against Comrade Stalin, eh?"

He stared at the people. Only the distant sound of an old M-1 bouncing along over the ruts in the dirt road disturbed the silence.

"The enemy, the fascist, is advancing on Moscow. Soviet people are blocking his way, giving their blood to save the motherland, but you . . . you traitors should be shot, the lot of you. It's a pity I didn't know what you were up to here last night. I would have come and shot you all myself. What use are you, you sons of bitches? Today, right now, a hundred men must be ready to leave for the front. I'm really going to put the screws on you! I'm transferring Orlov to another camp, under somebody else's command, to stop him from making a complete mess of things for me here." He had turned completely red and his right hand rested on the holster of his pistol. "And as for your technical chief, the main instigator, I'm going to have him shot as an example, right here and now. Do you understand? A fish always rots from the head first." He waved at Angarov. "Hey you, come here!"

Angarov came and stood in front of him. He kept his eyes fixed on Degtev's crimson face, trying desperately to think of some way of avoiding what looked like certain death. Mukhin hadn't killed him, but this one would. Silence hung over the gray mass of people.

"It was you who organized this rebellion. You! There's a war on, and we've got no time to bother with traitors." He pointed Angarov toward the fence, which was made of long branches blackened with age. "Over against the wall, on the double!"

Angarov did not move. It was as if his legs had taken root. If he threw himself at Degtev and struck and killed him, they would shoot him just the same. Colonel Degtev was not Lieutenant Mukhin. This time it looked like the end.

"Up against the wall!" Degtev roared, losing control of himself. He had drawn his pistol and was almost poking Angarov in the face with it. Angarov sensed that the pistol might go off at any moment and, to gain just a few seconds in which to hope for the miracle that all condemned men hope for, he went and stood with his back against the wall.

"Your face!" Degtev shouted. "Your face to the wall!"

Angarov turned to face the fence, which was overgrown with grass, and glanced longingly at the forest and the morning sky. Was this really how his life would end? He was not afraid. He tensed his body, waiting for the bullet to strike. If only he would get it over with quickly!

"As you were!" Orlov's quiet voice made Angarov start. "As you were!"

"What!" Degtev turned to Orlov and half lowered his pistol. "You're giving me orders? I'll settle you! You're confined to quarters. Move! The court will take care of you . . . For destroying the rear . . . You bastard . . . I'm going to shoot this one so that the others don't get the habit."

"You have no right to shoot him," Orlov said. "Angarov was

confirmed by the Kraslag. You will be brought before the court."

"Me? Before the court? I place you under arrest. Guard! Take him away!"

The soldiers looked at Gusev in confusion. The senior sergeant had never found himself in such a situation before. He looked questioningly at Orlov, on whom everything now depended.

"Comrade Degtev!" Orlov stepped toward him. "The guards will obey no one but me." His deathly pale face was slowly coming out in red blotches. "My appointment was confirmed in Moscow. You will be tried for taking the law into your own hands. I now ask you to put away your pistol. Otherwise I will have you arrested. According to NKVD regulations I can be removed from my post only by the head of the Kraslag, with Moscow's consent."

"You filthy scum!" Degtev looked at Orlov in confusion. His hand trembled as he shoved the pistol into his holster. "I'll get you for this. Go and get your things. I'll die before I let you stay here. You want to arrest me? Well I'm going to report all this to Moscow right away . . . There's a war on . . . You'll get what's coming to you for tricks like this . . ." He nodded towards Angarov. "Tell this pig to get into my car. I'm taking him back to headquarters . . . Whatever happens I'm going to have everything changed here."

As he watched this scene, Angarov saw a car drive through the gates and he glimpsed Nadezhda Alekseyevna's blonde head. Almost at the same moment Orlov seized his chest with both hands, his mouth gulping for air. He gestured as if he was summoning help. Angarov ran to him and caught his almost lifeless body as it fell.

Orlov lay with his legs spread wide in their green breeches and gleaming boots. With an effort he raised himself on his elbow. His astonished gaze was fixed on his wife. Nadezhda Alekseyevna knelt beside him. With one hand she supported his neck, with the other she stroked his face. "Sasha, Sashenka! What's the matter? What happened?"

She raised her tearful eyes to Angarov, who was supporting Orlov's shoulders. Degtev remained standing by his car. He was now gazing around like a wolf in a cage. All his domineering ardor had vanished with this unexpected turn of events. Fear at what had happened and what might happen to him had driven every thought from his head.

For ten minutes not a sound had been heard from the gray crowd.

"Aleksandr Andreyevich!" Angarov bent down to Orlov's ear as he felt for his pulse. The red blotches had disappeared from the camp commandant's face and it had acquired a beautiful dull color. His eyes still gazed at Nadezhda Alekseyevna, but his head was slowly falling back. His body went limp and sagged in Angarov's arms.

"Sashenka, my love! Don't!" She pressed her lips on his face and squeezed his body against her own with both arms and sobbed. She did not know what to do or say, or how to help.

Angarov lowered Orlov slowly onto the grass. He stood over him with his head bent, hardly able to hold back his tears.

"What are you doing?" She raised her tear-stained face to Angarov. "Why have you put him down? Hold him! Keep his head raised."

Angarov shook his head sadly. "No, Nadezhda Alekseyevna, it's too late. There's no pulse. It was a heart attack, instantaneous . . . He should have kept himself quiet."

For a few moments Nadezhda Alekseyevna gazed blankly up at Angarov, then she passed her hand over her husband's tranquil face and brushed the unruly lock of gray-streaked red hair away from his brow. She got up from her knees and stood for a while over her husband's still-warm corpse in complete silence. The faces of the people around her and the gray silent crowd farther away appeared as in a mist.

Without realizing what she was doing or why, she turned abruptly toward Degtev, the blue-green figure with the red face that was now the repository of all the evil that existed under the sun. She moved closer to him. Degtev stepped back instinctively, but the sound of her two slaps rang through the camp.

"Bastard!" Orlov's wife shouted in his face, choking back her tears of grief and rage. She glared at the crimson face swimming before her eyes. "Villain! Slob! Filth! Scum! Upstart!" She struck at him again, but Degtev raised his arm to block the blow and backed away toward his car.

"Get out!" She sobbed. "Get out of here, you damn murderer! Brainless pig! I'll see you rot in a camp, you camp dirt! Can you really be a man? Was it you who killed my Orlov? A real man! Ah, you filth! I'll destroy you! Get out of my sight, offal! I'm going to fly to Moscow today and I'm going to see Comrade Beria. I'll have you flayed alive!" she shouted after Degtev, who had jumped into the car and slammed the door. Without looking back, he stammered hoarsely to the driver, "Step on it!"

Krasnoyarsk is the capital of Central Siberia and of the Krasnoyarsk

Territory, which could contain Europe several times over. The town is comparatively young. Three hundred years ago the Cossack troops of the first explorers forced their way east through the slumbering taiga and came out onto a high hill. Broad and powerful, an unknown river flowed below them in the valley. The swift current carried along, as if they were matchsticks, huge trees that had crashed down somewhere in the upper reaches where the river had undermined its steep bank. Beyond the river and the green treetops lay the foothills of the Sayan Mountains, which stretched away to the east, as far as the Pacific Ocean.

On this hill the Cossacks built a high watchtower of stout timbers and then moved on. Centuries passed. Gradually a town grew up in the valley, on the left bank of the river named Yenisei, after a Cossack who had perished in its rushing waters. Rows of single and two-story houses were built of wood, with tiny windows and walls of thick planks to ward off the fierce polar cold of winter and the terrible heat of summer.

Decades passed. The town grew and expanded, and with it the cemetery on the hillside. The watchtower stands to this day, dominating the whole town but separated from the its noise and bustle by the eternal quiet of the village of the dead.

At the beginning of this century the criss-cross ironwork of the railroad bridge was stretched from the left bank of the Yenisei to the right. With wheels screeching, the trains crawled slowly across the bridge and the passengers gazed warily at the eddying waters far below. Bearded businessmen of the first and second merchant guilds would be sitting in the first-class cars, drinking vodka as they traveled east in search of furs, gold, and profits. In the classless cars, other people would also be drinking vodka. They flowed here from Central Russia just like dirty rainwater does across sloping asphalt—adventurers, gold prospectors, thieves escaped from prison, half-baked revolutionaries, ruined noblemen and merchants, and peasants seeking freedom and sufficiency in the new lands. Yes, like lava from a volcano, the Russians flowed along the rivers and through the taiga to fill the social vacuum that history had created among the indigenous inhabitants of Siberia.

Seen in those days from the tower, the town looked like a big village, but it was something more. Krasnoyarsk lay on the long road from Moscow and St. Petersburg to Khabarovsk and Vladivostok in the east, to Taimyr and Port Dikson in the north, and to China and Manchuria in the south. Multidecked steamboats, their paddles churning, carried thousands of people to the upper and lower reaches of the rivers. Some of the settlers would return home after a few years, their purses full of money, but the majority disappeared in the expanses of that harsh territory, their skeletons indicating to future pathfinders the way things had gone.

The columns of political prisoners also passed through Krasnoyarsk, rattling along in chains or staring out through the bars on the railroad cars. They were on their way to the Narymsky Territory, as the northern part of the Krasnoyarsk region was then known. In exile here, Lenin had strolled through the dirty gray town, whose great future was still to come, admiring the beauty of the river and the mountains and preparing the theoretical justification for the world-wide upheavals that lay ahead. The young black-moustached revolutionary Soso Dzhugashvili had passed through on his way to and from exile, where he had studied the weaknesses of the prison system under the old liberal power. One day, many years later, he was able to use this personal experience to establish the largest centralized state machine the world had ever seen, administering hundreds of camps from which few prisoners ever escaped.

Under Soviet power, the development of the river's right bank went ahead. Heavy-engineering plants sprang up along the hills and two- and three-story wooden tenements spread around them.

In the fall of 1941, the Kraslag Authority was accommodated in a simple three-story building that resembled an abandoned school. Inside, however, everything had a solid look about it. The office of General Bukin was especially cozy. The large room with its pale-gray walnut paneling and green upholstered chairs created a relaxed atmosphere. The windows looked toward the Yenisei and the hills rising beyond it.

The general was standing by the window, absently admiring the way the office was furnished. There was, he noted, only one unpleasant detail. That detail was Colonel Degtev. A deep, soft, green armchair stood close to the general's desk. He could see the colonel's leg poking out from the armchair in its gleaming boot and dark-green gabardine breeches. The armchair was facing the middle of the general's desk. The colonel had not dared to turn the chair toward the window where the general stood. Instead, he sat bolt upright in his dark-green uniform, as if he had swallowed a broomstick. His red bull-neck hung down in folds over the white lining of his collar.

General Bukin's position obliged him to imitate the modesty of his leader, whose portrait hung on the wall in an enormous polished frame.

Like the figure in the portrait the general wore a simple pale-gray jacket, buttoned up to the neck, and his trousers were of the same material. The general differed from "Him" only in that he wore breeches, which puffed at the knees and were tucked into chrome-leather boots. It was necessary to show moderation in all things, even in flattery and imitation, for they could interpret every word and every move as they pleased. And how many of them were around him, these envious stool pigeons who were just waiting for a chance to take a knife to him, step over his fallen body, and sit down in his comfortable chair!

"What a neck he's got!" the general thought. "Well, his forebears were only workers. It would have been better if liberals like Colonel Orlov had remained in power. Orlov may not plow very deep but he doesn't ruin the furrows either. Give this fellow power and you'll be buried under the bones. He'd smash and mangle everything and everybody." The general gazed at the misted hills. Beyond those hills and across Lake Baikal, thousands of miles away and at an altitude high above sea level, was his home in the town of Chita. In the confusion of the Civil War, when he was a boy, the Whites had mobilized him. Then the partisans had arrived and enlisted him. There followed a stormy upward career. His advancement had been particularly swift in the mid thirties, when he was given a senior position in the NKVD. No one knew that he had served a few months with the Whites. His comrades in the White Army had all gone abroad, and most of his acquaintances had died in the Civil War. Still, he remembered everyone who might possibly have heard of the mortal sin he had committed in his youth and he gathered material and brought these men before the troikas under any article of the Criminal Code, so long as they disappeared from society forever. Subsequent events had troubled him. He had been deputy head of the NKVD Regional Authority when a top-secret order reached Chita that some senior officials of the region and town, including his immediate superior, were to be arrested and shot. The order came to him personally. He had sat for a long time in his office, staring at this list. Why, of the two of them, had they decided to kill his chief rather than him? He was now about to kill his chief, and before long somebody else would kill him. How should one behave, how should one live in order to survive? That night many of the senior officials of the region and of Chita were taken from their beds and driven off into the depths of the forest—where pits had already been dug—and shot. No sentences were read out. The pits were filled with damp earth and covered with grass and fallen branches. No one remembered the place because of the darkness, and the only map with accurate references was kept by a man from Moscow, who flew back the next morning to make his report. On his orders Bukin sent all the soldiers who had taken part in the execution on leave and subsequently transferred them to the Far North. The widows and children of the repressed officials were allowed to remain in Chita, and when Bukin drove through the streets in his closed black car, he would sometimes recognize people who had been his friends not long ago. It was torture to see these women. After that night he lived in a constant state of fear that someday he would be making the same journey into the forest. Unseen currents in the struggle within the Party continued to carry him steadily up the official ladder. But that was precisely where he did not want to go. Some nights he would wake up in a cold sweat and recall the details of his latest dream. He, Bukin, the head of the Authority, was being whisked up beyond the clouds in a balloon. He could not control it and he could not jump to the ground. He often had such dreams and he had even begun to fear for his sanity. Thank you, vodka helped. He indulged in bouts of drinking, and only his predeliction for the bottle saved him from the expected invitation to transfer to the Central Apparatus of the NKVD. Now that the main threat to Stalin's rule no longer came from internal enemies but from Hitler, who intended to settle with Stalin when the USSR had been defeated, there were fewer arrests and Bukin could find release from the constant fear. Or had been able to do so until this morning. The attempted uprising at Orlov's camp could so easily have ended satisfactorily, for what were those twenty-five men whom Orlov had sacrificed to calm the crisis? If it hadn't been for Degtev!

The general returned to his desk and sat down in his chair. He gave Degtev a kindly look and pushed a pack of cigarettes over to him.

"Have a smoke, Comrade Colonel!"

"No, thank you." Degtev shook his head.

Bukin was well acquainted with Degtev's shallow inner world. He was always aware of the danger to himself that Degtev's connections in Moscow could bring. How could he neutralize this dangerous man without pricking the vanity of his patrons in Moscow? They had placed Degtev under Bukin's command as a means of correction, and now Degtev was in trouble again. That meant that he himself was also in trouble. Degtev must be dealt with once and for all.

Bukin half closed his eyes and directed his gaze at Degtev. "I haven't invited you here, Comrade Degtev, to discuss with you the appropriateness of your conduct as my deputy. You are well aware that your conduct was inappropriate from every standpoint. You and I are communists, we are building a new society under difficult conditions. We must be more dedicated and united around the Party and Comrade Stalin than ever before."

Degtev nodded. He leaned forward and rested his chest against the edge of the table. He licked his lips, which had suddenly become dry. The course of the interview was alarming him.

"In the present situation the building of the new world demands effort and sacrifice, coercion and training, tact and cruelty—depending on the circumstances. The end justifies the means. You understand that the outcome of your interview with Orlov was extremely unpleasant for everyone—for the Authority in Moscow, for me, and, of course, for you." Bukin continued quietly. Bored with the sight of Degtev's face, he examined his own fingernails, glanced out of the window and then returned his gaze to the stony countenance across the desk. Degtev's intellect did not present any psychological or political problems for Bukin. All he needed was the time to program Degtev's mind for a specific course of action. This course of action was quite clear to Bukin, but Degtev had no inkling of it. These two men represented the two main camps in the ranks of the NKVD. In the constant collaboration and competition between these camps, the Degtevs were inevitably subordinate to the Bukins by virtue of the iron laws of logic, which operated even in such thoroughgoing upheavals as the Stalinist purges.

Bukin paused, expecting Degtev to say something. But Degtev continued to stare at his chief in silence.

Bukin struck a match and puffed a cloud of smoke across the desk. "Yes, this is your second serious mistake, Comrade Degtev. I'm telling you this as your senior comrade, as a communist, and as a man. You've overdone it again. You lost sight of one important point—you are not running a system of strict-regime camps, the basic aim of which is the gradual physical and moral destruction of the most dangerous enemies of our state. You are running a system of corrective-labor camps, the basic aim of which is the political re-education of a certain category of irresponsible Soviet men and women so that they will be able to expiate their guilt by honest work and then return to society. But the main thing is that these camps must supply the country with the wood it desperately needs. Orlov understood that and he made a good job of it. That was why many people in Moscow valued him; even Lavrenty Pavlovich made a flattering reference to him."

"But!" Degtev gave a start, as if he had just woken up. "He undermined the discipline," he said hoarsely. "That Angarov . . . He was in with the zeks . . ."

Bukin nodded. "Yes, you're partly right. Discipline must be maintained. I can't find fault with you there. But you've got to know just how far to go. You know that all Comrade Stalin expects us to do is to carry out his will, within the framework of the regulations, so that our efforts do good and not harm. You don't seem to have a clear idea of all the complexity of the relations within our state apparatus, and now this is the second time you've gone too far. It's quite natural that there should sometimes be attempted uprisings in our system—not all prisoners can be reeducated. Some of them remain hopelessly antisocial and have to be destroyed physically. Orlov was quite right to let their friends deal with them. It does him credit as a leader. Of course the whole hut could have been shot, but I want to assure you that neither you or I would have been thanked for it. It would immediately have reduced the rate of dispatch of timber, and the two of us would have had to answer for it. In our job, Comrade Degtev, we have to answer literally for everything. In other words, since none of your actions in this affair were necessary and since they contradicted the interests of our cause, I advise you, as a friend, to change the direction of your life and career for a while, if you want to avoid more serious trouble."

"But what can I say to the comrades who recommended me for this post with you?" A shadow of anxiety crossed his face. "You're not thinking of ordering me to Kolyma!"

"Well, of course not!" Bukin gave him a patronizing smile. "There would be no sense in sending you to the north. I simply want to suggest that you take Orlov's place."

"Me!" For a moment Degtev stared wildly at his chief. Then he sank back in the chair and hung his head. "Is this a . . . demotion?"

"Yes, temporarily. No, no, don't worry. I won't appoint anyone to replace you. I'll manage without a deputy for the time being. Orlov's camp is the largest and most complex in our system, and the most productive. I simply have no one to replace Orlov at the moment. I must wait until they send a suitable man from Moscow. And anyway, I think they will take a positive view of your action in the People's Commissariat. You've chosen the most onerous post yourself. They like that kind of thing. Time will pass, and Orlov's death will be forgotten. Everything is forgotten. Time heals all."

"Yes, yes!" Gratitude showed in Degtev's face. "I understand. Thank you. I'll do it gladly, just so long as that business in Moscow doesn't come up again. Damn Orlov! Couldn't he have picked some other time to die!"

Bukin smiled. "Surely you knew he had a weak heart?"

Degtev shook his head.

"You see! But I knew. You should know your subordinates better, their personal lives. You probably didn't know that Orlov's wife has powerful connections in Moscow, all the way up to Lavrenty Pavlovich?"

"Yes . . . no, I mean I didn't know but she said something to me back there in the camp about complaining to Comrade Beria. What right does she have to complain about me? Or to hit me in the face?"

"She has the right," Bukin said seriously. "She has the right to complain about you under NKVD regulations. And she has the right of the strong—her connections are stronger than yours, unfortunately. And she has a woman's right to slap your face—she's stronger than you there as well. We are living in difficult and interesting times, Comrade Colonel." Bukin looked at the man sitting opposite him almost with sympathy. The course of his future career was settled. From that moment it had started on a downward path and would never rise again.

"And I advise you to familiarize yourself thoroughly with Orlov's procedures so that you'll be able to justify yourself in this post. Understand one thing—it's the men who cut the timber. You won't make them work hard by force. They need food, and we haven't got much. So let them forage for it themselves. You'll need tact and you have to know how to rely on people and use them in our interests. Are you sure that you can cope?" Bukin's cold glance transfixed Degtev in the chair.

"I don't know. I'm not sure," he answered, scarcely audibly. He avoided his chief's eyes. "I've never had to do any managerial work. I've mostly been operational."

"That doesn't matter," Bukin continued in the same friendly tone but with a feeling of triumph. "I'll help you. I'll reduce your production plan temporarily, for a couple of months, until the people settle down. And I advise you to rely on the zeks and on their technical chief Angarov.

When you're dealing with a mass of people you must always rely on their representatives, the men who have their full authority. That way you'll win."

"But . . . I tried to shoot him . . . for treason."

"They're all traitors, Comrade Degtev, but their terms of imprisonment were set by the highest authorities and that must be our law. That is what you must do: go out to the camp today and apologize to Orlov's wife. She, as I hope you are aware, is planning to fly to Moscow after the funeral to make a complaint about you." He broke off, seeing the colonel's face suddenly turn white. "You will have to take part in the funeral and organize everything as it should be. A funeral committee has already been set up, and you have been appointed its chairman."

"Already?" Degtev raised his brows in surprise. "But you only just flew in . . ."

"Yes." Bukin interrupted him and stood up. "I phoned from Moscow so that everything would be done right away. You must learn to control people, Colonel, or they will control you. I wish you success!" He offered Degtev his hand. "If anything goes wrong this time, I won't be able to help you."

Degtev left the Authority, crossed the street, and sat down on a bench in the square. He was oblivious to his surroundings and had to fight back the lump in his throat. For several minutes he sat gazing at the old three-story Authority building, with its big windows, and at the four portraits flapping in the wind over the entrance. Then he stood up and moved off aimlessly toward the center of the town. He was surprised to hear himself mutter as he looked toward the Authority, "Damn you, damn you all!" He started at the sound of these blasphemous words and looked around in terror. There was no one there. "No! I mustn't give in to this weakness. It's my own fault. The Party won't dump me. It'll help me."

His spirits brightened a little and he turned up the collar of his gray military raincoat against the drizzling rain. He'd better get going and start work. Otherwise, he'd be finished.

6

THE THEATER

The women in the camp were not segregated into criminals and politicals. They all lived in the same hut—former office workers, the wives and daughters of men who had been imprisoned or shot, former revolutionaries, Soviet and Party workers, some of whom had been with Lenin when he set up the Party and had served terms of imprisonment or penal servitude before the revolution. There were even aristocrats, representatives of the old nobility, including the daughter of General Khabalov, who had commanded the Petersburg garrison before the revolution. They called her Ninon, but nobody knew her real name.

Women with criminal records were in a minority, and they tried to accommodate themselves to the remaining mass of prisoners. The women formed groups in the hut, according to their origins or outlook. There were a few lesbians among them, but the majority either accustomed themselves to do without sex or had affairs with men. Such affairs were not forbidden, but they often ended in death during an abortion. Only women about to be confined were sent to the district hospital. The women performed the abortions themselves, often without even seeking Lida's help. Fear of the consequences and the desire to live and to see the sky overhead were powerful deterrents.

The women criminals usually played cards, but they never gambled for anyone's life. The women brought all their questions to a group of older political prisoners. They could answer all the questions except one: why are we here? Only the criminals knew why they were there and when they would be released. The politicals never knew when their terms might be extended.

The descendants of the former aristocracy formed a separate group. They considered themselves victims of history and they looked forward to change. Ninon Khabalova was in this group. She had served half her term and had another five years left. Ninon had gone to seed. She carried her head high, as if to avoid seeing her gray jacket and baggy trousers. Her thick red hair lay on her neck in a tight knot. She rarely washed it until her neighbors threatened to wash it for her to get rid of the smell. She went on living simply because it was easier than dying. She obeyed everyone without a murmur, spoke little, and answered all questions with "Go screw yourself!" Sometimes out of boredom, a woman would go up to her with some question simply to hear her answer.

In the evenings or during work breaks the women sang songs: old ballads, Russian folk songs, revolutionary songs, Soviet songs—the whole cultural inheritance of the Russian nation was included in the repertoire of songs they sang at impromptu concerts that evoked nostalgia for their former, real lives. Often they sang with tears in their eyes.

The whole hut usually fell silent when the criminals began one of their discordant but resonant round songs, which caught at the heart. As the politicals listened they recalled all they had read and heard about the Russian "lower depths," about Gorky, about the degraded and dispossessed criminal element of the Russian people—who now, as before, could find no place among the secure and respectable. They felt that they were responsible for the fate of these women who had defied the whole social order and had spent the greater part of their lives outside society.

Sometimes the criminals sang in language that made their audience blush and be grateful for the darkness. Yet every song expressed a longing for true love, a friend's devotion, good fortune, freedom. The songs were a dream of happiness. All the women understood this, although many did not follow the meaning of the underworld jargon:

"Hello my Lyubka, little dove.
Hello my Lyubka and farewell,
You squealed on all my red raspberries,
Now take your olives just as well.
You used to wear those patent slippers,
Patent slippers, such high class,
But now you're wearing ragged sneakers,
Since you gave up your thieving past."

Long after the melancholy voices had died away, the listening women would guess at the meaning of "raspberries" and "olives." (Few found out that "raspberries" were connections to illegal money and "olives" meant exile or death.)

Sometimes the refrain of the Marseillaise would be heard from the old revolutionaries' corner. Then the whole hut would prick up its ears, sensing in the song something stern, durable, and unconquerable that affected the fate of each one of them.

By general consent the hut leader was Pelageya, a thin woman in her mid-sixties, with a knot of gray hair on her crown, a fringe on her forehead, and piercing eyes set in a wrinkled face. She maintained an iron discipline, but spoke rarely. Though she seldom struck anyone in the face, when she did, it hurt. This Pasha was the daughter of rich parents. When she was attending high school near the end of the last century, she met a man who was a law student at St. Petersburg University and connected with the terrorists called Narodnaya Volya, who supposed that by murdering the most hated ministers they could set the Russian people on the road to happiness. It had begun as an innocent love affair, but it ended in a police station after her arrest in connection with the attempted assassination of Czar Aleksandr III. Others were hanged, including Lenin's brother, Aleksandr Ulyanov, but Pasha got off with exile to Siberia. After that she was unable to restrain herself. She abandoned her family and attached herself to one movement after another. During her exile she married a czarist colonel, and at the beginning of 1917 went with him to France. But her head was still filled with ideas of universal equality and world revolution. She had no inkling of the constant struggle for power waged within the Bolshevik Party from the moment of its founding. She left her husband and returned to Russia.

When she was arrested in 1936 as a lecturer for the Bolshevik Party committee in an Odessa district, she did not understand what was happening. She wrote enthusiastic letters to Stalin and spat in her interrogator's face, shouting: "Traitors, butchers, czarist satraps!"

But that only aggravated her situation. Since the plan for the removal of the enemies of the people had been sent down from on high and must be carried out, the local NKVD Authority, in the face of its worthy representatives—the troika—sentenced her to twenty years in a normal regime camp, supposing that there was no role for Pelageya Kovrina in the society that was building the new world.

Here in the camp she finally comprehended what had happened. She accepted the situation and adapted herself to it, convincing herself of the correctness of the general policy of the Party and the Soviet state. What had happened to her had simply been an isolated error; everything she had fought for all her life would come to pass.

In her quilted clothing she looked like a little gray-haired old man. She would go up to the criminals and say, "Marusya, my dear, your group's on kitchen duty tomorrow. Do it properly!" And she would walk away without looking back. There were never any objections. Marusya would nod silently.

Only Ninon Khabalova ignored Pelageya's wishes. She willingly did everything required of her at work, but she would not tolerate individual instructions. One evening, after the idea of setting up an amateur theater had been broached, Pelageya stopped by Ninon's bed. "Madam!"

Ninon was busy with something on the upper bunk but began to climb down, her backside and legs dangling over the side of the bunk in their quilted trousers and *kerz* boots of canvas. Silence had fallen over the nearby bunks.

"Madam!" Pelageya said louder, losing patience. She detected an ulterior motive in Ninon's behavior. "I can do without your arse!"

The women lying on the beds smiled in anticipation of some entertainment.

"Go screw yourself!" Ninon answered calmly and jerked her boot. A chuckle arose from the several dozen prisoners. The laughter died away when Ninon jumped down to the floor and turned to Pelageya.

"Well, what can I do for you, m'lady?"

"Ach, that's enough of that aristocratic 'm'lady'!" Pelageya snapped. "Just call me 'Citizen Chief.'"

"But you call me 'Madam.'" Ninon twisted her thin sensitive lips into a derisive smile. "At home our cook was called Pelageya, and it's too long to call you 'Citizen Chief.' It hurts my tongue."

"But it doesn't hurt your tongue to tell everyone to go screw themselves?"

"No, that sounds nice," Ninon answered, squinting at the delighted faces around her.

"Well, well, that's a noble upbringing for you," Pelageya said with a bitter smile, disarmed by the directness of Ninon's thoughts.

"But, m'lady, you were also brought up in a noble family. And see

116

what you look like now! A Bolshevik commissar would die at the sight of you!" The whole hut laughed heartily.

"What's so terrible about me?" Pelageya was getting nervous.

Ninon shrugged her shoulders. "It's difficult to explain. But that outfit doesn't suit you. The pants fit you like a scarecrow's and your sweater's too short. It has no taste."

"And how do your pants fit you?" Pelageya said resentfully.

"What pants?" Ninon asked in surprise, glancing at the laughing faces around the hut. "I haven't any pants." She pointed to her legs. "These are not pants, they're Soviet work clothes."

"Well, all right," Pelageya interrupted. "So I'm a scarecrow. But you're no Petersburg beauty, either."

"That's your fault!" Ninon raised her voice.

"What do you mean, my fault?" Pelageya raised her fists.

"Yes, m'lady, it was you who thought up this revolution."

Pelageya choked back her tears and stepped up close to Ninon. "Let's leave history out of it. I want to ask you to take part in our theater."

"Go screw yourself!" Ninon answered plaintively. "Why are you bothering me? I've washed all the lavatories today, and the floors. I've fulfilled my norm!"

"No, Ninon, no," Pelageya said, trying to conciliate her. "This theater is for us, for our entertainment."

"What part will you give me?" Ninon asked suspiciously.

"Oh, you can choose it yourself."

"Well, all . . . right!" she drawled.

The theater was a popular idea, even among the criminals. The first performance took place on a warm spring evening atop a plank stage in a clearing in the forest. The play was written by one of the zeks, and its theme was the moral and political re-education of the inmates as a result of the beneficial influence of the Soviet camp system.

The new camp commandant, Degtev, who lived most of the time in Krasnoyarsk and entrusted all the work to Angarov, drove out that evening for the specific purpose of verifying the political content of the play. He was now sitting right in front of the stage on the only stool. Behind him sat Angarov and the whole camp guard on benches that had been knocked together quickly from planks. The women crowded at the sides, near the stage, in the "boxes." The male inmates of the camp occupied the space at the end of the clearing, sitting crosslegged on the grass.

An interrogation was in progress on the stage. The interrogator was being played by a political zek who had once worked as an interrogator. The subject of the interrogation, a fashionably dressed old woman, glibly parried the cunning questions, seeking to muddle the inquiry and wriggle out of the trap into which the other characters were trying so persistently to drive her.

With bated breath the fifteen hundred prisoners with one hundred soldiers strained to hear every word from the stage, on which each of them could see a part of his life unfolding, either in the role of the inter- rogator or of the prisoner—for each member of the audience was only one step between these two.

The tedious voice of the man in the familiar dark-blue uniform rang out from the stage. "Citizen Osipova, you're just wasting time. You can't lead us up the garden path . . ."

"I know, Citizen Investigator, I know all that," the old woman gab- bled. "But I'm not trying to lead you anywhere—you can go where you like without any help from me."

"And there's no need to play with words." The interrogator tapped his pencil on the desk.

"Well, what could I do, my dear?" The old woman gave a grating laugh. "You can tell a man by the company he keeps."

"What do you mean by that?" The interrogator stood up threatening- ly. "I detect a lack of respect for the authorities in your answer."

"Oi, oi, you do go on!" She waved her arms. "I was talking about my- self, about my terrible past. I've lived, don't you see, among ignorant, evil people, and that's why I'm like I am . . . Only it's not my fault, Citizen Comrade Investigator, as God's my witness . . ."

He pulled a wry face. "You can leave God out of it, Mother Citizen. This isn't a church. Why do you deny the obvious fact that your son, with malice aforethought, permitted his farm's winter crops to be damaged by horses from a neighboring kolkhoz? Do you deny that your son was the senior agronomist at the state farm at the time?"

"He was, of course, sonny."

"Don't get familiar with me! Were the winter crops damaged?"

"Of course they were, my dear boy, you know the horses ate . . ."

"I know it was the horses! But who was responsible for the crops?"

"Who was responsible for the crops?" The old woman repeated the question in confusion.

"Yes, who was responsible for these crops?" the interrogator said menacingly.

The old woman hesitated, and said nothing. The audience waited for her reply in heavy silence. One of the young criminals in the back row shouted at the top of his voice: "Hang in there, ma, don't let him get you!"

The old woman immediately stood up, strode boldly to the edge of the stage and shouted, "Go screw yourself!"

The stunned audience froze for a moment, and then the laughter broke out over the clearing like a cannon shot. The interrogator's shoulders shook, and he collapsed onto the desk. Ninon stood at the edge of the stage like a mythical goddess, staring down at the howling gray mass, from which issued enthusiastic shouts: "Bravo, Ninon! Encore! Go on, give us some more!" And sitting on the stool in front of the stage, the surly Colonel Degtev laughed for the first time in years.

The actors managed to resume after about fifteen minutes. At the end of the play they left the stage to a storm of applause. The audience remained in the clearing for a long time, exchanging their impressions and recalling their own theatricals of the past.

Vikenty had been shaken by the unexpected talent of the prisoner-actors, which had once more reminded everyone, including the prisoners themselves, that they were still alive. He sat on the edge of the bench until the last person had left the clearing; he wanted to be alone. His soul ached, disturbed by visions of the full life he had left behind and a confused desire, a hope of finding himself once more in a real theater, sitting next to a beautiful woman, strolling with her in the lobby during intermission, buying her cake.

He felt as if these terribly simple thoughts were suffocating him even under the dark-blue vault of the night sky. Hanging his head he picked his way in darkness through the benches toward the camp gates. He started, hearing someone whisper, "Vikenty Filippovich!"

"Lida?" He was astonished to recognize the voice, and peered at the dark figure sitting on the bench.

"Yes." Her voice sounded tender, but firm. "Sit with me a while, if you're not in a hurry."

"Thank you." He moved closer to her and sat down on the bench. "Aren't you afraid to sit here alone?"

"No," she answered softly, "the zeks don't bother me, and anyway, I knew you were here."

"You kept quiet all this time?"

"Yes, I couldn't call your name." She blushed in the darkness, and wrapped her gray jacket tighter around herself. "I feel so sad . . . it would have been better not to have watched the play. It was a great idea of yours, the theater. While you're watching, you're doubly alive. And after the play, even if you're depressed, you want so much to live . . . but life is passing you by . . . it's been four years now . . . nothing but work, the forest, the sky . . . Do you remember that night, after the Mukhin business?"

"How could I forget it?" he answered. He was sitting beside her and looking sideways at her face, half of which was covered by a thick lock of hair. She brushed it back with her hand and turned to him. The whites of her eyes gleamed in the darkness.

"Do you still remember it?" He looked her straight in the face. "It's almost four years ago now."

"You don't understand women very well." She smiled slightly. "We have rich imaginations. Richer than yours. It's because we have to spend more time waiting than you do. You can wait and seek, but we have to wait and hope. We are not allowed to seek. That's the way this silly world is arranged. The strong choose the weak. But our feelings are just as strong as yours—stronger even!" Her voice sounded hard, almost angry.

"I'll be frank with you, Lida. I had a wife, Katya. I loved her and I'll love her till I die . . . but I've been thinking about you."

"I've been thinking too. I realized that your heart belonged to someone else. I tried not to bother you . . . But I'm still a human being! This camp will not break me . . . It's better to die than . . . than to be like some of them . . . they're passed from hand to hand, to the depths."

"Yes," he said, "it's difficult for you women in this hell."

"Did you see Nadezhda Alekseyevna after Orlov's funeral?"

"Why would I? Why do you ask?"

"It's simple, very simple, Vikenty Filippovich. We women can read each other's thoughts. She was not indifferent toward you."

"It would never have occurred to me!" he muttered in amazement. "No, Lida, I didn't see her. She's been living in Moscow a long time now . . . And thank you for thinking about me. I've often thought about you too, these years."

He laid his hand on her shoulder.

"Let's go." She stood up and gently removed his hand. "I'm frozen."

He meekly took his hand away and walked beside her. At the gates he said, "Let's go to my room, Lida."

She raised her face to him and opened her eyes wide. For a minute she regarded him silently in the darkness.

"No, Lida, no!" he took her hand and pressed his lips to her slender, sweetly warm fingers. She did not take her hand away.

"I know what that 'no' means." Lida stressed the word. "Before I called out to you this evening I'd lived a whole lifetime with you in my imagination. I know you very well—four whole years. You're a strong and noble person. Of course, 'no'! I've been cleaning your room for four years now and I've never once seen you in it. You never once left your bed unmade. Why? You didn't like the idea of my hands soiling your sheets?"

"No, it's not that." He pressed her palm against his eyes.

"What a beard you have!" She ran her hand down his face, wreathed below with the thick red fan of his beard. "Aren't you tired of going about like this?" She laughed as she gazed up at him.

"It doesn't bother me," he answered, embarrassed. "I'll shave it off when I get out of here. I'm afraid of seeing myself as a simple human being. This way it doesn't look like me, but someone else, and that makes it easier . . . Yes, I didn't answer your question. I avoided meeting you in my room. I had my reasons. I loved my Katya. I was faithful to her and I will remain faithful to her memory."

"Her memory?" Her hand slipped down and went to her throat.

"She died some time ago, in a camp. She wasn't as lucky as you. And too, I was afraid of temptation, of being left alone with you—I wouldn't have been able to control myself, and you were dear to me. I made my bed myself so that I shouldn't smell the scent of your hands . . . I've lived without a woman for five years now."

"And now you're inviting me . . ."

"Yes, because my conscience is clear toward Katya. I've lived like a hermit these five years, but she was with me in my thoughts. She won't come back to me. I'm to blame for bringing her here to this unhappy country. But now it's too late to change anything."

"Any other reasons?" Her voice betrayed her hope.

"Where you're concerned all my temptations are now behind me. Because we must talk about important things. Because I need you."

"What if I hadn't called out to you this evening?"

"I would have come to you myself, if not today, then tomorrow. I still have a life ahead of me. I still have half my term to serve. You do too. There's still life ahead!"

She stood before him, holding the collar of her jacket up around her neck to keep in the warmth. "Can I speak frankly?"

"Yes, yes."

"Don't be angry. We women often dream more than men do and yet we're more prosaic too. Just now I simply wanted to have something to eat and drink a glass of vodka. I forget when I last had a tasty and satisfying meal. I suppose it was four years ago, at home. And I feel very sad too. I feel like some vodka . . . today's my birthday . . . I'm twenty-eight."

He pulled her close in his powerful arms and pressed his lips to her neck, as if he was kissing his daughter rather than the woman he loved.

She froze. She did not move away but she did not respond to his kiss.

"Come on, Lida." He took her arm. "It doesn't matter if they see us. The whole camp's been wondering for ages why we avoid each other. And it's dark now."·

She walked silently by his side . . . In his room he lit the kerosene lamp, placed the two old office chairs at the table, and sat down on the bed. She stood hesitating in the middle of the room.

"Do you know what?" He looked at her with an unusual light in his eyes. "Will you do something for me? I'm sick to death of the kitchen. You know where everything is . . . I just want to watch and do nothing. It's the first time my table will be laid by you."

He stood up abruptly, stepped toward her and pressed her hands to his face. Then he went to the window and turned his back.

She glanced at the powerful figure standing at the window and then raised her hands to her face, touching her eyes gently. Her palms were wet with tears. She swallowed to hold back her own tears and then set to work. From the small wooden cupboard by the door she took bread, herring, a tin of meat, two dirty cut-glasses, two rusty forks, and three flat china plates with the blue inscription *"Obshchepit,"* the state catering organization. She quickly washed all this in the washbasin, cleaned the herring, and cut it into thin slices, as her mother used to do when her father brought guests home. She spread a clean newspaper on the uneven plank table, poured out two half glasses of vodka, then stood back and examined the "laid table." "It's ready," she said quietly.

Vikenty came away from the window without looking at her, as if he was embarrassed by his momentary weakness. He took his glass. She sat down opposite him.

"Thank you, Lida. It's quite a spread! Drink! Here's to your birthday! This is the first real toast I've drunk all these years. So let's drink to everything at once! To you, to us, to the memory of our glorious Orlov, may he rest in peace! He was a real Russian, a real officer! People like him will conquer in the end—that's the guarantee of the survival of the nation. Let's drink to Nadezhda Alekseyevna too. She was a true friend to him. What else?" He was looking at her with his glass in his hand and an almost satanic light in his eyes.

She lowered her gaze. "We should also drink to the memory of your past, Vikenty Filippovich."

"Yes. I didn't want to think of Katya just now, but . . . since you yourself . . . thank you . . . you . . . you have a great heart. And to my son who's pining away somewhere with strange people, and to our future, to our survival! Drink! Straight down!"

He poured the vodka down his throat and watched as Lida, her head thrown back, tried to swallow the fiery liquid. She emptied the glass, glanced at him with slightly bloodshot eyes, and picked up her fork.

She ate in silence for some time, casting embarrassed looks at the man sitting opposite her and swallowing down an unbidden tear with the food. He too was silent as he watched her, her hands with slender fingers holding the fork, her thin young face flushed from the vodka, food, and excitement, the scarcely perceptible vein pulsing in her thin white neck. From time to time she brushed the unruly strands of hair from her forehead, avoiding his gaze, and when, at last, their eyes did meet, she stopped short for a moment, ceased eating, and hurriedly swallowed the unchewed mouthful. Then she decisively turned her gaze aside.

She cleared the table without looking at him. Then she went to the door, but glanced back. He was still sitting at the table, drunk, and was watching her with a mute request in his eyes.

He went up to her and pulled her to him. He pressed her head against his shoulder and buried his face in her grass-scented hair.

"If you . . ." He used the familiar form of address. "If you want to leave," he muttered, hugging her tenderly, "then leave. I won't stop you. But please don't go away . . . Stay with me a while. I won't harm you, you know that. It's as you decide . . ."

"Ah, you, my man!" She placed her arms around his neck, standing on tiptoe, and pressed her face against his beard. "Of course not! It isn't that at all. I'm ashamed of myself, not of going to bed with you. I decided long ago that I would be your wife. No, I'm ashamed of something else . . . I'll tell you later. Put out the light."

He moved to the table and blew into the sooty glass. He stood at the window in the darkness, listening to her undressing. When she lay still in his bed, Vikenty undressed and lay down beside her, his heart beating wildly. She turned her whole body toward him and laid her head on his shoulder. Then she lay still, her rapid breathing in his ear. "What are you puffing away like a squirrel for?" He pulled her head playfully toward him and kissed her on the lips. She responded . . . Then she propped herself on her elbow and looked down at his face. She took his hand and laid it on her breast. "Can you feel what this is? This slip is made out of an old mattress cover. Vikenty Filippovich! My love! Forgive me. I feel so ashamed in this slip . . . and I've nothing else."

She buried her nose in his chest and began to weep quietly.

"I'm sorry, Lidochka, my love." He laid her head on the pillow and stroked her face with his rough palms. He kissed her forehead, her eyes, her hair. "Forgive me. I forgot, just like a man! We're all fools in things like that. Just a minute." He jumped out of bed, went to the cupboard, and took out a bundle. "There are some things that the wives of the officers at the Authority collected for the prisoners. Choose whatever you like. Don't worry. They're nothing special."

He pulled the blanket from her and took her hand. She clung to him meekly, just as she used to hang on her father's neck. She kissed his beard, laughing a quiet happy laughter, and pushed him toward the bed. She stood over the bundle in the darkness and glanced shyly at Vikenty, who was lying in bed, his face turned to the wall. She knelt down and sorted through the bundle, trying to find what she needed. The clothes smelled of other women's bodies. Trembling with joy and cold, she pulled out a slip and a pair of panties. She glanced again toward the bed, then took off her mattress slip and put on the new underclothes. Hesitantly, she stepped over to the bed.

She lay down beside him and put her arm around his powerful back. "Vikenty," she whispered, "feel what a soft silky slip! I'm a woman. A woman again! I want to be a woman! I'm tired of being nobody. Come here, come to me!"

He lay on his back with his left arm around her. With his right hand he stroked her face, brushing back the strands of hair.

"Look, Vikenty, it's dawn." Lida raised herself on her elbow, leaning over his chest, and stroked his face, his beard, his strong muscular body. She peered into his eyes, which were gleaming in the darkness. "Forgive me for crying, Vitya," she whispered in his face. "It hurt. I'd quite forgotten that I'm still only a girl, do you see, I'd quite forgotten. And I'd forgotten that I'm a woman. I'd become something in between, a neuter sex. And now everything's different! We've been living side by side like strangers for four whole years. Do you love me? Oi, my bones are breaking! You'll crush me!" She playfully propped herself up with her hands on his broad, prickly chest, then collapsed and buried her nose in his neck. She was quiet for a long time.

"What are you thinking about?" he asked, as if in a sweet dream.

"I was just thinking about my home," she whispered. "My father was the manager of a big factory in Sverdlovsk. We lived very well. We had friends, guests. I was already in my fifth year at the medical institute when one night, in the fall, they came for my father. I remember it like yesterday . . . There were the three of them, in uniform. My mother was crying and wanted to go with him. They pushed her away and she fell down. They didn't even let me go to my father to say goodbye. He just smiled farewell at me and raised his thumb. He always made that sign when he wanted to cheer me up, ever since I was a child. They took him away, and I tried to bring my mother around, but I couldn't. She just lay there on the floor, from a heart attack."

"What happened next?" he asked gruffly.

"In the morning I went to the institute, but they told me in the dean's office that I had been expelled, for being the daughter of an enemy of the people. They wouldn't even let me go to my lecture room to say goodbye to my friends. The dean showed me to the door himself and he watched until I had turned the corner. I went off into the forest and wandered around all day, staring at the sky and the trees. I didn't believe that it was all true, that people could be so terrible. I had nowhere to go. I decided to go to our empty apartment. I didn't know why. A girlfriend from the institute, Ninka Kozyreva, met me on my street. We had grown up and studied together since the first grade. She grabbed my arm and pulled me into a doorway. She was crying. 'Lidonka, don't go home. The NKVD men are waiting for you. They'll arrest you. Come to my place! I'll hide you!'

"I went with her. On the way she told me that they had taken my mother that morning and buried her in a cemetery where they bury the destitute. No one from the family was there . . . Then I lived in my friend's house, in the attic so that her parents wouldn't find out. Her father and mine had always been friends, but her father worked in the NKVD. I lived in the attic nearly two weeks while Ninka brought me food and newspapers. Then I overheard her father telling her off because somebody had seen her with me in the street. He warned her that she'd end up in prison and so would he if they didn't find me. She wept but kept her mouth shut. I wrote her a note and left that morning. I went straight to the NKVD and told them I'd been hiding in the forest."

"Did they beat you?"

"No, they just arrested me and gave me a paper to sign. It said that I had violated a decree of the special commission that had tried my father and the other enemies of the people ordering the families of the condemned men to leave for Siberia within twenty-four hours. They gave me ten years in a normal-regime camp and sent me here . . . That's the story of my life . . . here I became a doctor, unofficially, but I've been able to put my five years in the institute to good use. I've saved a lot of lives, especially the women's. It's hard for them here."

"Yes, Lidochka." He laid her head carefully on the pillow and changed places with her. "That's enough about the past. Let's talk about the future. I'd be glad if . . ."

"You want a child?" She opened her eyes in terror. "Think of me and him! To be born in prison! It's terrible! They'd take him away from me, Vitya, I couldn't bear that."

"It doesn't matter, dear girl, we'll think of something." He stroked her face and breast. "We haven't any contraceptives and there's nowhere to get them. And it's also impossible to live apart any longer. You're my wife now. It will be difficult to prevent you from getting pregnant. I have connections, even in Krasnoyarsk. If it does happen, I'll take you to the hospital myself. Everything will be all right . . . There's a war going on and they need timber. They've begun to value people a bit more, and Degtev needs me like the air he breathes. He realized that long ago. He comes and looks, quiet as a mouse. You'll move in with me."

"Vitya! Darling, perhaps that's not wise?" she whispered, her eyes flashing with alarm. "They'll be jealous!" He shook his head. "The whole camp's been expecting this for ages. I think a lot of them even blame us for staying apart. People always condemn things they can't understand. So it will be quite natural. You're mine now, my treasure! I want to see you near me for the rest of my life."

He turned back the blanket. She was lying in a pink slip. She held her hands modestly to her girlish breast and pressed her legs together. Vikenty sat up and lowered his feet to the floor. He took her foot in two hands and pressed his lips to her tiny, childlike toes.

"Oi, it tickles!" She shook with quiet laughter and tried to pull her foot from his grasp. "Are you kissing my foot?"

"Yes." He kissed her tiny foot again. "I'm kissing this foot, this little foot." He picked her up like a child and sat her on his knee. She put her arms around his neck and whispered in his ear, "Today I remembered what happiness is. So they didn't take away my last drop of happiness."

"Yes, my girl." He rocked her on his knees like a baby.

"My dear one, my strong one." She looked into his face. "But our happiness makes me afraid when I see those fifteen hundred other people who are having a harder time than we . . . Will we really leave here one day and become people again? There's still such a long time to wait here behind the wire. How loathesome it is, to keep people like animals! Who's idea was it? The bastards!"

"It's better not to think about that." He kissed her eyes. "We will live and wait until we've served our time. We must endure and we must be careful. I beg you, Lidonka, be careful! Never say a word to anybody about politics, about yourself, about anything! They'll inform on you, destroy you! Trust no one!"

"I know, Vitya!" She got down from his knees, laid her hands on his shoulders, and bent down to his face. "I know all that. Let's get dressed. Our wedding night is over and our honeymoon's beginning—I have patients waiting in the isolation ward!"

He took her in his arms and whirled her around the room. Then he stood her carefully on the floor, like a porcelain statuette.

"Put on your clothes, my dear friend, and tonight you will throw them off and become a real woman again, at least for me, and that's not so very little!"

"Ooh, it's not little at all. It's a great deal!" She smiled at him. "And now I'll get breakfast."

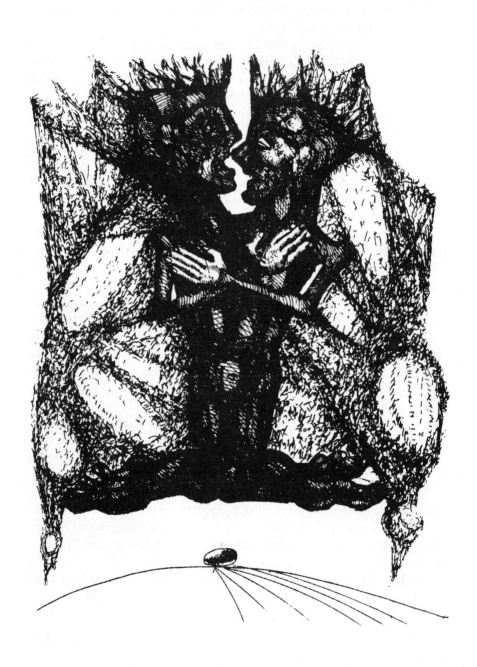

7

SPRING

Day succeeds night, sun succeeds rain, snow sprinkles the mud, and the frost freezes. Fall waters the pools with drizzling rain. Winter sets in, raging and storming, then flees to his father the sea with his last shreds of ice. And then the sun returns with spring in its arms. So, too, is it with the ages of man.

Summer! It's hot, the water's warm. No roof? Sleep on a bench! Don't feel like working? Take a vacation! A train to the country. There's a shallow stream there, with cold water. White geese are swimming there and squawk in alarm.

The train's wheels clack over the points. They sing you a song you heard in childhood, in your cot holding your dear father's finger while he told you wonderful tales. When you get off, take your time—this is your native land—here you grew up in the mud and dirt—your heart will remember it as green grass. The wisdom of memory is to take from life only what is good. The good that selfless people do is not dimmed by the ages. Walk along the ties. All around you is grass and the ancient trees that have stood here since the time of Genghis Khan, although he passed farther south, preferring the open steppe.

The centuries have passed, unfolding their history, and only the taiga has remained unchanged, damp and brooding, concealing its riches.

Stride beneath the shady pines. A squirrel, button-eyed, is gnawing his nut high in the cedar. An icy spring bubbles among the roots. The earth's water rises like home-brewed beer and nurtures the bark. The trunks stand for centuries, bound fast to the roots that dig into the earth, into the depths.

Here's an old village, there will be people here. The low huts are built of stout timbers cut two generations ago.

Knock at a hut at the edge of the forest and wait by the gate until the owner comes. On the other side of the gate there's a big gray wolf, and thank God it's on a chain! The woman of the house appears—she's about thirty, wearing a white kerchief, a skirt and boots. She stands astonished: "What do you want?" "I'm from the town. I'd like to stay a few days and rest here."

"Well come in, but be careful, my husband's jealous. There might be some fun and games and you'll end up in the pond."

Go in, don't be afraid, it's just a joke. The people here are decent.

The warm, tiny room has one little window, and on the floor a carpet woven by industrious hands, with a simple design—a reindeer in the forest. You lie down for a while, you close your eyes and doze off, but suddenly you're awake—a knock. In the doorway a muzhik, broad as a barrel, red beard, sharp eyes squinting at the guest: "Come to table!"

A pot of potatoes steaming fabulously, salted fat pork and a little vodka in ancient glasses, and bear meat, not in a stew but smoking straight from the coals. You lick your fingers—that was no trouble! You'll remember later when some waiter brings you roast beef, at the fashionable Bega or the Rossiya, that there's a village that smells of old Russia and a simple life. That is where the air is cleaner and the water clearer, where the shashlik is tastier for being bear meat, where the people are better, where your roots are, roots torn up in our headlong times.

"Vitya, what on earth are you thinking about?" Lida looked at him in amazement. She was sitting on a stool by the door, keeping an eye on the potatoes that were cooking on a primus standing on another stool. Vikenty had taken off his jacket and boots and was lying on the bed, wrapped up in his own thoughts. By the door of their tiny room, which the prisoners considered a palace, Lida was preparing their meal. Near her, in a wooden cradle, made in the form of a fairy-tale ship by skillful thieves' hands, slept Tolik, their son—born in the prison two years earlier. By special permission of the Kraslag officials, his birth certificate showed his place of birth as Krasnoyarsk.

The last five years had passed uneventfully. Scarface and his group had remained the leaders of the criminals' hut. Degtev had continued to trust Technical Chief Angarov with full authority. Gusev had been promoted to lieutenant and still commanded the camp guard; he was due shortly to be demobilized.

Lida had less than a year to serve, and Vikenty was leaving in the morning. The order announcing his release was hanging on the bulletin board, written in Colonel Degtev's sprawling hand on a strip of paper torn from an exercise book.

Lida was terrified by the thought of being left alone with her son amidst a thousand embittered, deprived people. Vikenty would caress her and describe to her their next meeting, outside the confines of the camp. She understood that the most difficult time was now behind them, but she was no longer twenty-three; she was thirty-three! What now?

"As a matter of fact, Lida, I was lying here thinking about my youth in Medvezhie village. I love the taiga and I love Siberia. The pity of it is I've spent ten years here as a nonhuman. A poem about Siberia even came into my head."

She sat beside him on the bed. "A poem? Well, well, Vitya, I never thought you were a poet! It's probably because tomorrow you'll be a free man. Freedom changes people's thoughts." She turned away to hide her tears.

"Come here!" He pulled her to him and wiped away her tears with his handkerchief. "No, my dear friend, I wasn't thinking about freedom. I was thinking about my native land. There cannot be complete freedom for people like me; it's a semifreedom everywhere in this country. It will be bad as long as Stalin's alive. I'll have time to get organized there, and then you'll come. You're of minor importance to the authorities and they will never harm you. There are plenty of people here to look after you—Gusev, the politicals, Scarface, and Degtev—who says you may stay in this room until your release. Scarface will be technical chief until the end of the year, when his term is over, and you'll be released a month before him, so everything will be all right." He sat up on the bed. "And now let's eat your potatoes so we won't get drunk right away. We must go, the people are waiting. My farewell party! Some of the thieves'll be there, and the politicals, even women from Pelageya's hut. And you must come too," he said in reply to her inquiring look. "Let Tolik sleep. It's already late." He glanced through the window at the deepening twilight and pulled on a boot.

Lida placed the pot of potatoes on the table together with two old stainless steel forks and two pieces of bread. She rested her head on her hands and watched Vikenty tucking into the potato.

"What are you looking at?" He raised his laughing eyes to her and stopped chewing. "You surprised to see me putting it away like a gannet? I've been all round this world and I know the best restaurants in a dozen countries, but I've never tasted such good potatoes! It's because they were cooked by your hands, and because here these potatoes are a luxury. And you—you're my luxury. Eat up! You must look after your health. We have life ahead of us!" He took her playfully by the nose and pulled it down into the pot.

"Stop that!" She looked at him with brimming eyes in which he read the joy of a woman who is loved.

The table was laid in the guards' messroom, a long, low, narrow room with whitewashed walls. Two long tables of planed boards had been placed together and covered with clean newspapers. They had been laid with unheard of delicacies: steaming dishes of boiled potato, herring with onion, a few tins of American stewed meat left over from the war, a five-liter tin jug of vodka, and two rows of aluminum mugs to drink it from.

Vikenty sat at the head of the table and gazed around at the people gathered in the room. Their expectant faces were turned toward him. Aged faces, but with joy in every eye. Prison would soon be over for Scarface and three other thieves from his hut and for the five men from the politicals' hut who had sat on the logs in the forest with him when the uprising in the camp had been discussed. Only Horse and his comrades were missing. Lieutenant Gusev was present on behalf of the camp administration. Degtev, as usual, avoided contact with the camp, sensing that the slightest trouble there would result in a further demotion for him. Orlov's wife had done her work in Moscow; Degtev remained in his post, but his standing in the NKVD had suffered a serious blow.

"Pour out, Scarface!" Vikenty nodded in the direction of the thieves. Scarface did not move. Two of his friends stood up and poured vodka from the jug into the mugs.

"Friends!" Vikenty raised his mug. "I'm not proposing our first toast to myself. My freedom is relative. Anything can still happen. Let's drink to our comrades in misfortune who didn't survive till release, and to the freedom of us all: may everyone who's sitting here see freedom and be able to live a little as a free man, and not behind the wire."

Gusev clasped his mug and stared at the table.

They all drank and began to eat. A quiet hum of conversation arose as they waited for Angarov to continue.

"Now I want to tell you something." He set aside his mug, which still contained some vodka, and took from his pocket a sheet of exercise paper covered with figures. "All of us here are ten-year men who arrived in one shipment almost ten years ago. In this respect we're all on an equal footing. On my recommendation and with the consent of Degtev and Gusev, the Kraslag Authority has confirmed Scarface as technical chief until the end of the year, when he'll be released."

Scarface turned away, avoiding the approving looks of his camp comrades.

"You, Scarface," Vikenty continued, "will assume responsibility for ensuring that there's no trouble in the camp and that the others get out of here. I recommended you because any trouble can only come from your hut, where the thieves don't give a damn about anyone else's life.

"Do you remember our first meeting, Scarface, in the railroad car?"

"I remember, Pirate," answered the thick-set man with the broad streaks of gray in his hair, "and I remember your promise about me not having any kids. You were wrong! I'll have kids all right, I've already proved it!"

"He's proved it!" Pelageya said out loud over the general laughter. "And now I've got to send her off to the town, your Nyurka. She's due soon, and Lida says she might die here."

"She won't die!" Scarface laughed wryly. "I'm serious about her. Let her have the kid, the two of us'll soon be out of this damn cage. We'll fix us up some place and we'll live. I'll have a family. I'm getting on, you know!" he said, clenching his fist on the table. "Look, Pirate, there's something, here, from our hut." He pulled a wooden box from under the table, opened it, and placed on the table an elegant model of a schooner under sail. Listing, the schooner was almost skimming over the foamy wave that was its wooden base. It was all made of birch and bark, carved with a knife, without a single nail or string.

For a few minutes they all gazed at the schooner in silence, struck by the delicacy of its lines and the skill of the carving.

"Well, thank you!" Vikenty lifted the model up over the table. "You made it?"

"No! It was our men, for you, to say thanks for being one of us, not a squealer, for not just looking out for yourself."

"Thanks, Scarface, I'll treasure this gift till I die." He placed the schooner on the table. "Now to business! Here's a list of those who arrived here ten years ago and here's what happened to them. Two hundred went to the front in forty-one and we don't know their fate. Almost a hundred escaped into the taiga and not one of them crossed the Chinese border. Almost five hundred died from illness, starvation, and other causes. That makes eight hundred. Three hundred more with shorter sentences served their time and were released. That means that out of those fifteen hundred, about four hundred are still here now. The others are all new—fresh blood. Nearly three hundred more are due for release this year. So the people are changing all the time. The year's now forty-seven, and we came here in thirty-seven! That, my friends, is how the days of our lives have passed!" He glanced at the political prisoners and the thieves. "The lives of many people remaining here depend on you. Hang on till the fall. There's not much food, it's a hungry year! Well, you know all this yourselves. . . ."

"Of course, Vikenty Filippovich, you don't need to tell us!" said one of the political prisoners sitting at the hushed table. He was the one who had spoken in favor of the uprising at the conference in forty-one. "We haven't died yet, so we'll live out our sentences somehow. There's not much left, as long as they don't increase them again."

Gusev ate in silence, occasionally giving the zeks an indifferent glance. He knew all this, just as well as Angarov or Scarface; he never reported to the authorities in Krasnoyarsk anything that might disturb the routine of camp life—it was in his own interest too.

They knew Gusev and did not fear him, but now they fell silent—life could depend on a single word.

Angarov waved his hand. "Nothing that we say or do will surprise Lieutenant Gusev. Or the Authority for that matter—they know perfectly well how we live and what we think. Now let's eat and drink, to smooth my road to the west so I won't feel any bumps."

For three hours Vikenty sat in the circle of people with whom he had shared his ten years of imprisonment. Several times they had to bring out more food and top up the jug, and they had to listen to many kind and many bitter words. The people sitting there had lost everything and now hoped to regain something—all except Pelageya, the "Commandirsha," as everyone called her, who still had ten years to serve.

It was midnight when the people began to leave. Standing in the spring darkness under the black sky, they breathed in the taiga-scented air. One by one, with tear-stained faces, they gave the Pirate the three kisses on his long red beard—it was impossible to penetrate to his cheeks.

"Well!" Pelageya went up to him with quick steps. In her gray trousers and jacket and with her gray mushroom shaped hair, she looked like a gnome from an old fairy tale. "Well, I'm glad, Com . . . Citizen Technical Chief!" She held him by a button on his jacket. Her eyes were shining. "I'm glad, glad . . . that you . . . that you're free now. Ah, what a happiness freedom is! Even if it is only temporary and conditional. How free I was! Long ago, in my youth, under the czar! How wrong we all were! How we lost! A whole lifetime behind the wire." She buried her face in his chest, shaking with noiseless sobs. It was the first time she had wept in ten years.

"That's enough, ma, what a row!" Scarface stepped up to her and took her by the shoulders. "Stop tormenting us. You'll see it through, you won't die. Look, if I'm still breathing when my release comes up I'll ask Degtev to make you technical chief. Now stop bawling. See you, Pirate. And keep that silver spoon in your mouth!"

"Good luck, Scarface!" Vikenty pulled Lida close and watched the two shadows melting into the darkness.

"Now it's my turn, Comrade Angarov." The lanky figure of Lieutenant Gusev loomed up. "I said 'Comrade' on purpose. I've been watching you people all these years. Let's talk frankly, eh? Comrade Angarov, there's no one here just now, and it's a dark night."

Lida walked away and waited. Vikenty and Gusev stood for a minute facing each other, saying nothing.

"Well, it's like this." Gusev shifted his weight awkwardly from one foot to the other. "You see, when I joined up in the army, I always dreamed of doing some great deed, as did all the boys in our village. But it all went wrong, Comrade Angarov, Vikenty Filippovich. I've been here fifteen years. I had power under Orlov, I've got it under Degtev and even in the Kraslag. Yes. And I was going to get demobilized once before, five years back, but the men in the guard asked me to stay—they were scared they'd get another chief like that fool Mukhin. If I ever meet up with him any place outside I'll smash his face in, for you, for the past. You know, in fifteen years I never did anyone here any harm without cause. I always knew in my bones that they'd all been sent here for nothing. Look, you're an educated man. Tell me what all this upheaval in Russia is all about."

Vikenty stared at his feet in silence.

"You know, Gusev," he said huskily, peering in the darkness at the snub-nosed face. "You don't know yourself! You dreamed about a great deed? In all this tragedy you kept your hands and your weapons clean. Think how many people have survived thanks to you and your kind! I'd hardly be alive today if anybody else had been in your place. Do you remember that time in the clearing, when I kicked Mukhin?"

"I do!" Gusev smiled, his white teeth gleaming in the darkness. "You really gave him one! I thought he'd croak! But he hung on, the bastard! According to the regulations I should have shot you."

"Why didn't you?"

"Intuition, Comrade Angarov. He got what was coming to him that time, made him human. You really gave him one! Our men in the guard were still talking about that kick five years later. I'll soon be on my way home too. I'm sick of the army. My wife's been living in the village, all these years, just waiting. She didn't want to live with me in the camp. She felt too ashamed."

"Well, you go to her and live, Lieutenant Gusev." Vikenty took him by the shoulders, pulled him close and kissed his clean-shaven cheek. "Thanks to you for everything. And as for your great deed, Gusev . . . it was a great deed. You remained an honest man. You risked your career, and perhaps your life. In such times, Gusev, it is a great deed for a soldier in the MVD troops to keep his heart and hands clean." He let go of the young man's shoulders.

"Ah, Comrade Angarov, you're a real man! Every happiness to you and don't you worry your head about Lida—she won't come to any harm. In six months time, I'll take her to the train myself."

Gusev marched off into the darkness.

"Lida!" Vikenty called softly.

She emerged from the darkness, and clung to him.

Half an hour later she was lying on her side, in bed, her arms around his chest, pressing her tear-stained face against his broad shoulder. "Vitya, are we really going to part? I had thought of asking you to stay here until my release, but then I was afraid."

"I thought of that too. What were you afraid of?"

"I thought that perhaps they would change their minds and not release you at all! Then what would I do by myself, free, with the child, but without you? I'm afraid of them, Vitya. Once they let you go, run, don't look back! They won't bother to keep me in here."

"I thought that too, but I didn't want to worry you, my dear little girl. I must go. I really must. I'll manage for the time being, and then you'll come. Everything is working out fine. Is Tolik asleep? It's going to be hard for me without you. Well, never mind, there's not long to go. Let's get some sleep."

"Sleep!" She ran her hand over his eyes, his lips, and down his beard. She took his hand and laid it on her hip. "I'm not going to see you for a long time, you know. Look, I'm wearing the slip you gave me on our first night . . ."

In the predawn the fifteen hundred men and women in gray uniforms resembled a huge indistinct rectangle overgrown with strange plants.

The soldiers of the guard stood toward the gates. Above them bobbed Gusev's crimson cap. Right by the gates was a green American jeep, and sitting in the rear seat was Lida, with Tolik asleep in her arms. Colonel Degtev stood near the jeep, chatting quietly with an unknown officer wearing the crimson epaulets of a major. "From the secret section!" Vikenty guessed. "They're checking to see how the departure goes."

"Friends!" Vikenty's voice sounded loud in the stillness. It seemed to rebound from the dark wall of forest around the camp. "My time has come. Exactly ten years. It's been a hard time for me, just as it was for you."

He squinted back toward the gates. Degtev and the major were no longer chatting. They were listening. "We are all the children of history, children of our country, of our Russia." He raised his voice. "Each one of us broke the law somewhere, and that is why we had to answer to the motherland and to Comrade Stalin. I have expiated my guilt in full and I expect you to do the same." As he addressed the crowd he felt an inner revulsion at the facility with which the loathsome falsehoods tripped from his tongue. "It is never too late to hope, friends!"

At these words a murmur arose from the gray sea of heads.

"All right, Pirate," a voice rang out from the crowd, "get on with it. Stop wasting time! Tell us something to cheer us up."

"Be patient, men." He raised his hand. "Hope, help each other, live, and wait—you have only one life. Here in the taiga the earth is rich. You have a vegetable garden on the camp. It's possible to live, and to serve out your sentences. Every day your terms grow shorter. To survive to the end you must love this earth, respect one another, and love life. You know your new chief. My wife will stay here another six months. Make sure you respect her. I did what I could for you. If I harmed any of you, don't judge me too hard. Farewell, friends! I'll be glad to see all of you on the outside."

"Goodbye, Technical Chief. Live, dear man!" Some one's sharp voice cut through the noise of voices in the crowd.

The car drove through the gates. Vikenty turned around in the rear seat. The gray crowd was flooding through the gates, filling the grassy area in front of the camp. The people were waving their hands and shouting.

"It's not pleasant for them to see someone driving off to freedom!" He pulled his wife's thin shoulder closer.

The major drove fast along the taiga road.

Degtev sat in front beside the major and said nothing until the tiny wooden buildings of Rodnikovo came into view. Then he turned his face to Vikenty and spoke. "Angarov, try to forget about the past, understand, if you get to talk to anyone in Moscow. I acted according to my duty. There was a war on."

Vikenty said nothing and looked away. The major did not respond to Degtev either.

The car crossed the small square at which the Krasnoyarsk bus stopped for only a minute. Angarov got out of the car and helped Lida, taking Tolik from her. He walked a few paces and turned round. Degtev and the major were watching him in silence. "Goodbye, Citizen Colonel," he said, avoiding the word "comrade" out of old camp habit.

Degtev nodded, but said nothing.

"Comrade Angarov!" The major spoke, startling Vikenty. "I wish you luck! You've served the state and the Party well these past ten years. You have truly expiated your guilt. Everyone thinks well of you. Bon voyage! We'll take care of your wife—she'll be released soon. And now goodbye, the bus is coming."

Vikenty did not answer the major. He hugged his son's fair head and with his other arm he embraced Lida.

"Oi, dear Lord!" she sobbed on his chest. "I'm so glad and so unhappy! If only these months will pass quickly! Then we'll have a real human life together!"

"We will, my love, we'll have everything." He kissed her face. "It'll all happen, but don't make any mistakes, just wait. And every week, every week expect a letter from me, even if it's only a couple of lines. I will wait for your letters and they will give me life. For the moment write to Moscow General Delivery. Here's the bus. It will take me to the train, Lidochka, that I've spent ten years waiting for." He let go of her. "Goodbye, my precious friend. Take care of our son. I'll soon . . ." he shouted from the steps as the bus started up.

The young woman with the child was left standing on the road, holding the child close.

8

AFTER TEN YEARS

Angarov spent very little time in his compartment as the Vladivostok–Moscow express sped to the west. He was wearing a new naval uniform with the gold rings of a captain, second rank. From morning to night he sat at a table in the restaurant car, eating, drinking, and gazing at the fields, forests, and stations flashing past the window.

In 1931 he had traveled with Katya and his son along the Trans–Siberian Railroad from Vladivostok to Archangel, after his first arrest. He had traveled along this steel highway for the second time five years later, after his successful arctic voyage to Vladivostok on the icebreaker *Arktika*. Then the star of his career had been shining brightly.

Several months later he had found himself traveling the route again, eastward, in a prison train. And now, ten years later, he was riding to the west to find the grave of Katya and to look for his son Valery, who was living in a children's home in Vologda.

In Krasnoyarsk he had talked with General Bukin of the Kraslag and realized that they were all perfectly well aware he had spent ten years in prison for nothing. The MVD did not wish to have anything further to do with him.

The general shook his hand and the cashier paid him almost twenty thousand roubles, which had been set aside for him from his camp "pay" over the ten years. He found out his son's address and, having passed a decent bribe to the station clerk to procure a sleeping car, he left at night on the express.

The train stopped for half an hour in Novosibirsk. Vikenty did not even look through the window at the station where in the spring of 1917 he had been among the crowd welcoming Soso Dzhugashvili, released from exile by the February Revolution. Here, not far from the station, was the high school where he had spent three wonderful years and first experienced the tender feeling of platonic love for his deskmate Svetlana. Nineteen years had passed since the night he had left Novosibirsk, and a Russia torn by civil war, to go to his father in Harbin. Where should he go now? Should he go to Archangel to thank Pogodin, the interrogator who had saved his life? No, first his family.

He changed trains at night in Sverdlovsk, and on the morning of the following day he got off at the small station in the little town of Kustanai. Forty kilometers from town, Vikenty pushed fifty roubles into the hand of the grateful cabdriver and strode off toward the distant cluster of barrack buildings where Katyusha had died.

On all four sides lay the boundless steppe; not until he was almost at the camp did he come to a small birch copse that stretched away in a narrow band nearly to the horizon. The sun was already up and shining brightly on the green steppe. The sky was cloudless; the day would be hot. The narrow dirt road wound between fields green with the young shoots of winter wheat. Quails were hovering over the fields and swooping down after insects. The air was filled with the fragrance of grass, with the smell of the hot earth, and of dew.

Carrying his bag in his left hand and with his raincoat thrown over his right arm, Captain Angarov slowly approached the forbidding building. Involuntarily he slowed his pace. It was difficult to reconcile the beauty and peace of the morning steppe around him with the thought that close by were people deprived of the joy of living. And somewhere nearby lay Katyusha, who had been less fortunate than he.

Beyond the high barbed-wire fence with its searchlights at the corners, female figures in gray uniforms were digging in the yard.

He stopped at the entrance checkpoint, a wooden booth with a narrow iron door and a small window, from which a pair of eyes watched him. The women stopped digging and stared silently at the man in naval uniform.

A guard carrying a submachine gun emerged from the booth. "What do you want? You're not allowed in here."

"I want to see the camp commandant." Vikenty looked him firmly in the eye. "On business."

The soldier was wearing a dirty green uniform and the cap with the crimson band. He examined the visitor for a few seconds, then turned grudgingly back to the booth and picked up a telephone.

"Comrade Lieutenant? Yes, reporting somebody for you. What about? Won't say. Asks for you. Yessir!"

He came out again, stood indifferently beside Angarov, and watched the door. From it emerged a short, smart sublieutenant who reminded Angarov somewhat of Mukhin, except that the eyes were different—alert and clever.

"Ah! Comrade Captain!" His face dissolved in an ingratiating smile. He straightened his sword belt and held out his hand. "How can I be of service to you? I'm Sublieutenant Kozodoyev, officer commanding the camp guard. The camp commandant is away. I'm his deputy. Forgive me for not inviting you into the camp—it's against regulations."

"Comrade Lieutenant, I, er . . ." he said gruffly. "I've come to see my wife, I mean, to visit her grave."

A shadow of alarm crossed the sublieutenant's face, which had turned crimson.

"Yes, by all means, if you have the relevant document." He made an effort to smile at the tall man in the naval uniform.

Vikenty silently held out to him the order concerning his release signed by General Bukin, which included the general's request for the bearer of the document to be permitted to visit the grave of his wife.

The sublieutenant glanced closely at the document and disappeared into the booth. After a minute he reappeared with a map case in his hand.

"Come along, Comrade Captain, I'll show you the cemetery. Er, there's a lot of graves there. It might take time to find the one you want. I've brought a map; they're in alphabetical order. Her name?"

"Angarova, Ekaterina Sergeyevna," Vikenty answered bleakly as he walked beside the sublieutenant toward the birch copse that stretched away to the horizon.

The first birches began about a hundred yards from the camp, and here he saw the graves. Under almost every tree was a tiny mound with a number on a wooden cross that poked up through the thick grass. There were no names. The sublieutenant walked ahead in silence, holding the map in front of him as he picked his way between the birches and the graves. He stopped on the edge of the copse, by a birch that stretched its bright white trunk up to the sky. Trickles of sap ran down the trunk. The bright green leaves rustled softly in the wind. Right at the base of the tree, on the side facing the steppe, he made out the scarcely discernible mound of a grave overgrown with the long, thick grass. Only the tip of a wooden cross showed above the grass.

Angarov dropped his bag and raincoat and knelt beside the grave. He looked at his companion in confusion.

"This is it." The sublieutenant spread his hands, as if apologizing for something. "I remember her. A lot of them died at that time from brucellosis. We had no means of treating them or anything to feed them with. Her name's on the cross too. I learned from her dossier that her husband was someone important. That's you of course. As an exception, I told the soldiers to carve her name on the cross."

Kneeling, Angarov parted the grass around the cross. He could hardly read the name carved in the wood: "Ekaterina Angarova, died of illness, June 1937."

"And this is all," he whispered. He looked around. The sublieutenant had moved away and was almost hidden by the trees: "This is all that's left of you, my Katyusha. Katya!"

He lay down along the grave, closed his eyes, and buried his face in the scented grass. It seemed that he could see her skeleton down below him. A bitter rage constricted his throat. He had no tears. Fragments of thoughts and memories whirled in his mind like leaves in a hurricane. "Katya, do you remember the Parkers, our first meeting?" he whispered into the grave through his clenched teeth. "How beautiful you were then! And our first night, after the theater. You loved me, you loved life. You would have lived happily if I hadn't brought you here to this country of mine! Forgive me! Forgive me, Katyusha."

He stretched his neck and kissed the cross with dry lips. For a long while he lay silently on the grave, digging his fingers into the earth. At last he got up. Mechanically he picked up his bag and coat and stumbled away in the direction of the camp. Kozodoyev, who was waiting for him, gave him a brief sympathetic glance and fell in step with him.

As they approached the camp, Vikenty saw the gray figures of women standing behind the fence, their faces pressed against the wire.

"I can't bear to look at them!" He stopped short and gazed about helplessly, but there was nowhere to hide.

"Wait here." The sublieutenant set off toward the booth at a run. "I'll get a truck and take you to the station."

A minute later the gates creaked open and an old one-and-a-half-ton-

ner emerged with the comrade sublieutenant at the wheel. He opened
the door.

"I can't look at those faces!" Angarov repeated, as if in a trance. He
covered his eyes with his hands and sat swaying on the seat beside Kozodoyev.

"I understand," the sublieutenant said somberly. "I've been here so
many years, seeing this . . . seeing the women slowly dying, first their
minds, then their bodies. But what can I do? Orders are orders. If you
don't carry them out, you end up behind the wire yourself."

The train from Karaganda reached Moscow at dawn. Waking, Vikenty regarded the other passengers with a mixture of surprise and hostility. "They're so busy, traveling, laughing! As if there wasn't a camp in Siberia where I left Lida, or a camp in Kazakhstan where I left Katya.
They've got time only for themselves. What kind of people live in this
country?"

"Attention please, comrade passengers." The announcer's voice
came over the loudspeaker in the car. "Our train is arriving in Moscow,
the capital of our great motherland. Have a good day! Don't forget your
tickets and baggage!"

"I hope you lose your voice, you pig!" he muttered as he made his
way through the crowd toward the exit.

The tide of passengers carried him straight toward Yaroslavl Station.
The familiar platform, the familiar square! With the three stations at the
corners: Yaroslavl, Kazan, and Leningrad. And the towering building of
the Hotel Leningrad opposite, where he had dined once, after his talk
with the People's Commissar for the Merchant Marine.

He stood in the square for half an hour, by the taxi rank, letting other
people go ahead of him, gazing with moist eyes at this wonderful living
world.

He paid off the taxi at the children's store, Detsky Mir, and crossed
the street into the lobby of the multistory granite building of the Ministry
of the Merchant Marine. He obtained a pass at the window and took the
elevator to the fourth-floor reception office. The familiar blonde secretary
was not there. A middle-aged woman glanced at him sternly and wrote his
name on the list of persons wishing to see the minister. His turn came.

Sitting by the huge desk, Vikenty waited with a certain indifference
to hear what the man in the minister's chair would say. He was about six-

ty, a short, gray-haired, thick-set man with rings up to his elbow. The minister leafed through Angarov's dossier without raising his eyes, then smiled affectedly. "I'm glad, Comrade Angarov, that you've been released. Fate is fickle, but it can't be helped. We are all servants of the State, the Party, and Comrade Stalin. In the present situation I can't give you a ship right away, even a coaster, and you won't be able to get a visa to sail to foreign ports, not for a long time. I think the best thing will be for you to work on shore until a few things are cleared up. I can offer you the post of harbor master of the port of Riga. If you don't accept it, then you'll have to try your luck at the Ministry of Fisheries of the Central Authority for the Arctic Route—they also have large fleets."

"No thank you," Angarov said drily, easily holding the minister's piercing gaze. "I began my career in the Merchant Marine and I want to end it here too. I accept. We'll see how it goes!"

"Well, that's fine!" The minister stood up and came out from behind the desk. He took Angarov's elbow and showed him to the door almost like a friend. "Accept things the way they are, Captain. Live for the future. In time I think you will get a ship, but for the moment . . . I'll call Comrade Bude right away—he's the minister for Fisheries of the Latvian SSR—and ask him to help with your arrangements and papers. You'll cope with the work—I've no doubt of that."

Vikenty shook his hand. He glanced back from the doorway. He wanted to ask, "And how are Sukhov and the former People's Commissar Rusakov?" But was it worth risking what was left of his life? They were either dead or on the sidelines. Where else could they be?

After his interview, Vikenty went to the Central Post Office and wired five thousand roubles to Lida for her to buy some things in the camp store—sometimes they had dried fish, and pryaniki made in the thirties—hard as iron, but spicy enough when soaked in water.

Cafes and restaurants invited him with their open doors, and the crowd that surged along the sidewalks beckoned him into this bustling life, but he was living in his own mutilated inner world, a deep and gloomy world that was like an underground lake contaminated with poison gas. Angarov crossed Red Square and stopped outside Lenin's mausoleum, mingling with the crowd waiting to see the next changing of the guard.

He could not remember how long he had been standing in the crowd

in front of the mausoleum when the small bells of the clock in the Spasskaya Tower in the Kremlin began their melodious chiming at five minutes to eleven and the guard emerged from a side door in the wall. The
two young soldiers and a sergeant, all dressed in dark-blue breeches and
green jackets and with the concertina folds of their chrome-leather boots
gleaming, slow marched along the asphalt path. Their rifles were on their
shoulders and they kicked their toes high in front of them and banged
their heels on the ground.

"Goose step!" Vikenty thought bitterly. "They're marching the way
they did under Paul the First."

The crowd surged closer to the guard, cameras clicking. Vikenty did
not move from the spot. His gaze was fixed on the crenelated red-brick
wall that rose up behind the mausoleum. In one of the buildings whose
roof was just visible above the battlements lived the man whom Angarov
had seen in 1917 at the Novosibirsk railroad station, the man who clung
like death to Angarov's throat and controlled his every step, the man who
had killed his first wife and kept his second wife behind barbed wire, the
man who might still take away his freedom. He swore under his breath.

"Citizen!" A man in a civilian suit and a raincoat tapped him on the
shoulder. "Come with me."

As if in a trance, and with sinking heart, he meekly followed the gray
raincoat. They stopped a little farther along the fence, near the reviewing
rostrum. There stood a second man, somehow resembling the first.

"Papers!" The civilian held out his hand. He took the papers from
Angarov's sweating palm, read them, and raised his eyes sternly. "You're
just out of prison? Who authorized you to come to Moscow? What are
you doing here on Red Square?"

"I . . . I . . ." It was as if he had just come out of shock. "I'm going
to my new job, as harbor master at Riga. I stopped in Moscow to see the
minister for the Merchant Marine . . . You can check . . ."

The two men exchanged looks. "I beg your pardon!" He handed Vikenty the papers. "You may go. I must ask you not to loiter on the Square
in front of the mausoleum. We get all kinds of people here. I hope, now
you've served your sentence, that you, as an educated man, have ac-
knowledged your guilt and don't hold a grudge against the Soviet government."

"Well of course not! What grudge could I have? You're my own people!" he answered almost joyfully, seeing the faces of the MGB men soft-

en at his use of the insider's slang for "informer." He saluted them, took his bag, and set off toward the National Hotel. After a few minutes he glanced back. The two men had still not moved. They were watching him. "Hell!" he cursed to himself. "You're never rid of them. They're like locusts!"

In the lobby of the National he handed his bag to an obliging porter, tossed him his coat, then climbed the carpeted staircase to the restaurant and into his old familiar world. He looked down and caught the porter watching him. As he made his way to an empty table he joked to himself, suddenly in high spirits, *"Et tu, Brute!* You're one of 'my own people' too. They're all my own people here!"

There were few guests in the restaurant during the day. He sat near the window and leaned blissfully back in the comfortable chair. He lit a Kazbek and glanced around the room. There were no Soviet people, only foreigners. They sat up straight and chewed slowly—they were in no hurry. They made themselves quite at home. Good people! He laughed to himself. He knew that he must not utter a sound here—everything was picked up by the microphones.

"What would you like to order, sir?" The waiter had appeared at the table almost unnoticed, as if he had hopped down from the ceiling. Short and bald, with a shiny face and a thin nose and a mouth like a chicken's rectum. He stood by the table in his black tail coat, leaning forward deferentially, a pencil in his right hand, a note pad in his left, his gaze fixed somewhere above Vikenty's eyes, on the crown of his head.

"Are you one of 'my own people' too?" Vikenty wondered. "What are you? A lieutenant? Or something higher? You're a poor worker. You've fattened yourself on state victuals!" Out loud he said:

"I want three hundred grams of vodka, some herring, kharcho soup, duck with apple, ice cream, and a bottle of narzan."

"Right away, sir!" The waiter finished writing, tucked the pencil behind his ear with a neat movement, and disappeared into the corridor.

A few minutes later Vikenty was pouring himself a full glass of vodka. He raised the glass, drinking a silent toast to someone. He glanced out of the window at the square that separated the National Hotel from the Kremlin.

"Well, Soso," he thought with bitter pleasure as he regarded the red battlements beyond the square, "here I am alive and well, and free for the time being. Permit me to raise this glass to all those whom you have murdered and those whom you will yet murder. Here's to their memory! And to you, Soso, to your death!"

He drank off the glass in a single draught and began to eat, rediscovering that there was real food in the world, not just potatoes and bread.

It was growing dark when Angarov got off the streetcar at Smolenkskaya Square. He continued on foot toward Zubovskaya Square, agonizing over the next task that he had planned for his short stay in Moscow.

Ten years earlier, on the way to the camp at Krasnoyarsk, he had spent one night in a transit prison at Chelyabinsk. There he had managed to exchange a few words with Vasily Nikolayevich Semenov, the former head of the planning section of the People's Commissariat for Agriculture. Semenov, who was dying of dysentery, had shoved into Angarov's hand a short note for his family, with an address in Moscow. Vikenty had lost the note, but he remembered the address very well. He was now finding it difficult to go to this family that possibly knew nothing about what had happened to Semenov. There would be tears, questions. But he had given Semenov a promise just before he died. Such promises must be kept. Vikenty sighed as he stopped outside the house. He climbed to the second floor and pressed the bell at one of the four doors on the landing.

He heard soft footsteps on the other side of the door, then silence. He rang again.

"Who is there?" It was an old woman's voice.

"You don't know me. It's a private matter," Angarov answered as gently as he could.

"What is it about?" said the voice, frightened now, after a few second's silence.

"I can't tell you about it through the door. We need to talk."

"I will not let you in!" Irritation as well as fear sounded in the voice. "There is nothing for us to talk about. Go away or I will call the police."

"It's about Comrade Semenov!" Vikenty shouted at the door. He was losing patience.

He heard the muffled thud of something hitting the floor, then hurried steps. The door was opened by a man of about thirty. He was wearing an old sweater with holes in the elbows, and worn trousers. His pale nervous face looked at Angarov in terror. Then for some reason he whispered, straight into Angarov's face: "Don't just stand there! She's fainted. Quick, help me get her to the sofa."

149

Vikenty recovered from his astonishment and stepped into the vestibule, dropping his things straight onto the floor. He helped the man lay the old woman on the sofa. She was dressed in black and her long gray hair was tied back in a knot on her neck.

She lay unconscious on the narrow sofa in the dark room with its old-fashioned furniture while Vikenty and the man tried to bring her around by splashing water on her face. He whispered to Angarov, "Semenov, Vladimir Vasilyevich." Vikenty whispered to him, "Captain Angarov," as he stared anxiously at the old woman's pale face.

She recovered consciousness, and they helped her to sit up. She fixed her misty gaze on Vikenty, a gaze that reminded him of the eyes of the gently insane Olya—Olya, who had not survived until her mother's release; one day she had not returned from her walk in the taiga.

"Do you mind if I smoke?" Angarov took out a pack of Kazbeks.

"No, but tell me quickly!" She kept her intent unblinking gaze fixed on him.

Vikenty told her the details of his meeting with her husband, of his last words before the orderlies took him away on a stretcher. Vladimir Vasilyevich walked nervously up and down the room, tugging at his cheek and giving the captain looks of amazement. This was the first news of his father since his arrest in 1937.

"He died?" the woman asked huskily.

"Yes, he was dying when they took him away. I don't think he survived. They didn't treat people there. He asked me to give you a note, but I lost it—I was ten years in prison. You could lose your life there, let alone a note. But I remembered your address and so here I am, in memory of him."

"So you saw him and spoke with him?" she asked again.

"Yes, I had the bunk next to his for nearly twenty-four hours." He felt uneasy under her unnatural gaze and he asked, to try to distract her, "But how have you been living all this time?"

"Oh!" She smiled almost imperceptibly. "We lived well, before. My husband was one of the old czarist officers. He joined the Red Army in 1917. Tukhachevsky knew him well. Then he retired and took the post of deputy head of the planning section of the People's Commissariat for Agriculture. They arrested him right in his office. I waited for him, then I went there. There was a new man sitting in his chair. He shouted at me, 'You are the wife of an enemy of the people! Get out of here or you will go where he has gone!'

"I went to the NKVD, to the Lubyanka. I asked them to arrest me, but they would not let me in. They laughed and said that they knew what they were doing and they did not accept volunteers for prison. They drove me away."

She was sitting unnaturally straight, watching Angarov with wide-open sparkling eyes.

"Mother, that's enough! Don't go on about the past like this!" The son was walking to and fro in exasperation, giving his mother anxious looks—the next attack might end badly.

"I was in a mental home," she continued without answering her son, "then I worked as a cleaning woman. You know, I was an actress before." The hint of a smile flitted across her face. "But you must not think I am unbalanced! No, it only seems that way. It is just that I have this ache in my heart all the time. Vasily Nikolayevich comes to me every night, we talk, and I am happy. Only at night. He is not here during the day and I hate it without him. You do not believe me?" She frowned, staring at the man in the naval uniform. "But he is my husband. They destroyed his body but they cannot destroy his soul. He often calls me to his side, and I hurry to him."

"Mother!" said Vladimir Vasilyevich. "What are you saying?"

"It is all right, Volodya. This is the first man with a human face who has entered our apartment all these years. He has brought us a little of our father. My Volodya was a student in the law faculty at the university then. They expelled him. He has had a hard time, my boy. But, you know, the years passed, and he managed to get an extramural degree. He earns a little money . . . He is a lawyer, but they only let him take divorce cases. You are not annoyed with me for telling you all this?"

"Of course not, madam. You have my fullest sympathy." Vikenty stirred in his chair and glanced at the narrow dark window beyond which he could hear the noise of the Sadovoye ring road.

"Good. God sent you to me. I have been going to the church for many years now and praying to God to send me news of what happened to my husband. And now, see, you have come. Our God sees all. Oh, I know it! And you cannot deny that he sent you to me. I will tell him everything tonight . . . Will you come to see us again? Please do! Even if only once a year. I will wait!"

"I'll come, madam, I promise, without fail," he answered, glad that the painful visit was over.

When he had taken his leave, he stood in the courtyard for a few minutes. "Well, there you are, Vasily Nikolayevich," he muttered, "I've carried out your dying wish. You can rest now. Your memory lives."

That evening Angarov sat alone in a corner of the restaurant of Yaroslavl Station, occasionally fingering the ticket to Vologda in his breast pocket. He had taken a small table in the far corner and removed the other chairs. He wanted to be alone. He closed his eyes wearily and tried to put into order the events of his first day after ten years on the sidelines of life. His face was flushed with brandy, and it still felt somehow naked without the beard.

The huge hall of the restaurant reminded him of the waiting room, from which the noise of a thousand voices carried through the wooden wall along with the indestructible odor of Russia on the move—sweat, bread, onion, and something else that constricted the throat. But still it was better here than in the waiting room, where hundreds of people were lying about and hundreds more picking their way to the counters for steaming coffee and sandwiches, or to the ticket windows.

Beautiful images of the saints gazed down from the walls through the blue haze of cigarette smoke. Their elongated faces seemed embarrassed by the disorderly spectacle. Hundreds of ill-dressed people sat at the numerous tables, which were covered with once white tablecloths stained with wine and sauce, gulping shchi that only smelled of meat, drinking vodka by the glass, grimacing and hastily chewing a crust of bread or a pickle. The fat waitresses scurried about, their full figures underlining, as if on purpose, the difference between them and their half-starved customers, many of whom were thinking that it must be good to be a waiter in such hungry times.

Vikenty even noticed, in a corner of the ceiling, the ubiquitous "Three Knights," who, unlike the saints, were looking away, as if this drunken rabble did not interest them. He laughed at the comparison and squinted at the far left corner of the room where an elderly waitress with a shock of yellow hair under her dirty cap was leaning over a table, moving her lips in concentration as she counted some money. "She's counting and won't make a mistake," he thought bitterly. "They act as though there wasn't any violence in this country, as though millions weren't dying in camps. She's counting her money! Next she'll buy a country villa, then a car. This dirty gray old crone is living! She steals and cheats, and she lives! And at the expense of her fellow citizens as well. And she didn't end up in a camp of course!"

He tipped a half glass of brandy down his throat, swallowed, and struck a match. "That's the way it always will be. For some, camps and prisons and death; for others, who are in with the regime or simply don't give it any trouble—for them, money, cars, life. Divide and rule! Joseph can't be such a fool if he's managed to divide and rule these millions."

Vikenty was now regarding the waitress almost with hatred. She had finished counting. With a quick movement she rolled the thick bundle of notes into a tight wad and hid it away somewhere in her bosom; then she disappeared behind the buffet counter. The almost square bull-neck of the barman rose up from behind this counter. He was a man of about fifty, his face red with health and liquor. He silently poured the vodka and brandy from the bottles into the tumblers and wineglasses on the trays, and paid no attention to the impatient looks and urging of the waitresses standing in line. Each of them mentally cursed the barman for giving short measure, but each of them just as silently took what they were given and disappeared into the blue haze of smoke. There were people sitting at the tables to whom they could themselves give short measure, almost at a run and with a single habitual deft movement.

"If you don't cheat, you won't survive!" Vikenty's mood turned sour and he tossed a hundred-rouble note onto the table and moved toward the exit. Out of the corner of his eye he saw the waitress hurry eagerly to the table and shove the note into her pocket.

He stood for a few minutes in the waiting room gathering his thoughts and watching the noisy sea of people. On the right, just by the entrance to the toilets, sprawled an old man wearing ancient resoled felt boots and quilted trousers, both patched in various colors. His old thread-bare military pea-jacket was buttoned up. Strands of straight hair hung down from beneath an ear-muffed cap of indeterminate age and fur. The old man was sleeping, his chin resting on his chest. He was hugging a birch-bark knapsack, perhaps containing bread. Vikenty's own father could be lying around somewhere like that! He felt sick at the thought and turned away. Only when he reached the exit did he remember the telephone. He could call them: his parents and sisters in Zhitomir. He had last seen them in 1936, before his voyage to the Arctic.

He rushed out into the station square and took a taxi to the Central

Post Office in Kirov Street—where he placed an order for a long-distance call. As he waited he squeezed the receiver with relief. It was a good thing they had a telephone at home, otherwise he would have had to put off the conversation.

"M . . . Maria? Wh . . . who's that?" he asked hoarsely.

"It's me, Maria. Who is this? What do you want?" The faint voice sounded strange.

"It's me!" he almost shouted into the mouthpiece, smiling joyfully. "It's me, Vikenty!"

With tears in his eyes he looked in surprise at the silent receiver. Then, as if something had just dawned on him, he asked, "Are the old people still alive?"

"No." He recognized the voice of his younger sister, and yet it was the voice of a stranger.

"What do you mean 'no'?"

"You know what I mean. They're dead, that's all. They died!"

"They died?"

"Yes."

"When?"

"Years ago."

"And the others? Genka?"

"The others are alive. But not Genka," his sister answered. "But where are you calling from?"

"From Moscow."

"Where've you come from? Where've you been?"

"Maria Ivanovna!" shouted a fat man with an affable face in the next booth, giving Vikenty a wink. "I bought everything you told me! Yes. In GUM. Fabulous! Well, what's the weather like there in Norilsk? Eh? What did I buy? A fur coat for four thousand. No, a silver fox. Five suits and some dress material. What? In the commission store, in Presnya. Yes, and I even managed to pick up some black caviar. I'm flying back overnight. Eh?"

"What are you shouting for?" Vikenty yelled, glaring with rage at the fat man through the glass. The man's face turned sour; he banged down the receiver and vanished from the booth.

"What was that you were saying?" He heard his sister's alarmed voice from Zhitomir.

"Nothing. Someone was bothering me. There's all kinds of riff-raff here!" He spat viciously on the floor and smeared the spittle with his foot. "Look, I want to come down there. We must meet . . . Why don't you say something?"

"I . . . I don't know!" she said after a few moments' silence. "You write first, where you are and what you're doing. Then we'll talk about your coming down. Send us a letter. It's crowded here. There's nowhere for you to sleep."

He said nothing and replaced the receiver. Staring at the ground he walked past the line of people sitting along the wall waiting for their calls. He was thankful for the darkness. Wiping his eyes, he walked slowly down toward the station. "So there's no one left. They died 'years ago'! So investigator Bydlin wasn't lying when he interrogated me in 1936 . . . They killed my brother Genka."

With his hands thrust into the pockets of his black raincoat he strode along the Sadovoye ring road, not noticing the passersby. Suddenly he stopped. *Encounter on Elba* announced the poster above the entrance of the Zvezda cinema. "*Encounter on Elba*! Who's in it? Americans, no doubt. Our allies! Let's go to the movies! What a crowd!"

He stood there watching the flood of people pour from the cinema amid a cloud of steamy air and disperse noisily along the sidewalk.

Two hours later he was striding along the corridor of the sleeping car thinking only about the approaching meeting with his son Valery. He was oblivious to the passengers around him and to the dark-green northern woods flashing past the window. The years of suffering and anxiety had taught him to shut himself off completely from the outside world, to live in his own inner world where all the events of his past were laid out on shelves: the happy events, closest; the unhappy ones, in remote corners, where they would not weaken his spirit.

He spent the whole night striding up and down the green-carpeted corridor. Every half hour he took a pull at a rapidly emptying bottle of brandy, and he threw his cigarette butts through the window into the dark night. What was he to say to his son? Would the boy recognize him?

Morning greeted the town with mist and rain. Single- and two-story wooden houses, wooden streets, and sidewalks overgrown with grass. An ancient bus, rattling like a gypsy's cart, took him to the outskirts. At the end of a street, almost up against the forest, stood a four-story, box-shaped building built of wood and painted pink. The rows of identical windows had no balconies. Behind the building he could see volleyball and basketball courts, and beyond them the forest.

He went into the lobby, trying to control the trembling in his legs, and asked the old man sitting at the desk by the door, "Where can I find Valery Angarov, dad?"

"Right away, chief," the old man wheezed in a north-country accent as he fussily placed the chair on one side. "I'll get his house mother for you." He minced away up the stairs, and Vikenty followed him. They were met on the second floor landing by an elderly woman wearing an old-fashioned dark-gray dress, almost down to her ankles, with a white collar. Strands of gray hair poked out from under her colored kerchief.

"You're here to see Valya?" She nodded understandingly. "Come with me." They entered a small room with a large window. Four iron bedsteads stood in a straight line along the walls. In the middle of the room was a bare table and four chairs.

"He lives here, this is his bed." She sat down on a chair and motioned him to sit. The old man gave the visitor a last indifferent glance and closed the door from the outside.

"Are you his father?" Alarm showed in the woman's watchful eyes.

"Yes, why?" He was embarrassed.

"Nothing, of course, nothing." She put a handkerchief to her moist eyes. "Where have you come from just now? Where do you live?"

"From prison. I was ten years inside," he answered grimly, lowering his eyes.

The woman said nothing.

"But where is Valery?" Vikenty glanced at her.

"He should be here so-on," she replied. Her long "oo" reminded him of the old doorman. "His last class is just finishing. He's a go-od boy. You'll take him with you, of course?"

"Are you sorry?" he asked irritably, and immediately regretted it.

"No, I'm not sorry." The woman smiled sadly. "It's just that I've grown used to him. When they brought him here, ten years ago that was, he called for his mama and papa every night. He called and cried, he broke my heart with his crying . . . Later on he stopped crying but he turned gloomy and sulky. He'd hardened his heart against people. There's only me he loves, and he promised to take me in when I'm old . . . You know, since that night when they brought him here an orphan I haven't left him for a day. But, if he's found his father . . . Then of course I'm glad, just as long as Valya's happy. I'll live out my time some-how by myself. Here he is!"

A tall lean youth in the regulation gray uniform was standing in the doorway holding a briefcase. He turned pale, then threw the briefcase onto a bed and stood looking questioningly at his foster mother and the unknown man in the handsome black uniform.

Vikenty stood by the table, white as a sheet, hiding his trembling hands behind his back.

"Valyusha! I'm sorry, I didn't introduce myself." She turned to the visitor. "My name's Anna Ivanovna. Valyusha, this is your father."

Valery swayed and gripped the bedstead. With compressed lips he stared at the man, not knowing what to do or say. Something seemed to be constricting his throat and forcing tears from his eyes. A feeling of heaviness overcame his arms and legs. For a few seconds he saw blurred images of Archangel and Dvina. He could no longer remember his moth-er's gentle hands and his father's bristly cheek, but he remembered the people who had once torn him from his mother's arms. He had wept long then, months and years, and had called out for his father and mother, but they had not come. Time had passed, and Anna Ivanovna had been there. He had grown used to her and he loved her, but in his heart there was a deep wound, covered over by a scar of time.

Now he stared eagerly at the gray-haired captain standing by the ta-ble. He did not remember his father.

"Are you my father?" Valery whispered, although he thought he was speaking loud.

Vikenty stood silent, as if struck dumb. He was afraid that by one wrong word or movement he might frighten off this boy who was almost a stranger and yet so dear to him.

"Are you my father?" Valery repeated. He stepped toward the table and stood behind Anna Ivanovna's chair.

"Yes, Valery, I'm your father," Vikenty answered huskily. He was afraid to raise his hand to wipe his cheek.

"But where were you so long?" Valery asked. This time he had used the familiar form of address, but he still did not move.

"I was in prison, son, in a camp."

"So long?"

"Yes, son, ten years."

"What for? Were you guilty?"

Vikenty glanced helplessly at Anna Ivanovna. She stood up, holding her handkerchief to her eyes with both hands.

"Don't cry, mama." Valery took her hand. "My father's come to see me. Has my mother come too?"

"No, son, she's not here. She died in a camp, of an illness."

"When did she die?"

"Long ago. You were still small."

"Have you seen her grave?"

"Yes."

"And will you be able to show it to me?"

"Yes, but later."

"Go on!" Anna Ivanovna almost shouted, and pushed Valery on the shoulder. She burst into tears, but was unembarrassed. "Go to your father. Embrace him!"

Valery gave her a startled look, then turned to his father. His eyes filled with tears.

"Can I embrace you?" he asked quietly.

Vikenty stepped forward and pulled his son close, burying his head in his light gold hair. Valery's whole body was trembling. He slowly put his arms around his father's shoulders and pressed his face against his chest. He began to cry.

"My son!" Vikenty murmured, choking back his tears. "My son! How you've grown. Forgive me. I couldn't come. I thought about you all the time. All these ten years, every day, every minute. And I thought about mama. She's not with us any more. We'll go to her, to her grave, later. Will you come with me now?"

Valery nodded silently. Then he raised his head and asked, "Where to?"

"Riga. I'm going to work there."

"But what about Anna Ivanovna?" He turned to her.

"She'll come too. She can live with us."

"Will you come, mama?" He went up to her, took her by the shoulders, and turned her face toward him.

"It's all right, son." She smiled at him through her tears. "You go by yourself. You've found happiness again. And I'll stay on here by myself."

"No, I won't go!" He went up to his father. "Don't be angry, father, I can't leave Anna Ivanovna here, I can't go without her. I'll stay with her. And in the summer we'll come to visit you, or you'll come to us. Alright?"

With a chill in his heart, Vikenty gazed into his son's wide-open eyes, in which, as in a mirror, he saw reflected his own confused feelings.

He would have to wait, for years, perhaps, until the thin thread linking him to his son grew strong again, for it had only just been re-established over the abyss of ten long years. It was still weak and might easily break, for the second time and forever.

"All right, Valyusha," he said more cheerfully. "Live here for the time being, with Anna Ivanovna, and I'll send you money and come to see you in the summer. Then we'll all be one family. And later we'll be together . . . here's some money—five thousand." He placed a newspaper-wrapped package on the table. "Let Anna Ivanovna put it in a savings book. It's for both of you. I have to go to Riga, to begin work in the port. Will you see me off?"

"Can't you stay until tomorrow?" Valery was disappointed.

"I will!" he agreed suddenly. "Now let's eat!"

Vikenty took from his bag some wine, sausage, cheese, and candy. Valery and Anna Ivanovna watched in silence.

"We never have things like this to eat, we live very simply." She shook her head.

While Anna Ivanovna was laying the table, Vikenty observed his son furtively, searching for likenesses of himself and of Katya. The boy was like Katya, and only the build and eyes were his.

After the meal they went for a walk in the forest. Anna Ivanovna hung back and followed them at a distance, both sad and happy at the development. That night they pushed two beds together and he slept with his son. Anna Ivanovna accommodated the other three occupants of the room elsewhere. Vikenty laid his son's fair head on his shoulder and lay listening to his regular breathing until dawn, afraid that the slightest movement might disturb the sleep of this boy who for him was the dearest person in the world. That night he forgot even about Lida and his little son Anatoly, who were living out the last months of imprisonment.

Comrade Bude, the Latvian Minister for Fisheries, was glad when the new harbor master arrived—he was short of experienced men. He smiled politely at Captain Angarov, who was sitting across the desk from him in his office. "It's true," he said. "We do have passport regulations, the same as in the rest of the country. It's difficult to get a visa, especially as this is a port open to foreigners. But we'll help you. I've already made arrangements. The personnel officer will direct you to the ministry's hostel for senior staff—you'll have a room of your own. And I'll ring the chief of the passport section of the militia about your visa."

"Thanks for that too," Vikenty thought as he listened in silence to the tall, narrow-faced man with the straw-colored hair and blue eyes. He felt as if he was talking with a foreigner; the Baltic people were not coarse and rude like the Russians.

"Thank you, Comrade Minister." Angarov stood up, supposing that the interview was over.

"That's not all." Bude came and took his elbow. "I'm just going out on business and I'll drop you off at the militia station."

He telephoned about the visa and ordered a car. In the street he dismissed the driver with a nod.

"I like to drive myself!" he said in response to Angarov's silent look of surprise, as he steered the car around a bend. "It takes my mind off work, and makes for fewer ears too."

He glanced searchingly at the captain sitting beside him. "By the way," he continued. "I used to know Comrade Sukhov, your former chief at Archangel."

Vikenty said nothing. He waited for Bude to tell him more.

"I know all about it, Comrade Angarov," Bude said softly. He was taking a roundabout route so as to have longer to talk. "These are stormy times. I've been lucky, you haven't. But you know, in the year you were arrested I was a mere seiner captain, working the Atlantic. I don't think Sukhov came back. He was a good man. We once did some training together on the old tall ship *Tovarishch*, after we had finished at the Merchant Marine school. I . . . I . . . ." He paused. "I advise you never to show any interest in what happened to him. You can't do anything about it, Vikenty Filippovich," he said familiarly. "You must be patient and wait. Think about yourself, you still have a life to live. I'll try to help you in personal matters. What do you think of your new job? Riga port is a big concern, and you've had a break . . ."

"Break? Bullshit!" Vikenty answered, his voice suddenly hoarse and his eyes sparkling. "I've really missed the water, and my work."

Bude squinted at him approvingly. He stopped the car and held out his hand. "Please, come straight to me if there's any problem, anything at all."

A few minutes later a lieutenant-colonel of the militia was leafing through Angarov's papers, looking not at what was written in them, but at the signatures. Then he gave Angarov an encouraging look. "It's a complicated busines, Comrade Angarov. According to the law I have no right to give you a visa for Riga, not after you've been in prison. But I'll make an exception in your case, especially as the minister himself has requested it. We always pass people who are needed." He breathed on the stamp and banged it down on one of the pages of the passport. "Here you are, Comrade Angarov. Live. I hope no one will trouble you any more."

"I hope so too!" Vikenty shook his hand with feeling.

He moved into a furnished room on the second floor of the four-story hostel for senior staff of the merchant and fishing fleets of the Latvian SSR. He sent parcels to Valery and to Lida at the camp, then buried himself in his work. He would rise at 5 A.M., boil water for his tea on the electric plate, shave carefully, and brush his uniform. Then he would stride through the still-sleeping harbor, breathing in the beloved aroma of seaweed and sea. He would inspect the whole harbor, then pay visits to the captains of the vessels moored at the piers or standing in the roads—cargo and passenger ships, trawlers and seiners. During these talks he listened to the captains' advice and complaints, knowing in advance what the essence of the matter was and what action to take. This was his element.

Angarov was no longer the same bold, fair-haired navigation officer who had once climbed so briskly up the mast to reset a sail. Now a tall, thick-set, gray-haired captain, he sometimes found it difficult to climb up a too-steep companionway. The habit acquired over ten years of walking on level ground told on him.

Yet the goose necks of the waterfront cranes, the hoots of the steamers, the splashing of the water against the piers, drew him like a magnet. He often stayed to spend the night with some captain, sitting with him over a glass of brandy. But he never spoke a word about the past with anyone. The past, those ten years, no longer existed: it was as if someone had taken a pencil and deleted them from the total number of years assigned for his life.

In the evenings, unless he stayed with one of the captains, he tried to arrive home late. In his room he would hang his jacket on the back of a chair, place the teapot on the electric plate, which stood on a stool by the door, lay the table with clean newspaper, and slice up some of his favorite freshly pickled herring or open a can of sprats. Then he would sit there a long while drinking the thick tea. He would take out a box with photographs of Katya, Valery, Lida, Anatoly, and the dozens of other people, friends and enemies, who had crossed his path. He would lay all the photographs out on the table and sit for hours gazing at the faces.

Then he would lie down on the bed, on top of the covers, in his trousers and undershirt, and smoke. The smoke would drift out through the open ventilator, and from outside he would hear the noise of streetcars. Riga Harbor Master Angarov was alone in his room, feeling good if a little sad.

Fall came, and with it a new joy. Valery wrote that he was finishing school and in May he would arrive with his "mama." Shortly afterward, Vikenty was notified to take a long-distance telephone call. He arrived at the post office half an hour early, having drunk a glass of vodka on the way. His heart had suddenly begun to ache.

When he heard the faint, beloved voice he squeezed the receiver till it hurt.

"Vitya, is that you?"

"Yes, yes, Lida!" he almost shouted, smiling into the receiver. "It's me! Go on, go on!"

"Yes, yes, my dear, I'm free! Do you understand, free!" Her tiny voice came to him over several thousand kilometers. "I'm calling from Krasnoyarsk. I'm leaving tomorrow."

"What time?"

"In the evening."

"By air?"

"No, by train, its too expensive."

"What do you mean? To hell with the train!" he roared into the mouthpiece. "Go to the post office. I'll wire the money to you right away by express, two thousand. Come by air. Wire me with the flight number."

"All right!" She laughed joyfully. "I'll fly. Love and kisses!"

When he had wired the money to her, Vikenty went home. He sat down on the bed fully dressed, not knowing where to go or what to do. Today he could not sit drinking tea by himself, he could not be alone for a minute, a second. He went out into the street. It was ten in the evening. Riga lay wrapped in mist, through which a fine drizzle was falling. The very "sea" weather that he loved.

He turned up the collar of his raincoat, pulled the cap with the crab emblem down over his eyes, and luxuriated in the feeling of the rain on his face. He strode through the dark, narrow streets and along the river, then returned to the harbor. He kept on walking, tirelessly.

He called at the post office before five the next morning and joyfully read the telegram from Lida: "Flying. Arrive Leningrad 5 A.M. Riga time. Riga 9 A.M." That meant four hours to wait. He did not feel at all sleepy. He made his way to the railroad station on foot. There would be plenty of people there! The sight of the bodies sleeping on benches and on the floor, the crowds of people at the ticket windows and the buffets, and the noise and familiar odor of Russia calmed him down, and he began to feel drowsy. He sat down on a bench in a corner and dozed off, his nose tucked into the collar of his coat.

He woke with a start and glanced at his watch. Eight o'clock! He rushed out into the square and into the first taxi. "Airport! Fast as you can! I'll pay for the risk!"

It was 8:45 when the taxi pulled up outside the airport building in a spray of mud. The plane from Leningrad had already arrived and was taxiing toward the arrivals building. Standing on tiptoe, Vikenty scrutinized the column of passengers walking away from the plane with their suitcases and bags. Lida was not among them.

He walked away from the barrier and stood wondering what could have happened. The passengers all passed by; the tarmac was empty. Vikenty set off along the metal railing toward the exit where he saw the solitary figure of a fashionably dressed woman. He stepped aside to avoid bumping into her and walked on.

"Vikenty!" He stopped dead and spun round. There was no one there except for the young woman. She was carrying a bag. He could see the lower part of her face below her hat. She was holding the hand of a small boy, who resembled a bear cub in his fur coat. Vikenty looked from the boy, whose face was muffled up, to the woman, and only then did he recognize Lida's familiar, loving eyes.

"Didn't you recognize the prisoner?" She pulled off the hat and her marvelous shock of hair scattered in the wind, covering her eyes.

Vikenty went up to her without speaking, took her face in his rough hands and pulled her close, kissing her hair, her forehead, and her eyes, which were wet with tears.

"Didn't you recognize me without my prison clothes?" she asked playfully but with a hint of bitterness. "This is what I was like when they arrested me as a student. The ten years simply flew by, didn't they?"

"Ye-es!" He looked at her with delight and with sorrow. "You're a student again, and I'm an old man already."

"Huh, some old man!" Her eyebrows shot up in amazement. "You're the best man in the world, for me . . . Take us to your home!"

He picked up Tolik and aimed a kiss at his nose, which was hidden behind a scarf. He kept glancing in astonishment at the beautiful young woman, trying to remember the gray, quiet, thin creature who had cleaned his room for so many years in the camp. What imprisonment did to people!

"Where did you get these things?"

"Aha!" She huddled up close to him and gazed into his face with happy eyes. "They're my things. Before I turned myself over to the NKVD, I left a suitcase of clothes with a friend. She had kept everything! She brought it to me at the airport at Sverdlovsk. We had a good cry together. What a friend! Thank heavens there are such people. I changed right there, in the rest room. Now I'm the same student I was ten years ago. Only, I'm older in my heart, and I never had wrinkles before." She snuggled against his shoulder and fell silent.

He squeezed her tighter, picked up his son and the suitcase, and walked in silence toward the taxi rank.

To Vikenty's and Lida's secret delight, Tolik had fallen asleep in the taxi after staring fixedly at the road and he did not wake up when Vikenty carried him up the stairs. While Lida was putting his bachelor cell into some kind of order and preparing their breakfast, Vikenty sat by the table, unable to take his eyes from her shapely figure, from this simple irresistible creature who filled his room and his heart with peace and happiness.

During breakfast they were both silent for a while, and then Lida asked, "Did you go to Katya's grave?"

He did not reply, but went and stood beside her and kissed her eyes. "How many good people have perished before my eyes!" he said. "But I've been lucky in life. And you love me."

She stood up and put her arms around his neck. "Yes, I love you. You're not like the others. You're a romantic at heart, Vik, and that's a hidden strength. I couldn't tell you before, but now . . . well, six years ago, immediately after Orlov's death, that cretin Degtev took a fancy to me." She blushed. "He offered to transfer me to another camp if I would become his mistress, or even to set me up in Krasnoyarsk in a secret apartment. He promised he would marry me later."

"He did?" Vikenty was stupefied. "And you refused that chance of freedom. Because of . . ."

"No!" She shook her head. "Not 'because of,' Vitya, but 'for the sake of,' for your sake, for our sake, for the sake of our love. Even as a zek you were a real man for me, and a human being. Not like Degtev."

Vikenty shook his head and took her face in his hands. He stared into her eyes. "All the same, you did refuse six years of freedom! What if we hadn't come together later? Would you have gone to him?"

"No!" She looked stubbornly up at him, and her face grew dark. "I was and I shall always be honest, the same student that I was when they arrested me. They could have killed me but I would never have become anyone's whore."

She moved close to him and ran her palms over his face, beardless now. "And I know, my dear captain, that you've been half a year without me, but remember that I've been half a year without you . . . It's still a long time till evening! Have you got anything we can hang over the window? Undo my blouse for me." She turned her back sharply to him.

With trembling fingers he began clumsily to unfasten the buttons. She threw off the blouse with a light movement, revealing her narrow pale shoulders. "Turn your back," she said.

He went to the window and pulled down the blind. He could feel his heart jumping in his chest, like a sparrow in a cage.

"Vitya, I'm ready!"

He turned round. She was standing by the bed wearing only her slip, elegant like a girl of seventeen.

"Lida!" He stepped forward and took her by the shoulders. "I'm not used to it any more . . . I'm sorry . . . it doesn't feel right."

"I know, I know," she laughed softly. "I'm not expecting anything of you. I just want to lie near you for a while, to lie with my husband. I'm afraid that you'll run away or there'll be an earthquake or something."

When he lay down beside her, she turned onto her side and snuggled up against him. She lay still, with her nose tucked into his neck, and began to fall asleep, but after a few minutes she felt his firm hand on her shoulder.

"You men are all crazy," she whispered affectionately in his ear half an hour later as she smoothed his damp forelock with both her hands. "You never know what you're capable of. You're not sorry we didn't wait till tonight? You're confident of yourself now?"

"Yes, doctor." He covered her eyes with his palm.

"Tell me," she said after a while, "is our happiness forever? Could they still remember about you and me?"

"Hardly. We served our time. Put it out of your mind! I'll rent a cottage soon, on the beach near Riga. My son Valery's coming in the summer with his foster mother."

"Yes?" Lida raised herself excitedly on her elbows. "How old is she?"

"Sixty, I think. She's an old woman. Alone . She's been bringing Valery up these past ten years. Let her live with us. But I didn't tell Valery about you."

"Why didn't you?"

"Well, there was enough news for one meeting as it was. Let's leave the past alone for a while. I'm sure he'll love you. It'll be all right. But we'd better get up now; otherwise, you know, appetite grows with eating!"

"Let's get up!" She hung on his neck and Vikenty stood her on the bed. He took a long time to dress her, having trouble with the fastenings. Lida stood looking down at him and laughed the happy laugh of her childhood—it was just the way her father used to dress her in the mornings, when she was still very small.

There was already a long line in the ZAGS registry office in town. Some twenty persons were sitting on the chairs in the narrow gloomy corridor, their eyes fixed on a door that bore the inscription: "Registry of Marriages, Divorces, Births, and Deaths."

"That's a good door," Vikenty thought bitterly as he took a seat near the entrance, farthest from the door. "Grief and joy. They've got it all in one room." Lida was silent, intimidated by the surroundings.

A young couple was sitting next to the door, holding hands and gazing happily at the other people. A little farther away a middle-aged man and woman were quarreling quietly, drawing up the accounts of their life together.

At last they were ushered into a small room, the white walls of which had not seen paint for a long time but which displayed the usual four portraits. A middle-aged woman sitting at a desk motioned them to two chairs and gave them a confused look. "It's like the preliminary detention room," Vikenty thought, looking at the grill over the window.

Lida sat down on the chair and looked anxiously now at Vikenty, now at the woman. She felt as if she was about to be sentenced again. She pulled her son closer.

"What is it, Comrade Captain?" The woman broke the silence.

"Madam, we want to register our marriage, we love each other." Vikenty said quietly but firmly.

"I realize that!" She laughed. "Here are the forms. Fill in all the details, think about it for a month, then come back and we'll register you."

"Madam!" He glanced at Lida's face, which had immediately fallen. "We spent six years thinking about it in the camp. We have a son, he's four years old . . ."

"Can't be done!" the woman declared. "The law's the law."

"My dear woman!" He stood up and looked her straight in the face. "My wife just flew in from Siberia yesterday, from the camp. I've been waiting six months for her. I have to register with the authorities today and find her a job, otherwise we're going to have another hard time of it. Unless you formalize our marriage I can't register her with the authorities. Meet us half way. It's no great crime to register a marriage before the waiting period's up."

"It's easy enough for you to say that." She looked away. "But they hammer us for the least little thing. They don't care about the spirit of the law, only the letter."

"Lida, wait for me in the corridor," he said quietly. When the door had closed behind her, he turned to the registrar and placed a newspaper-wrapped package on the table. "Madam, we're alone here. There's five thousand in this package, for the risk. Although some important people will speak for me, if necessary. It's quite safe."

"You're a clever man, Comrade Captain." The woman put the package away in a drawer of the desk, having made a preliminary check of the contents. "I'll make an exception for you. And I'll take the money, for the risk, as you say. Call your wife and write out an explanation."

Fifteen minutes later they were standing before the registrar, solemn and happy, as groom and bride. They listened as she read quickly, as if she were announcing the agenda of a trade-union meeting: "In the name of the Latvian Soviet Socialist Republic I declare you man and wife. I wish you happiness. Sign here."

"That's all." She looked at them impatiently.

"Madam, there's just one more small thing." Vikenty stopped and took a tiny velvet box from his pocket. It contained two gold rings he had bought a month earlier. Lida blushed crimson, held out her hand, and watched him place the ring on her finger.

"Now you do mine." He handed Lida the ring. Her fingers were trembling with emotion and she fumbled as she placed the ring on his finger. At first she had not been able to remember which finger wore the wedding ring.

The registrar blushed and looked at them in silence.

"One other detail, madam." He sat down at the table decisively. "Give me the form—this is our son." He nodded at the boy, who was sitting on the chair wrapped in a blanket, watching the people silently.

The woman sighed in resignation and gave him another form.

"And now, let's push the boat out!" he said when they had signed the form stating that they were the parents of Anatoly Vikentyevich Angarov, born in 1943 in Krasnoyarsk. From his briefcase he pulled out a bottle of champagne and three glasses.

"Ah!" The registrar stared at him in amazement. "You're a man with style! I've been sitting here twenty years and I've never seen such a bridegroom. You've lived abroad, I suppose?"

"It's nothing to do with abroad, madam," he answered as he poured out the champagne. "It's simple humanity."

"We don't run things very well here," the woman said sadly, sipping her champagne. "There's not much comfort. But it will improve one day. I wish you happiness!"

That same day Vikenty called Bude and his colleagues at work and told them that his wife had arrived. That evening the table was laid for fifteen persons in the cabin of one of the captains. From vessels anchored in the harbor came three or four captains, with their wives, and a few of Vikenty's colleagues from the port administration, who were told that the old sea wolf, once deputy chief of the Northern Steam Navigation Authority, and later a convict, had just married a beautiful young "lady doctor" whom he had met after his release from the camp. He preferred not to reveal Lida's past to anyone, so as not to hurt her. Lida found it difficult to accustom herself to the deception, to deceiving so many people at once. But then she forgot about such things. She sat next to her husband, glancing at the gold rings on his sleeve, listening to the incomprehensible sea talk, feeling the curious looks of the women turned upon her, and the approving looks of the men. If this evening was not happiness, what was?

PART TWO: GOLD

9

EXILE

Lida began work as a doctor in the port sanitary inspectorate. At the same time, she was studying for her final examination in medicine. She usually arrived home first. Vikenty would appear by nine and open the door with a smile, in anticipation of seeing what he had been thinking about all day: supper on the table, the cozy greenish glow of the table lamp, and Lida, who shone upon him as the pole star had shone upon him in his youth. Life took on a rhythm. Work, then home, a kiss for her beloved face, and the scent of her hair. Trips to the country and to the shore on Sundays; visits with captains he knew. The days and months flew by unnoticed, like an immeasurable honeymoon.

Summer came. He rented a cottage at the shore, right on the sand dunes so that he would be able to hear the noise of the surf. Then one day he and Lida and Tolik went to the station to meet Anna Ivanovna and Valery. Vikenty's sizeable salary, his connections, and the "compensation" he had received for his ten years of imprisonment enabled them to live well, although the situation in the country was difficult. Their house was well stocked with food, which he and Lida and Anna Ivanovna went to market together to buy, or which he obtained straight from some warehouse—"under the counter."

His whole noisy household would sit down to breakfast in the morning and discuss the day ahead, an evening visit to the movies, or a trip into Riga. He never interfered in the noisy arguments at the table. He just ate in silence, but his shining eyes showed his gratitude to the fates for these weeks of family happiness.

His apprehensions about how Valery would accept his new family were proved groundless. Everything seemed to develop naturally and simply, with the unnoticed but vital assistance of Anna Ivanovna, who understood the inevitability of all that had happened and the pointlessness of any recriminations: all four of them had been hurt by life in some way; they all felt and understood this and assiduously avoided in their conversation any hurtful topics.

Valery had finished school and had enrolled in an electrical engineering college at Vologda. It had been decided that he would continue to live with Anna Ivanovna in her cottage not far from his school. He was to receive money from his father every month, and they would spend the summers together. This arrangement pleased everyone, especially Anna Ivanovna, who would be able to keep her foster child. Only occasionally did Vikenty feel a pang of of conscience about Katya, when he remembered that he had not succeeded in reuniting her family. But he consoled himself with the thought that he could never have brought back the past completely. Life was pushing him in a different direction, away from death and the past.

The month's vacation passed like a dream, like a happy day. Just before their departure he took his whole family around the shops in a taxi, and they chose some things for Valery and his foster mother. Valery blushed with embarrassment, but he took the gifts: for the first time in his life his father had bought him something. This was unfamiliar and pleasant and filled his heart with pride. At the station just before his train left, as he kissed his father and his father's new wife and his own little brother, he felt that he was parting from something good, important, and dear for him, something that he had not had before.

On one of the clear sunny days of the spring of 1949, Angarov was returning from the harbor to his office in the Authority where he had scheduled a conference with some tugboat captains. He stopped involuntarily at the sight of the gray Volga automobile standing at the entrance, just as he always stopped when a black cat ran across his path. Then he gestured in disgust and went up to the second floor. In the lobby three men in raincoats and caps got up from their chairs to meet him. He started as if he had been given an electric shock. He tried to pretend that he had not seen them, and turned to the right into his office.

"Vikenty Filippovich!" one of them called. He stopped and looked at them with a guilty smile.

"I beg your pardon, Vikenty Filippovich." One of the men walked up to him with a similar smile. "Don't get angry and don't despair. Nothing terrible's going to happen this time! But you must come with us."

"Where to?" he asked quietly as he walked meekly between them.

"To MGB Headquarters."

"I've done something wrong?"

"No, Comrade Captain." One of them shrugged his shoulders. "We have nothing against you. It doesn't depend on us. You'll find out when we get there."

The car drove into the courtyard of the headquarters building. All four of them went up to the third floor and stopped outside one of the doors. The leader of the group gripped Angarov's elbow. "Keep calm, Vikenty Filippovich. Don't lose heart. We're simply carrying out an order. It's nothing this time. They're expecting you." He opened the door.

Vikenty entered a spacious reception office. At a desk straight ahead of him sat a woman of about thirty-five wearing the epaulets of an MGB major.

"Sit down, Comrade Angarov." She smiled at him like an old acquaintance and nodded toward a chair. "I regret that we have had to disturb you again. You have not been arrested and this is not an interrogation. Not only you but everyone who has been released during the past two years is to be exiled to Siberia. That is the order of Comrade Beria. There is nothing to be done about it."

"Exile?" He could hardly speak; his tongue seemed to have turned to wood, but he felt a new surge of hope. "Whereabouts?"

"To the Krasnoyarsk Territory, to the village of Medvezhie."

"What!" he almost shouted.

The woman recoiled, startled. Her face paled.

"But I was born there!"

"Yes." She reddened. "We did take that into account. The places of exile, you understand, are determined according to a plan. We try to think of everything! But what's bad about it? You'll stay for a while in your home country. You are exiled for five years. Don't be downhearted, Vikenty Filippovich." She looked at the gold rings on his sleeve with respect. "Don't bear a grudge against us. This is just our work. The interests of the state and the orders of our leaders are more important than anything else. You will understand that of course."

"I understand everything." He hung his head. "But what about my apartment? My work? My family?"

"You'll lose your apartment and your job. I'll help your wife myself as far as I can. Unfortunately, you won't be able to see her before you leave, which is right away, in a few hours. But I'll give her your new address and I'll help her with the arrangements if she decides to join you."

"Is that permitted?" He raised his head.

"Yes, she can join you in exile . . . " The woman turned toward the window. "To tell you the truth, Vikenty Filippovich, I feel sorry for you, but there's nothing I can do. If you were in my position you would carry out the order too, wouldn't you?"

"Yes, of course." He nodded.

"We fought for you here a whole week." She smiled.

"With whom?"

"With Moscow! With the Ministry of Internal Affairs. Comrade Minister Bude even telephoned Comrade Beria about you, but they told him that the order had been signed by Comrade Stalin, and so there couldn't be any exceptions. But I'm sure, and I hope, that this time you won't have to suffer. You'll settle in there."

"What about clothing?" He glanced at her; the memory of the prison uniform was painful.

"No, no! Wear what you like. It's not prison, you know, just exile. You'll be traveling with a whole group, in a reserved car, but you won't be permitted to get out anywhere . . . you understand."

He nodded but said nothing. He wanted to cry like a child, and to complain to somebody. But he was ashamed to cry, and there was no one to complain to.

"Will I be able to write to my son and send him some money?"

"Yes." She pushed a sheet of paper toward him. "And write an instruction to the savings bank. They'll be able to transfer as much as you like to him."

He quickly scribbled out the instruction: of the twenty thousand roubles in his account, five thousand were to be transferred to his son in Vologda, ten thousand to remain in his wife's name, and five thousand to be transferred to the savings bank of the Krasnoyarsk MVD Authority.

Then he wrote to his wife. He could feel the MGB major watching him. He was nervous and kept crossing out words as he tried to console his wife and strengthen her spirit, which had still not recovered from the last experience, for the next ordeal, the latest trials and humiliations.

"My dear Lida. Your fears have come true. I am being exiled again, to Siberia, for five years. I'm going to Medvezhie village, where I was born. If you decide to join me there, sell all our things. We will be able to live together—'with love in our hearts and paradise in our hut'! I've left you money in the savings book. Let me know what you decide. They'll give you my address at the MVD. I'm leaving today. My native parts are waiting for me once again! I'm not downhearted and I don't expect you to be either. Everything's for the best! I'm sure that this will be our last trial. I've told Valery everything and sent him some money. I kiss and embrace you and Tolik. Chin up, student! I shall be happy to embrace you again soon. Your Vikenty."

When he had finished he looked inquiringly at the major. She nodded and continued to stare at him, wanting to speak some words of encouragement, but there were microphones in the walls, and she had her own family to think of.

He took a second sheet of paper and paused to think. This second letter would be more difficult. "My dear son. I want to tell you that I have to go to take up an important post, in the east, perhaps for a long time. Lida is going with me. I have transferred five thousand roubles to you. It's for you and Anna Ivanovna, for your support. I'll soon be able to start sending you money again. You'll be leaving the technical college soon and I expect you'll join the army. Serve honestly, and be a good soldier. I'll be looking forward to seeing you and Anna Ivanovna again. Take care of her. Be brave, fight for your happiness, and look forward to our meeting. It will take place. I'll send you my new address soon. Lida and I embrace you both. Your papa."

The woman put the letters in envelopes and stood up and held out her hand. "I'll post the letters today and I'll get in touch with your wife. A car is waiting for you downstairs. I hope you won't hold this against us, Vikenty Filippovich?"

"There's no helping it." He smiled dolefully and shook her hand. "It's my fate. Thank you for everything. I hope things go better for you."

She stood at the window and sadly watched the gray Volga drive out of the courtyard, taking the man wearing the uniform of a captain, second rank, to the station.

Vikenty had been badly shaken by this latest misfortune. For the whole four days of the journey to Krasnoyarsk he lay on his bunk in the sleeping car, staring at the ceiling and speaking to no one. His comrades in misfortune understood how he felt and did not disturb him; not one question. So his happiness was ended! Once again Soso had his hands on him! He lay for hours, his eyes closed. Riga, the port, the work and the woman he loved, his two sons, the career he had begun to rebuild; it had all vanished in a moment. Here was this goddamn Trans-Siberian Railroad again, a highway to captivity and death. He wept frequently. The thought of doing away with himself floated in his mind, then faded, giving way to more sober thoughts: Lida, Tolik, Valery, Anna Ivanovna. Lida would surely join him! Such a faithful camp friend would never betray him in his need. He must get down to business again; again prepare to fight for what was left of his life. Exile was not prison, after all.

He stared at the ceiling. He did not want to see people or the Russian countryside flashing past the window: for people and for this country he now felt only revulsion and hatred. He felt it was wrong for him to become embittered, for bitterness deprived the soul of its vital forces. But this latest blow had fallen upon a deep wound that had hardly healed.

In Krasnoyarsk their car was uncoupled and shunted onto a siding out of sight of the passengers. Then the whole carload of about a hundred and fifty people, all from Riga, was taken into a deserted side-street behind the station, where the open trucks were already waiting. It took a few minutes for the exiles to be loaded into the trucks, where wooden benches had been set up for them. Vikenty sighed with relief when Krasnoyarsk had been left behind in a cloud of dust. A soldier with a submachine gun sat in the driver's cab. There were about fifteen other men in the back of the truck. The number was gradually reduced as they got off at the villages along the road where they were to serve their terms of exile. By evening he was left alone on the truck. Then the soldier climbed down from the cab and handed him a bundle of papers. "Here, Captain, here's your transit papers. Give them to party organizer Troshkin in Medvezhie village. There's no militia there, so he's the one to keep an eye on you." The soldier grinned and gave him a friendly wink, pleased that his responsible mission was over.

The dirt road ran along the right bank of the Yenisei. Dusk was falling quickly. On the right the river was revealed only by the silvery strip of moonlight and the noise of the water lapping against the rocks at the bank. The black taiga stretched away on the left. Huddled in a corner of the truck Angarov pulled his cap down over his eyes and turned up the collar of his raincoat. For the first time in many years he gave himself up to memories of his childhood. The river from home must be somewhere nearby. In 1913 he and his father had drifted down it on a raft from Medvezhie, on their way to the high school in Novosibirsk. How many years had passed since then? Almost thirty-five. A whole lifetime.

The truck stopped. The driver tapped on the dusty window in the back of the cab and waved his hand. Vikenty jumped down and climbed into the cab. He gave the soldier a grateful look, but he could not see his face in the darkness.

"Cold?" the driver asked, squinting at the man in the corner.

"I'm all right, thanks."

"Here for long?"

"Five years, exile."

"Oh, that's nothing!" He shook his head as if trying to dislodge a fly. "Hardly no time at all for these days. Your voice sounds a bit familiar. Say, this your first time inside?"

"N-no!" Vikenty answered, hesitating. "The third."

"Well, hell, I've heard your voice some place." He stopped the truck, took out a flashlight and shone the beam on Vikenty's face. "Pirate!"

He seized Vikenty's arm and gazed joyfully into his face. "Well, I'll be damned! I know you, but you don't know me!"

"How do you know me?" Vikenty smiled at him, and felt a bit more cheerful.

"I was in your camp near Rodnikovo. I was a thief."

"What are you now?"

"Oh, I'm going straight. You remember, Pirate, when you saw the volunteers off to the front, in forty-one? Well, I went with them. Straight to the front."

He started the motor and accelerated. He said nothing for a while, expecting questions, but Vikenty waited in silence. The meeting was unexpected, somehow pleasant and hurtful at the same time—the nearer he came to captivity, the more he remembered the previous time.

"Then some Kraut gave me a bullet in the leg," the soldier continued thoughtfully. "He was a smart one, that Kraut, he knew what to aim at. They carted me from the battlefield near Rzhev straight to the hospital, and from there—free, a clean slate! Was I lucky! But plenty of our men didn't come out of that fight. Almost all of them. They got their freedom all right! But I was lucky, Pirate, Comrade Angarov. See, I even remember your name! We all liked you, even the thieves, and them dopes of yours, the pols."

"What have you been doing, then? In the army ever since?"

"Yep. Since my luck was so good in the army, I decided to stay in. Grub's not bad, and they rig you out okay. And liquor, a shot a day. The men are all right, and there's girls too, when you go to town. And I like driving. Anyway, I'm too scared to leave the service. I'd go on the booze again. My old pals'd catch up with me and they'd make me start thieving again. And I'd soon be back inside. No, I'm through with all that. I'm staying in till they kick me out."

"That's fine for you, old pal," Vikenty said thoughtfully, "but I'm back in exile again, in Medvezhie, where I was born."

"What? How lucky can you get!" The soldier was genuinely amazed. "They send a guy to his own home village! By the way, my name's Stepka—Stepan Zhmyrev, but in the hut they called me Zhmyr. You don't remember of course. How could you remember fifteen hundred zeks. But I bet you remember that pig the Intellectual? Boy, were we all glad when you killed him in the forest! We were all scared of him, the pig . . . What happened to Scarface?"

"I think he came out, freed, six months after me."

"Well you hang in there, Angarov." He passed Vikenty an open pack of Belomors. "Don't let it get you down. Stick it out and you'll be okay. You know, back then, you only had to walk into the hut and we'd swallow every word you said, just like it was some kind of God talking to us. We wanted to live, and you gave us the strength. We weren't much ourselves, not much guts."

"Did you really think that about me?" Vikenty looked at the soldier with interest and was grateful for an inner sense of joy. He took a cigarette and struck a match. For the first time since his arrest he felt his spirits reviving.

Zhmyrev nodded. "When people are in trouble and expecting to die, they'll always believe their leader and listen to what he's got to say—he can make or break them. You were keeping us alive, and we knew it. Well, here's your village." He nodded ahead. Through the branches of the trees Vikenty could see the dull lights shining in the windows of the huts looming in the darkness. "I'm on my way back right away. The order's to deliver you and get back. Well, here you go, old pal!" He held out his hand. "Stick at it, like you did the last time. A long and happy life to you! If you ever get to Krasnoyarsk, look me up." He pushed a bundle of papers into Vikenty's hand.

Vikenty stood in the road until the red tail-lights of the truck had vanished in the taiga. Then he made his way toward the first of the huts.

A hundred yards along the road became a street. On the right side the huts showed up as dark masses, like burial mounds. Beyond them, and lower down, he could hear the rustle of the river. On the left side of the street the taiga rose up in a black wall. The village straggled along the river for a good two kilometers, without ever making up its mind to cross the road and displace the taiga. Even in the darkness he recognized the familiar bend of the forest by the outermost hut, the timber for which had been felled half a century earlier by his grandfather, an exile too. Over there, about five hundred yards into the taiga, his grandfather rested in the village cemetery, under a tall old birch. His father had told him that in Harbin; that he had buried the grandfather just before he left for China in the stormy days of 1918.

And here was his own house. He went closer to it. It was almost unchanged, except that some kind of extension had been built on at the back, toward the river, perhaps for livestock, or even for people; he could not tell in the darkness whether there were any windows in the low sheds, which were partially hidden in the dense growth of bushes and trees between the house and the river. And the fence was different: low, askew, with its wooden stakes sticking out in all directions. The gate was hanging only by its upper hinge, almost barring the way into the yard. Who lived there? What did it matter? He walked slowly along the dark street, hoping to find the "Forestry Office," as was indicated in his transit papers. It was impossible to plow the land in the impenetrable taiga; it was also difficult to raise livestock because there was no grazing. On the other hand, the hunting grounds were limitless and rich, but hunting was strictly controlled by the state. Thus the villagers had no alternative but to cut timber and float it down the river, and in winter to go to the town to earn money. The villagers' free and easy life had changed with the arrival of Soviet power. The Soviets had revoked their former status of "escaped convicts" hunted by the czarist regime and designated them "fully enfranchized citizens" of the land of the Soviets, making it difficult for them to go to the town without permission of the forestry management.

He stopped outside a low single-story structure, the timbers of which showed through the plaster shell like huge ribs. Three small windows looked straight onto the street; there was no fence. This was all that distinguished the forestry office from the private houses.

The door, made of thick, time-blackened boards, was locked. He climbed the three creaking wooden steps, deposited his bag, and sat down. He lay his head on his knees and closed his eyes.

He woke with a start: standing before him was a short man in a ragged sheepskin coat and a cap with earflaps. Below the cap a beard and moustache could be seen. The man stood with his legs apart, pointing the barrel of an ancient rifle straight into his face.

"Well, what's this, dad?" Vikenty laughed sleepily. "Are you arresting me too? What do you want me to do?"

"I ain't your dad. To hell with your dad!" the old man hissed. "Where you from? What you want? I'm watchman here but who are you?"

"I'm a new resident, come to spend my exile here. I'd like to see the management."

"Management? Get moving!" He pointed with the barrel. "Or I'm pulling the trigger. I'll find the management for you right away, don't you worry. Don't want you wandering about at night without a roof over your head, do we?"

Vikenty stood up obediently and followed the watchman. They stopped at a tall hut with carved window frames. The watchman tapped cautiously on a window. After a few moments a light came on in the hut. A shadow showed behind the curtain, and a deep thick voice said, "Why can't you let people sleep, you old goat?"

"But Petr Yevgrafovich," the old man bleated in a thin goatlike voice, "it's an important matter. Grabbed a bandit."

The figure vanished from behind the curtain and a few minutes later the door creaked open. Angarov placed his bag on the ground and regarded Petr Yevgrafovich in silence. He was a muzhik of medium height, broadshouldered, wearing an old coat that hung straight as a board, a cap, and dirty boots. He resembled neither a peasant nor a worker; he resembled no one.

"I'm Troshkin." He came closer. Vikenty examined the face with its wide cheekbones and sparse beard, and the pair of wide-set eyes that seemed to be looking in different directions.

"Angarov," he said quietly.

"Let's go. And you, Afanasy, well done!" Troshkin gave the old man a patronizing slap on the back. "Go back to your watch."

"You going to let him go?" The old man did not move from the spot.

"That's none of your damn business!" Troshkin said nastily. "I told you to go and that means go. Otherwise you're in for it. Move! You've taken to thinking too much, granddad. If you don't watch out, I'll put you back to herding cows."

"All right, all right, Petro Yevgrafovich!" The old man made for the gate almost at a run. "I was only thinking about the security."

"All right, beat it!" Troshkin waved his hand and set off toward the forestry office.

He lit the kerosene lamp that stood on the narrow wooden table in the long whitewashed room. Some of the benches along the sides of the room had been knocked over, and Troshkin righted them in a business-like manner. He sat down, motioned Angarov to a seat across the table, and held out his hand for the papers.

He read for a while in silence, then raised his eyes to his visitor; one of them looked Vikenty straight in the face but the other stared past him. This created the impression that someone else, in addition to Troshkin, was sitting at the table. Vikenty waited with sinking heart to hear what this latest controller of his fate would say.

"Well now, Angarov." Troshkin laid the papers aside and regarded his visitor fixedly. "You'll have to get that uniform off." He used the familiar form of address.

"Why are you being familiar with me?" The color rushed to Vikenty's face.

"Already started giving me lessons, eh?" Troshkin had turned lobster-red, as if he had just taken a steam bath. "I'll remember that! You'll give me that black and gold outfit in the morning. You have no further use for it. If you manage to serve out your five years, I'll give it back to you. But now you'll wear boots and some kind of working clothes. I'll find you something in the morning. You'll be in my dairy gang—you'll muck out the cowshed."

"That's all?" Vikenty asked calmly. He could feel the hatred pinching his heart.

"That's all," Troshkin repeated, "and if you don't want to work, you'll starve. And if you don't die, I'll send you to prison as a parasite. That's all, Angarov. I'm boss here, understand? You'll work hard these five years, hard labor. Like it says in your papers, 'for correction by hard labor.' That means no mental work for you. Now you can stay here till morning, on a bench. I'll fix you up tomorrow in some old woman's cottage."

"I have a family in Riga . . . " Vikenty called questioningly after Troshkin's departing figure.

"That's your affair. Let them come, if they think they'll like it. They can work in one of my other gangs."

"Well, greetings, native village!" Vikenty said grimly when the door closed behind Troshkin. "Party organizer! So I'm to muck out the sheds. All right!" He swore viciously. "I'll muck out the sheds."

Angarov moved in with an old woman who lived alone in a hut that was just as ancient as she was. He put on the old cloth trousers and faded army jacket—Troshkin's "gift"—rolled up his sleeves and in two days had put the hut in order for the old woman, who was called Avdotya. He made a broom out of nettle stalks, washed the inside walls, blocked up the cracks with rags, then plastered and whitewashed. He replaced the floorboards, but there was nothing to paint the floor with. He crawled around on his knees all day planing and polishing every knot until, at last, the floor was as smooth as a parquet made of huge blocks. The old woman Avdotya watched him in silence from on top of the Russian stove.

Then he went around the outside of the house, noting what needed to be replaced if they were not to freeze to death in winter. He prepared his materials with an axe and handsaw and worked late into the night cutting away the rotten pieces of the timbers, inserting new wood, and blocking up the cracks. The roof, too, was scarcely holding up; the sky showed through the gaps in the rotted boards.

Passing villagers would stop and stare at the new resident frenziedly wielding the axe on the roof of the old woman's hut. Even Troshkin came and looked, chewed his lips contentedly, and went away.

The manual labor with the axe, the stupefying aroma of honey and pine needles wafting from the taiga, and the pot of milk that the grateful Avdotya placed before him for dinner raised his spirits. When he thought that Lida might soon arrive with his son, his heart would begin to pound: he wanted to do more to make this cowshed more like a human dwelling, so that Lida would be able to accept this latest misfortune in their lives more easily, so that they would be able somehow to endure the five years.

The hut consisted of one large room with two windows; there was a nook behind the big stone stove, which was also almost falling apart. Vikenty rebuilt the stove and whitewashed it. He threw out into the street the two stools and the rickety three-legged table—old Avdotya's "furniture." He nailed together a large table, two benches, a few stools from freshly planed boards, as well as a bookcase that reached up to the ceiling, and two beds—a small one behind the stove for the old woman, and a broad platform in the room for his family. To his great joy he discovered some old pieces of tarpaulin in the shed. Armed with a needle and four thicknesses of thread he sewed together a huge mattress, and stuffed it with dried grass. He hoped that Lida would bring sheets and blankets.

Two days later Troshkin stood in the middle of the room looking at Angarov with one eye. "You're a strong one then," he observed softly, "and you can handle an axe."

"Yes, there's plenty I can handle." Vikenty stood by the table, tall, looking like an old woodcutter or hunter.

"Yes, strong." Troshkin shook his head. "The other huts need patching up, but there's no authorization. I can't do it myself. The postman's going to town today, so you can send your missus a letter."

"He's a pig, that one," the old woman muttered from the stove when Troshkin had left. "Worse than the policeman they sent here long ago, when there wasn't none of these communists. Stupid women gave birth to them. But you, my dear, you've got a heart in you, I can see that. And a strong arm! You'll survive, you won't die. Only watch out for that Troshkin." She ended the first speech she had uttered during those two days. The stove was roaring and shaking with the blaze of pine logs. Potatoes were cooking in an iron pot in the oven, and the old woman lay on top of the stove on a tarpaulin mattress stuffed with soft grass.

"Tell me, ma." He sat down at the table and regarded his work with satisfaction. "Do you know anything about Troshkin. Who is he?"

"Don't you know?" Avdotya raised herself on her elbow, and a long strand of gray hair drooped down from the stove. "He's not a man, he's a devil. No one knows where he's from. But he's been here all of twelve years now, doing mischief to people. He's the Party boss. Folk's all scared of him. But not me. I don't give a cuss for Troshka! The Lord's already waiting on me, getting impatient I expect. I keep on waiting, lie awake at night, but the black visitor still don't come for me. And now look, you've mended my hut. And the stove's warm again. I shan't die now. I'll wait a bit . . . Your wife a good woman, eh?"

"Yes, ma, I have a good wife, but she's been unlucky with me—first the camp, now exile."

"Well, don't you fuss! Have patience! You've still got your health. Lord, you're like a farmyard bull! You'll outlive Troshka all right!" The old woman stirred and jumped down from the stove, landing nimbly on the floor in her bare feet. She hitched up her skirt, which was the same color and age as her jacket and resembled an old gray sack, shuffled over to the table and sat down beside him. She turned toward him her wrinkled little face, in which a pair of clever eyes shone out from a dense crosshatch of fine lines. Her eyes were quite out of keeping with the rest of her face. She laid her shrunken yellow hand on his shoulder. "Your trouble, my dear, is your strength. You've got plenty of strength, all right. That's why you scare that flabby muzhik. You wake the envy in his black heart. You must hide your strength. Bend like a weeping willow in a night storm. Don't stand up there like a cedar in the forest, showing your strong body, or else the wind'll break you down. The wind's blowing now, son, and it's a bad wind, bringing dust and thistles the likes of Troshka. You take heed of what I'm telling you. And don't you forget it. God sees everything, but he don't say much. This wind will stop, it won't blow forever, and then the sun will shine for you too. Just you make sure you outlive Troshka. He ain't done you no harm so far, he's just trying to think, the devil, how to start. Don't you cross him in anything. Have patience. Your woman'll soon be here. What'll you feed her on? What's she do?"

"She's a doctor, ma, and I'll feed her well enough."

"A doctor, you say?" The old woman smiled contentedly. "That's good—for you, for her, and for all the folk hereabouts. She'll cure the people and the animals. The town doctors don't come out here." She crossed herself in the direction of the tiny icon standing in a corner under a white cloth. "And as far as food goes, you're my guest. My old cow very nearly died of hunger this last winter. She ate up all the straw in the shed, but she survived. There's no one to see to her. She grazes in the taiga all day just now and she's putting on fat. She's a clever old beast, she knows she'll be all swollen up with hunger again in winter. So you mend her shed for her and cut some hay and store it up, then you'll have milk to drink all winter. I don't mind meself, and she'll gladly give you everything God gives her. And when your woman gets here, just you live your life, and God grant you happiness. I'll be here with you, and I'll be watching to see what it's like, happiness, I mean. I never had happiness of my own."

She stood up and moved away a step, inclining her head and looking at Vikenty. "You know, used to be a muzhik living here, long ago, in the end hut—Filipp he was called. Well, you're the spitting image of him. He went away, sold up his house, when that red-white carry-on came through these parts."

"Mother Avdotya!" He stepped toward her and took her hand. "He's my father, Filipp Angarov. Maybe you remember his eldest son, Vikenty? I'm sorry but I don't remember you. I was small."

"You mean it's you, you're Vikeshka?" The old woman shook her head in bewilderment. "I'd have died before I recognized you! You was a proper little rogue, fair hair you had. And now? . . . Oi, what a life it is! But what became of Filipp?"

"He's dead." Vikenty hung his head. "After the camp I rang him in Zhitomir. My sister answered. My mother had died too. And my brother Genka. There's only my sisters left."

"Well, God preserve you, Vikeshka!" The old woman hobbled toward the stove. "Don't tell a soul you're from these parts. Keep your mouth shut, Vikeshka, and live quietly. Folks are hungry these days."

"Thanks for the good advice, Mother Avdotya," he said with feeling. He went over to the stove and pressed her hand to his lips. "You live too. We'll help you."

"Well now, you see, we're settled in again." Lida glanced fondly into his face. They were walking in the taiga not far from the village. "It's hard, I must say, to treat cattle as well as people, but I'm getting used to it. I know enough. Let's go down to the river. It's getting hot." She began to walk faster, pulling him along by the hand. Forcing their way through the dense undergrowth they almost slid down to a narrow strip of sandy beach, where the river had washed away the bank on a sharp bend. The beach was surrounded by a solid wall of trees and grass. They stopped at the water's edge. Lida dropped her jacket onto the sand and snuggled against him in her skirt and light blouse. She was quiet for a while, then she looked into his face.

"I know what you're thinking. Not long ago we had Riga and life. It's terrible! What century are we living in, Vitya? Still, we have to live. I'm free now, and at least you're not in a camp. We *can* live! But don't you slip up anywhere—I beg you. I know how bad you feel, but we can endure it for five years. We're together. We have a home. Our son's growing.

Please be calm, Vitya, reconcile yourself."

"I know, I know." He brushed the hair away from her forehead and gazed into her eyes. "But it's not easy for me. Even the camp was better than here. But I'll endure, don't you doubt it. Every day I'll muck out the cowshed. . . . Farther down the Yenisei, there is Shushenskoye, where Lenin spent his exile, in his own house with his own library . . . He should have spent a few days here, in my cowshed."

"Vityusha, don't!" Tears came to her eyes as she put her arms around his neck and pulled him to her. "It scares me when you say things like that. We can live here as long as we avoid other people. Keep your eyes on the sky and the taiga, it's safer. You know, Stalin's not immortal, and remember, you wanted to outlive him."

"Yes." He shook his head stubbornly. "And I will outlive him, just as I will Troshkin. This is just a temporary depression. It'll soon pass. You know, I found an old rusted diesel engine in a dump about ten days before you arrived. I cleaned and greased it and made some parts for it myself in the workshop. I got it to work again. I was thinking of using it for sawing firewood or for lighting. But, no sir! Troshkin saw it and ordered the workers to take it to the district office. 'You,' he said, 'are allowed to do only manual labor. A diesel's mental work. If you don't comply with your regime, I'll report it and your sentence'll be increased.' Bastard!"

"Don't!" She stood on tiptoe and kissed him on the lips. "I want us to survive this and live the rest of our lives like other people. Well!" She hung on his neck and tucked up her legs like a girl. Then she released her grip and fell onto the sand, giving him an inviting look. Her hair was spread out in a fan on the yellow sand. Her shoes had fallen off and lay almost in the water. He took off his jacket in silence, knelt down, and pressed his face to hers. She wound her arms around his powerful sunburned body and turned her face away, gazing up at the blue sky, hearing the rustle of the taiga and the splashing of the water at her feet. Her eyes filled with tears of joy as she sensed her power over her strong man.

"You're a bear, my love," she whispered later, propping her hands against his chest, "you'll crush me to bits. I'm tired."

"Yes, you don't need a sledgehammer to crush a fly," he muttered apologetically. He lay beside her and placed her head on his shoulder.

"Just look," she said after a few minutes silence, "how beautiful it is! This taiga, the river, the silence."

"Yes." He leaned over her and kissed her eyes. "I love these parts.

This territory is tremendously rich; it's only that the people live bad lives."

He stood up, holding her in his arms like a small girl, and carried her to the water. She clung to him and gazed anxiously at the river surging past. The icy water flowed straight from the Sayan Mountains, freezing his legs as he walked in up to his waist and sat down, immersing himself and his wife. He felt her slender body tremble in his arms.

"A-a-a-h!" she squealed as she emerged from the water in his arms. She gazed at him with a mixture of fear, delight, and love. "What a child you still are! Could you kill me?" she asked, her face grown serious.

"Can't you think of anything cleverer than that?" He tucked her playfully under his arm, tight against his right side, and carried her to the bank, laughing at the desperate flailing of her arms and legs.

He stood her on the sand and picked up her skirt. "Here, hop into your uniform." Holding on to his shoulders with both hands she meekly allowed him to dress her. Then she said quietly "Vitya, you've never once undressed me, but you always try to dress me yourself. Why is it?"

He turned her face toward him. "In these things I prefer to leave all the initiative to you. I can live for a year without this. But you can't. When you take your own clothes off, you become more a woman than ever. If I start undressing you, it seems to diminish you. You're a woman, you expect and want me—and this means you must do all that yourself. For the man this undressing before bed, when there's real love, must always remain a little mysterious, unfathomed. The woman must not reveal her whole being to him, down to the last detail. But when I dress you, I feel it's my little girl standing there, a daughter I never had, or my best friend, my treasure, whom only I have the right to dress. There's something platonic in this, but true love and life always retain an element of the platonic. The cautious looks and contacts, the fluttering of the heart at the merest touch of the hands, all the things that two people live for until they first know each other. I always remember that I've never undressed you, so there's still something between us that I haven't experienced."

He put on his own, for the time being his only, gray cloth trousers, his army jacket, and ancient boots. He stood up from the sand, picked her up in his arms, and set off along the river toward the village, avoiding the prickly bushes.

"Are you going to carry me like this all the way?" she whispered in his ear as she clasped her hands around his neck. "People will see. Sharp tongues are worse than a pistol . . . I really did like what you said just now. And soon we'll be home, in our hut. Tolik will be asleep or playing in the yard. I expect grandma will have cooked the dinner in her oven. You know, that old woman's come back to life before our eyes. And to-day's Sunday, and we're together! Of course we can't go to the theater or visit someone, but we have the taiga and the silence, and our love. It real-ly is possible to live like this, isn't it? We can bear it, eh? You know, Vitya, I don't want to go to Krasnoyarsk. There's nothing for me to do there. They'll buy some other clothes for you. I'll ask them. I won't leave you for a moment. Your life is my life."

He hugged her silently and stood her on the ground, seeing through the trees the first huts of the village.

Within a few days after Angarov's arrival the whole village had known that there was an exile living in Avdotya's hut who was a good car-penter. Since then, he tried to remain on formal, although friendly, terms with everyone and not to strike up acquaintanceships or indulge in over-long conversations, but this did not impede the growth of his pres-tige in the village. By day he cleaned the cowsheds, carrying out the order of Party organizer Troshkin. Out of his sailor's habit he scrubbed the old warped floor boards until they shone; he sluiced them with water and spread fresh hay in every stall. The foreman and the milkmaid, who re-sembled old Avdotya with her ancient outfits of gray skirt and jacket of the same thick coarse material, watched in silence as this husky man skill-fully wielded pitchfork and shovel, but they did not bother him with ques-tions; if a man kept silent, it meant he preferred it that way. In this village of former convicts and fugitives, people were not talkative.

In the evenings, he would go to some hut to mend the roof, or the walls or floor. Often he worked alongside the householders. He would not take money for his work, but he gladly accepted a jug of milk or a bag of potatoes, or occasionally even some bear meat.

They had no radio at home. Lida listened to the radio loudspeaker at her clinic and tried to tell him the news, but he would simply gesture dis-missively. "Don't, Lida, I don't want to hear it. Just tell me when he dies." After that she preferred not to bring *Pravda* home; she did not want to dis-turb his inner world, grown calm, like the sea after a storm.

At night when everyone else was asleep, he would leave her in bed and go and sit at the table. He would make sure that no light was escaping through the window and then he would write till dawn on paper torn from school exercise books. What he wrote were his observations about people and life, about other countries, and about Russia, where he had already spent so many years behind the wire. The idea of starting to write something for other people had come to him quite recently, unexpectedly and simply, spontaneously almost, as the logical result of the whole of his life. Every morning he hid the completed pages in the cowshed, and at the end of each week he buried the accumulated material in a corner of the shed in an earthenware pitcher.

Lida knew but she did not ask him about it. He knew that she knew; sometimes at night he would feel her sleepy, inquiring gaze on him. Later he told her, "I'm writing my life story. It's better for you not to read it, it's dangerous. If they find out they can arrest you, and you'll have a hard time under interrogation. But it'll be easier if you haven't read it. It's always obvious to an interrogator whether a person is lying or not. This is my 'mental work.' Do you know where I hid the pitcher?"

She nodded, but said nothing.

"If anything happens to me, keep it. In time perhaps you'll be able to publish it somewhere, for posterity, in memory of me."

She blinked back tears and turned away. She said nothing to prevent his working at night. Occasionally, pretending to be busy with something else, she would go out into the street and examine the window to make sure that the light was not visible from outside; but the windows were two black patches.

He did not know how to write and was sure that he would never have thought of becoming a writer. What he was producing on the sheets of exercise paper was not so much a story as a diary: impressions of schooners under sail remembered as clearly as people, of steamers, ports, captains, sailors, stokers, Red Guards, White Guards; low haunts in Cape Town, Singapore, Hakodate, Shanghai . . . Then came other images: his first wife, Katya, her father and mother, rich White emigrants in Shanghai, John and Mary Parker, his friends and companions who had warned him against returning to Russia . . . He wrote eagerly, with pleasure, trying to get as many lines as possible on each precious sheet of paper, delighting in his unexpected discovery. He realized that his diary was simply a catalog of everything he had seen, experienced, and thought; there were no conclusions, no harmony of subject matter, no moral or message for posterity. But these pages and lines and sleepless nights had unexpectedly opened up a new world to him, a world of genuine "mental work" inaccessible to Troshkin. "Well, you son of a bitch!" He smiled with bitter pleasure as he thought of Troshkin. "So you've broken me, eh, you pig? You live like a pig and you'll die a pig, without ever being a man." He sketched in detail impressions of members of the Soviet trade mission in Shanghai and impressions of interrogators, seamen, prison warders, prisoners, thieves, and politicals—"dopes" as they had been called by Zhmyr, the driver who had brought him to the village.

Sitting at the wooden table, dipping his slender school pen with the squeaky "Rondo" nib into the inkwell, he lived a true spiritual life. He felt joy filling his heart as somewhere within him the horizons expanded. "You must be born a writer!" went the old saying, but perhaps it was not necessary to be "born" a writer after all; couldn't you simply become one by enduring hardships? By understanding people: their cruelty to each other, their silliness, greed, nobility, generosity? Their blindness and wisdom? Their mistakes? His mistakes? He had been homesick for Russia and had returned. That was *his* mistake. And what was the mistake of the Russian people, who were now paying with so much suffering and blood?

In the search for an answer he was brought back time and again to one man—to Stalin. How could it happen that Soso Dzhugashvili had become "the great Stalin," imposing his will on this vast land and its people? Was it really possible for one man to accomplish such things? It sounded like fantasy! But the more he thought about it the more he became convinced that Stalin was, like himself, not a maker of history but its product, and that Stalin too lived his life as a prisoner: a prisoner of himself, of his nation, of history.

It was an astonishingly simple discovery, which, once arrived at, filled Vikenty with spiteful pleasure. It soothed his wounded soul. And as the picture grew clearer the images began to spill from his pen:

Moscow. The spring of 1948. Early morning. The huge city sleeping. The buildings of the Kremlin are wrapped in silence, protected from the city by the massive crenelated wall of red brick.

The silence is broken by the hollow echo of the steps of a guard pacing the sidewalk by the wall on the Moscow River side. One hundred paces forward, one hundred paces back. For the whole watch, the whole night, the whole year, for every one of the thirty years since glorious 1917 a guard with a submachine gun has paced along the perimeter of the wall.

On the third floor of one of the buildings a window is open. An old man, shorter than medium height, is standing at the window. His rumpled gray military jacket is buttoned up to the neck and the gray trousers are tucked into chrome-leather boots. His face, with its drooping moustaches, is pouchy and tired, with the lines of old age under the eyes and at the corners of the mouth. His dark-brown eyes bear a hint of melancholy.

The clock in the Spasskaya Tower is striking the hour. The gentle, quiet chimes of the tiny bells echo across the city. Then they fall silent, yielding to the main bell.

Bom-m-m, Bom-m-m . . . The man at the window listens, as he has listened for years, to the deep sounding of the clock. To him it is an ominous sound, for it marks the irreversible march of time. And time is now his enemy.

The bell struck five. Silence once more, disturbed only by the occasional automobile horn sounding faintly from the nearby streets. The man glanced over himself quickly and ran his hand over his unshaven stubble. His lips twisted into an almost imperceptible smile; it was good that no one could see him now, after a sleepless night. He looked about the room at the plain furnishings: a simple green velour couch on which he often slept without undressing, a few red carved chairs with soft cushions, a deep armchair near the desk, and a fireproof steel safe in a corner. The room was small, twelve feet by fifteen, with armor-plated walls and door and an armor-plated shutter for the single window, which looked onto the courtyard from the third floor of the inner building of the Kremlin.

He filled his lungs with the fresh morning air and went slowly to a discreetly placed wall cupboard. He opened the door to reveal a row of bottles gleaming in the darkness, took out an opened bottle of Armenian brandy, removed the cork, and poured the brandy into a broad goblet.

The fragrant amber fluid sparkled with a peculiar light, enticing and mouth watering. He took a sip and felt the revivifying moisture spread a pleasant warmth through his body. Brandy! Brandy in moments of reflection; wine in those rare moments when the clouds dispersed from his heart and the bottomless blue sky of his native Caucasus seemed to be shining overhead. He sometimes drank vodka too, at his country dacha among dignitaries—"for company's sake." But he had to force himself to do it.

The old man resumed his position beside the window. The sun was already tinting the high cumulus clouds with pink. A short distance away the big gold cross on the Cathedral of the Archangel gleamed dully, and just to the left shone the ruby star on the Spasskaya Tower.

The cross and the star! For him this combination held a meaning intimate and profound. Those two symbols, the one of former times, which had lasted two thousand years, and the other of the new order, which was not yet fifty years old! He smiled bitterly. Those two symbols had followed him everywhere, ever since his youth, when he had first hitched his own star to the revolution. And for three decades now, throughout his self-imprisonment within the Kremlin walls, he had seen the sun glowing upon them.

Which did he prefer, the cross or the star? Which did he love more? The star, of course, out of habit. Before the revolution he had imagined a red star hanging over the whole world, the symbol of all five continents of the earth inhabited by free and happy people. Then it had all come true, and red stars had appeared on caps and greatcoats, everywhere . . .

And the cross—not that rich gold cross gleaming atop the cathedral, but an iron or wooden cross—always reminded him of the Russian people and of Russia herself. It was the Russians, with their monstrous history, their barbarity, their kindness and cruelty, their sensitivity and indifference to each other's fate, and with their revolution, who had carried him to the summit of human possibilities. He loved this country in his way, and its people, a significant part of whom continued to bless themselves with this cross.

Many churches with such crosses had been sacrificed to the cause of the star as he implemented what had been planned—the transformation of this people and then of the whole world. But he had left some churches intact: not so many that they were obtrusive but enough so that the symbol of the cross should not disappear. Since the believers did not attend Party meetings, let the Holy Church keep them in its hands and guide them in the true faith of service to Stalin.

Nothing and nobody, not a single person, must remain outside the scope of his plans. Let him be Stalin's servant or an enemy, but not an outsider. There must not be any outsiders. The whole nation was divided into those who revered him and those who concealed their deadly hatred behind a subservient smile. With none of them, least of all the dignitaries closest to him—Beria, Molotov, and the others—could he utter a single careless word, show a single moment of weakness or uncertainty. For they would tear him to pieces. Nothing but an iron will, an iron fist, fear of death, canine devotion to himself, absolute faith and obedience, absolute!

Nothing else was safe.

He lowered himself slowly onto the couch, struck a match. Puffing a cloud of smoke from his pipe, he fell into reverie. He remembered the Caucasus, his childhood, the mountain ridges, cliffs, gorges, and precipices where he had walked with his friends, training himself not to be afraid, to keep a sharp watch and see far. Like most mountain people he could not swim, and so he always mapped himself a path on solid land.

Then had come the underground, the 1905 revolution. At first he had simply been caught up by events. Later, his youthful infatuation with revolution was bolstered by vanity and the frustration of the means to satisfy it. Could he truly flourish in Georgia and find something worth fighting for? It was doubtful. But Russia! Russia was something else!

Even then he had sensed Lenin's strength. What of those other drivellers, the Plekhanovs and the rest of them? What could they have achieved? Could they really have spearheaded that revolution? That bloody civil war? No, when it came to the actual take-over of power in the country, a firm fist was needed, a real leader. Lenin played that role well. And Comrade Koba, Joseph Dzhugashvili, had stuck close to Lenin until the end, following him, respecting him, envying him, waiting. He, Stalin, had a sixth sense; he chose his path infallibly amid the prevailing chaos and it led him to the top of the world. But was he really a revolutionary? In his heart, no. Revolution was simply his work, the profession in which he had made his career. The higher he was carried by the struggle within the Party, the less time he had to analyze the motives of his actions, the less opportunity to look back or change the course he was taking.

Yes, he had lived a long and eventful life. His policies had killed many people. Well, what of it? They would have died anyway, sooner or later; the whole history of mankind was one long crime. But what would happen after his own death? Out there beyond the window lived two hundred million Russians who had been under his personal control for more than twenty years. And why? Why did they all flatter him, try to catch his eye, glorify him, set him up as a god? Because they were afraid, because they were deluded, because people could not live without an idol. Slaves!

Oh, he knew people very well! He was no theoretician, but he understood how to win people to his side, how to organize and deceive them. But did he really know Russians? What kind of people were they? He had been obsessed with this thought all his life. And it sometimes seemed that he did not know them at all, could not fathom the deeply buried motives for their actions. They were a people with a strange soul. Never in history had any nation displayed so much heroism, courage, self-sacrifice, resourcefulness, and endurance as the Russians had displayed in the war. Physically strong, bold, hardy, simple-hearted, generous, hospitable, indifferent to each other in time of peace, ready to give their lives for each other in battle, cruel to each other, as were no other people. But they were politically feeble. That was the main thing! Both the people and their rulers. They had been ruled by foreigners for too long. Most of the czars after Peter the Great had had some foreign blood. And now he ruled: Dzhugashvili, another foreigner.

How easily, almost with their connivance, he had removed them all from politics and life! In no other country would anyone have been able to destroy a whole political party with such ease. And how had it been possible? It was not he, after all, who had prepared the course for Russia. It was Europe and the old Russian ruling class. It was Marx with his doctrine, Lenin with his theory and practice and his Party. But it had fallen to him to lead Russia along the road to her bright future. In his way had stood the Leninist Party intelligentsia, who did not understand the road Russia had to follow, and who could have ruined everything. He had removed them all. Many innocent people had perished; many former revolutionaries, partisans, and army commanders had cried out "Long Live Stalin!" as they fell before the firing squad. Millions had been sent to camps, in the huge expanses from the Urals to the Bering Strait. Their places had been taken by unthinking, loyal people. He had not spared even his wife.

He felt no remorse until he began to grow old, and then it terrified him to look back. His fears had increased; he could not sleep and so he had begun to work at night. It seemed that he had climbed to the very top of a high mountain and was sitting there in utter solitude, awaiting death, which alone was stronger than he. He could not bring himself to go down to the people who shouted his praises only so long as he remained in lofty solitude. But they would tear him apart if he descended to their level, if they saw that he was a common mortal and not a demi-god.

"Yes?" He picked up the receiver of the internal line. "Joseph Vissarionovich!" It was the chef. "It's already noon—don't you wish to order something?"

"Yes, all right, shashlik, as usual."

He replaced the receiver. In a few minutes he opened the hatch and took from the tray a silver dish of fragrant lamb shashlik, without a scrap of fat. He poured a glass of dry red wine and lifted the receiver. "Lavrenty?" he asked in Georgian. "Come over."

He ate slowly, quite alone. After twenty minutes the red lamp above the door flashed on. He glanced through the spyhole. In the corridor the guard commandant was searching Beria.

"What's the matter, you dog, don't you like it?" He laughed at the sight of the grimace distorting Lavrenty Pavlovich's round flushed face.

"Sit down, Lavrenty." He welcomed Beria in Georgian. "Sleep well?"

"Yes, thank you, Joseph Vissarionovich." Beria's pince-nez gleamed as he straightened his black suit and sat down on the edge of the chair.

"Well, I didn't sleep at all. I've been thinking."

"Yes?"

"Yes! Why not—don't you believe I can think?"

"I didn't say that."

"Just as well! What's there in the file?"

"Lists, Joseph Vissarionovich, for your signature."

"What kind of people?"

"The comparatively young ones released from the camps since the war. The embittered ones. It'll be better for them to serve another five years' exile, in Siberia. By then a lot of things will be settled here, and, at the same time, they'll have grown older, less dangerous."

"How many?"

"Ten thousand in all."

"So few?"

"The rest are retired, or invalids. I've chosen the most active. The others can be left alone."

"How long and where?"

"They'll all get five years in Siberia, without deprivation of rights or confiscation of property."

"And you haven't slipped in any death sentences for me to sign? I know you!" Stalin's moustache twitched as he glanced sharply at the man opposite him.

"Joseph Vissarionovich!" Beria cringed, sensing the aura of death. "I've never once tried to deceive you!"

"Listen! There's no need to kill people. It was necessary once, but it isn't any more. Understand this, Lavrenty: if I hear of a single case of you killing someone without cause, I'll hang you by your feet from that win-

dow. Is that clear or not?"

"Quite clear, Comrade Stalin!" Beria paled as he held Stalin's gaze.

"And you'll just hang there," the old man with the gray moustache said slowly in Georgian. His eyes bored into Beria. The man who held such terror for others was now sitting before him like a naughty schoolboy. "You serve me, Lavrenty, and you serve the state, but not yourself. Everything I did, even the purges, I did not for myself but for the sake of the state, for an idea and a policy. That's why they think I'm a great man. But I'm afraid you haven't got my brains. You can try to use your power for your personal ends. But be careful, Lavrenty. What I've created will not tolerate mistakes. If I find out anything I'll have you killed. And if I die others will kill you. Try to think a little more. You must think, you must learn."

Beria said nothing and lowered his gaze.

Stalin walked round the desk and stood in front of him. "Nothing else to suggest?"

"No!" Beria stood up, startled.

"Sit down!" Stalin waved his hand. "You're sending ten thousand into exile?"

"Yes."

"And how many are still sitting there behind the wire?"

"About thirteen million."

"And are they all so dangerous that you can't release any of them?"

"N-no, it's just that I haven't had time to think."

"Rubbish! You've had no time! But I've had time! I'll sign this list. Let them spend a little longer inside; it won't grieve history very much. But by this evening you'll have on this table a report on the release of politicals and criminals from the camps—the sick and all those over fifty who have less than five years left to serve. How many will that be?"

"I think . . . somewhere in the region of two hundred thousand."

"Well, all right. Let them go home. I've been waiting for you to make this decision, but you didn't. You keep putting people inside, but who will release them? Me? You must rule the people with a carrot as well as a stick. Now, leave me! I'll expect you this evening."

Beria left. Stalin went to the window again. A fresh breeze blew in his face. The phone rang. "I told you I'm busy."

"Joseph Vissarionovich!" It was the guard commandant. "Please may I see you, on a personal matter?"

"All right, come on in."

"Well, what is it?" he asked in Georgian, glancing affably at the burly soldier standing at attention.

"It's not about myself, Comrade Stalin. It's about a girl."

"What, you fallen in love?"

"No." The mountain man blushed. "She works on the radio. She's an announcer. The Minister for Communications wanted to see you, but you're not seeing anyone today, so he asked me to help."

"What's it got to do with me?" Stalin asked. He liked having to make decisions about these simple people who represented no danger to himself, for he could be generous and help to foster among the masses the opinion that he was their protector against his own officials.

"She's been sacked," the guard commandant continued. "She was reading a statement last night and she said 'for the final victory of capitalism' instead of socialism."

"Oh-ho!" He smiled to himself. "No one would have said that on purpose! What do you think, could she have said that on purpose?"

"Impossible!"

"Well then, there's nothing to punish her for. How long a shift do announcers work? Did the minister tell you?"

"I asked him myself. Eight hours."

"That's bad. The minister should be reprimanded for that. Tell him to forget about what happened. Reinstate the girl. And reduce the working day for all the announcers to six and a half hours. Understood?"

"Perfectly! Thank you very much." The guard beamed, stepped back and closed the door behind him.

Stalin refilled his pipe. He gazed into the cloud of blue smoke and frowned, his thoughts returning to the past. Whom could he hate? Who was to blame? Marx? Yes, he had written a lot of nonsense, and all about his own times. He had observed the suffering and poverty of the workers in England during the Industrial Revolution. "The dictatorship of the proletariat!" Utopians! He clenched his teeth on the pipe. Well, all right, it would have made no difference if Marx had never been born. Some one else could have come up with the same idea; all the theoretical and practical data had been available. Just as Stalin had had all the necessary data for establishing the absolute power that enabled him to carry out the Marxist doctrine. Marxism! It had deceived him, subdued him and held him captive all his life, him and millions of others.

But why exactly in Russia? Why had Marxism not taken root in the

West where it had been born? The old Russian ruling class had gone too far, of course, in driving the people to the limits of their endurance. But was it alone to blame? Why had the people permitted themselves to be oppressed? Other peoples had resisted. What was that fatal characteristic of Russian life? Why had the people permitted their ruling class to "divide and rule" until it was too late to change and the revolution was inevitable?

Yes, all power was based on the unity of the rulers and the disunity of the people. And the geographical dispersion of the Russians made it difficult for them to unite in defense of their interests.

So what had happened in Russia seemed to be rooted deep in history, in the geography of the Russian nation. Perhaps he was wrong, but that seemed to be it, the main link in the chain of doubts that was tormenting him. That was why the cross had always attracted him like a magnet: in the cross lay the root of events, not in the star. But what could he change now? Nothing! He could not even hint at the truth to these millions of people, for their only happiness was their blind faith in him, their leader, and in the idea, in Marxism-Leninism.

Well, let events take their course. Even after his death, the force of inertia would continue to carry forward the state machine he had created. Some day people would begin to dig into the past. But which one of those future hacks would uncover the truth? Which of them would be able to see into the recesses of his soul? Who would write The Sufferings of a Tyrant?

Vikenty put down the pen and pushed back his chair. He was exhausted and his eyes burned from working so long in the poor light. But he could not resist picking up the pages and reading them from the beginning. He read the lines slowly, enjoying every word. He relished Beria's discomfort under Stalin's gaze and smiled at Stalin's talk with the guard, the radio announcer's slip of the tongue. Vikenty had heard about these things when he was still in Riga, never imagining then that his own name was included on Beria's list.

He looked over the pages once more. He was pleased with what he had done and thought of showing the story to Lida. But no, better not. Better to let the pages lie in the ground until better times.

The old woman stirred, breaking Vikenty's concentration. He had installed her bed behind the stove on purpose, persuading her that sleeping on top of the stove would shorten her life. She slept there obediently until, as now, she woke up to answer the call of nature. Quickly he pushed the papers into a drawer and picked up a copy of Lenin's *What Is To Be Done?*, which he always kept at hand in case he was interrupted.

One pitcher of his writings had already been buried in a deep hole, and a second was filling up. Every night some twenty or thirty pages disappeared under the muck-covered floor of the shed. He wrote hurriedly, as if he was trying to make up for what he had omitted, for what he had not written during the past decades, as if he sensed that this happy time might end unexpectedly.

"Look, Angarov," the foreman said to him one morning. "Last night they sent us in some more exiles like yourself, and I'm giving you two of them to help out. Teach them how to hold a pitchfork so's they don't stick it to the cows, these geniuses." He was a powerfully built but short muzhik, almost square, with the strange surname "Shkvoren." He stroked his thick, spade-shaped beard thoughtfully, then took a pouch from his ancient patched trousers. "Smoke?"

Vikenty did not want one but he nodded. He did not want to refuse.

"Can't manage it?" Shkvoren laughed as he watched Vikenty trying to roll a cigarette from the strip of newspaper.

"No, I used to smoke factory-made!" Vikenty lit the cigarette from the match the foreman held out to him and took up his fork again.

"You're a good worker," The foreman nodded understandingly. "But you're mighty silent."

"That's the way I have to be. I'm a political exile. Every word can cost me dearly," Vikenty replied over his shoulder.

"I can understand that." The foreman went toward the door. "It doesn't matter. I'll just send them along now. These foreigners can't tell a cow's nose from its tail. But they have to live and work for their bread."

The word "foreigners" put him on his guard, and reopened an old wound. He stuck the fork in the manure and stood gazing after the foreman until he disappeared behind the corner of the hut. Then he made another round of the whole cowshed: it was about a hundred yards long with a row of stalls on each side separated by a narrow walkway in which a channel had been set into the boards to allow the water to drain away. He carted the muck from each stall along these narrow boards in a wheelbarrow and dumped it on the heap in the yard. The manure was then carted to the various vegetable patches squeezed into the clearings.

A half hour later two people approached the cowshed. One was a short, middle-aged man with a bald head above a round, clean-shaven face; he was wearing blue shorts, brown ankle-boots, and a sweater. With him was a woman of about forty, elegant in similar sports clothes, and with her chestnut hair done up in a pompadour.

They stopped in confusion at the entrance to the cowshed, listening apprehensively to the lowing that came from within. They looked expectantly at the tall man with the pitchfork who was standing still as a statue and gazing at them.

The faces were oddly familiar. He racked his memory, but he could not remember anything about them.

"We've come to work for you," the man said, gesturing in perplexity at the cowshed. The woman watched, her eyes brimming with tears.

"Why are you dressed up like that?" Angarov asked the man. "This is dirty work. You'll need different clothes."

"We haven't anything else. We've come here straight from abroad."

"Where from exactly?" he asked.

"From Shanghai. What's the matter with you?" the woman exclaimed. "You've gone white as a sheet. Can I do anything?"

"I'm all right." He forced himself to smile, squeezing the handle of the pitchfork until his fingers hurt. "It's just . . . memories. I was a sailor once. I was often in Shanghai."

"Oh!" The man stepped forward, smiling broadly. "I'm very glad . . ."

"There's nothing to be glad about," Angarov interrupted him. "You've landed here like chickens in the soup. Why are you here? When did you arrive?"

They exchanged looks. Then the man glanced over his shoulder as if afraid of something. "We arrived a month ago," he said, "on the *M.V. Ilich;* we disembarked at Nakhodka. You know there's been a revolution there, in China, and the communists have taken power. People like us, from Russia, we didn't know which way to jump. Some, the smarter ones, went to America or Australia, but others, like us, were longing to return home. We were afraid to travel farther away from Russia. The Soviet representatives promised us the earth if we returned to the motherland . . . But what are you doing here? Are you a local?"

"No, I'm an exile. But why are you here and for how long?"

"Why?" The man shrugged his shoulders. "Who can tell? Apparently they don't know why themselves. For returning to our native land! They arrested us straightaway in Nakhodka, when we got off the boat. Then they put us in a barracks. They spent a month interrogating and classifying us. They released a few—to the west, to Moscow and Leningrad. Others went to a camp, and they sent us here; exiled for five years. That's the motherland for you!"

"Don't Pasha, that's enough!" The woman took his arm. "You mustn't think about it."

"No, I must!" Pasha stubbornly shook off her hand. "And all our things were confiscated. They took away a whole truckload of things. We're beggars now."

"You can thank God you're still alive," Vikenty answered. He could hardly restrain himself from going to the woman and kissing her hand. At the name "Pasha" a memory had flashed in his brain. "Pasha Zubov!" he said to himself. "And you, Svetlana! So fate surrendered you to the clutches of this Zubov after all!"

"Excuse me, are you married, or just acquaintances?" he asked.

"We're married," the woman said, "more than twenty years."

"Have you been happy?" Vikenty asked absently, paying no attention to the husband's look of bewilderment and displeasure.

"Why do you ask that?" the woman exclaimed, blushing. "We've come here to work."

"Svetlana!"

"What did you say?" Her jaw fell open in astonishment. Her bewildered husband gazed from the man to his wife and back again.

"I said 'Svetlana,'" he repeated quietly. "Don't you recognize me? Vikenty Angarov, from high school."

Turning deathly pale, she steadied herself on her husband's arm and stared at Angarov in stunned silence.

"What's this all about?" Zubov demanded. "Who are you? Are you Vikenty? You can't be!" He could hardly remember the well-built, fair-haired youth in the high school who, thirty years earlier, had fought and beaten him in front of the whole class because he had insulted Svetlana.

"I can. You have a poor memory, Zubov."

Svetlana smiled wanly. "Pasha, it's Vikenty. You remember!"

"Yes, I remember now how he punched my teeth in on account of you!"

"Yes, but you did begin to have more respect for me," she said, relaxing her grip on her husband's arm. "How you've changed, Vikenty! I would never have recognized you."

"But I recognized you." He smiled at her and winked at her alarmed husband. "No, don't you worry, Zubov, I won't take your wife away from you. It's too late now—I've lived my life."

Zubov pulled Svetlana close, but her face was not joyful.

"Well, all right, distinguished guests." Vikenty picked up the pitchfork and became serious. "I never expected to meet you like this. Please come to my house this evening and we'll drink some tea and have a talk. But now let's do some work. I advise you not to say a word to anyone about your past. And be respectful of Troshkin. He's the local Party boss—and he's dangerous!"

The arrival in his domain of the exile Angarov had thoroughly shaken Petr Yevgrafovich Troshkin. One look at the tall man with the gold rings on his sleeve had been enough to remind Troshkin of the past and to revive his hatred for the privileged classes.

Troshkin had been nineteen when his father had been dispossessed of his land and sent to Siberia. Up till then they had had an allotment of land, with a dozen sheep, pigs, chickens, geese, ducks, a cow, and an old horse. The whole family worked from dawn to sunset, but they lived amidst plenty, and every Sunday his father would harness the bay to the cart, load up the produce, and take it to market. All that ended. In a small room on the outskirts of Krasnoyarsk, where the family lived in poverty, Troshkin's father died, never having recovered from the ruin of his life. Troshkin's mother quickly followed. The younger sister married a Cheka man simply as a means of organizing some kind of life for herself. The elder brother was drafted into the army. He served many years in the Far North in the MVD defense force. Troshkin decided to return to the land, but in an even more remote area, where no one would ever be able to get their hands on him again. He hitched his way deeper and deeper into the taiga until he found himself in Medvezhie, beyond which there were no more villages. But he soon realized he had made a mistake; it was no longer possible to get some land together and build up a farm. So he joined the Komsomol cell and later the Party; he was assiduous and modest with his superiors and decisive and authoritative with his subordinates. At first he had been an ordinary worker in the timber industry, then in the cowshed; later he had worked on the hauling and floating of trimmed logs. Everywhere he contrived to be among the "outstanding workers."

The MVD approved of him. Subsequently Troshkin's affairs took a sharp turn for the better. He was elected Party organizer of the village and became the manager's right-hand man. He soon occupied the best three-room hut in the village. He brought furniture and a wife from the town and began to put the village in order, displaying the same acumen, cunning, calculation, and cruelty that he had observed around himself for many years under the new power, and in whose name he now controlled this small world of defenseless people.

He realized that the higherups had forgiven him his dispossessed father only conditionally and that this power would never trust him all the way. But at this level they trusted him fully, reasoning that there was nowhere for him to flee to, that he would seek to advance himself at any price, and that he was useful.

It had been his idea to set up the dairy farm and he had had the cowshed built. Since there was nowhere to graze the cows except in the small clearing near the village, where bears could attack them, he had appointed a herdsman with a rifle. There was more than enough grass in the forest. They cut it by hand and stored it in a rack near the cowshed. The cows did not starve in winter and Troshkin triumphantly dispatched dozens of cans of milk to neighboring forestry enterprises and even to district headquarters.

This initiative was warmly appreciated "at the top." The whole operation had gone smoothly, apart from one small setback: he had tried to persuade the other villagers to surrender their scrawny beasts to the common cowshed and then to buy the milk, cream, and butter, at "hard" prices. They refused, terrified of losing their last private source of food. Afraid to compel them to do it by force—for he had received no official instructions to dispossess the villagers—Troshkin worked all kinds of mischief against anyone from whose tumbledown shed a hungry lowing could still be heard: he gave the owners of livestock the kind of work that left them no time to lay in fodder for the winter. Still the people went out into the taiga at night, after a hard day's work, to cut hay . . . The cows provided the main source of life for the majority of families.

Now, without realizing it, Troshkin took to thinking day and night about Angarov—"from there," "one of them"—who by some chance had turned up here. It seemed to him that some small part of the hateful power was subordinate to him and was just as afraid of him as he was of it.

He inspected Angarov's work every day, pacing back and forth over the floorboards in the cowshed, which were as sparkling clean as a ship's deck. He never engaged Angarov in conversation, sensing that he was dealing with a man who stood two heads taller than himself in intellect. It even occurred to him to poison a couple of cows or set fire to the cowshed so that he could blame the cowman for it, but his cowardice conquered his hatred. He simply awaited an opportunity to settle with Angarov.

He had wanted to employ Angarov's wife in the cowshed too, but he was afraid to do so, since there was no other doctor or veterinarian in the village.

For the first time in his life, Troshkin began to lose his self-control. He concentrated his attention on this odious figure whose naval uniform was lying in his own storeroom, on the floor. His inbred fear of authority caused his legs to tremble whenever he met Angarov. He would spend all day thinking about what he should say to Angarov tomorrow, what he could invent in order to demonstrate his power and to humiliate, wound, and destroy the spirit of this calm enemy, who greeted him with a smile and obediently carried out his orders.

Angarov cleaned his cowshed in silence, deliberately dragging out the work to fill the whole day, so that no one should ever see him unoccupied. Things were going well with Lida and at home. The cache of completed pages under the floorboards was gradually increasing in size. Yet he felt sick at heart. He began to grow tired of the forest, which seemed to occupy the whole of the rest of the world; tired, too, of the sight of Troshkin who was forever lurking about, reminding Angarov of a summer gadfly that he lacked the "length of tail" to brush away and which was always keeping watch in the vicinity in the hope of finding an opportunity to sting him.

Somewhere over there beyond the taiga lay the outside world, going about its business without him. Then he thought about his son Tolik, who was already playing in the yard with their neighbors' boys, about Lida, about Valery far away, waiting for money and letters from him. These thoughts relieved his depression for a while, but as soon as Troshkin appeared his spirits would fall.

He gladly accepted Lida's suggestion that they go to a party on the seventh of November holiday organized by Troshkin to remind the villagers of the great Socialist Revolution.

In that same long, shedlike room in which Angarov had spent the night of his arrival, they whitewashed the walls and covered the tables with some red material left over from the posters and slogans made for the holiday. By eight in the evening on November 7, 1950, the forestry building was full to overflowing. The women's dresses smelled of mothballs, and the men had cleaned their boots. Angarov and his wife sat in a far corner, enjoying the opportunity to be among people, even if on account of the revolution.

Drawn up in a row in the middle of the tables stood the tempting green bottles of "sawdust" vodka, which was distilled from wood waste. There were also wooden platters of boiled potatoes and bear meat and pickled cucumbers. The villagers sat listening to a long and confused speech that Troshkin was delivering from the plank stage, where he sat at the table reserved for the presidium. They all knew that Troshkin did not believe in what he was saying, but they listened attentively, correctly supposing that this speech would end sooner or later and they would be able to tuck into the vodka and food, chat with their neighbors, and sing a few soulful songs, which could never be sung without vodka.

Next to Troshkin at the head table sat the forestry manager, reigning but not ruling, a pale gaunt man in a peaked cap. Shkvoren, the dairy foreman, was at the table too, with the forestry foreman and two dairy maids, who were smiling broadly at the whole room, keeping their hands hidden under the table. They were not listening to Troshkin; they were simply burning with pride and shame, in the face of the whole village, and longing for the moment when they would wriggle out from behind the red table and merge with the ordinary members of the audience.

"Hail to the Great October Socialist Revolution!" Troshkin was exclaiming to the room at large while squinting down at the text of his speech, "which opened up a new era in the history of mankind! The era of proletarian revolution and the conclusive victory of socialism throughout the world! Hail to our great motherland—the Union of Soviet Socialist Republics, the first workers' and peasants' state in the world, the state of genuine sovereignty of the people! He who was nothing will become everything! Hail to our glorious Party of Bolsheviks, which, under the leadership of our great and wise leader, Comrade Stalin, is leading our people from victory to victory on the glorious road of the building of a communist society! Hail to our great Russian people, who, under the wise leadership of our Party and Comrade Stalin, are bearing liberation from the slavery of capitalism to all peoples of the world! Hail to our great leader and teacher, Comrade Stalin! Hoorah! Comrades!"

Setting his speech aside, Troshkin turned his triumphant face to the room and began applauding furiously, watching closely to see which members of the audience were clapping—this was a true indication of a person's moral and political character. They all clapped as hard as they could, because they were tired of sitting and listening, because they sensed Petr Yevgrafovich's sharp little eyes watching them, and because each of them felt a tiny ray of happiness in his heart—the speech was over, and now they could eat and drink.

Long into the night, uproar reigned in the forestry building. On the benches and under the tables lay unfinished scraps of bread and meat. In the pools of vomit and spilt vodka lay the muzhiks and their women, blind drunk, who had not had the sense to eat something before pouring a glass of "sawdust" down their throats, or who had failed to set off for home in time.

Petr Yevgrafovich was also drunk, as was Vikenty Angarov, who was sitting at the end of the room, his eyes merry and his face red from vodka. He gazed at the bacchanalian devastation that had overtaken the tables; in all his long career he had never witnessed such a drunken spree. Lida had become drunk immediately and had long been tugging at his sleeve to go home, but he did not want to leave. The Zubovs, who had been sitting next to them, withdrew from the room, dragging Lida with them.

Angarov was left almost alone at the table, quite inebriated. He was quietly sipping vodka and smoking hungrily. He felt someone's hand on his shoulder. Troshkin's drunken face with its wandering eye was thrust close up against his own. He recoiled, but Troshkin seized him by the sleeve and slobbered into his face, drowning him in a revolting stench of vodka and bad breath. "N-no, my darlin', don't y-you leave! Y-you're such a p-pig! D-don't you l-love me?"

"No!" Vikenty turned his head in an effort to escape the stench issuing from Troshkin's mouth. "I love my wife!"

"But not me?" Troshkin insisted, wrapping his arms around Angarov's neck and almost collapsing on the table as he gazed into his face.

"Not you!" Angarov said quietly.

"Wha-at about C-comrade Stalin? L-love him?"

"Yes, I do!" Vikenty answered firmly, staring at Troshkin's roving eyes.

"So wh-why don't you love me, y-you b-bastard? An aristocrat, eh?"

"I'm not a bastard or an aristocrat, and I don't love you." Angarov's eyes were filling with blood. "You're a drunken pig. Let go of me while you've got the chance."

"Foo-oo-ey!" Troshkin flexed his back, spat in Angarov's face, then recoiled in terror, immediately sober, flinching from the expected blow.

Angarov wiped the spittle from his face, spat on the floor, and got up from the table. He staggered toward the door, watched by Troshkin and Shkvoren, who was sitting at the other end of the room, a grim expression on his red face; he could never drink enough to be really drunk.

When Angarov had gone, there were only the two of them left. Shkvoren walked unsteadily up to Troshkin: "Why you tormenting that fellow, you gutless bastard? Haven't you got enough people willing to bend their necks to you? How would you like me to beat your face in?"

He grabbed Troshkin by the collar and pulled him forward. "Well, just what are you anyway? You nit! You pox-ridden son of a louse!" Almost lifting Troshkin from the floor, he spat in his face. "Well, why don't you say something, eh? Or don't you fancy me as much as Angarov? Don't you love me, Petr?"

Troshkin hung from his hand in silence. The spittle oozed slowly down his cheek.

"Never mind. Do you really want me to smash your face in?" The foreman gripped Troshkin's collar furiously until he squealed.

"N-no, don't!"

"Don't what?"

"Don't hit me!"

"Why not?" Shkvoren said in astonishment. "Why musn't I hit you? Who else do you want me to hit? It's you, my dear, what needs a beating. Should have done it long ago, but I never had the chance."

He clubbed his left fist into Troshkin's face. One of his eyes flared crimson, and blood spurted from his nose and streamed onto the floor.

The foreman released his grip and Troshkin flopped softly to the floor. He immediately rolled over onto all fours and tried to stand up.

"Don't" Shkvoren kicked him in the ribs. Troshkin dove face first into a pool of vodka and some other mess. He got to his knees again, groaning, and wiped his face on the back of one of the muzhiks lying on the floor. "Don't!" the foreman repeated. He stood swaying over Troshkin, staring down at him with muddy eyes. "That's for all of us, for the whole village, d'you hear, Petro Yevgrafovich? D'you hear me or not? Answer me if you don't want another dose!"

"I hear you!" Troshkin whimpered, squinting up at Shkvoren.

"That's good. Now you come down off your high horse, d'you hear, otherwise you'll find yourself in the graveyard. This village is miles from nowhere. This is your first lesson, Yevgrafovich, in all these years. It's a good thing, education, eh? Now run along home, and keep your pig face shut! You let out one squeak about me decorating your ugly mug for you, and it'll be your last. And don't forget about Angarov. You leave him be, Yevgrafych, you bastard!" The foreman made his way toward the door, stepping over the bodies of his fellow villagers.

When the people's judge had finished his short statement, an uneasy silence fell over the office of the first secretary of the district committee of the Party. All four participants in this special secret meeting were silent. They exchanged glances: the chief of the district militia, a short, corpulent man wearing the uniform and epaulets of a lieutenant-colonel; the people's judge with his shock of red hair above a pale, narrow face and beak of a nose, and his dirty-collared shirt; the district prosecutor, a swarthy, stern-looking man with evasive eyes; and the first secretary himself, the sovereign ruler of the district, a middle-aged man with a good-natured Russian face from which gazed a pair of tense, wary eyes; he was wearing a khaki-colored jacket of military cut, buttoned up to the neck.

"Well then, comrades! Is the picture clear?" the first secretary said. "What are we to do? Any suggestions? What does the custodian of the law think?"

The prosecutor gave his colleagues an anxious searching look. "In accordance with existing legislation, for inflicting bodily harm on a representative of the authorities I will demand fifteen years solitary confinement. Especially as we're dealing with a political criminal."

"Ahem!" The lieutenant-colonel drew their attention to himself. "According to our information, this Angarov's clean politically. I've been in touch with the regional MVD Authority and with the Kraslag. It's a complicated case. General Bukin's in Moscow, and new men are in charge there now, but there are still plenty of people in the MVD who are well disposed toward Angarov. We must take all aspects of the situation into account if we don't want to come unstuck. Especially since he didn't lay a finger on this Troshkin, who can rot in hell for all I care. Before I passed the case to the people's court and the prosecutor I checked out all the details myself," the lieutenant-colonel continued. "I don't care about Angarov, but I do care about my own position. Troshkin was beaten up by one of the villagers, and not so much because of his humiliation of Angarov as for all the little deviations from the norms of Party control that Troshkin has inflicted on his villagers in recent years. I consider that our comrade has overstepped the mark and it is no longer appropriate for him to remain in this post; my view is confirmed by this business with Angarov. We must get rid of Troshkin. . ."

"You're right." The first secretary nodded. "We'll transfer him to another district. We've already found another job for him—head of the rural consumers' co-op. If he puts a foot wrong there, then he can go to hell. There's no need to expel him from the Party for the moment, comrades. Let's give him one more chance."

They all smiled approvingly.

"How was Angarov arrested?" the prosecutor asked.

The militia chief shrugged his shoulders. "In the evening, after work. We took him straight from the cowshed, to avoid any trouble."

"Do you think there's any point trying to find the man who did beat up Troshkin?" The first secretary leaned toward the people's judge.

"Yes." The judge smiled uncertainly and for some reason fidgeted with the file on the assault, which was lying on the table. "We might even find the culprit, but what use would that be? Whoever beat up Troshkin did so with good reason and thinks he did the right thing. That means that any punishment will only have a negative effect."

"Ye-es." The prosecutor shook his head. "But even if we don't investigate further, we can't just overlook an incident like this. Somebody must be convicted! I think it should be Angarov. Otherwise this case might have harmful effects on the people's attitude."

"But they know that Angarov didn't assault Troshkin," the lieutenant-colonel put in.

"Yes." The first secretary raised his hand a little, requesting silence. "That's true. But they know lots of other things as well and they manage to live with them. The people must know, must take on faith, that any action of the authorities is always correct, not subject to any kind of doubt or criticism. That is the basis of our rule. Minor errors do not matter. Let the whole village think that the authorities made a mistake in convicting Angarov. But they will still know that our power is capable of dealing with anyone, innocent or guilty, who gets in our way and interferes with us

. . . However you look at it, the people must have fear in their hearts and they must obey. I can understand the leniency of our distinguished people's judge, who wants to have his cake and eat it. But, unfortunately, we must be realistic. If we follow the judge's wise counsel and do not seek out the true culprit, it will arouse the whole village, and that's not in our interest. We must find a clear-cut and more appropriate solution for this small but dangerous conflict. And our decision must include the following points: first, immediately after the trial we must remove Troshkin from the village and transfer him to another district: second, we must hold a show trial in the village, in which anyone who wants to may take part, and if no one wants to, we'll choose people from the register and order them to attend; third, Angarov's sentence must not be too harsh—to avoid any undesirable reaction from the MVD and the territorial committee of the Party, but at the same time the punishment must be stiff enough to satisfy all the others—the witnesses, etc. It's decided then, comrades," he concluded in a tone that indicated he would not tolerate any objections. "Are there any suggestions as to the sentence?"

"Fifteen years' imprisonment!" the prosecutor said.

"Ten years!" the militia chief objected.

"Fifteen is rather a lot for a case like this."

"I . . . I . . ." the judge began indecisively. "I think that since our sentence will be purely arbitrary, er, I mean of an exemplary nature, not based on an actual crime, then I think that in a case like this it would be undesirable to change the category of the sentence of imprisonment, or in this instance, exile . . . It would be better to leave the sentence as exile and simply to impose some additional term . . ." He looked expectantly at the others. "We would thus absolve ourselves of any responsibility and, at the same time, we would not be raising the question of the original article of the code, under which he was exiled here from Riga."

"There's some sense in that!" The lieutenant-colonel nodded. "What do you think?" He turned to the prosecutor.

"I'll go along with the majority decision."

"It's a problem!" The first secretary looked wearily through the window; outside it was fall. "There's no sense in leaving Angarov in the village or even in our camps' system. We can't send him to the West. That leaves the East. I propose that we leave his sentence at five years but replace exile with imprisonment in a strict-regime camp, in the Magadan region."

"The decision is adopted unanimously, then," the first secretary said after a few moments' silence. He got up from the table and glanced at his watch. "Let's leave it there, I have work to do." He shook hands with the people's judge last. "Be firm but be careful. I want you to come to see me immediately after the trial."

"Yes, of course." The people's judge shook the first secretary's hand and went out into the red-carpeted corridor where the prosecutor and militia chief were waiting for him.

"It's a shame!" The lieutenant-colonel shook his head. "But it can't be helped. That's life! I'm inviting you all to my place Saturday evening. There'll be Stolichnaya and black caviar, straight from Moscow."

Although the Sunday was rainy, the whole village crowded around the forestry office, where the court had already been in session for several hours. The court consisted of a judge and three jurors, who were sitting at the same table from which Troshkin had delivered his anniversary speech a few days earlier. Lida was sitting on the front bench, holding Tolik in her arms. Her face was drawn, and she did not take her eyes from her husband. She could feel the sympathetic gaze of the whole room upon her.

Angarov was sitting on the stage between two militia men. His pale face had a heavy stubble.

He did not know who in fact had assaulted Troshkin, or why. He had accepted his arrest calmly, as inevitable, and he was even surprised at the politeness with which the district militia had treated him in the preliminary detention room. He had been there for twenty-four hours in all, but no one had interrogated him. He had been well fed, and after a day he had been taken back to the village, to the court . . . He understood the whole of this charade perfectly well; he understood the position and mental processes of the district authorities. He expected a new sentence, but could think only of Lida. He avoided her eyes; he felt in his heart that this time he was parting from her forever.

He listened indifferently to the judge's statements, the witnesses' replies, and the jurors' questions, which clarified every detail of the situation in the room after the celebration and the manner in which Angarov had assaulted Troshkin. Troshkin was also sitting on the stage, behind the judge and jurors. He hung his head. For the past few days he had been walking around as if submerged in water. He sensed that he had harmed his own cause, and he cursed Angarov, himself, and everyone else.

Later the room was filled for an hour with the noise of subdued conversations, while the court deliberated in an adjacent room. At last the door opened, and the loud voice of the militia man sitting on the stage rang out: "All stand! The court's in session!"

The people rose noisily to their feet, then grew quiet in order to hear the sentence.

"In the name of the Russian Soviet Federal Socialist Republic!" the judge read in conclusion, ". . . the court orders that the exile Vikenty Filippovich Angarov, for the crime he has committed, shall be delivered to the strict-regime camp in the Magadan region to complete his current term of five years. This sentence is not subject to appeal and shall be carried out immediately." Then followed the names of the judge and jurors.

The woman sitting in front of the judge on the first bench let go of her child and fell to the floor in a faint. Vikenty closed his eyes and pressed his hands against his face. Some people ran to the woman, lifted her up and carried her from the room, together with the boy, who was crying.

The noise in the room had begun to die down when the foreman who had beaten up Troshkin forced his way right up to the judge's table and said in a loud voice, "It was me who smashed his face in for him! Why d'you want to condemn an honest man, eh, judge? Why don't you speak up, you, Petr?" he shouted at Troshkin, who had turned quite white. "Or you forgot them shiners I gave you here? Well you're a bastard right enough!"

"Si-lence!" the judge shouted, wiping his sweating face with a trembling hand—events had taken an unexpected turn. "This is provocation!" He glanced down at Shkvoren, then at the two militia men near the door. "Take him away! I'm removing you from the court for disorderly conduct," he told the foreman sternly. "But it was me beat him up!" the foreman shouted at him as the two militia men seized his arms and began to drag him toward the door. "Ah, you people!" Shkvoren cried out. "What are you doing? Where is your justice?"

When his voice had died away beyond the door, the judge ostentatiously closed the bulky file on Angarov's case, which was lying on the table. "That's all! The court has passed sentence. Please leave the courtroom." A hubbub arose as the crowd trickled from the stuffy room. A stream of fresh air rushed in through the door, beyond which was visible a patch of gray, rainy sky.

The two militia men climbed up onto the open one-and-a-half-tonner and waited for Angarov. He stopped beside the lorry and looked around. The crowd had quickly dispersed to their homes in the drizzling rain. The only ones left were Svetlana and Pashka Zubov, whose frightened faces could be seen in the doorway of the forestry building. They were supporting Lida's limp body. Tolik was sitting in the mud and crying as he gazed up at the adults. Disregarding the order prohibiting leavetaking with families, he leapt to the door and bent down over Lida. He saw that she was in a deep faint, but was in no danger, and that she would soon regain consciousness . . . He seized his son, lifted him high in the air, then hugged him, covering his little face with kisses. He passed him to Svetlana and said, "Will you help them? I beg you!"

"Yes, yes, of course," she answered quickly, glancing over his head at the militia men running from the truck. "We'll help Lida, don't worry. For heaven's sake! They're coming after you!"

He kissed Lida's face and whispered, "Goodbye, my friend. Farewell. It seems you'll have to live now . . . without me." He turned and ran toward the truck, almost colliding with the militia men.

A minute later the truck skidded out onto the forest road, leaving Medvezhie village behind. It was followed by a small automobile carrying the people's judge, who had to report the next day to the office of the district committee of the Party.

Late that evening the first secretary of the district committee of the All-Russian Bolshevik Party dialed the number of the administrative section of the Territorial Authority of the MGB. "Comrade Smolin? Yes, this is Vostrikov. I held the meeting and issued the instructions as we agreed. The trial has already taken place. Everything's in order. What? No, he managed the whole business very well. There was a minor incident, with the foreman who actually assaulted Troshkin. What are we doing about it? Nothing. The foreman's been left in the village, by himself. He's an illiterate worker. We can let him off, yes. In any event, if he causes any trouble we'll pull him in and transfer him to another village. Yes, I consider the matter closed. I have more important things to deal with. Yes, I regret it too, but it can't be helped. We'll leave the wife where she is—let her work! Thank you! Good night." He replaced the receiver. "Idiot!" he hissed, referring to some person unspecified.

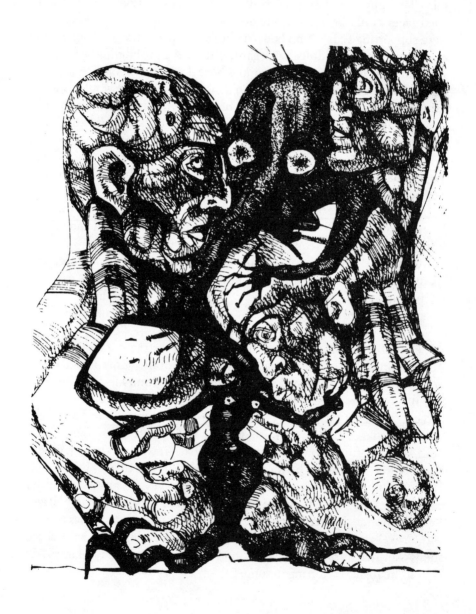

10

THE COLD SEA

That year the winter in Vladivostok was very windy and frosty. The city is open from the north to the cold winds that range over thousands of miles of the Far-Eastern and Ussuri taiga. The icy winds slacken in the dense forests, but when they reach the coast of the Sea of Japan they whistle and howl through the stone-paved streets of Vladivostok, raising clouds of snow and sand. The chill pierced to the bones the several thousand convicts waiting for transportation in the transit camp at Pervaya Rechka station. Some dozen huts built of logs, boards, plywood, and sheets of iron hugged the steep mountainside as if trying to escape the icy breath of the bay a dozen yards away. Not far off, on the other side of the mountain, steam locomotives hooted incessantly. There, life was moving forward, full of bustle; but here it was dragging on toward death.

In the huts were people in gray quilted jackets and trousers, in old army shoes, footcloths and puttees, and earflapped caps whose peaks still bore the marks of five-pointed stars. These people did not work, had no families, no books or papers, no decent food. Twice a day they each received beet or potato soup and two hundred grams of black bread. Many of them still tried to think, but it was not easy. Ahead lay Magadan, for stretches of five to twenty-five years. Only a few optimists dared hope to come out alive from the "Glavdalstroi," the Central Administration for the Development of the Soviet Far-Eastern Regions.

Not all the huts housed the living. Some contained the bodies of the dead. Every night a few more people succumbed to physical exhaustion, dysentery, and the many other diseases that attack a man the minute he grows weak and stops fighting for his life.

Vikenty was glad to get down from his upper bunk in the dark, damp hut when, in a voice crackly from the frost, the guard outside cried: "Ou-t! Line up! Dee-pa-art!"

Vikenty climbed into the cattle car standing in a siding for the mass transport of human freight. He helped up his weakened comrades. For them to remain in this camp would mean certain death; none would last till spring. Ahead there was perhaps something new, a ray of light. Ahead lay the sea! Perhaps he would manage to jump overboard and swim to Japan? Oh, Yoko from Hakodate! If only you could see me now, the dashing blond mate from the schooner *Yankee Clipper* who long, long ago deceived you, my Chio-Chio-San! How dearly one paid for mistakes, one's own and others'!

In the cattle car, pressed against the side wall among his gray, half-dead companions, Angarov kept counting the hours, the minutes, the clicks of the wheels on the rail joints . . . When the train finally came to a halt, he peered through a chink in the door, straining to see where they had been brought to: Nakhodka? Sovetskaya Gavan? No way of telling! Perhaps the Tatar Strait? To drown them straight away? He almost shouted for joy when the bolts clanked and the doors were rolled open. Vanino! That meant . . . the sea!

The fifteen hundred convicts dropped down from the cars like sandbags and got to their feet to drag themselves to the pier. Night fell over the piers along the small bay, which was equipped for the transportation of thousands of people to the east.

At a solitary berth loomed the hulk of a passenger and cargo steamer. Angarov read the faint white letters on the bridge: *Dzhurma*. A sullen mass of men huddled near the ship's bow, surrounded by soldiers with sheepdogs on leashes. A light, sparkling snow was falling; through it could be heard the muffled sounds of commands. Farther away, near the main gangplank, clustered a throng of women convicts. They had been given the privilege of boarding first.

Vikenty could make out the figures dimly in the darkness and hear the embarrassed, almost girlish voices of the women clambering up the steep gangplank carrying suitcases and bundles, clinging with one hand to a bag and the handrail and with the other trying to hold down their skirts in the wind. What innate modesty! They seemed to be firmly convinced that they were still expected to play the role of women, to look after men and bear children. Although they had long since been deprived of that function they could not wholly believe what had happened to them. A few, however, had already thrown away their skirts and wore quilted trousers; they walked up the gangplank silently or swearing horribly. They had crossed one psychological barrier on the way to moral and physical death. Death does not come to everyone at the same time, except in an epidemic. In prison people die by degrees, depending on the strength of their minds and bodies.

At last the gangplank was empty—the last female figure had disappeared into No. 2 hold, right by the windows of the wardroom, where it was warm, cozy, and smelled of food.

"Move!" The escort officer's bark interrupted Angarov's train of thought. The male prisoners began to make their way noisily and briskly up the gangplank. There they were met by a line of soldiers, their crimson epaulets dimly visible in the darkness, and their submachine guns slung across their chests. As each convict stepped onto the deck, a soldier handed him a gray bag containing something. The convicts took the bags without a word and walked along the deck, which crackled with frost, toward a short companionway.

Vikenty stepped onto the deck, took the bag handed him by the soldier and, by force of habit from the days as a captain, cast a swift glance at the bridge. Two heavy machine guns, their muzzles blunt and menacing, stared back at him from the wings.

When all the convicts had been packed into No. 1 hold in the bow, and the doors had been shut on them, the soldiers walked off the deck. As in the good old days of the slave trade, there would now be a formal wardroom signing of the bill of lading for the living cargo. The Glavdalstroi received a constant supply of manpower from the western regions for round-the-clock work in the uranium mines and gold fields of the Soviet Far East.

The wardroom had a green, wall-to-wall carpet, an oval table of polished mahogany, upholstered chairs, seascape paintings, and the four portraits. It was warm and comfortable. Two men sat at the table: the captain, a tall, furrow-faced man in a black uniform with rings on the sleeves, and the colonel, a kindly looking, corpulent man wearing a dark-green uniform with wide, red-trimmed epaulets and red stripes down his trousers, and felt boots. A gray astrakhan cap and greatcoat hung on a rack by the door.

On the table stood an opened bottle of cognac and two long-stemmed crystal liqueur glasses.

"Please, Comrade Captain, sign for the cargo." The colonel pushed the bill of lading toward the captain. "Fifteen hundred men, thirteen hundred women. You'll deliver them all?" The colonel leaned back in his chair and took a sip of cognac from his glass.

"Does it matter?" The captain shrugged his shoulders as he affixed his signature to the document. "It's not the first trip, and won't be the last. There's spoilage on every trip. With the kind of food they're getting, the rough seas, you know. But it's the security that worries me. With La Perouse Strait still icebound we'll have to steam part of the way through the Sea of Japan, and the Tsugaru Strait. Then the Pacific. Only a fifth of the voyage will be by the way of the Sea of Okhotsk. What's all the rush?" the captain asked; he sounded irritated. "Couldn't we wait a few weeks for the ice in La Perouse Strait to break and make the whole run in our own territorial waters instead of taking chances? Just think what could happen if there's some accident in international waters, with cargo like this! If the news got abroad!"

The colonel gave him a troubled look. "I sympathize with you, but there's nothing I can do. It's Comrade Beria's orders! Magadan wants the manpower, and in a hurry. The sick and the dead and those who get released must be replaced. The work in the mines mustn't be interrupted even for a minute! In case of an accident at sea, however, there are the flood valves . . . "

"The flood valves," the captain said softly. "That was understandable in time of war but not now, when life is just beginning to return to normal . . . "

"I understand how you feel, Comrade Captain," said the colonel. "But the war has come to an end only for the others, not for us communists! We have a lot still to do, and we must take chances. Especially you and I, who are in the front line. If the convicts revolt and overpower the guards, I'll be blamed for poor security and I'll be shot. Our only hope is the soldiers, our machine guns, and you—if you get them to Nagaev Bay quickly and without any trouble. Your voyage will be monitored by the special center in Vladivostock that's in communication with the warships at our bases in the Kurile Islands, and with the fighter planes. Help will arrive within ten minutes, should there be any provocation by the Japanese or Americans . . . Bon voyage!" The colonel stood up from the table and extended his hand to the captain.

With nearly three thousand human beings in its forward holds and general cargo in the aft holds, the *Dzhurma* cast off quietly, moved away from the pier in the frosty predawn mist, and out into the Tatar Strait, buffeted by huge waves driven by a raging force-9 northeaster. The wind screamed in the rigging and the ship rolled heavily as it set its long and difficult course toward the northern shores of the Sea of Okhotsk.

The vast No. 1 hold in the ship's bow was lighted by four dust-covered bulbs that gave hardly any light through their thick wire-mesh protectors. The convicts lay on the bare planks, beneath which could be heard the splashing of the water. On both sides the steel ribs of the ship's frame rose steeply to the deckhead. A wide iron ladder led down from the deck on the port side to the middle of the hold. The door to the hold was bolted tightly from the outside. Down below, by the ladder, stood a large steel drum that was used as a latrine. There was a wooden latrine on deck, suspended right above the water, but the convicts were allowed to use it only at night, when the door of the hold was opened for airing. The drum was then carried out and emptied overboard. A sign hanging on the ladder handrail warned: "Keep inside! The soldiers shoot on sight!"

After several hours at sea the door was opened a crack. Through it could be seen a sliver of gray sky. A stream of cold, fresh air came rushing in but dissipated at once in the heavy stench of the hold. "Bring it up!" a guard yelled. Two convicts got to their feet, took hold of the drum, and dragged it up the ladder to the deck. They set it down on the bulwark and emptied it into the sea. Then they spent a long time rinsing it, lowering it into the water on a rope, deliberately delaying their return to the hold, and greedily inhaling the crystal-clear sea air.

The machine guns and two submachine gunners looked down from the bridge. Two other guards with machine guns stood on the spar deck, by the companionway, and two more by the hatchway to the hold.

Vikenty lay on the boards, in the thick of the convicts, close to the fore bulkhead behind which the anchor chain clanked in its locker. Farther on was the storage room and a secret passage to the deck, the entrance to which was covered with a steel plate fastened with nuts and bolts instead of rivets. Vikenty lay there, his shoulders against the plate, and thought about the rusty nuts and bolts. Could he possibly loosen them with his bare hands? And what if he could? Where could he escape to? The water was cold in winter, even in the Sea of Japan, and he wouldn't make it to the shore without a life jacket.

In the bag, which he, like everyone else, had been given when boarding, Vikenty found a loaf of black rye bread, two hundred grams of salt, a packet of coarse tobacco, matches, several pieces of hardtack, and about six pounds of salt fish. A small water tank stood under the ladder, opposite the drum latrine.

The splashing of the water under the bows lulled and soothed his soul, and instilled a little hope. When, according to his calculations, they should have turned into La Perouse Strait but did not do so, Vikenty became alarmed, wondering where they were being taken. The gale-driven waves continued to strike the starboard beam as before. Could they be going by way of the Tsugaru Strait?

At last the pounding of the waves subsided, indicating that the ship had entered the strait. Angarov covered his face with his hands, attempting somehow to still the pain in his soul. Not many miles to the north was the city and port of Hakodate, where in 1927 he had abandoned his Yoko-San, who was expecting a child by him. Perhaps she was still living there now and remembered him, as she said she would. She could not know he was passing by, in a hold, on his way to penal servitude or death. He tried to drive away the thoughts of Lida and their little Anatoly. They must be getting along somehow; they were having an easier time than he.

As the pitching decreased, the mood in the hold became more cheerful. The convicts began to stir, conversations were struck up, and cards were slapped down noisily on the boards. They were playing for bread and for punches on the nose.

The Pacific greeted the *Dzhurma* with a force-11 gale. After passing the traverse of the island of Hokkaido, the ship ran immediately into an almost hurricane-force wind. It pitched forward, and the whole deck was awash with foaming water. The guards hurriedly made the bars on the hatch fast and rushed to the spar deck, slipping on the wet deck that kept running away from under their feet. A mountain of green water lifted the ship effortlessly and, rolling forward, pitched her nose first into the next wave. The terrible impact, accompanied by a sound like the thunder of a cannon shot, caused the vessel to come to a stop momentarily, then it moved on slowly northward through the thousands of great waves of water that the tireless wind was driving to the south.

All talk ceased in the hold. Outside they could hear clearly the furious breathing of the winter ocean, which was not as pacific as it had seemed to Magellan five hundred years earlier. The boards of the deck creaked, water slopped in the bilges, and the hull shuddered from the impact of the waves and the laboring of the screw far away at the stern.

And through the tumult of the sea could be heard the striking of a hammer on iron. Taking turns every few minutes, the convicts were chiseling away the rivets on the oval steel lid that covered the manhole in the watertight bulkhead between No. 1 and No. 2 hold. In the second hold were the women. No one knew where the chisel and hammer had come from, but the work proceeded without interruption, one or another of them kept chiseling away at the next rivet that still held fast. On the other side of the bulkhead there was silence.

The storm raged uninterrupted for a week. During that time several people died of exhaustion or from lack of fresh air: they were thrown overboard at night. Right now there were several dead bodies lying near the ladder, their noses buried in filth. In the evening the door would be opened, and the sea would receive them. Hunger, darkness, both spiritual and actual, and the howling sea outside—that was the reality that "determines one's consciousness," as Marx had said. That consciousness changed slowly and imperceptibly. What only yesterday appeared fantastic, today became simple and comprehensible. Yesterday they had not yet begun to stake their lives at cards, but today that was almost the only thing they bet. Everyone understood that the price of life had gone down on the stock exchange. So why not stake it? What difference did it make? What did they have to look forward to? And there really was nothing else for them to gamble with.

For over an hour now Vikenty had been listening to the noise of the game going on about fifteen yards away, in the center of the hold. Several convicts were sitting in a circle, their eyes gleaming with hunger and strain. Occasionally they cursed obscenely. Somewhere to the side someone began to sing tunelessly:

> "Rages and roars the ocean,
> Our native element sighing,
> We're bound for Magada-an,
> Where we'll all be a-dying."

One of the players got up from the circle and waddled off in the direction from which the song was coming.

"Shut up, you pig! Stop torturing us!"

The singing stopped. The man came back and sat down again in the circle.

"Where the hell . . . ?" Another player, with a long, lean face like that of a holy man, jumped up and demanded shrilly: "What did you do with that card? Where's the ace?"

"Awright!" One of the others gave way. "Sit down! We'll play again. Last hand."

The game—not for life, but death—resumed. From all sides dozens of eyes were riveted on the players. As if spellbound, Angarov also kept his eyes fixed on them and waited to see what would happen.

The "holy man" was again out of luck. He jumped up without a word and ran toward the ladder. Someone tripped him, and he was dragged back to the circle.

"You can't do that, sweetheart," a deep voice admonished the loser. "We're playing fair. You lost, you pay!"

The man struggled silently in the strong arms encircling him and looked around with terrified eyes. He was bound and gagged, but he managed to plead through the rag in his mouth: "Bro-o-thers! Let me off, eh? I didn't think! Let me li-ive . . . "

He fell silent. Two convicts sat on his bound legs, which were still twitching, two others wound a filthy towel around his neck and pulled it toward themselves in opposite directions. They watched as the gurgle coming from his throat died away, the trembling in his legs slackened, and his face turned blue. At last his tongue flopped out and lolled sideways like a piece of rotten meat. His small beard turned upward and his face looked calm, almost peaceful, under the thick growth of bristle. They picked him up, carried him over to the ladder and dropped him down near it.

Angarov turned away. He felt that he was going to vomit and his hands were trembling slightly. Directly in front of him he saw the face of his neighbor, white as chalk. Angarov noticed the collar of an old army blouse poking out from underneath his grimy padded jacket.

"Listen, dad," whispered the fellow in the military blouse, "let's kill them all, eh?"

"Who?" Vikenty stared at the face, which was that of an old man, although the eyes were young.

"Them over there, those that killed him! First they'll kill off their own, then they'll begin to stake us . . . "

"Lie still!" Angarov murmured. "You won't kill them, they'd get you first. They won't stake any of us—there are still plenty who want to die. And cut out the 'dad'—I'm not so ancient . . . How old are you?"

"Twenty-five," he answered quietly, with a sad smile on his lips. "Petya's the name. And have you been to Moscow?"

"I've been there," Vikenty said with a shrug, "in passing. I'm a sea captain."

Petya raised himself on an elbow and contemplated the man with the long, red beard and blue eyes. "And how come you're here?" he asked.

"What about you?"

Petya paused, then resumed the conversation almost in a whisper, breathing straight into Vikenty's face.

"We lived on Begovaya Street, near the racecourse. A large, wide street. On one side of it is Leningradsky Prospect, on the other Khoroshevskoye Highway with the Vagankovo Cemetery behind it. All sorts of people are buried there. When I was in the ninth grade, before the war, our literature teacher took our entire class to the cemetery, to the grave of Sergei Esenin. She told us a lot about him. It seems he was quite a man, Esenin. Did you read about him?"

"No-o," Vikenty drawled, embarrassed. "I was too busy to read, but I've heard of him. They say he quarreled with Mayakovsky . . . "

"Perhaps he did, I wouldn't know. But the teacher told us that he went and hanged himself, in Leningrad, in the Astoria, and that the girl he loved shot herself and asked to be buried with him. God! they were people! And us? Cattle, that's what we are! By the way, where do you think they're taking us?"

"Where? To Kolyma, to dig for gold. Are you thinking of making a break from there?"

"I am!" Petya lowered his head. "Would you believe it? I want to live so very much that it gives me the shivers. After all, I haven't lived yet! I'd just finished school when I was drafted, when the war began. I was seventeen then. At school I was in the Komsomol, like everyone. And I had a girl I loved, Tomka, she was called. She saw me off to the front in forty-one at the Leningrad railway station and promised to wait for me to come back. She looked thin. She was wearing an army coat, and a knapsack on her back . . . Our girls, too, you know, were taken to the front, as nurses."

Vikenty smiled with his lips only. "Well, what happened to you next?"

"Next?" Petya flashed a smile of gratitude at his companion. "Next we got to the front, outside Leningrad. We walked all the way at night to avoid the German planes. We didn't know how to shoot, and there was nothing to shoot with—just one rifle for every three soldiers! Half of our boys were slaughtered in the first battle, mowed down like grass. The rest were taken prisoner . . . as I was, too. The things we had to endure! . . . Then some Russian officers came and told us Stalin was a traitor, that we must liberate Russia from communism. We would rule Russia ourselves. And they assured us that the Soviet troops would not resist, that it would all soon be over. Those of us who refused to join General Vlasov's army would rot in camps, they said. Well, we thought and thought. But how could we make head or tail of all that? We wanted to live, and you know how things were in the German camps! So I became a soldier under General Vlasov. But Hitler and Vlasov had miscalculated somewhere. The Soviet Army didn't fall apart. Yes, and then we fought a defensive action against the Soviets in Prussia. I was wounded in the neck by a piece of shrapnel, and came to in a Soviet field hospital. Then the labor camp and the coal mines on the Pechora. Ten years they gave me, for being a traitor to the motherland. And in camp they added another ten, just like that, without an interrogation even, and sent me here. So there you have it, stuck in camp since the age of seventeen! There are a lot of us here who were with Vlasov . . . And who needed the war anyway? Whose fault was it all? I've got a mother at home, and a younger sister, Katyusha. In forty-one she was already in the third grade. Now she's grown up. And they must be getting it hot on account of me! Who knows, perhaps they'll be forgiven if I die . . . "

"What's there to forgive?" Vikenty hissed at him almost angrily. "What are you guilty of? Stop thinking that you're guilty! We must survive! I intend to survive. Let *him* croak!"

"Who's 'him'?"

"The evil spirit!" Vikenty did not dare to name the name.

"Hey!" came a shout from above, and at the same moment a guard stuck his head in the door. "Come on, move the dead. Any volunteers?"

Without a word Vikenty stepped forward, giving Petya's sleeve a tug. It was their chance to see the sea, sky, and horizon—simply to have a look at the world. They grabbed one body by the arms and legs and dragged it up the ladder. The fresh breeze took away their breath. The sea had calmed a little. The ship rolled gently and the spray kept hitting the deck. Row upon row of whitecaps stretched as far as the horizon, beyond which rose a narrow strip of coastline—the Kurile Islands!

Vikenty knew the region well. He took in the ship, the sea, and the sky at a glance. He nodded to Petya and they dragged the corpse to the bulwark and heaved it up and over the side. The gray body plopped quietly into the water and disappeared.

Several men watched them from the bridge. The submachine gunners standing nearby looked away gloomily. Panting, Petya and Vikenty kept dragging out the corpses. Down in the hold they avoided their comrades' eyes. Then they spent a long time rinsing the latrine drum they had lowered over the side.

"That's enough!" A soldier went up to Vikenty and touched him on the back with the stock of his submachine gun. "Move! We're locking up."

Tired by the unfamiliar work and intoxicated with the fresh air, they lay stretched out below for a long time without saying a word. Through his half-closed lids Vikenty saw three figures standing nearby, with what looked like knives concealed in their sleeves. He could not make out their faces in the gloom, but he realized that trouble was brewing.

"Get up, my darling," one of the three said quietly, "we've got accounts to settle."

Vikenty did not know what "accounts" there were to settle, but past experience—at sea and in the camps—told him that he was only one step away from death. There was no time to think or say anything. Moving completely automatically, instinctively, he got up and, still bent over, kicked the one standing in front of him in the stomach and the other in the groin. Both went down as if struck by lightning. The third man hurled his knife, which clanged against iron—missed! Petya threw himself at his legs and pulled him down.

The hushed hold watched the sudden outbreak and equally sudden end of the skirmish in the bow.

"Well, why don't you look me in the eye?" Vikenty pulled the third man toward him by the collar. "Shall I kill you or not? You decide. And what did you have against me?"

"You broke the rules!" The man turned his stubble-covered face to the side. "You carried out the corpses without asking us . . . We're the masters here." He motioned in the direction of his two comrades who were still lying unconscious nearby. Petya had hidden their knives under his bag.

"I'm sorry," Vikenty said quietly, realizing that it was advisable to come to terms. "How was I to know? You might've told us. Why this, why go straight for our throats?"

"And we're sorry too." The man's eyes gleamed approval. "We didn't know you were one of us. We won't touch you again, but don't you interfere with us. Who are you?"

"A seaman. I was a captain." Vikenty gave him a crooked smile.

"So-o!" The man looked at Vikenty with respect. "You wanted to have a peek at your dear old sea! But you can certainly hand it out! Well, mum's the word for now! We'll have another chat later on."

He walked off to his cronies by the bulkhead. After a minute they carried away his luckless friends.

Vikenty lay with his eyes closed, feeling the curious glances of the people lolling around him.

"You certainly gave it to them!" Petya whispered with admiration. "Aren't you afraid they'll kill you for it?"

"No, I'm not afraid. They kill only the weak or enemies. They understand that I'm neither weak nor their enemy. Now they'll try to make friends with me."

No one counted how many "locksmiths" had taken turns at the hatch to No. 2 hold or how many blows they had given the tiny steel chisel. But the days passed and finally the last rivet was chipped away and the steel plate dropped to the floor, opening a window for a thousand semihumans. For several minutes everyone stared in silence at the dark, gaping manhole, behind which there was also silence. Then someone stepped forward resolutely and plunged through the opening.

In the women's hold, the zek stared frantically at the somber, motionless crowd of gray shapes. He backed toward the manhole in the bulkhead, baring his teeth in an evil smile. "So, you whores receive guests?"

No one answered. All around him in the hold were hundreds of blurred faces, the eyes filled with desire, curiosity, fear. Under the gaze of these feverish eyes the terrified muzhik pressed himself against the steel bulkhead, beyond which he could hear the tense breathing of his hundreds of comrades. Keeping his eyes fixed on the women crowding close around him, he quickly bent down and put one leg back through the manhole.

A powerfully built woman wearing a quilted jacket and trousers and with a shock of unwashed hair hanging down onto her shoulders in a filthy mane stepped forward, took hold of the zek by the collar of his jacket, and lifted him effortlessly away from the manhole. "Come on, darling, come over to my bunk. Don't be scared. I'm tired of playing butch. I'd like a real man for once!"

The zek's face twisted with rage and he kicked her in the stomach. But she held him with one hand and gave him a resounding clout with the other. Then she dragged him off toward her bunk.

Two other gray shapes grabbed hold of the dishevelled muzhik and tried to pull him away. "Why, you bitches!" She hissed viciously at her friends as she beat them off and dragged the muzhik after her. "Ain't you got enough men, you whores. Ain't there a hold full of them over there!"

The crowd of women near the bulkhead began to shout: "Hey, in there, you men or what? Come on through!"

The women's shouts from the other side of the bulkhead seemed to rouse the men, and the whole gray mass rushed toward the manhole, trampling on one another in their haste. In the other hold the women at once divided into several groups. Some of them crowded around the manhole and began to pull the men through by their arms and hair. They dragged them off eagerly to their bunks, tearing off their clothing on the run.

"Girls! We've got men!" A woman's piercing cry resounded through the hold.

The far bunks were quickly occupied by couples who filled the hold with the animal grunting of people who had forgotten what love was. The men continued to stream through the manhole and dispersed throughout the hold.

Some of the women tried to retain their sense of modesty, a kind of innate instinct of reserve. The men seized them, paying no attention to their terrified pleading. Gray shapes were running and struggling among the bunks. There was a ceaseless screaming from those who were being raped. In a few minutes the entire hold had turned into a battlefield.

The door to the women's hold had been left open for airing and now about fifty younger girls, scared to death by the spectacle of the mass rape of their friends, rushed up onto the deck, ignoring in their terror the shouts of the guard, who hesitated to shoot at the thin, emaciated girls pouring out of the hold followed by the screams of a thousand women.

The entire guard was ordered on deck. Two men stayed in the cabin: the captain and the guard commandant, a lieutenant. The captain stared through the porthole at the foredeck, where the fugitives from the hold were huddling together on the wet iron. The lieutenant watched the captain nervously twisting a cigar and struck a match for him. The captain drew on the cigar, nodded his thanks, and looked up at the guard commandant.

"What do you plan to do, Comrade Lieutenant?"

"I don't know," the lieutenant gestured hopelessly. "Just imagine them breaking through the bulkhead like that! Perhaps we ought to open up the steam and wipe them all out? Their fate's sealed, whatever happens. What difference does it make whether they die now or later?"

"Well, that's more easily said than done!" The captain turned in irritation. "You're responsible for the cargo to Comrade Beria, and I answer to the steamship line and to the Central Committee. We have no right to kill people without proper written orders! We must inform Magadan, and the head of the local Glavdalstroi office. I'll also report, in code, to the Ministry of the Merchant Marine. To be on the safe side, I'll request a warship as escort. If the zeks broke through the bulkhead, they're capable of anything and they may manage to get up on deck. Will your machine guns be able to mow down all fifteen hundred men?"

"They're not so many now." The lieutenant shook his head uncertainly. "Some of them have died in transit . . . ."

"How many?"

"Well, about thirty . . . "

"You must be joking! What's thirty out of fifteen hundred? In the meantime we must put these girls in the messroom aft. The crew will be transferred to the bridge house. I must ask you to reinforce the guard at the hatch."

"Yes, I'll divide the entire guard into two watches. It's not long now to Magadan, they'll bear it . . . " The guard commandant stood up. "May I go now?" he asked.

The captain nodded. "Yes, but check out the machine guns tonight, and make sure they won't misfire if we need them. And we'll have hot steam ready for pumping into the hold . . . "

"Very good, Comrade Captain! Don't worry. Even if your bulkhead let us down, our machine guns won't!" The captain forced a smile.

The orgy in No. 2 hold did not let up during the three days that remained till the vessel reached port. Vikenty, Petya, and about a hundred men who were ill or weak or did not want love-making and rape stayed behind in the hold, listening to the screams and moans coming through the gaping manhole.

Toward evening it turned colder and the rustle of ice floes outside grew louder. The sides of the hold were covered with a thick layer of frost. The ship had entered the strip of coastal ice. Magadan! The hull stopped quivering from the rotation of the propeller shaft. The men in the hold crowded around the ladder, waiting for the tightly locked door to be opened from the deck.

"That's all we need!" the captain grumbled. He was standing on the bridge in his brown fur coat, reading the radiogram from the port controller: "Drop anchor at the entrance to the bay and wait for a berth!"

"What do they use for heads? After all, we are carrying people! Live and hungry people, not dead ones! Damn them!"

He glanced angrily in the direction of the port and went down to the cabin. Hemmed in by two-foot thick ice, the *Dzhurma* dropped one anchor and stopped dead several hundred yards from the entrance to the ice-bound Bay of Nagayevo. In the distance, closer to the port, the silhouettes of several ships could be seen. Among them was a tugboat, cracking the ice as it moved slowly ahead and leaving behind a black strip of steaming water. The captain sat on the divan still wearing his fur coat, his eyes closed with fatigue.

"Comrade Captain!" A sailor of the watch stuck his head in through the half-open door; he looked frightened. "Something's on fire . . . "

"Where?" The captain jumped up.

"In the bay!" The sailor clattered up the companionway, back to the bridge.

The captain followed him and picked up the binoculars.

Almost in the middle of the bay the captain could see a heavily laden vessel; above it, from the first hold, a thick black column of smoke twisted its way into the frosty sky. He shouted over his shoulder to the sailor:

"Tell the radio operator not to leave his set for a second!" With a chill in his heart, the captain scrutinized the outline of the vessel, pressing the binoculars to his eyes till they hurt, but he could not make out its name. He knew that at least one ship stood waiting to unload several thousand tons of ammonite for the mines. It was the ammonite burning! Was it carelessness? No, out of the question! People were careful, they wanted to live. Could it be the convicts' doing? It wasn't all that simple to set ammonite on fire, but then it was practically impossible to put it out! Perhaps the convicts on that vessel had gambled away their own lives in card games? They had nothing to lose! What utter stupidity! Whoever had dreamed up the idea of employing doomed people to load explosives?

The captain glanced at the deck. The entire crew and escort had come out of the cabins and were standing at the port side. In silence, as if at a funeral, they watched the column of smoke grow above the doomed vessel. The tugboat kept circling the ship, vainly pouring jets of water over its low sides, which were already beginning to glow red-hot. The vessel was enveloped in the steam rising from the ice melting along its glowing sides. The ammonite was burning in all the holds.

On the white snow he could see clearly the figures of men who had jumped overboard onto the ice and were running toward the steep, wooded shore.

He was now glad that he was carrying live cargo and not explosives. And he felt sorry for his colleague, the captain of the burning vessel; he sensed that the outcome was bound to be an unhappy one.

Farther to the left, beyond the burning ship, lay the piers and port buildings. Tied up at one mooring was the huge freighter *Wellen*, which he recognized merely by its shape.

Again he trained his binoculars on the blazing vessel. In the swiftly falling icy dusk it glittered over the entire bay like some fantastic, red-hot flatiron shrouded in a cloud of steam and smoke. Over the entire surface of the bay, on the white ice, he could see the figures of people running toward the shore from the ships held fast by the ice. At the very entrance to the bay appeared the prow of an icebreaker, steaming at full speed toward the site of the accident.

Suddenly his heart skipped a beat. Through the lenses of his binoculars he read the name *Vyborg* on the bridge of a ship anchored not more than a mile from the *Dzhurma*. But the *Vyborg* was loaded with detonators! If it exploded . . . the flying pieces of steel plating and ice could bring down the *Dzhurma's* whole superstructure.

"Reduce pressure in the boilers, below the red line," the captain turned to his first mate who was standing next to him, "so that there won't be an explosion if we hit bottom. Have all the men, the crew, and escort, move to the engine room below the main deck. Tell them all to hold on firmly to the railings until I cancel the order. Two sailors of the watch will remain with me on the bridge. After the explosion . . . . if something should happen to me, take command of the ship."

The first mate walked away in silence. The deck emptied.

"Bo'sun!" The captain picked up the microphone and waved his arm at the man at the windlass on the forecastle. "Drop the second anchor, four chains."

The anchor crashed through the ice into the water, and sank to the bottom. "Slow astern!" the captain said in a low voice to the chief engineer in the engine room and put his ear against the copper earpiece of the tube. "Slow astern!" came the familiar voice of the chief engineer. The captain decided not to use the engine telegraph for the time being—it was safer this way!

The ship crunched softly against the ice and moved astern. Straining at the two anchor cables, it turned its bow toward the burning vessel. Now the shock wave would strike the bow instead of the beam, which should help things, whatever happened.

The sailors standing at the wheel and on the wing of the bridge stared anxiously into the blackness of the night illuminated by the blazing mass.

"Hold on . . ." He did not manage to finish. A huge column of steam and water spurted up around the flaming vessel and, at the same moment, a deafening roar shook the entire bay. The captain instinctively threw himself to the deck: the reinforced concrete bulkhead should protect him! The two sailors, their faces dead white, were also sprawled on the deck.

The enormous wave caused by the two explosions swept out from the center of the bay, breaking up and throwing onto the shore the mass of white ice dotted here and there with human figures. The wave engulfed the piers and in an instant demolished and washed away most of the port buildings.

Taut as rubber, the shock wave pressed the *Dzhurma* to the bottom of the bay. A wave of air and ice rolled along the vessel from the direction of the bow. Several times the ship struck bottom and its entire hull shuddered like a fallen horse. Then the water surged back from the shore and seized the ship, spinning it like a matchbox. Both anchor cables snapped like thread, but the ship did not go down: its superstructure held, and the main mass of ice swept over from bow to stern, partly under the bilges, scraping the sides but not breaking through—and that was what saved the people in the holds.

The captain was certain that not more than half a minute had passed since the explosion. Seizing the binoculars, he stared into the darkness till his eyes ached. The bay was once again filled with water. Instead of the solid cover of ice, small, isolated floes spun about here and there; the rest of the mass of ice could be seen piled up in a broad white belt along the shores. All the ships were spinning slowly, anchorless, in the currents of water, but the ice had disappeared, as had the people on it, and the two ships: the one that had been burning and the *Vyborg*. They had simply vanished.

From the entrance to the bay the icebreaker was moving at full speed, picking up from the floes the individuals who had survived by hanging on to the ice till their hands froze to it.

The all clear was given. The pale, frightened members of the crew and escort crawled out from the engine room onto the deck and stared at the unrecognizably changed aspect of the bay from which two ships were now missing . . . And for the first time during those terrible minutes, many of them recalled that the destroyed vessel had also contained people, people like themselves, but marked as convicts; people who also wanted to live, but who had blown themselves up together with the ship and cargo. The crowd stood around for a long time on the night-shrouded deck, looking at the bay, the dark waters of which were steaming from thirty-five degrees of frost.

"Vasily Petrovich!" The captain nodded to the first mate who was standing nearby. "Keep an eye on the situation and on communications from the port, if it still exists! I'm tired, I'll be in my cabin."

The first mate, dressed in a black sheepskin coat and wearing the cap with the crab emblem pulled down over his forehead against the frost, nodded back and watched the tall figure of the captain descend the companionway to his cabin.

Not until morning did special army crews begin clearing the piers of the debris from the buildings and ships. An MVD commission had flown in immediately from Moscow and had begun to investigate the causes of the explosion.

Of all the ships in the road, only the *Dzhurma* carried people in the holds. The port radio station was not yet back in operation, and so all instructions from the port controller's office were brought to the ships by tugboats.

In the afternoon the *Dzhurma* tied up at a pier still covered with sand and silt from the shock wave. Farther away, near the half-demolished port buildings, stood some army trucks.

First the guards opened the door to No. 2 hold where the women were. A mass of fetid air came pouring out. None of the prisoners emerged. The guard commandant stood in confusion near the door for several minutes. He glanced almost fearfully at the line of soldiers on deck. He was at a loss what to do.

It was impossible to stand for long in one place in the thirty-five degrees of frost, not even in felt boots. The soldiers stamped their feet, waiting impatiently for an order.

"Hey, you down there!" The lieutenant stepped onto the first rung of the ladder and looked down. He could hardly make out the hundreds of male and female faces. "Come on out, we've arrived!" he tried to joke.

"Come down here! You eunuch!" came a woman's spiteful, hoarse answer. "We'll tie them up for you with a thread and make a man out of you . . ." The entire hold burst into approving laughter.

"You coming out or not, you sonovabitches?" The lieutenant was losing his temper. "Perhaps you'd like me to set up a machine gun and shake you up a bit?"

There was no response. In the suddenly hushed hold several dozen people rushed threateningly toward the ladder. The commandant jumped back onto the deck, hardly managing to slam the door behind him in time. The soldiers quickly replaced the hatch cover. From inside came shouts: "Sonovabitches yourselves, you damn pigs! Where you taking us? To die? You'll all croak too some day! We're not coming out, we'll all die in here!"

The guard commandant walked away from the door and glanced down at the pier. There stood the guard battalion of the special MVD troops that had just arrived. An MVD colonel wearing a tall, gray astrakhan cap, his face red from the frost, slowly climbed the gangplank to the deck. He nodded to the guard commandant who had come to attention before him, and went to the captain.

A few minutes later the captain lifted the mouthpiece in his cabin. "Engine room? Hot steam into No. 2 hold!"

The grease-stained engine-room men exchanged glances and, under the gaze of the chief engineer, silently opened two valves, one on the port, the other on the starboard side. Steam poured from the boiler under high pressure into the hold.

Within a few minutes white steam, which vanished instantaneously in the frosty air, began to seep through the invisible cracks around the hatch cover. The sun blinded the eyes of the men who waited on the deck and on the piers. At last the hundreds of prisoners started a loud knocking. The door was opened.

Fetid steam poured from the hold and was precipitated in a layer of frost on the deck and on the faces of the circle of soldiers. Then two pink shapes appeared in the steam. A man and a woman, wearing only their underpants and carrying their clothes in their arms, hesitated for a moment in the entrance to the hold, gasping in the frosty air. Then they stepped down onto the deck, the soles of their feet sticking to the icy metal. They were followed by the rest of the prisoners, also carrying their clothes in their arms, staggering out onto the deck, their skins lobster-red from the heat.

Looking out at the deck from the wardroom, the MVD colonel said something to the guard commandant standing next to him. The commandant jumped out onto the deck and shouted. "All get dressed! Move!"

Shivering on the icy deck, the prisoners began putting on their clothes.

Then they opened No. 1 hold. For a half-hour Vikenty, Petya, and some others went up and down the ladder, dragging from both holds those who could not walk themselves.

Cleared of its cargo, the *Dzhurma* moved out and anchored in the road. Vikenty saw its silhouette once again when the truck, loaded with zeks, and with a submachine gunner in the driver's cab, left the port and headed in the direction of the Great Northern Highway that joins Magadan with Pevek on the Arctic Ocean.

11

"PEOPLE PERISH FOR THE METAL" *

The snowflakes drifted slowly down from the gray sky, large and fluffy, like tiny parachutes. They touched down smoothly and immediately turned to slush, which squelched and gurgled underfoot like the surface of a bog. The fifteen degrees of frost rarely reached down here where Vikenty stood in the bed of the pit. The pit was three yards deep, three wide, and about ten in length, like a big trench or a common grave. The bottom of the pit was a little deeper in the middle than at the sides, so that the water flowed into the middle from the walls.

Fine and coarse grains of gold gleamed in the dark-brown sand. The sand was so rich that you could pick the gold out by hand, except that your fingers would not bend. They were always slightly frostbitten, and the skin on the fingertips cracked and came away in strips; the nails ached and turned blue like a corpse's.

So the sand had to be sifted. The rusty sieve with fine and coarse meshes had been set up on a piece of tarpaulin laid straight onto the mud. One side of the sieve rested on a log about fifteen inches long.

You had to work deeper than the six-foot layer of permafrost, which, frozen for thousands of years, would take neither spade nor pick. But below six feet the sand was powdery and the spades cut through it like butter. They dug deeper and wider. The open cutting resembled a trapezium with its base downward. The sides of the trapezium hung menacingly over the middle, but the eternal frost held them fast; landslips were rare.

These trenches were usually worked by three men. They dynamited

*A line from a Russian opera.

the upper layer of earth over an area some ten yards long and then dug to a depth of four to five yards, until the water began to flood the pit. Then they abandoned that pit and started a new one. Another group of three worked alongside them in a similar pit. This organization of labor into gangs of three had been introduced by the camp commandant for greater safety—so that no more than three could gather together and so that it would be possible to maintain more accurate control over the daily output in terms of the amount of gold extracted from a given quantity of sand.

Above the pit stood the gray, doll-like figure of a soldier in a sheepskin jacket and felt boots, holding a submachine gun across his chest. His narrow, wary eyes squinted out from under the winter cap pulled low over his forehead. This soldier, like most of the soldiers in the guard, was of a national minority, perhaps a Kazakh or a Kirgiz. But prisoners belonging to national minorities were guarded by Russian soldiers, in order to exclude the possibility of mutual understanding growing up between the zeks and the guards.

From the mound of earth near the pit, the soldier could see several other pits where the gangs were working. The soldier knew nothing of these gray people, but he was prepared to carry out orders—to shoot anyone who raised his head from the pit without being ordered to do so. All the zeks knew this and so they waited for that order from first light until sundown.

It was rare for anyone to glance into the pits at the prisoners: work if you want to; if you don't, just stand there. But you could not "just" stand there for long without freezing to death. Work was the only means of keeping warm and work was the only means of obtaining your ration of rye bread and potato; daily norms had to be met.

Three dark figures in quilted clothing, caps with earmuffs, and torn rubber boots were working on the bottom of the pit. Two of them, with their heads propped against the frozen wall, were chopping out the sand with spades and throwing it onto the sieve. The third was kneeling on the tarpaulin, rolling aside the dully gleaming nuggets and simply brushing the fine grains off with his glove. The sand filtered back into the surrounding slush, where the tiny specks of gold looked like grains of millet scattered on tilled earth.

"I'm tired!" Petka backed out from under the frozen overhang. He rested his spade against his leg and smiled sheepishly. The quilted trousers, the sweater, the rubber boots, which were still in one piece, and the long forelock poking out from underneath his ancient army cap would have given him the appearance of a soldier in a field-engineer battalion if it had not been for his gaunt, thickly stubbled face and his feverish eyes.

"Tired?" Vikenty asked softly, getting up from the ground. "Then take a rest. There's enough gold here for a thousand years!" He gave Petka a sympathetic look. "You know, when they brought us here two years ago, you were quite a different person. We haven't been working for an hour yet, and already you're exhausted." The second digger, a thin little muzhik with a long hooked nose projecting comically from a face that resembled a flat area of wasteland overgrown with stunted bushes, also crawled out of the stope. He leaned on his spade and gave his two comrades a silent, questioning look. No one knew his name, but since he hardly ever said anything, the nickname "Dummy" had stuck fast.

"You tired too, Dummy?" Vikenty turned to him.

He nodded silently.

"How many years have you been inside already?"

"He knows but he's not telling!" Petka joked.

Dummy said nothing.

"You've been sleeping in the bunk above me for a year already," Petka exclaimed reproachfully. "You should be ashamed. Just like a mute. It's sickening to live like that."

Dummy smiled guiltily, hung his head, and stared at his feet.

"Wish we had something to eat," Petka said quietly, forgetting about Dummy. "Look, Vikenty, it's snowing. It snowed just like this on my last New Year's in Leningrad. We had a New Year's dance at school. That was when I first waltzed with Tomka, and afterwards in the corridor I kissed her. And in the spring we had a graduation ball, but no snow. We promised each other that we would spend our lives together, no matter what happened."

"W-well?" Dummy asked with interest, lifting his head. His voice sounded like the grating of rusty hinges.

"What do you mean 'W-well'? I've told you this story a hundred times!" Petka looked at him angrily.

"Doesn't matter if it is a hundred times," Vikenty sighed noisily like an old tired horse. "Tell it for the hundred and first. I like to hear it as well."

"But I don't like remembering it so very much!" Petka hung his head and turned away. "Then the war came . . . I never saw my Tamara again and I never will see her. She was at the front. She may be alive, married to someone now, with kids . . . Or perhaps she was killed in the war. That was the end of my youth, our youth together. You're both older, it was easier for you."

"That's true." Vikenty stepped forward and shook him sympathetically by the shoulder. "My youth passed like a fairy tale. You can't imagine! That's why it's easier for me to endure all this—I have something to remember. And you, Dummy, maybe you saw good times too, eh? But you just keep silent, you devil. But don't you lose heart, Petka. Don't lose your hope of life."

"There's so much gold all around us," Petka said mournfully, pushing his cap onto the back of his head. "And I'd give every bit of it for a piece of bread. I could eat a loaf in one swallow. It seems like I haven't eaten my fill once these twelve years." There was hatred and bewilderment in his voice, and his eyes filled with tears. "We might as well be dead. We'll never get out of here anyway."

Dummy turned and disappeared into the stope. Vikenty dropped to his knees without looking at Petka and began to rake off the gold. For a few moments Petka stared in silence at his friend's sullen face, realizing that he had said too much; he had said what everyone thought but no one ever stated aloud. He picked up his spade, dived under the arch of frozen earth, and thrust the spade viciously into the sand. He could hear Dummy's hoarse breathing on his right.

The three men worked in silence for several hours, reluctant to renew the conversation. The instinct of survival lived in each of them, an instinct that fed on hope. None of them wished to admit anyone to those depths, for a careless movement might destroy the last spark of life.

"What have you got there?" Vikenty asked, hearing a spade scraping on metal.

"A nugget!" Petka's excited voice came from the darkness. At the same time Dummy crawled backward out of the stope and suddenly said quietly, "Impossible to go any farther. The overburden's about to give way!"

"What are you going on about?" Vikenty said in surprise.

"The roof's going to cave in." Dummy shook his head stubbornly. "I know. I was a mine foreman in the Kuzbass for fifteen years. Call Petka out before it's too late!"

"Get out!" Vikenty bellowed, suddenly realizing the danger.

"Just a minute, stop horsing around!" came the cheerful voice, and then Petka himself appeared, his face radiant. In his hand he held a huge nugget as big as a fair-sized beetroot.

"Ah!" Dummy gasped.

"Look!" Petka said joyfully, displaying the nugget on his palm. "Just look! You could buy a house with it! Maybe they'll set us free for this, eh?" He tossed the nugget to Vikenty. "There's more there, I saw them! I'll get them all. They'll give us a good feed. Maybe they'll even let us go."

"Stop!" Vikenty shouted with anxious irritation into the darkness at the shape that had disappeared under the overburden. "Get back here! It's collapsing! Dummy says so! Do you hear, Petka? Dummy says it's collapsing. Never mind the gold. Get out of there!"

He paused, listening to the blows of Petka's spade in the darkness. Then he pushed Dummy aside and threw himself under the overburden. At that very moment the ground shook under his feet. "A-ai!" The sharp cry from within was immediately drowned in a muffled rumble as the inner part of the overburden, a thickness of about five feet, gently caved in. The upper, frozen part of the earth roof did not move.

Vikenty knelt for a second with his arms buried in the loose soil, staring dazedly in front of him at the solid wall of sand in which Petka had disappeared.

He jumped back and to his feet. For a few seconds Vikenty and Dummy looked at each other. Then, as if waking from a trance, Vikenty seized a spade, dived under the overburden onto his knees and began digging frenziedly. A solid stream of sand flew out behind him.

"Stop it!" Dummy's muffled voice carried to him. "There's no point. You won't dig him out before evening. I know. We shouldn't have gone in at right angles without props. I'll get help. While there's still time."

"Stop!" Vikenty poked his head out of the darkness. "The soldier'll shoot! Come and dig!"

"We've got to save Petka," Dummy said calmly as he clambered up the narrow ramp that they had left at the side of the pit.

Vikenty threw aside the spade, covered his face with his hands and dropped onto the sand. A hollow shot rang out. A few seconds later he heard a slithering sound and Dummy's body flopped into the icy slush on the bottom of the pit. He crawled toward Dummy on his hands and knees and glanced at his face.

"My leg!" Dummy whispered, hardly able to part his lips, which had immediately turned blue. Vikenty dragged him toward the side of the pit, where it was drier. He pulled off Dummy's quilted trousers and felt the bullet wound in the flesh of the right leg just below the knee. He took off his belt and bound it tightly round the wound. Then he pulled Dummy's trousers back on and dragged him farther away from the water, under the overhang where the snow was not falling. He propped Dummy up with his back against the wall, but he collapsed unconscious onto his side, his mouth open and his legs wide apart.

Vikenty got up and turned back to the stope. He stared at Petka's huge grave of yellowish sand, gleaming with specks of gold.

"A golden grave!" He sat down in the mud, buried his face on his knees, and began to weep. After a while he jumped up, ran to the wall and began to crawl up the ramp. Hugging the ground, he shouted, "Hey, soldier! A man's been buried. He's dying! And the other one's wounded! He needs a dressing. Soldier, man, countryman! Have a heart! Help me!"

He peered hopefully into the darkness, then he heard a firm voice with a non-Russian accent coming from over the edge of the pit.

"There's nothing I can do. It's an order. Don't come up, or I'll shoot!"

Exhausted, he crawled down through the mud. He glanced at Dummy lying nearby and at the red stain on his leg, then at Petka's fresh grave under the overhang. Like an automaton he bent down and picked up the six-pound nugget from the mud. He stared at it in bewilderment for a moment, then hurled it into the sand at Petka's grave. He crawled after the nugget, picked it up again and crawled further into the opening. He began to dig the nugget into the sand, right in the corner, hissing through his tears, "You wanted gold? Ah, Petka, my son! Did you get your gold? Dummy told you it was dangerous! Did you get your gold? Freedom? Bread? My poor boy! My poor boy! This is a memorial to you from me!" He flattened the place where he had buried the nugget with his palm, then he crawled alongside Dummy, lowered his head onto his knees, and dozed off into oblivion, sobbing and trembling.

"Home!" He opened his eyes at the sound of the soldier's voice from above. No stars were visible. The overcast sky had turned from gray to black and was pressing against the earth in an unbroken black blanket. Vikenty shook Dummy by the shoulder. He did not move. His face was icy to the touch.

Shivering with cold, hunger, and nervous exhaustion, Vikenty crawled out of the pit and staggered toward the small column of zeks from the other stopes. The men either knew or guessed what had happened, but they stood silent. The soldier could fire without warning if they talked; conversation in the ranks was not permitted. As he marched along with the others Vikenty caught a few glimpses of the soldier with the submachine gun looming up on his right, but he could not think. The men in the column stamped their frozen boots quickly along the dirt road, which was covered with a dusting of snow. Ahead, between the small white dunes, which were set with the dark shapes of pine trees, twinkled the lights of the camp.

With a feeling of doglike joy he opened the door of the long earthen hut. The hut's few small windows level with the ground were blocked with snow, and the gently sloping roof with its blackened chimney was also covered with a thick white blanket.

On either side of the narrow aisle stood two rows of two-tier bunks. Each bunk had a mattress stuffed with straw or grass and two coarse blankets. Pillows and sheets were not provided. The two electric lamps in the ceiling, covered with metal grills, were never switched on. Near the door was a large table made of a few roughly planed boards. A kerosene lamp burned on the table next to a big iron pot of soup. The line of weary men with mess tins grew rapidly. Their mouths were watering, and their eyes were fixed on the food.

All aspects of life in the hut were strictly controlled by the criminals. One of them was now standing by the pot ladling into each aluminum mess tin a little mush smelling of rotten potatoes and salt fish and handing out pieces of boiled salt fish and the bread ration of three hundred grams, for evening and morning. He gestured impatiently. "Next!" Two other thieves stood near the table, watching the serving of supper. They had already taken what they wanted, and what was left was divided up on a strictly equal basis. Everyone, both zeks and officers, knew this and accepted it as the only sensible means of resolving the complex question of sharing out the food.

No one tried to argue with the thieves. All three huts in the camp were full of criminals and politicals, and other small fry, who had ended up here for petty theft, for telling an anecdote, for embezzlement, even for homosexuality. It was easy to find your way into the camp, but there was no way out. The thieves' group, strongly organized and ruthless, held the whole hut in a vise of terror, but it guaranteed everyone minimum rations and some protection against one another. This form of authoritarian power was even welcomed by many of the prisoners, who were accustomed to subordinating themselves and playing the role of semihumans.

When he had obtained his bread and bowl of soup, Vikenty went straight to his bunk in the middle of the hut. He sat in the darkness and ate everything, licking the edges of the mess tin, which had not been washed for six months now. Then he lay down on his bunk, the bottom one, and covered his head. Petka's and Dummy's bunks were empty. The bottom bunks next to his were also empty. But replacements were expected soon. Usually a bunk left empty by the death of a prisoner was reoccupied within a week.

When the noise died down in the hut, he realized that the camp commandant, Major Sinichkin, had come in. He was short and wore the usual sheepskin coat, green quilted trousers, and felt boots. His narrow face was always freshly shaven and always shone with a peculiar kind of humor: for him everything that happened in the camp had a secret, humorous aspect. He never displayed exceptional cruelty toward the zeks, but he looked on them as human cattle, there to be exploited and liquidated.

Accompanied by two soldiers with submachine guns, he walked slowly along the aisle, glancing at the dark faces in the bunks with his usual absent gaze. He stopped by Vikenty's bunk and stood there for a while, as if trying to remember something. Then he asked softly, "What's happened to these two men. Escaped? Playing the hare?"

"No, Citizen Commandant." Vikenty jumped up and stood by his bunk in the approved manner. "They died."

"Died?" Sinichkin sounded genuinely amazed. "That's very sudden. Unusually so. Well, tell me the truth."

"One was buried in a roof fall. The other was wounded by a soldier. He died in the pit."

"Sounds like a real adventure story! Alexandre Dumas—read him?"

"No, Citizen Commandant," Vikenty answered quietly, looking at the floor.

"You must be quite illiterate!" Major Sinichkin shook his head. "But how did the soldier come to wound the other one? I don't understand."

"He climbed out of the pit to call for help to dig Petka out."

"What a funny fellow you are!" He looked round with a smile, as if expecting to see the others smiling too. But there were no smiles. "Surely he knew the soldier would shoot. He knew he must not leave the pit unless ordered to do so. That's my order! It's the law!"

"He wanted to save the man."

"Why? Is he any the worse off now than before?"

There was no answer. The soldiers accompanying the major held their submachine guns at the ready, listening uneasily to the deathly silence in the hut. Sinichkin sensed something too.

"I'll send out a burial squad right away. They'll bury the one that's in the open, but the one who's already buried can stay where he is. It's no one's fault if the roof collapsed on him."

He turned away abruptly and went toward the door. The soldiers followed him, aware of the hundreds of eyes filled with fear and hatred boring into their backs. After a few minutes' silence the subdued noise of conversation started up again. "That Sinitsa's a kind-hearted murderer. He won't lay a finger on you himself, but he drives you into your grave all right—they can't keep up with replacements!"

Vikenty lay with the blankets over his head, listening drowsily to the snatches of conversation. He was beginning to fall asleep when someone touched his leg. He opened his eyes. The short figure of Misha Osekin stood by the bunk.

"What do you want?" Vikenty asked huskily, with an inward shudder of revulsion.

"Do anything for you?" The shape simpered in a feminine voice.

"Beat it. I haven't got anything. I've eaten it all."

Misha moved on silently, along the bunks, offering his services for parts of the bread ration or some scraps of soup on the bottom of a mess tin. He soon managed to make a deal with somebody. They disappeared into the far corner of the hut, where Misha lived behind a screen of pine branches.

Misha had been the leader of a village club in the Pskov region. In the fall of forty-one the Germans had attacked by surprise and all the members of the Komsomol had left for the east or to join the partisans. Misha alone had remained, to look after his paralyzed mother. He could not leave her to die. The Germans had not bothered with him and he had worked abjectly in the fields with the other villagers. When the partisans came back, Misha expected liberation and the beginning of a new life.

But the partisans arrested him. The trial was held in his own village club, and although no one gave any evidence against him, Misha was sentenced to ten years in a camp for "betraying the motherland."

Finding himself in a camp in Kolyma, in a human jungle ruled by laws he had never encountered before, Misha immediately went to pieces; he fawned on everyone, accepting their insults in silence, but then weeping quietly in his bunk. With his short build, almost childlike face, clean skin and full figure, he quickly attracted the attention of the ruling group of thieves, at one of whose meetings a decision was taken determining the future of Misha Osekin. Since none of the inhabitants of the hut dreamed of ever seeing a real woman again, Misha was selected to play woman's noble role.

One night they tied his hands, gagged his mouth, and laid him on the table. There were former doctors in the hut, and, by the light of the kerosene lamp, Misha was neatly deprived of his prospects as a father.

Afterward he lay in his corner for several days, neither dead nor alive. But he did not have the strength of will to die. He began to live in his new capacity. Everyone agreed he played his role well. During the day, on the orders of the boss thieves, Misha stayed in the hut; he cleaned the bunks, washed the floor, and did all the other domestic work, even mending clothes and boots. He did everything except prepare the food—the thieves drew the line at that, and the soup was cooked by the sick or by the guards. But Misha's main work began at night and continued, with breaks, until morning. He gradually reconciled himself to his fate, offering himself in return for anything edible when hunger began to torment him.

A month had passed since they buried Dummy, and rumors spread though the camp that a delegation from the American Red Cross would soon arrive. It was March. There were still hard frosts, and almost every week a blizzard would blow up, burying the camp and its chimneys in six feet of snow. Work would then cease and the men would stay in the huts, taking turns digging trenches through the snow to the other huts and the kitchen. Without work life was even worse. There was no radio or newspapers; there was nothing except the bunks, the men on the bunks and their sick, mutilated souls. The news about the Red Cross delegation was received like the announcement of an imminent revolution. For days the men talked of nothing else.

One day at the beginning of April, Major Sinichkin's car stopped at the door of the hut. He emerged from the vehicle, chewing his thin lips contentedly, watched as two soldiers unloaded some cans, brushes, and sacks and carried them into the hut past the puzzled zeks.

Sinichkin followed them and gazed proprietorially around the hut. "Here you are, men," he said affably, "soap, paint, brushes. They're just bringing the linen! Wash and clean the hut. Put new sheets on the bunks. There's a celebratory dinner today to mark the arrival of the delegation from the American Red Cross. They'll be here tomorrow. In the morning, when the whole hut will be bright as a new penny, you're all to go into the forest to cut fir trees. Decorate all the walls and the whole yard with firs so that it looks pretty and smells good. And you'll get a good dinner today—I'm feeding you up for the inspection!" He guffawed and went back to his car.

The men rushed excitedly to the cans and bundles of linen. The dust rose in clouds in the hut as they swept out the ten years of dirt. They brushed down the cobwebs and dragged the mattresses out into the frost, colliding with one another in their excitement, their faces shining with delight. Two hours later the neat rows of snow-white bunks and the shining-clean wooden walls and floor looked more like a military summer camp than the last refuge of the prisoners of the Tishina gold mine. Toward dinner time a mobile kitchen arrived with two steaming coppers. This time the cook himself—one of the guards—served the food. The aroma of real meat borshch had a stupefying effect. In a funereal silence the whole hut lined up. The soldier sat between the coppers in his sheepskin coat and handed each man half a loaf of tasty wheat bread and ladled out a full mess tin of borshch. They could have as much of it as they wanted.

Vikenty could hardly prevent himself from pouring the whole mess tin of borshch straight down his throat. He sat on his bunk hastily gulping it down, and he hid half of the unexpected bread ration under the mattress. Then he joined the line again and received another helping of borshch. He broke out in a sweat as he forced himself to finish it. He looked around at the other zeks chomping away against a background din of spoons and belches.

They served only one helping of pearl-barley kasha. When both coppers had been emptied, the cook took the wheel of the supply vehicle and drove off.

The starved men reacted to the meal in various ways. Some lay back contentedly on the white linen, their beards turned upward, belching noisily as they digested the food. Others sat or lay about, holding their stomachs. By evening several men had died and a dozen had gone to the sickbay as a result of the heavy meal.

Vikenty had listened to Sinichkin's speech that morning with a feeling of alarm. And the feeling had stayed with him all day. The news of the expedition into the forest had shocked him by its patent stupidity and deceit. There were as many firs as anyone could want right outside the huts. Why go into the forest? His anxiety increased when he left the hut after the meal. "We haven't had a blizzard for some time now," he thought suddenly. On the horizon the edges of the pale-blue sky were covered with broken clouds—a wind was blowing somewhere. In the old days at sea, such clouds in the evening had indicated a typhoon by morning.

Why had Sinitsa decided to hide them? Was he afraid to show them to the Americans? That was understandable! But it wasn't worth it to him to bury the whole camp. Vikenty was already in his second year in the camp; he had a chance of getting out. With so much time already served! And now this! He was sure of his intuition. Sinitsa was sending the whole camp into the forest away from the visitors, who would meet with the soldiers. What would happen to the prisoners? Even if he didn't have them all shot in the forest, they might still die in a blizzard.

With sinking heart he watched some unfamiliar birds swoop out from behind the roofs and fly off almost hugging the ground. Pressure! That was how birds behaved when the barometer was falling. Should he tell Sinitsa? No, that would be fatal. It would cost Sinitsa nothing to kill a man, or rather, to have others kill him. All these years they had never sent the zeks out to work before a blizzard; the guard received a weather report from Magadan. What would happen now? Either Sinichkin had gone out of his mind or he had forgotten about the forecast. What should he do?

He went back to his bunk, exchanging nods on the way with a few of the men he knew best. He lay down and pulled the blanket over his head out of habit. The others suspected nothing!

Vikenty lay on the bunk thinking furiously, as he used to have to think on the bridge when his clarity of mind determined whether the ship would cope with the raging sea or go to the bottom. He turned over all the possible options, but could find no solution. Even in the summer of 1936, when his icebreaker *Arktika* had lost the screw off Cape Shmidt, in the eastern sector of the Arctic, even then he had not lost his presence of mind; he had brought the vessel out into the open sea under sail. And there had been other dangerous moments, but he had always been confident, sensing that fortune would leave him an outlet somewhere. Now for the first time he was in the grip of panic. He felt condemned to death.

The delegation's visit was an accident. Sinichkin's desire to clear everyone out of the way and clean up the camp was understandable. And now Vikenty was beginning to comprehend the final detail—the major had obviously been carried away by events and had forgotten about the weather forecast. In such weather, with fifteen degrees of frost, a blizzard meant quick death; even if you dug yourself into the snow, the treacherous frost would reach you and turn you into an icicle in half an hour.

He lay until morning and then went out into the yard with the others. They lined up in a festive mood: they had a walk to look forward to and a meeting with representatives of the American Red Cross. Sinichkin had promised they would be able to ask questions about the international situation.

Still undecided what to do, Vikenty glanced at the sky, a morbid anxiety in his eyes: in the west the cloud cover had increased, but the air had not grown warmer, as it usually did before a blizzard.

Ten soldiers with submachine guns stood in a chain alongside the column. "Atten . . . shun!" The voice of the officer commanding the detachment rang out at the head of the column. Without realizing what he was doing or why, Vikenty went behind the hut to the place where firewood for the stoves was always chopped. It was as if he was in a hypnotic trance, acting not according to the dictates of reason, but instinctively. He gave one last misty glance around him, picked up an axe, laid his left arm on the scarred tree stump, and chopped through his wrist. His left hand flew off and lay in the snow like a red pancake. Dark red blood was spurting from the stump of his left arm. He gripped it with his right hand and staggered out from behind the shed. He caught a glimpse of the astonished faces in the gray column of men, then crashed onto the snow.

"It's a bad sign!" the major thought irritably as he watched the column of prisoners and guards march away. "A bad sign!" He glanced angrily at the bloody zek lying in the snow and the medical orderly kneeling beside him. Two soldiers had quickly brushed away the strip of blood-stained snow.

"How is he—is he going to die or not?" he asked the medical orderly.

"No, Comrade Major, he should live. He's a strong fellow, although he's lost a lot of blood. What do you want done with him?"

"What can we do?" Sinichkin shrugged in perplexity, alarmed at the thought that such a strange incident might reach the ears of his enemies in the MVD Camps' Authority at Magadan. "Get him to the sickbay, and make sure he doesn't die. What was he up to there—chopping wood? Or did he do it on purpose?"

"On purpose?" The soldier rose to his feet and shook his head. "Hardly on purpose, Comrade Major! He'd have to be an animal!"

"Mmm. Well, put him in the soldiers' sickbay and feed him up so he doesn't die. I'll have a chat with him later!" He turned away abruptly and went toward the duty office. A telephone operator rushed out of the door to meet him and banged his head against the major's chin at a run. His teeth rattled.

"What's up with you! Lost your prick?" the major blurted, rubbing his bruised chin.

"Yessir, Comrade Major!" The soldier came to attention.

"What do you mean, 'Yessir'?"

"Yessir, lost my prick!" the terrified soldier gasped.

"To hell with you!" the major cursed. He had quite forgotten the joyful mood that had possessed him in recent days. He went into the duty office, picked up the receiver and broke into a smile.

"Yes, Comrade General, I hear you!"

"Sinichkin!" The voice of the general commanding the Authority came hoarsely from the receiver. "Is everything ready there, as I ordered? The huts must be sparkling, and keep the men away in the forest till evening. I'm sending some more soldiers today. They're experienced men, they'll know what to do. And two photographers are coming, from our paper. Well?"

"It's all right, Comrade General." Sinichkin spoke rapidly into the receiver. "Everything's going according to plan. Everything's ready. When can we expect them? In an hour? Yes, sir, I'll see to it all, Comrade General. Goodb . . . Thank you! All the best!"

An hour later two green, broad-wheeled, cross-country vehicles drew up in the camp, around which there had never been any need to put up wire. A group of well-built soldiers climbed out of the vehicles.

At noon the line of vehicles at last appeared; the general's green car was followed by a long, black ZIS-101 carrying the visitors. A closed truck

with a platoon of guards and MGB men brought up the rear of the caval-
cade. In the yard, near the camp office, stood Major Sinichkin and a few
soldiers; behind them, steam rose from the kitchen where a tasty dinner
was being prepared for the "prisoners" working in the pits two kilometers
away from the camp.

The major ran briskly up to the car, opened the door, and came rig-
idly to attention.

"Well, well, hello there, comrade!" the fat general bellowed affably.
He was wearing his general's overcoat with the astrakhan collar, a tall astrakhan hat, and felt boots. There was a single star on his epaulets. "Here
we are then, and we've brought our visitors from across the ocean. They
want to acquaint themselves with your establishment, with our system of
re-education!"

"I serve the Soviet Union!" Sinichkin rattled off as he saluted.

"Good man, you serve well!" The general reached out to shake his
hand. The major almost fell over with astonishment. It was the first time
he had shaken a general's hand. He gave the two women and two men a
look of curiosity and gratitude. They were wrapped up in fur coats and
hats and were listening attentively to the interpreter, an MGB captain
dressed in an expensive fur coat, a musquash cap, and felt boots. These
boots were cut in a distinctive big-city style: narrow, and of a beautiful
grayish color.

"Welcome, comrades ladies and gentlemen!" Sinichkin ran up to the
group and clicked his heels.

"Dis iss head of de kemp, Medjor Sinichkin," the interpreter quietly.

"Oh! Very good!" One of the men held out his hand. The major
shook it vigorously, then stepped back and listened attentively to his visitor's long speech.

"Mr. Cherston, the head of the delegation," the interpreter translated, "is glad to say hello to the major and all the soldiers in the camp on
behalf of the delegation. Now they would like to learn something about
the prisoners' routine and take a few photographs, if it's not prohibited.
The press of free America will be delighted to have some shots taken in
cold, remote Siberia."

"Yes, of course." The major waved his hand. "Please follow me!"

"But where are all the men?" The captain translated the questions of
the members of the delegation as they moved slowly down the central

aisle in hut No. 1, feeling the freshly laundered, crisply starched sheets in surprise.

"They're all at work just now. Their dinner has been taken to them. They'll be back this evening. With us, gentlemen, work is a matter of honor, valor, and heroism!" Sinichkin smiled radiantly at his own fluent utterance and noticed the general's ironic but approving glance.

"Mrs. Brady," the interpreter said, "is pleasantly surprised. She had heard a lot of critical reports about the living conditions of Soviet prisoners and suddenly—such a pleasant surprise! Of course you Bolsheviks, she says, have many enemies in the world who either do not know the true state of affairs or make a point of not knowing."

Mrs. Brady took a few photographs.

A minute later the delegation was already driving in a crosscountry vehicle toward the pits, where Petka, the former Vlasov man, was buried.

"Where is the gold mined here?" the other American, who had said nothing so far, asked in a puzzled voice.

"You'll soon see!" the general roared, without giving Sinichkin a chance to open his mouth. "Right here. The gold is mined in these pits in the sand. We don't build underground shafts because it's too dangerous for the men—sand is an unstable substance, gentlemen. Come with me, please!" He jumped out into the snow and offered his hand to one of the women.

The car had stopped on the side of a small hill. The visitors climbed out into the hard, crunchy snow. They were smiling happily, either because of the fresh frosty air or simply at the thought that they were at the very center of the Soviet hell and were now about to see things that their colleagues back home in the States had never even dreamed about.

From the hill they could see spread out below them like a cupped palm a broad valley, several square kilometers in size, hemmed in on all sides by identical hills with their growth of stunted firs and gray bushes. The white blanket of snow covering the valley was studded with yellowish mounds of sand, beyond which, they supposed, lay the pits.

The visitors were chatting animatedly about something and gesticulating toward the valley.

"They say this valley reminds them of a battlefield," the MGB captain said, "trenches and earthworks. They ask where we've brought them!"

"A battlefield! That's very witty!" MVD Major-General Vasily Zakharovich Nikonov gave the visitors a relaxed smile and invited them to follow him with a broad gesture. "In fact this is a battlefield—the battle is for the establishment of the material and technological base of communism in our country and for the re-education of man! We re-educate by labor. Nothing but labor, ladies and gentlemen! This way, please."

The group began to descend the hill toward the first trench. The sheepskin-coated soldier standing watch on a nearby mound came to attention and saluted. Vasily Zakharovich, his face red from the cold, waved affably at the soldier, and led the visitors to the edge of the trench. Far below three men in quilted clothing were wielding their spades.

"Is this where you mine the gold?" The second woman, Mrs. Morrison, was genuinely astonished. "I would like to see how they do it. If the general would be so kind?" The interpreter could hardly translate her throaty gurgling.

Sinichkin glanced at the general and made a sign. The soldier dropped his submachine gun and ran to help. The three gray-clad zeks received the men and women at the bottom of the pit. The three-yard descent down the steep ramp was accomplished successfully, and the visitors crowded round the iron sieve, under which a sprinkling of large and small nuggets and a layer of gold dust gleamed on the wide strip of tarpaulin. The husky well-fed prisoners, with only a day or two's stubble on their faces, smiled shyly at the visitors. The guards and the MGB men crowded around the top of the pit, and the two special correspondents from the MVD Authority, who looked like foreigners, clicked their cameras.

The visitors stood around the tarpaulin in silence, examining the precious metal that gleamed with an even, dull color.

"Can we touch?" asked Mr. Cherston, the head of the delegation. The general and the major nodded simultaneously. Cherston squatted down, tossed aside his black fur gloves, and buried his hands in the gold. He stared at the beautiful cold nuggets cupped in his hands and became oblivious to all else. His three companions also scooped up handfuls of nuggets and stood gazing at the gold as if they were bewitched. Silence reigned for several moments.

"Ahem," Vasily Zakharovich coughed. "Perhaps the visitors have some questions."

"Oh, yes, a lot of questions." Cherston gave a start and poured the gold back onto the tarpaulin. He stood up and smiled in embarrassment.

"I'm sorry, but I've never seen such wealth in all my life, if you don't count movies about Aladdin's cave! What riches you have, gentlemen. How much gold do you have here?"

"We, Mr. Cherston," Sinichkin answered, after his chief had nodded for him to go ahead, "we have enough of this gold to last a thousand years. And this is only one field! We have hundreds of fields like this," he said proudly, watching the visitors' faces. "We are the richest country in the world!"

"Oh, yes?" the second man asked, coming to himself after his contemplation of the gold. "But this wealth doesn't prevent your having a very low standard of living, gentlemen. We in America are convinced that you do not know how to use your wealth correctly."

"And you want to help us?" The captain hastily translated the general's mocking retort.

"Well, why shouldn't we help you?" Mrs. Brady asked.

"All right, ladies and gentlemen." Vasily Zakharovich yielded. "We're not against help, but unfortunately my rank does not permit me to decide such questions. They are decided only in Moscow, and anyway I think we'll manage to cope with our gold and with our other problems by ourselves. But thanks for the canned meat all the same. And for the military supplies and the rest of it. You certainly helped us out during the war. And in exchange we'll give you gold. We're not greedy people . . . Well, then, ladies and gentlemen." Nikonov had decided to change the subject. "There are three of our prisoners. Please question them, if you wish."

The three zeks came closer. Their clothes were old but still sound.

"Can I snap them?" Mrs. Morrison pushed her fur cap, which she had acquired in Moscow, onto the back of her head, and took her camera from its leather case.

"Of course!" Vasily Zakharovich smiled at her aimiably. "Take any pictures you want."

"Will one of them take off his jacket?" Mrs. Morrison asked, blushing. At a sign from Sinichkin one of the zeks stepped forward, quickly removed his quilted jacket, then his old but clean army shirt, and gray woolen undershirt. He stood in front of the group, smiling in embarrassment.

"What a man! What do you feed them on?" Mrs. Brady asked as she examined the gold miner's hairy chest and powerful muscles.

The other two zeks also stripped to the waist. The delighted visitors clicked their cameras, taking shots of each zek separately, then all three together, now holding their spades, now with handfuls of gold.

"They eat the same as we do, dear visitors," Vasily Zakharovich explained in a businesslike manner. "With us, the men come first. Our system of re-education is the most humane in the world. The guards are absolutely forbidden to lay their hands on the men. It's true, we do have some difficulty with provisions, after the destruction we suffered in the war, but we see that the prisoners working in the gold mines get the best of everything."

"Yes, of course, that's perfectly natural," Mr. Cherston nodded. "After all, they pay good money for it!"

"Exactly! Good money!" The general laughed cheerfully.

"And why are you here?" Mrs. Morrison asked one of the prisoners timidly.

The zek listened to the translation and blushed. He glanced anxiously at the officers, then said in a firm voice, "I collaborated with the fascist army against my own people."

"You must be sorry for what you did?" replied Mrs. Morrison.

"I'm very sorry about everything. Now I'm expiating my guilt. I have no complaints against anyone."

"And why are you here?" Mr. Cherston turned to one of the other zeks.

"I killed my wife, out of jealousy."

"Heavens! And you're in a camp for that? I suppose you were an honest man before the murder? And you killed her for innocent motives?"

"Of course! I loved her very much. I could not bear to see her with another man," the zek answered in a loud voice, squinting at the tense faces around him.

"How cruel your country is! How can you punish people this way for committing crimes of passion?" Mrs. Morrison exclaimed to the general.

"It can't be helped, dear visitor." The general shrugged his shoulders. "We have our laws. Human life is sacred for us. Taking somebody else's life carries a heavy penalty. In this respect our legislation is more humane than yours. In your country men have been known to murder as many people as they liked and have remained at liberty. We isolate such people and make them expiate their guilt through work. Our laws are socialist laws, more advanced than yours. It's quite possible, ladies and gentlemen, that the time will come when you will have to learn from us how to organize people and society . . . And now please follow me."

He held out his hand to the first of the soldiers forming a chain up the ramp. The three zeks quickly put their clothes back on, while the men boisterously hauled the two furiously blushing women out of the pit.

"What is it?" Sinichkin went anxiously to meet the signalman from the camp guard who was hurrying toward them. The official camp car had stopped a short distance away.

"Here, Comrade Major, it's urgent!" The soldier handed him a white message form. He was breathing heavily and had forgotten to salute.

"What's wrong, Major?" The general hurried up to him, sensing bad news.

"A blizzard!" The major handed him the message. His face as he looked at the general was just as white as the paper.

"Ladies and gentlemen!" Nikonov turned abruptly to the visitors. "We have received an emergency weather report. A heavy snowstorm is on the way. Please get back to the car immediately. We're returning to the camp. Quickly!"

The soldiers ran to the cars, dragging the bewildered visitors with them. On the way the interpreter explained to them hastily what a blizzard in Kolyma meant.

Sinichkin spoke into the face of one of the soldiers, making him recoil. "Tell everyone to get back inside the camp immediately! Immediately! At the double!"

"Send a truck for the men in the pits!" He shoved the signalman in the shoulder. "And have it here in fifteen minutes!"

The guard ran toward the pits and the signalman to the car, which disappeared with a roar over the top of the hill. Two men were left on the hillside—the general and Sinichkin. Nearby stood the general's car with an army driver at the wheel.

"Well, what happened to you? Fell asleep, eh?" Vasily Zakharovich said coldly, watching the major's pale face. "In our job you can't afford to miss anything, Comrade Sinichkin. Will you have time to get the men back?" General Nikonov continued his interrogation as he got into the rear of the car and sat down in the corner, gesturing for the major to sit beside him.

"I h-hope so!" Sinichkin answered hoarsely. Forgetting the general, he took the driver by the shoulder. "Back to the camp! And step on it!"

The car roared off along the bumpy frozen road. Just outside the camp the driver turned sharply aside to leave room for the crosscountry vehicle that was speeding toward them on its way to pick up the men from the work site, who were already running helter-skelter along the road toward the camp.

"Did you receive the forecast?" The general wiped his sweaty neck with his handkerchief. He was sitting on a chair in Sinichkin's office, staring into space past the major's white face.

"I forgot about the forecast, Comrade General, on account of the visitors arriving. I completely forgot!"

"Did you forget or was it the signalman?" Vasily Zakharovich stopped wiping his neck and squinted at Sinichkin.

"No, it wasn't the signalman. I forgot it myself." Sinichkin's chin dropped onto his chest. "The signalman put the forecast on my desk yesterday." He raised his head hopefully. "Er, Comrade General, did you know about it at the Authority?"

"Don't be ridiculous!" The general laughed. "What do we care about a blizzard? In Magadan a blizzard's nothing to worry about! You should have taken care of it. But you missed it. Over tired, eh?" He glanced sympathetically at the major, who immediately seemed to be diminished in stature. "Will you manage to save the soldiers? It can strike at any moment."

"The men!" Sinichkin said suddenly. He stood up and looked through the window. "The men!"

"What men?"

"I forgot about the zeks, all three huts, almost a hundred and fifty men!"

"Where've you got them, far away?" the general asked, paling slightly. It was on his orders that the men had been removed from the camp.

"They're cutting firs, a kilometer away. There's a hollow there, called Volchya Pad." Sinichkin leapt to the telephone, his face suddenly hard. "Pakhomov? Yes, shut up! Listen!" he shouted into the receiver. "How much rope is there in the camp? You've never counted it? I'll count your ribs for you, you blockhead! Get all the rope from the storehouse, all of it, anything that's narrow and will stretch, everything, even trouser belts. Understand? Get it all together and fall in with the men. All of them! We've got to make a line a kilometer long, to Volchya Pad, to the zeks. At once! Don't stop if the blizzard sets in. Keep going until you find them. Everyone must be suitably dressed. You'll answer to me with your head! That's all! Don't come back without the zeks—alive! Take a radio with you."

He banged the receiver down. Silence fell. Then he opened the door into the corridor. The duty soldier saluted.

"Where are the American visitors?" Sinichkin asked in an altered, vicious voice.

"Right here, sir!" the soldier mumbled.

"What do you mean, right here?" the major demanded.

"Sitting in the mess room, Comrade Major."

"Settle them in my room, quickly! And they'll be there several days, remember. The blizzard's going to be a long one. Move!"

The soldier vanished. The general's and the major's eyes met for a moment, then darted aside, like frightened birds that had collided in mid-air. Neither of them was now thinking about the zeks, but about himself. When prisoners died gradually, so that the arrival of new shipments enabled the camp to maintain the rate of extraction of the gold, then it all passed smoothly and normally, without any unpleasant consequences. But the death of the whole camp amounted to an Extraordinary Occurrence, for which someone would have to answer. Each knew he was to some degree responsible, but the major realized that Vasily Zakharovich had the power to put all the blame onto him, the subordinate.

Considering himself as good as dead and therefore more independent of the general, the major left him and went to his quarters, a room fifteen feet square where three extra beds were being hastily arranged. The visitors were sitting at the table, anxiously watching their busy hosts.

"I must apologize," Sinichkin said to them through the interpreter. "There's an unexpected blizzard on the way. You'll have to stay a few days with us. So make yourselves comfortable. Tell the interpreter what you would like to eat this evening and tomorrow," he concluded drily as he closed the door behind himself, silently cursing the foreigners.

Through the window he could see the soldiers who had been playing the part of zeks a half hour earlier and who were still sweating from their long-distance run. They were now hurriedly preparing for another run, disappearing beyond the buildings, carrying coils of rope and waterproof capes on their backs.

Sinichkin went out into the yard. He gazed sadly at the camp buildings, which were hardly visible under the blanket of snow, and then up at the sky. A gray, leaden mass of clouds had crept up from the south, quickly blotting out the last patches of blue sky. The air had become noticeably warmer. After a minute a warm south wind began to blow, making breathing difficult, as if a pillow was being pressed against his face. Another minute and snow was mixing with the wind. Clouds of snowflakes whirled and twisted in the air, as if they were performing a round dance at a New Year's party. The wind grew stronger every second. A minute later the camp was buried in darkness, through which the relentless wind drove a solid wall of snow. This kind of blizzard never caused any destruction, but it would blow long. Covering his face against the blinding snow, he gripped the line stretched across the yard and made it to the door. As he was shaking off the snow in the corridor he caught sight of the signalman's anxious face.

"Well?" Sinichkin asked bleakly. "What have you got to say for yourself, Private Kuzmenkov? You'll be court-martialed for this!"

"Yes, sir," the soldier answered quietly, standing motionless at attention. "But, Comrade Major, I did put the forecast on your desk as I usually do."

"And if I forgot about it, why didn't you remind me?"

"But you don't ever forget anything, Comrade Major. I've never had to remind you about anything before. I just waited and when I guessed you hadn't noticed the forecast, why I got on to Magadan again and they gave the blizzard warning. And I brought it out to you right away. Just as well I did, otherwise they'd all have been left in the field."

"Yes!" Sinichkin turned away. "It's just as well you did. All right, don't leave the set for a moment."

"It's begun!" he said as he entered his office.

The general nodded in silence.

"Can I count on your help, Vasily Zakharovich?" he asked hopefully. Outside the window at which he was standing swirled a black curtain of snow.

"I'll do all I can." The general shrugged, avoiding the major's eye.

"Comrade Major!" Signalman Kuzmenkov poked his head into the office. "The men have reported . . ."

"Well?"

"They've gotten to the zeks and started passing them back. The rope just reached. The blizzard's heavy. They've found a lot of the men and are looking for the others."

The signalman glanced at the two officers, then closed the door.

"Yes?" General Nikonov picked up the receiver and sank back in the deep armchair in his luxurious office, the office of the head of the Magadan Camps' Authority of the Glavdalstroi. He glanced through the window at the red roofs of the Magadan "skyscrapers"—the ten-story buildings that seemed to promise a big future for the capital of the Kolyma Territory.

"Vasya?" It was his wife's voice. "They're doing Ostrovsky's *Don't Get into Another Man's Sled* at the theater tonight . . . "

"I know, Klava," he interrupted her quietly. "But some very important business has come up. Go by yourself or with the girl. And don't be angry! I may have to stay here in my office until morning, until I get the call I'm waiting for . . . What business? Men's business! And you need to know even less about it than I know about your women's affairs. Be sensible! Don't call me and don't worry! That's all."

He replaced the receiver and sighed sadly as he thought of the large comfortable auditorium of the Magadan theater with its rows of red velvet seats and its buffet with beer and salmon and caviar sandwiches; the actors—exiles and prisoners—were just as good as in the Moscow theaters. But he had no time for the theater now.

He had returned to Magadan only that morning, having spent three days with Sinichkin on account of the blizzard. He had brought with him the American visitors, who were flying off to Moscow before dinner, on their way home. The representatives of the American Red Cross had obtained a wealth of impressions about the condition of Soviet prisoners at the Kolyma gold mines, about the great intelligence of the officers of the Soviet correctional system, and about the enormous deposits of gold in this icy land. They had even learned something about this harsh territory, with its blizzards and frosts.

They knew nothing about the fate of the inhabitants of the camp; they had even forgotten to ask about them. In general, the visit had passed off very well and had produced results: a half hour earlier, Nikonov had received calls from the Ministry of Internal Affairs, from the Glavdalstroi, and even from the Ministry of Foreign Affairs of the USSR, thanking him for having organized the foreigners' stay so well.

The twenty-five soldiers of the camp guard and the platoon that had accompanied Nikonov from the Authority had unreeled a kilometer of rope and had dragged back through the blizzard the majority of the zeks who had been "cutting firs." They had failed to find only ten men, who had been buried so deep in the snow that even after the blizzard a search had proved fruitless. He had simply had to write them off. The remaining one hundred and forty men had reached the camp. These one hundred and forty, suffering varying degrees of frostbite, had been sent to the hospital at Magadan, together with a few of the soldiers whose hands and feet were frostbitten. Under the circumstances it was a good outcome!

The camp was empty. Work had been temporarily halted. Men would be brought in immediately from other fields so that work could resume until the arrival of the replacements.

The general had ordered the major to be removed from his post and arrested. He was now awaiting his fate in the prison within the MVD building. Nikonov had simply observed the regulations! He was sorry for Sinichkin, and he was now waiting impatiently for the call from Moscow in reply to his coded report about what had happened. In this report the general had stressed Major Sinichkin's long and irreproachable record of service and had requested mitigation. General Nikonov was still sitting in his office when, two hours later, the expected call came.

"Vasily Zakharovich?" wheezed the familiar husky voice of the lieutenant-general commanding the Glavdalstroi.

"Yes sir, Comrade General." Nikonov drew himself up in the armchair.

"Well, I tried to help you in this matter." The voice sounded relaxed and friendly. "It's a bad business, you understand. I've just reported to Lavrenty Pavlovich. He's displeased. But he remembers you very well. He's grateful to you about the Americans."

"He is?" Vasily Zakharovich said excitedly. "Thank you very much, Comrade Lieutenant-General."

"Yes, but he said the camp commandant must be shot."

"Shot?"

"Yes, yes, shot! Bring the case before the court right away and have it all finished with tomorrow. We have more important things to worry about. Shall I send you a new camp commandant or will you appoint one yourself?"

"N-no, I have some capable officers. I'll choose someone. However, Comrade Lieutenant-General, if I can find some means of saving Sinichkin from the firing squad, what view will be taken there with you? Can we possibly appeal to Comrade Stalin for mercy?"

"What's the matter with you? You getting old or something?" The voice sounded harder now. "I thought of that myself. To go to Joseph Vissarionovich on such a trivial matter, and over Lavrenty Pavlovich's head into the bargain! What's this major to you anyway? . . . Well, all right, Vasily Zakharovich, for the sake of our old friendship! Let the court pronounce sentence—the death penalty—and then commute it to twenty-five years' imprisonment on your own authority. Inform me of the sentence officially. If I can't confirm your decision, at least I'll keep it under wraps for a while, and there it'll be forgotten. It'll all be smoothed over. And send him somewhere as a guard. He's our man after all! But Lavrenty Pavlovich's order is the law. You understand that."

"Well, thank you, Nikolai Sergeyevich. Thank you very much. You've made an old man happy," he muttered into the receiver. "I'm indebted to you."

"I know, I know you've got a soft heart!" laughed the general in Moscow. "So this matter's closed. When you come to Moscow, don't forget a nice barrel of my favorite brand . . . "

"Red and grainy, Nikolai Sergeyevich?" Nikonov smiled broadly into the receiver.

"Precisely! Well, till then! Send me the documents on this case."

"Yes, sir, Comrade Lieutenant-General, I'll get them off tomorrow. Thank you!"

Vasily Zakharovich stared at the telephone for a minute, then he stood up and went to the clothes hanger near the wall. With a groan he began to pull on his general's overcoat with the gray astrakhan collar. It was now only eight o'clock. So there was still time to catch the performance at the theater, the second act at least . . . *Don't Get into Another Man's Sled!* Hm . . .

None of the occupants of No. 1 hut had been able to get any sleep on the clean sheets. Ten men had been left behind in the snow, forever. In spring their bones would be found in the forest, gnawed by foxes. The others had been taken to the hospital. Some of them had died there, and the rest had been sent to the outside world, either for release or to a normal-regime camp. Major Sinichkin had lost his place on the social ladder of the inner world of Soviet reality. At last he had been given an opportunity to become more closely acquainted with the prisoners' mentality and way of life, farther north in Pevek.

When Vikenty returned from sickbay, the hut contained new people. He had spent nearly a month in bed, but his powerful constitution and the ample soldier's rations quickly put him back on his feet. His left arm had healed and now hung down his body in a long stump. He could not work and was made storekeeper of the provisions warehouse, where the food for the soldiers and the zeks was kept in two separate sections. After the affair of the blizzard, when he alone out of a hundred and fifty men had been left behind in the camp, he made up his mind to escape at the first opportunity, on foot, not to Magadan from which there was no way out except by sea, but to the west, to Yakutsk. It was a deadly dangerous undertaking, but it was better than waiting for death here on the edge of the world.

In the hut he tried to avoid all conflicts and intimate acquaintanceships. He would not argue with anyone about anything. Staring at the stump of his left arm, the history of which they already knew, the new zeks limited their interest in the storekeeper to curiosity, supposing that a man who had cut off his own hand could just as easily cut off another man's head.

He did become acquainted with his neighbor on the next bunk, a young Yakut named Ivan Kotov. Sometimes, he managed to bring back with him a piece of mutton fat, which Ivan ate at night under the blanket. Vikenty did not reveal his plans of escape to Ivan, instead he decided to wait and watch, in case the new man was simply a plant put in to find out what Vikenty was thinking.

After his appointment as storekeeper, the torment of starvation affected him more frequently. The constant contact with food—he only occasionally managed to take a piece of mutton fat from the huge barrel—reminded him that he never had enough to eat. If a single gram was discovered to be missing, they could shoot him without trial right there outside the hut. The new camp commandant had made that perfectly clear to him.

In the dim light of the hanging kerosene lamp he busied himself for hours in the warehouse, studying the various products there, their weight, quality, packaging, and method of distribution, seeking a means of getting something for himself without risking his life. But there was no loophole. It had all been carefully thought out. All the items were accurately weighed, to the gram, when they were issued either to the soldiers' kitchen or for the prisoners. The weighing always took place in the presence of the cooks and Pakhomov, the quartermaster sergeant.

He would sit for hours in the warehouse, swallowing his saliva in an effort to allay the hunger pains in his stomach, gazing helplessly at the abundance of food, and thinking . . . Then he would make a round of the barrels and boxes, prodding the mutton fat with his finger, plunging his hand into the barrel of pickled cucumbers for the soldiers. But he could not bring himself to remove a cucumber; he simply licked the brine carefully from his fingers. He began to dream about food at night and he slept badly. He sensed that the situation could drive him out of his mind.

One day in the fall, Vikenty was sitting on a block of wood in the middle of the refrigerated warehouse, staring with tired empty eyes at the sheep's carcass hanging directly in front of him; his mouth was watering. Suddenly a thought struck him. He stood up, took the carcass down from the hook, laid it on the scales, and checked the weight carefully: 45 kilos, 430 grams. A minute later he returned with a bucket of water, which he placed on the floor. He half filled a glass with water and, after a few moments' thought, splashed it over the carcass. The scales immediately registered 45 kilos, 480 grams. The water spread over the carcass, covering it with an invisible layer of ice. Wonderful! And no one would notice! Trembling with impatience he cut a piece of frozen meat and fat from the carcass, then another piece, until the scales again registered 45 kilos, 430 grams. Joyfully, he swallowed the meat straight down without chewing, then splashed some more water over the carcass.

During the next few days Vikenty gained experience at this method of obtaining food. He did it skillfully and unobtrusively, weighing out to the cooks meat covered with a transparent film of ice; no one could suspect a thing. Warned by his inner sense of caution, he tried to eat only enough meat to overcome the sharp pangs of hunger. He kept the same permanent blue rings under his eyes, but he could feel his body growing stronger. He must build up his strength for the crossing to Yakutiya. And he must choose himself a companion. He kept thinking about Ivan, feeding him at night and waiting. He was waiting for an opportunity, for some unusual event; and he was waiting for the onset of winter. He would not get far in summer, not with the swarms of midges and the bogs.

12

THE WOLVES

The storm struck as suddenly as an ocean squall. The settlement disappeared in a solid cloud of snow, in billions of flakes driven northward by the raging wind. The continuous howl of the wind over the roof of the earthen hut reminded Vikenty of the old familiar voice of rigging in a storm.

Everything had long since been ready for the escape. They had only been waiting for a blizzard. And it had come. Judging by the ferocity of the wind it would not last long. A blizzard is like a man: if it builds up gradually and does not rage too strongly, then it will blow for a week. As much as six feet of snow will pile up and bring all activity to a stop, locking everything living behind the protective walls where a stove drones in the corner, where it is warm, where life glimmers. If that condition between life and death can be called life.

But if the storm strikes suddenly, striving with a furious howl to sweep all from its path, piercing the door cracks, taking your breath away, then, like an outburst of rage in a man, it quickly dies down and moves on along its natural path . . . And woe to the man caught in the open in such a blizzard—he cannot see his own hand in the swirling snow. But the air loses its freezing bite and grows a little warmer.

Vikenty tugged Ivan's sleeve and moved closer to the corner of the squat wooden storehouse, behind which the figure of a soldier in a sheepskin coat was just visible. Not more than half a yard farther . . . He stood still, his heart beating wildly. It was difficult to keep his frozen eyelashes open. He clenched his fist, hating himself for the nervous trembling in his legs and sweat on his palm . . . Weakness! That was all he needed! The decision to leave had been taken long ago. Everything was ready. Delay now would be fatal. They had nothing to lose anyway. Every day several men died in the typhus epidemic that had broken out in spite of the winter cold. Here death seemed inevitable.

He stepped forward decisively, seized the bayonet jutting above the sheepskin coat with his one hand and yanked it hard toward himself. Taken unawares, the soldier fell face down in a snow drift and became stuck in it, writhing in the snow like a great gray lump.

"His mouth!" Vikenty hissed to Ivan. Ivan threw himself on the soldier, groped for his face in the snow, and with trembling hands began to stuff a gag made out of a foot bandage into his mouth. Vikenty tied the soldier's hands and dragged him to the wall. The door of the storehouse was only latched. They dragged the soldier into the dark passage and threw him into a corner, near a barrel of pickles.

While Ivan held the flashlight he had taken from the guard, Vikenty, who had been in charge of the storehouse for two years, stuffed two pairs of dog-skin boots, woolen army underwear, and wool-lined gloves into a tarpaulin sack.

The howl of the wind was quieter inside. The soldier sat tied in the corner, staring at them wide-eyed.

"I'll kill him!" Ivan's narrow eyes flashed angrily. He stepped toward the guard and pulled a knife from his belt.

"What for?" Vikenty stopped packing the things and straightened up, almost touching his head on the timbered ceiling of the hut. "Why kill him?"

"Why? They don't have pity on us!" The Yakut looked at him almost with hatred. Vikenty's heart faltered. It was a bad sign. The boy was proving to be weaker than he had thought.

"Leave him alone!" He glared at Ivan. "We came here for food and supplies. Will you do what I tell you? Or do I have to start explaining? You won't touch him! Listen, Ivan! One of us has got to be the boss, like we agreed. Otherwise, we'll die before we leave this hut. So get moving!"

The Yakut did not budge, but stood over the guard with the gleaming blade extended in his hand.

Vikenty stepped forward and jabbed him in the chest with the stump of his left arm. Ivan fell toward the door, leaped up, and stared wildly at the big man standing before him. Tears poured down his brown face, which was blackened by the dirt and the northern sun and covered with wisps of long black hair. Vikenty went up to him, grabbed him by the collar and pulled him forward. "What's wrong with you, Vanya? For God's sake! We agreed, didn't we? We've got to go. They may come any moment. Then we'd be shot on the spot. Well!" He shouted into Ivan's face. "Either you come or I'll kill you! Move!" He shoved Ivan toward the sack. "Take it. Or I'll finish you off, if that's what you want! It's up to you."

Ivan came to himself and hung his head submissively. He took the sack and stood by the door, avoiding Vikenty's furious eyes. Vikenty stood by the shelves, stuffing another sack with boxes of matches, cigarettes, old newspapers for kindling, canned meat and fish, and rusks. He then ripped a piece of tarpaulin from the shelf, rolled it up, and tied it with string. He used his right hand and the stump of his left arm deftly. He tossed the second sack to Ivan, took a sheep's carcass from a hook, threw it onto his shoulder, and moved to the door.

"There was a rifle here!" Ivan shouted above the storm into his face.

"To hell with it! We don't need it. Let's go! You lead." Vikenty pushed him forward.

The Yakut moved off into the blizzard. With the instinct of a native of the tundra he could follow the path under the layer of the snow. It led from the settlement up the side of a hill, beyond which, for several thousand kilometers to the north and west, lay the half-tundra, half-taiga region of eastern Siberia: endless hills and low mountains overgrown with stunted spruce, fir and cedar, and northern berry bushes. All was now hidden beneath the snow, and the tops of the sickly evergreen spruce were bent to the ground by the force of the wind.

Quilted trousers and jackets, old military caps with ear flaps pulled down over the forehead almost to the eyes, military boots with foot cloths, tarpaulin mittens—none of these saved them from the piercing wind. Bending under the weight of their loads, the two fugitives struggled up the hill. They had to make it to the top before the covering blizzard ended.

Finally, soaked with sweat and by the snow melting on their faces, they collapsed in the snow at the top of the hill under the dense foliage of an old spruce. The blizzard was still raging, but the wind was less strong under the tree. They lay for a long time, their faces pressed together.

"Why didn't you let me kill the red tab? Why did you leave the rifle?" Ivan tore the crust of snow from his eyelashes and saw before him the long handsome face of a saint. "You look just like Santa Claus!"

"No killing!" Vikenty raised himself on an elbow and stripped the icy crust from his face with his right hand. "We didn't harm the guard or take the rifle. That makes it a different crime. They won't come after us. They're going to think that without a rifle we'll die anyway. You're a real dope! If they send an aerosled they'll find us in no time. But this way we just left, and that's okay. They'll write us off as perished in the blizzard. That suits us and them . . . Look, the storm's dying down."

From under the branches of the tree the lights of the Tishina settlement seemed to be just below them. The blizzard had died as suddenly as it had begun. "How quiet it is!" Ivan murmured. "They don't call it 'Tishina'* for nothing! It's quiet as a graveyard."

"And a graveyard it is! Perhaps, we won't survive either," Vikenty answered, avoiding his friend's eyes, "but at least we're fighting for our lives. Hey, it's getting colder!"

He stood up and untied his pack.

"Quickly, Ivan, let's put on the soldiers' underwear and the rest of the things. Without the boots we'll be corpses inside an hour."

Ivan smiled quietly to himself. He was at home here, in the snow and frost. It was even colder in his native Yakutiya. But he silently obeyed.

Blue from the cold, they changed right there behind the spruce. The new woolen underwear tenderly embraced their bodies, filling them with a pleasant warmth. Now even the quilted clothing seemed less stiff and cold. When they had collected everything together, they started off westward, away from the cluster of earthen huts where each of them had left a piece of his life.

Ivan carried two packs: the food and other items. Vikenty carried the sheep's carcass on his back. It was attached to a rope that he slung over his shoulder and held in his right hand. The stumps of the carcass occasionally struck the snow, leaving a blurred trail.

After an hour they stopped to rest for a few minutes. Vikenty watched in silence as the Yakut stripped the bark from a short time-blackened spruce with his knife. He was making skis. He took four pieces of bark, each about eighteen inches long, and laid them on the snow with the slippery side downwards. He trimmed the edges and made a line of small holes along them. Then he threaded a thin string made of soft bark through the holes. He placed his feet on his skis and tied them to his

*Russian for silence.

boots with two skillfull movements. Then he helped his friend. Vikenty took one step and collapsed on the snow, cursing viciously.

"Slowly does it," Ivan laughed, "take your time. We won't make it on foot, that's for sure. Only on skis. You'll get used to it."

Vikenty took a few gliding steps and picked up the rhythm. He smiled to himself as he began to make better progress. His legs did not keep giving way and his stride grew longer. They started to move faster.

The Yakut glided along in front. He was humming something to himself, and he turned his happy face to Vikenty from time to time and waved. They kept moving all day, skirting the steep slopes, since climbing them took too much energy. They spent the night on the top of a small hill. They chose a tiny clearing between three firs, and in half an hour they had built a cozy shelter of branches. Vikenty broke off some more branches and stuck them in the snow around the shelter, while the Yakut set about building a fire. First he placed two thick damp branches parallel to each other and a little distance apart and scooped out a hole beneath them in the snow. He smiled at Vikenty. "For air!" He laid a few thinner and drier twigs over the hole, then a sheet of newspaper and more criss-cross layers of twigs. Finally he added a few layers of branches. He struck a match. The fire blazed up immediately, casting a red glow onto the faces of the two men and sending clouds of sparks into the air. The snow around the fire turned dark and began to melt. But beneath the fire it remained frozen.

"You're really good at that!" Vikenty blurted out delightedly.

"I learned it when I was a kid." Ivan squatted on his haunches and stretched his hands out to the fire. "I used to look after a herd of reindeer with my grandpa. I learned it from him. All us Yakuts know the tundra and we won't come to any harm as long as we've got a knife. Without a knife it's impossible."

"What about wolves?"

"There's none around here."

"Why not? There's wolves everywhere. Even in Australia! Are you trying to tell me there's none in Siberia?"

"This isn't Siberia. It's Yakutiya. The eastern part. There's no wolves here because the wolves always follow the other animals, the ones they eat. There's nothing for them to eat here."

"Why not?" Vikenty shivered suddenly.

"Because there isn't." The Yakut shook his head stubbornly. "This is a dead area. There's hardly anything living here. Maybe only a few squir- rels. Farther on toward the west there'll be a lot of squirrels, and arctic foxes, martens, brown foxes, hares, and then reindeer later. And wolves of course. You'll find them all to the north as well. But there's nothing here except you and me. We must cross this area quickly. I think it's a thousand kilometers at least."

They were silent for a while. A dead area!

Vikenty stuck some pieces of mutton on two sticks and put them to roast over the fire. Ivan got them two rusks each and poured some liquor into two wooden mugs that he had carved himself before the escape.

"Here, friend!" He squatted in the snow holding the skewered mut- ton in one hand and the mug of liquor in the other and gave Vikenty a friendly trusting look. "Let's drink. To our freedom, eh? We're free, aren't we? Well, tell me, are we free or not?" Tears suddenly filled his eyes and froze in white tricklets as they ran down his face.

"Yes, Vanya, we're free now," Vikenty answered thoughtfully. He was trying to put the distasteful words "a thousand kilometers" out of his mind. "There's no one guarding us now, we're free of the soldier boys. But they are just as much prisoners as we were. And they're not all ani- mals, just as we're not all human. Well, here's to our freedom, to the free- dom of our people, who have the rottenest luck of all—drink, Vanya!"

Ivan drained the cup. He sat for a moment with his eyes squeezed shut, then he wiped away his tears and smiled. "I like drinking, but it doesn't like me." He slipped the savory pieces of meat from the stick and swallowed them almost without chewing. "Tell me, Vikenty, there's no one to be afraid of now. When you cut your left hand off two years ago, was it an accident or not? You could do with another hand now!"

"No, Vanya, it would be no use. If I hadn't cut my hand off that time, I probably would have frozen to death at the felling area, like those others did. I had to sacrifice my hand to save my life. You know, there's a lizard like that. You tread on its tail and—snap!—the tail breaks off. The lizard leaves it under your foot and runs away. That's what I did, just like a lizard. You have to become a lizard if you want to survive."

"Were you scared when you cut if off?" Ivan had stopped chewing.

"Yes, I was scared. It's hard to remember what I was thinking. Could you have chopped yourself across the wrist with an axe?"

"With an axe!" He shook his head. "No, I couldn't. I would have died with all the others."

266

Vikenty nodded, "Yes, you would have died. But I didn't want to die. I'm stronger than other people, Vanya, because I understand more. A man's strength depends on his willpower, on his mind. Have you ever studied medicine?"

"No. I just went to a teacher-training school, not an institute. Of course, we did a bit of medicine."

"What did you learn?"

"Well, human anatomy, but not much about the brain."

"Pity. I've never been able to understand how you managed to drop that bust of Stalin. Did you do it on purpose?"

"No, Vikenty! How could I have! I loved and believed him, like everyone else. The republic inter-school athletic championship was being held at our school that year. My boys were doing well. Then during a training session I knocked the bust over and it smashed to pieces, almost as though it wanted to spite me. I remember I almost cried. I had dropped my dear leader . . . I picked up the pieces—the boys helped me—and we carried on as if nothing had happened . . . Next morning they arrested me. It wasn't my boys; one of the visitors informed on me."

"Did they beat you?" Vikenty asked gruffly. He remembered his own interrogation, which had lasted five days, and the difficult victory that had won him his life.

"No, they didn't." Ivan smiled and poked the ashes with a stick. "They placed a paper on the table and said, 'There's ten years in the camps for you. Sign it. It's for deliberately breaking the bust. If you don't sign, we'll think up crimes you haven't even heard about and make you sign. We'll beat you until you're dead or until you go before a firing squad!'"

"Were the investigators Russians?"

"Yes, Russians, and Yakuts as well, my own people! The International! I had another friend, the literature teacher from our school. I don't even know what he was arrested for. He was well-read. When they put the screws on him at the NKVD—you're a Japanese spy, confess everything—well, he kept calm and began to lie. He dictated and they wrote it all down. He invented a whole book, an adventure story. He put in various towns and people and names. He told me all this one night when we were waiting for it to get light . . . Yes, the next morning the Cheka men came and dragged him out of the cell straight onto the street and chased him away. I've never understood why. Perhaps they were ashamed because he'd lied to them a whole week. God knows. He was lucky. It's useful to be a literary man and know about history. But they sent me here. When I'd signed my sentence, the investigator—a major—said to me: 'You're a good man, Kotov. I'm sorry for you. Don't be angry at me. Anyone else would have dealt with you differently. Go to your camp, work hard. It's your North after all! It'll be easier for you than for the others. You'll be released one day and you'll come back here and start teaching physical culture again. But,' he said, 'don't drop any more busts of Comrade Stalin.' And I haven't, either!"

He paused and hung his head dejectedly. Then he asked, "What's the time, do you think?"

"About ten."

"How can you tell?"

"I'm a navigator, Vanya. I know the map of the sky." He nodded up at the light northern sky, glittering with a myriad stars. "You can find your way by the stars and tell the time. How many degrees of frost do you think we've got at the moment?"

"This is nothing!" Ivan shrugged and raked the ashes in the hole under the fire. "Not more than thirty degrees. Let's hope it stays this way. But it's winter; we can expect worse. Let's get some sleep, eh?"

Vikenty stood up, stretched his numbed legs, and followed Ivan into the shelter. They dragged in the two packs, and while Ivan arranged them among the branches to make pillows, Vikenty hauled in the sheep's carcass and pushed it underneath the branches, directly onto the snow. The thin beam of the flashlight illuminated the two men wriggling about on the two-foot layer of branches, and the branch walls, which filled the shelter with the intoxicating aroma of pine needles. They blocked the entrance with more branches, then lay down, snuggling close up against each other. Vikenty pulled up the piece of tarpaulin he had brought with him, and they began to feel warmer.

They lay in silence for a long time, listening. But there was nothing to hear. The silence was broken only by the sound of their breathing and the occasional crackle of the branches beneath them.

"You asleep?" Ivan whispered.

"No." As he answered Vikenty breathed out a cloud of steam that formed a layer of frost on Ivan's face.

"Do you think they've missed us yet in the camp?"

"Don't be a fool!" Vikenty wriggled irritably. "They'll have missed us as soon as the blizzard ended, and they've forgotten about us already. We no longer exist. They'll put ticks against our names in the register of arrivals and departures. They'll write us off—frozen to death in a blizzard. Later on, they'll pass our dossiers to the permanent archive in Moscow."

Ivan opened his eyes. "What do you mean 'permanent'?"

"Well, the archive of the dead. They'll keep the dossiers there for fifty years, or even longer."

"They keep dossiers on the dead? Why?"

"Who knows? It's the Soviet state that thinks all these things up. They keep those dossiers underground somewhere so that no one can get at them. They'll keep them until this whole era is ended. For the record, for history perhaps, for future generations."

"But why? What does Stalin want with future generations?"

"Who knows what he wants!" Vikenty swore obscenely. "But of course they must keep the dossiers. The entire history of man has been written from such records."

"Vikenty, do you think we're ever going to reach a settlement?"

"Yes, provided we keep up a good pace and use our heads. We're bound to."

"But what are we going to do if we reach the West? How are we going to live? And what if they catch us again?"

"We've got to get there first! Then we'll see. We can't let ourselves be caught. We've got to be smarter than they are and we've got to cross this dead zone alive."

"Yes!" Ivan breathed right into his ear. "I'll find my own people there, Yakuts. They'll hide us somewhere on a farm in the wilds. We'll herd reindeer, right up to the Arctic Ocean. We'll be safe in the tundra. There's no bosses there, and the herdsmen won't give us away."

"But how many years will we have to live in the tundra?" Vikenty asked doubtfully.

"All our lives, if need be. Until the government changes. Maybe it'll change, eh?"

"Maybe, Vanya, maybe. But it'll be hard for me to live my whole life in the tundra, waiting for that change. After a while, I'll probably move on, into the center. Well, go to sleep. We've sniffed freedom. Freedom, Ivan. A man is born with it . . . Only later is it taken away from him . . ." Vikenty was falling asleep and could hardly get the words out. Ivan was already snoring.

The sun hung over the horizon in a blue sky. It had no warmth but its light shown piercingly bright upon the snow. They kept their lids half closed to prevent their eyes watering too badly, but then after a while their lashes would freeze together, and they would have to pry off the crust of ice with their fingers. If they kept their eyes open they would water freely from the unbearably bright light and their eyeballs would begin to ache.

They had already crossed the steepest hills. But now even these lower ones seemed like insuperable mountains. Their legs felt leaden in the badly worn boots.

Vikenty went in front; slowly he would lift one foot with its tightly bound bark-ski, take a step, transfer his whole weight onto the front foot, then drag up the other. Another step forward, then another, thousands, millions of steps.

He stopped and turned to face Ivan. "Do you remember how many days we've been going?"

Ivan shook his head in silence. He glanced guiltily at Vikenty.

"It's four weeks now, Vanya!" Vikenty gave him a friendly prod in the shoulders with the stump of his left arm. "We've covered the worst part. See, the hills are coming to an end. Now we'll be descending into the plain. There must be people there."

Ivan nodded but still did not speak. He stood leaning on a thick gnarled stick, which had been trimmed into three short twigs at the end and made progress easier, especially on the slopes. Vikenty had a similar stick. With a practiced movement he threw off the single pack, which now contained only two boxes of matches and a little salt; all the food had been finished long ago. He laid the skeleton of the sheep down beside the pack. They had finished the meat about a week earlier. Now, during their brief halts and before sleeping at night, they boiled some finely chopped bones in a pot and drank the bouillon. They would glance regretfully at the bones—they had nothing to gnaw them with: blood oozed from their gums; their teeth were loose but by some miracle they stayed in place.

Ivan was not carrying a load. About a week earlier Vikenty had gone up to him, silently removed the pack and heaved it onto his own back. Ivan had said nothing. He felt sorry for his friend and ashamed of his own weakness, but he realized that he was growing weaker and was beginning to slow Vikenty's progress. They must keep moving forward.

Their provisions had proved insufficient. But it was too late to start feeling sorry about that; not that they wanted to—the food had been difficult enough to carry as it was.

Seeing Ivan's questioning look, Vikenty took the blessed scrap of tarpaulin from the pack and threw it on the ground. Ivan almost collapsed onto the tarpaulin. He said nothing for a while, leaning against Vikenty's shoulder, then he nudged his arm.

"Listen, Vikenty, we should . . ." He broke off.

Vikenty sat facing toward the west, picturing that longed-for life out there beyond the hills. He waited for Ivan to continue his thought, the same thought as he was thinking himself. There had been escapes from the camp before. The prisoners usually escaped in twos. They agreed beforehand, by casting lots, which of them was to die first so that the other could continue to the end. Although Vikenty and Ivan knew of that rule, they had avoided talking or even thinking about it; after all, they had had a good stock of food.

Vikenty laid his hand on Ivan's shoulder and squeezed it gently. "Look, Vanya, we've been friends and we'll stay friends until the end. That's the rule with seamen. You've been doing fine. Hang on a bit longer. There's not far to go. But let's cast lots, if you want. No one should feel a grudge when he's about to die."

He took off his cap and ran his fingers through his tangled mane of filthy hair and through his vast red beard, as if reflecting over something. He placed the cap on the snow in front of Ivan. "Put in five chips and write 'R.I.P.' on one of them!"

Ivan broke a twig into five pieces, scratched the letters on one of them and tossed them into the cap. "Will you draw first or shall I?" Vikenty asked quietly. Ivan said nothing.

"All right, I'll draw!" He turned his back to the cap. "Shake them up!"

Ivan shook the cap and replaced it on the snow. He watched indifferently as Vikenty lowered his hand slowly into the cap, his fingers spread, and pulled out the first chip.

"R.I.P." Vikenty read aloud. "You're in luck! Perhaps you'll make it." Ivan did not reply.

"Let's go." Vikenty stood up and helped Ivan to his feet. "Let's keep moving. We still have four days in hand, there's still a few bones left."

He walked on a little way, then looked back. Ivan had not moved from the spot. He was standing almost collapsed over the stick.

"What's the matter, Vanya, you giving up?" He smiled gently at the Yakut. "Let's go!"

"Vikenty!" Ivan raised his blackened face, which was streaked with frozen tears.

"I won't be able to kill you! Go on by yourself. I won't be able to kill you. I can't . . . I won't be able to touch you . . . I can't . . . eat another man . . . I'm weak . . . You're stronger than me. You must get through . . . go on alone . . . I'll sit down here . . . for a bit."

"Vanya!" Vikenty went up to the Yakut and hugged him. Ivan began to weep, clinging to Vikenty's chest, his shriveled body trembling.

"Come on, now," Vikenty muttered, holding him with his right arm while his left stump soothed the long black hair, straight as a mane. "Come on, you gymnast, you athlete. You mustn't think about dying. This is your own native territory, after all. We've got to keep going, Vanya, keep pressing ahead until our last breath. Hey, I'll sing you a sea shanty. I've forgotten the words, but it goes something like this:

> "There beyond the stormy weather
> Lies a land of calm and peace,
> Where the skies are cloudy never,
> Where the silence never ends."

He broke off. "See, I've forgotten the words. Anyway it goes on:

> "To that land the waves will carry
> Only those with strength and heart."*

"Do you hear, Ivan? Only those with strength and heart! Only the strong-hearted! Look at me! I've been through typhoons, I've been arrested, interrogated, I did ten years in a camp and got another five years, I lost my wife in a camp, my son is living somewhere with other people, an orphan, I lost my second wife . . . Do you hear, Vanya!" He was shouting into the Yakut's ear, wiping away his streaming tears with his sleeve. "Do you hear, my dear zek? Well, look at me! I'm alive! Vanya, this earth of ours is round and life is wonderful! If you go to paradise, there's no coming back. Never! It's for hundreds, thousands of years, for eternity! You'll never

*From "The Seafarer," by N. M. Yazykov.

come back from there. Look, the sun is shining down on us and calling us on. It makes no difference if you're weak. I can hardly stand up myself! But you're still a man!"

He took hold of the Yakut's head and turned his face toward him.

"And you mustn't be afraid to kill me. My life doesn't have any value for me any more. We can hold out for a few more days. And then, at night when I'm asleep, you cut me with the knife just here." He ran his fingers across his throat. "But make sure I'm asleep. It won't hurt if I'm asleep. I love my life, but I lost it to you. You won it fairly, and I'm ready to pay. Sometimes a moment comes when you have no choice . . . But you'll make it! There's no need for us both to die. No need! Well?"

The Yakut set his teeth and stepped forward determinedly, but he swayed and almost collapsed onto Vikenty's arm.

"Take your time. We'll go together." Vikenty pulled him close. "Hang onto my arm."

The two black figures, merging into a single shape, walked slowly toward the sunset. The four skis and two sticks left a blurred track in the snow. Even the most experienced hunter could not have read it.

Another week passed. For two days Vikenty had been almost carrying Ivan on his back. Every fifteen minutes he stopped to rest. As he heaved the Yakut to his feet after every halt he felt that he was himself hanging by a thread; his legs were trembling and buckling beneath him.

They spent that night on a hillside in a hole he had dug in the snow beneath the roots of a huge cedar. It was warmer in the snow. Vikenty fell into a deep sleep, only to awake suddenly as if from an electric shock. He gave Ivan a furtive frightened glance. Ivan was breathing weakly, his face buried in his friend's sleeve, his lips parted. So he was still alive. Vikenty was terrified by the thought of being left alone in that wilderness. Ivan could not kill him. He could no longer even hold a knife. He just had the strength to lift himself, grunting and groaning, fill his mouth with snow and cling to Vikenty's sleeve, dragging himself along with slow childlike steps.

The snow crackled. Vikenty tensed his whole body and listened. The sound came again. There was someone there. He pushed Ivan aside and crawled up out of the hole, through the narrow opening in the snow. Then he crawled back, seized the Yakut by the arm and dragged him out. The sun blinded him for a moment. When his sight returned, he rubbed his eyes and lifted Ivan by the shoulders. "Look, Vanya, life!"

Ivan lay motionless. He blinked his eyes to show that he was alive and could hear.

"Vanya, wolves! Look, wolves! We're out of the dead zone! Soon . . . soon we'll find people!"

Propping himself up on his elbows and with his spade-shaped beard thrust upward, Vikenty gazed at the three predators, which were now standing six feet away, warily examining the two strange beings that gave off an odor of dead flesh. These three wolves had broken away from their pack. Abandoning the age-old route, they had come farther south, where there was no food, but no danger either. They had long been aware of the presence of the two strange animals that reminded them of humans. They had been following them at a respectful distance, sniffing the unpleasant odor that neither allayed their hunger nor promised a tasty meal—living flesh smelled different.

Hunger was not yet tormenting this family of wolves. Fifty kilometers to the north, the direction from which they had come, wildlife was plentiful. These semihumans who had just crawled out of the snow did not stimulate the salivary glands that caused their muscles to grow hard and tense, ready to spring or give chase.

The wolves' thick, fluffy fur gleamed in the sunlight; their wary green eyes stared unblinkingly at the two men.

"Wolf! You, wolf!" Vikenty hissed softly. Holding the knife in his pocket against his body, with his right arm, he crawled toward the leader, which was standing just in front of him. He did not take his eyes from the wolf for an instant. The wolves jumped back in unison, without even baring their fangs.

"Hey, you, wolves! You running away?" he muttered hoarsely as he pulled the knife from its sheath. "Don't run away, my dears." He hurled the knife.

The steel flashed in the sunlight. The wounded beast somersaulted backward with a hoarse yelp and ran off after its fleeing companions, leaving the knife and a trail of blood in the snow.

Vikenty crawled to the place where the wolf had been standing and buried his face greedily in the bloody patches of snow. The still-warm blood melted in his mouth. Gulping down the pieces of red snow he crawled along the trail of blood. After ten yards it stopped. The wolves had gone.

Vikenty went back to Ivan and carefully raised the knife to his lips so that he could lick the blood from the dull steel. Ivan did not stir. Vikenty wiped the blood off with his finger and poked it into Ivan's mouth, feeling his thin rough tongue. Ivan swallowed convulsively and licked the blood from the finger. He half opened his eyes.

Vikenty leaned over him. "Tasty? It's wolf's blood. I almost killed one. We've arrived!"

Vikenty paused. Ivan's eyes told him to lean down closer. He dropped down beside him and put his ear to his mouth. He heard the Yakut whisper, as if in a dream, "I'm dying. Forgive me, my friend, that I didn't . . . didn't make it . . . with you . . . as we agreed . . . Go ahead . . . Eat me . . . Otherwise you won't make it . . . either. Go to Yaku . . . Yakutsk . . . my people there . . . tell them . . . everything."

Vikenty carried Ivan until evening. As dusk fell he collapsed in the snow, holding onto Ivan by the sleeve of his quilted jacket. Ivan was silent. When he had rested a little Vikenty rolled over to Ivan and looked into his face. His heart seemed to drop into an abyss and his eyes clouded over. Terror gripped his heart. He lay there beside his friend's corpse for a long time, his whole body trembling and his teeth chattering with cold and fear. Sensing that he was beginning to freeze, he pulled off Ivan's boots and cap and tossed them aside; he took the knife and cut off the ragged jacket and trousers and wrapped them around himself. He dug a hole in the snow, something like a grave, and lay down in it, pulling the corpse on top of him. He then scrapped a layer of snow over them both and fell into a deep sleep, hugging, out of habit, the icy body of Ivan Kotov in its woolen underwear.

The next morning he sat by Ivan's body, screwing up his eyes against the bright sun. He was numb with fatigue and hunger and felt that he was beginning to lose the will to live. This thought sent a wave of terror through his being and he began to shiver. He had never had such thoughts before, even in the most difficult moments of his life. For him the thought that the struggle was hopeless was the most terrible of all. And now he could feel these black thoughts taking root in his consciousness. Weightless, intangible, yet terrible in their simplicity. Ivan had not had sufficient will. He was younger and stronger but he had lacked the will. This was not Ivan any more. It was a frozen corpse, heavy as a tree trunk; Vikenty had dragged him along all the previous day and would continue to drag him as long as his own heart beat. Ivan would have done the same for him.

Ivan lay stretched out to his full length, as if he was training in a gymnasium, his serene, frost-white face staring up at the sky. A gentle icy breeze ruffled the strands of straight black hair on his forehead.

"So you've left me, Vanya," Vikenty muttered as he stared at the familiar face and thought over recent events. "And you were so close to making it . . . I don't like being alone. I feel so sad. You couldn't kill me! Perhaps my blood would have helped you survive. But you couldn't do it. Ah, man! You spared another's life and sacrificed your own. But perhaps you wouldn't have made it anyway . . . Perhaps . . . Perhaps I was wrong that time, in forty-one, when I stopped the thieves from staging an uprising and striking from the rear. Perhaps they would have been able to get to China or at least have died from a bullet . . . But now . . . how many years in the camp? It's as if I was born there—I can't remember anything different."

Vikenty fingered the knife in the leather sheath. He stood up and fell down again, almost losing consciousness. Everything spun before his eyes in a wild dance. He lay for several minutes, holding his head in his hands. Then he filled his mouth with lumps of snow and swallowed the life-giving water. Slowly, without making any sharp movements, he stood up. He laid the corpse on the piece of bark and slung the rope across his shoulder.

He walked on for a few more days, eating snow and covering three or four kilometers each day. He dragged Ivan's corpse behind him; it rustled as it slid over the snow. Toward evening, sensing that he was losing consciousness, he dug himself into the snow, using his last strength. He could not drag the corpse into the hole; he just managed to pull Ivan's rock-hard hand toward him before he lost consciousness. Ivan lay like a white log, his arm plunged into the snow, as if he was trying to reach his friend who was buried there, still alive.

After several hours Vikenty began slowly to come to his senses. He opened his eyes and gazed at the layer of snow above him. He saw the hand hanging down right in front of his face and shuddered at the thought that the man whose hand it was lay up there in the snow. Then he sank back into oblivion. His withered body still retained some heat under the warm clothing. Although his boots were badly worn, they were still in one piece, and the heavy beard which grew right up to his eyes protected his face from the frost. But his vital forces were almost exhausted.

He had forgotten how many days had passed since he had eaten the last rusk he had found in his pocket. Since then he had taken only water produced by melting snow in his mouth and occasionally some unfamiliar berries from frost-rimed bushes.

He lay in his snowy grave, a foot below the surface, not yet dead, but not alive either. He had begun to lose his reason. For a few seconds at a time the main centers of his cortex would function together and clear his mind. Then a wild terror would seize him. His heart would seem about to stop, but then his brain would switch off again, as if to preserve the last sparks of life still glowing within him.

His exhausted brain continued to work like the staff headquarters of a defeated army, gathering together the remnants of its forces, distributing its scant reserve of energy to the various parts of the body, sending to the memory only those scenes from the past stored in the secret recesses of the mind that had a positive potential and might somehow prolong the life of the organism. The brain was nursing itself, unwilling to rely any longer on a body that was already almost dead.

Without opening his eyes Vikenty smiled into his beard at some pleasant thought or other. Then he began to whisper, although he thought he was speaking out loud. "Mr. Headmaster? Er, er, excuse me, Comrade Blyukher? I find it difficult to understand you. What's the proletariat got to do with it? I'm simply a navigator . . . Eh? Comrade Spinoza! The ph-philosopher. No, no! What is it? The Roman Senate? Gaius Julius Caesar? How long will you abuse our patience, Catiline?"

He opened his eyes for a moment and stared with clouded eyes at the blackened hand hanging in front of his face. Then he slipped back into delirium.

"Ha, ha, ha! Philosophers! Marx? Karly Marly beardy wierdy! Your beard's nonsense. The wisdom of the people. Here they come, in columns. Who are you? Ah, scholars! Was it you who thought it all up? It's cold here. No, what the devil! I know that music! In banana-green Singapore, in a storm! Ah, Vertinsky, how beautifully you sing! The Russian nightingale! Katya, is that you? My dear Russian girl! The friend of my hard times . . . They arrested you too, then? You called me, didn't you? But of course you knew that . . . that . . . Valerik, where are you? Bom-m, bom-m! Moscow! This is Moscow calling! All the radio stations of the Soviet Union are operating. Well, Ivan Nikolayevich, forgive me for signing that paper. It was Izakson made me do it. I've never seen anything like it in my life! . . . Did they really shoot you? It's nothing, the merest trifle. Ready . . . fire! And it's all over. Farewell! But I'm alive, ha, ha! I'm a living, crawling reptile. He's beating me, Joseph is, but I'm alive, he's beating me again, but I'm alive again! Ha, ha! And I'll beat him too, right here in the temple, no, in the throat, with the edge . . . of my . . . p-palm . . ."

He raised his arm, as if about to strike someone, but then he came around for a moment. He rubbed his eyes with trembling fingers and pressed his hand to his face.

"No, no," he said in quite a loud voice, hearing himself as if from a distance, "is this really the end? I'm going out of my mind? What's Blyukher got to do with it? Who's hand is this? A-a-ah!" A terrible cry broke from his breast. "I'm frightened! There's no one here! There's no one anywhere! There's nothing living! Everything's dead. I want to live, I still want to live. As long as I don't lose my reason," he whispered. He made a tremendous mental effort not to fall back into the abyss where he had just been rambling deliriously and from which he felt he would never again be able to escape. "No, up there, it might be better . . . up there . . . I'm going out of my mind here . . . I want to eat."

He swallowed some snow, pushed away Ivan's hand, and began to struggle up out of the hole, brushing away the snow with wooden arms. He poked up his head and went rigid.

It was quite light: the night sky was burning and flashing with bright strips of fire; orange, blue, greenish, and pink strips, singly and in clusters, appeared in the northern part of the sky, quickly increased in length, reached their zenith and descended in an arc to the other side of the sky. It was like a child's kaleidoscope in the hands of a skillful manipulator. It seemed to Vikenty that someone gigantic and invisible, beyond the bounds of the earth, was creating and dissolving different pictures and patterns, changing them every few seconds.

It was the first time the Aurora Borealis had appeared during the entire six weeks since their escape. Kneeling with his hand resting on Ivan's back, he gazed at the sky as if bewitched, feasting his eyes on every explosion of light from the magnetic storm caused by solar radiation somewhere beyond the horizon. These northern lights were part of his being, part of his manly past, when he had lived among real people and had been a human being himself. He remembered the *Arktika* and its voyage from Archangel to Vladivostok along the Great Northern Route a year before his arrest.

Now the beacon that he had loved best in his life was shining down on him from the sky, a beacon that set his mind working again, refilled his heart with the desire to reach the shore. He must go on, he must get through; he must eat . . . nothing to eat . . . Eat . . . Ivan. He sat down in the snow near the corpse and hung his head.

"Forgive me, Vanya, forgive me," he whispered as he turned the corpse over onto its stomach so that he would not be able to see the face. Then he cut the underwear away from one of the legs and plunged the knife into the frozen flesh. He cut off a piece of flesh and tried to open his mouth. He had to force the meat between his lips. He sat for a minute without swallowing, fighting down the feeling of nausea caused by his hunger and the thought of the human flesh. The meat began to melt in his mouth. He gulped down his saliva convulsively, his body shuddering from the feeling of insatiable hunger. His whole being seemed to cry out: "Swallow it, swallow it! Quickly!"

He swallowed without chewing. The piece of meat almost stuck in his shrunken gullet. He had lost half of his teeth and the others were loose in his gums. He could not chew. He had forgotten about the lights, about the cold, about the whole world. All he could see was the greenish-red flesh of the leg. He began to cut the meat off rapidly in small pieces. He melted them in his mouth, then swallowed. He kept peering about, like a predator as it tears its prey to pieces. Almost fainting from the sharp pain in his stomach, he collapsed face down onto the corpse and lay there for a long time. As he came to himself he tried to calm the frenzied pounding of his heart, which had suddenly revived. There was a roaring in his temples. With his glove he wiped away the sweat that was streaming down his face. He lay motionless, listening like a doctor to what was happening inside his body. The body would now determine whether the brain survived.

Gradually, the pain in his stomach eased. He rolled over onto his back and gazed tranquilly at the starry sky. He felt sure that the danger of starving to death had passed. "Forgive me, Vanya," he whispered again and turned his head, which was resting on the corpse's back. The left leg, from which he had stripped the flesh, now looked like a thin white stick.

How many days had he been walking? How many? He could not remember. But his many years' experience of journeying on land and sea told him that he had crossed the larger part of the snowy desert, that he would find people and life in these parts. But he must not fall asleep. He must keep going until sunrise.

Cautiously, as if he were afraid of falling apart, he got up from the ground. Tears of joy came to his eyes as he realized that his legs no longer trembled with weakness and he could stand in the snow without swaying.

He tied on his skis and attached the corpse securely to the other pair. Then he leaned forward and moved off down the hillside. But after a few minutes he had to stop for breath; his weakened system could not cope with the double burden. He stood over Ivan for a moment, then mechanically, his mind a blank, he took out the knife. He squatted down and gazed at his friend's face for a long time. Then he turned the corpse over onto its stomach, propped the stump of his left arm against the back of the head, and struck at the neck with the heavy knife. The head rolled away a few inches and lay on its side. The face still had its former serene expression. He rolled the body over again, cut away the underwear and plunged the blade into the stomach. He worked with the knife, cutting out the innards in pieces, until at last the corpse had acquired an astonishing resemblance to the sheep's carcass he had carried on his back for the first three weeks of the journey. He buried the head and the innards in the snow and set off, dragging the headless, disembowelled body behind him. The going was easier now.

For the next several days he walked only while the sun was up. Soon he was carrying the skeleton with its remnants of skin and flesh on his back. That was now easier than dragging Ivan's remains over the snow, and the flesh was less likely to catch on bushes and lumps of ice and be torn off. He stopped every half hour and swallowed a few scraps of meat. Then he heaved the skeleton back onto his shoulders and pressed ahead.

During one of his halts he carefully scraped away the last scraps of flesh from the stripped bones, cut them off and buried them in the snow. His burden was gradually growing lighter.

He no longer saw in his mind's eye those movie stills from the countless scenes of his life. The range of his thoughts had narrowed to a minimum: the snow and frost, the sky, sun and stars, the half-skeleton with the remnants of flesh on his back, the clumps of firs with their thick branches facing south, the occasional pink cloud in the west, toward which he was heading and where safety awaited him. He had long since forgotten about politics, about everything that had tormented him in the past. Even the image of the hateful Georgian did not disturb his almost petrified mind, every cell of which was now permeated with a single biological imperative: survive.

The day came when he could walk almost unencumbered, carrying only one arm which he had tied around his neck with a piece of twine; this way it was easy to cut off the pieces of meat without having to lift the twine over his head. Every movement required a great effort.

He sat with his back against the trunk of a cedar, his face turned up into the slanting rays of the sun, which was shining straight into his squinting eyes. He was smiling quietly at something as he hugged the remains of his food to his chest. Since the time when he saw the northern lights he had had no more periods of delirium; instead he sometimes drifted into oblivion, breathing and walking without a thought in his head.

He was now smiling at the unexpectedly pleasant sounds penetrating into his consciousness, sounds that reminded him of a dog barking. He knew that his reason would not give way again, that he would experience no more delirium or hallucinations, but that noise . . . it sounded astonishingly like a dog barking.

He opened his eyes and immediately closed them again. He gulped in the frosty air and tried instinctively to calm the pounding of his heart. Three feet away from him stood an enormous dog with shaggy, yellow-white fur. It stared at him for a few seconds, then took an indecisive step forward.

Vikenty pulled the long knife slowly from his belt. He could see the dog's muzzle right in front of him. With a feeling of impotent rage he gripped the knife in his feeble fingers; he did not have the strength to lift it. The dog came right up close and examined the strange man without hostility; it sensed that he was not dangerous. It had stopped barking. Perhaps he had imagined it? He shifted his position, the hand with the knife resting on the snow, and slowly raised his eyes.

The dog could not hold his gaze. It turned away and loped off down the hill toward a scrubby wood. Vikentry opened his mouth, but no sound emerged, only a husky muffled whisper: "Where are you going? Come back! I'm still alive! Ali-i-ve!" He burst into tears and buried his face on his knees.

He started at a strange sound. Was he delirious again? It wasn't a dog barking. It was the sound of a sled crunching over the snow, and human voices. Trembling feverishly, he clawed the ice from his lashes. A dog team was heading up the hill straight toward him. He could make out human figures in the sled. The big dog with the yellow-white fur was running ahead of the team. Breathing hoarsely and with his eyes bulging with tension, he got to his knees and began digging frenziedly at the snow with his knife. Hardly realizing what he was doing or why, he shoved the arm bone into the hole and filled it in with snow . . .

The sled came to a halt near the tree. The four pair of huskies lay down in the snow, whining and sniffing in the odor. The yellow-white dog sat down next to him, shifting its gaze back and forth from its master to the man it had found a half hour earlier.

An elderly, thickset Yakut jumped down onto the snow. He was wearing boots trimmed with reddish-yellow fur and a jacket and trousers made of reindeer hide with the hair outside. A reindeer-hide hat covered the whole of his head and his shoulders. A pair of wary narrow eyes peered out through the slits in the hat. Wrinkles could be seen on his brown, deeply tanned face. A woman and a boy of about ten were standing in the sled. They were wearing similar clothes. They were gazing fearfully at the lifeless body lying under the cedar.

The old man came closer. He bent down on one knee and ran his fur-gloved hand quickly over the body. Then he picked him up and carried him to the sled. He wrapped him in a reindeer skin. The woman and the boy sat down on the edges of the sled, staring timidly at the bundle and at the beard projecting from it. The old man threw an ancient rifle across his shoulder and jumped nimbly into the sled. He looked around. The dog was standing under the cedar, snuffling at the snow. The Yakut went over to the place and dug the snow away. He examined the stripped human bone for a few minutes, keeping his back toward his wife and son. Then he reburied the bone and stamped down the snow.

The Yakut picked up his long stick, and the dogs whisked the sled away down the hillside. When they reached the old sled trail he stopped the team and took a bottle, containing a clear liquid, from underneath the skin. He bent over the man whose deathly pale face was just visible under the long red beard; he looked dead. The old man pulled the cork and poured a little of the liquid into his palm. He parted the stranger's tightly closed lips and poured the liquid into his mouth. He replaced the bottle and said to his wife in Yakut, "He's still alive. We're going to the far camp and we'll live there for a while. No one must know about this man. Give him some antler juice in half an hour. I want to have a talk with him. He must be kept alive."

The woman nodded silently. The old man turned to his son: "Feed the dogs! We're going to be traveling fast and far." The boy threw the dogs some coarsely chopped dried fish, then climbed back into the sled.

The woman gave her husband a questioning look. "What do you think?"

"It's bad!" The old man turned his tanned face toward her. He pushed his hat off onto his shoulders, uncovering his straight, black, gray-flecked hair. "He's a Russian."

The woman waited for him to continue.

The old man glanced at his son. "You forget everything you saw and heard!" The boy said nothing.

"He wasn't alone. There was one of our people with him."

"A Yakut? He killed him?" the woman asked. "What makes you think that?"

"I don't think it, I know it! Back there, near the cedar, there was a piece of bark that someone had made into a ski. The way we do it. A Russian wouldn't have made it that way. The Yakut didn't get this far. He was left behind in the taiga."

"He killed him?" she asked in the same indifferent voice.

"I don't know if he killed him or not. But he ate him. He's a strong man. I'll have a talk with him. We'll go to the far camp, then I'll come back by myself. I want to go back over their trail . . . Hup!" he shouted at the dogs. The rested animals pulled at the traces in unison and hauled the sled off on the snowy, hardly perceptible road.

13

LIFE!

The spacious yaranga was all but dark inside. In the center stood a rough-hewn pole, from the top of which the reindeer-hide walls sloped down in a pyramid. The wind was howling outside the walls, but inside it was warm. The floor was spread with a thick layer of skins. In the middle, on a low tree stump near the pole, a large kerosene lamp stood smoking, throwing a dim light onto the faces of the occupants. The elderly Yakut, dressed in hide trousers, high boots, and a black shirt, was sitting cross-legged, holding a wooden cup of strong-smelling green tea. The woman, similarly dressed, came into the yaranga, placed an iron pot of boiled reindeer-meat, some black bread, salt, and an aluminum flask of liquor in front of the man, and then sat down beside him. The boy, who had been turning the pages of a book, near the lamp, joined them.

The man poured some liquor into an iron mug, drank it off, poured out some more, and gave the mug to the woman. The son drank last. Then they ate the meat, picking the pieces from the pot with their fingers, sprinkling them with salt. They ate hardly any bread. Bread was brought from the town, infrequently, and they did without it. They threw the bones to the dogs, which were lying by the entrance to the yaranga, their eyes fixed on the meat.

"Look!" The woman stopped eating. "He's coming around!"

The Yakut glanced at the corner where a man was lying on some skins. Two deep-sunk eyes glittered back at him. He took another pot, containing meat broth, and sat down beside the man. Spooning up the broth, he poured a little into the man's half-open mouth. The man gulped it down and shuddered; he asked, barely audibly: "Who are you?

Where am I?"

"You're in my yaranga," the Yakut answered in pure Russian. "This is the camp quarters of a large reindeer-raising sovkhoz, about five hundred kilometers north of Yakutsk. I'm the herdsman and veterinarian. You're a convict? From Magadan?"

The man nodded and asked in a firmer voice: "How do you know? Where did you find me? How long have I been here?"

"I found you fifty kilometers from here. My dog, Nord, found you. You owe him your life. Don't be surprised at my Russian!" His face spread even wider in a smile. "A lot of us speak Russian now. I lived in Yakutsk for many years, I studied and worked there. What was the name of the Yakut you ate?"

"Kotov, Ivan Kotov. I didn't kill him!"

"I know. I know a lot about you and him. When I brought you here, my wife took care of you. You were already dying. You would have died that evening for sure, if the dog hadn't found you. I found a hand in the snow and your knife and a ski, made out of bark by your Kotov. I know that name. His parents live on the next sovkhoz, three hundred kilometers from here, toward Yakutsk. He was arrested at school where he was teaching . . ."

The man listened in silence, then he asked, "Are you going to turn me in?"

"No," the Yakut shook his head, "you tried to save a Yakut. You carried him on your back, alive at first, then dead. I followed your tracks eastward for two hundred kilometers . . ." He paused and half turned toward his son and wife who stood up and went out through the door, which was hung with a skin, into the other yaranga.

"I found everything!" He looked intently at the man. "Is it hard for you to listen? We can put off our talk."

"No," the Russian breathed with an effort, "please go on . . ."

"I found everything." The Yakut stood up and left the yaranga. After a minute he came back carrying a small hide bag. "His head's in here! I left his innards there, in the taiga, where you buried them. But I took the head!" He pulled a round object out of the bag by the hair. Ivan's face gleamed in the lamplight.

The man on the furs groaned, bent almost double, his mouth gaping convulsively, and vomited the contents of his stomach straight onto the skin. Clutching at the floor with a hoarse groan, in time with the contractions of his stomach, he brought the rest of the gastric mucous up. Then he fell back, his whole body trembling, staring vacantly in front of him.

The Yakut pulled the soiled skin from under him, flung it outside the door, where the blizzard was raging, sat down again beside the man and poured some liquor into a mug: "Drink this, it'll clean your stomach and your conscience. You can drink now. For six weeks my wife and I have been feeding you on antler juice and meat broth. You won't die. Now you can drink and eat a little. Here's a piece of bread. You'd better not eat any meat for the time being . . ."

He watched the man greedily swallow the liquor and a few pieces of black bread, then fall back and close his eyes.

"According to our northern laws, you saved a man. If you had not reached here, we would never have found out about him. I'll take his head to his yaranga when the storm dies down."

He shoved Ivan's head into the bag, went out, came back again, sat down and smiled gently: "I buried your knife along with his innards, but his head and hand will be buried in his camp, where he was born."

He was quiet for a while.

"We're not Russians, we're Yakuts. We've adopted your laws and we obey them, but we've kept our own too, our old laws, subject to no one. It's in our blood, ineradicable. Look at me—I went to a Russian-Yakut school, studied everything in Russian. I've even read all of Pushkin in Russian, and I've been to Moscow on vacation. I was in the Komsomol for many years, where I carried out the decisions of the Yakut Republic Committee. They dragged me into the Party . . . I've been reckoned a communist for God knows how long. But I've no use for that kind of thing—I love this yaranga, this meat, this snowstorm. We had all this long before the communists arrived."

"You're a communist?" Fear showed in the Russian's eyes.

"Yes," the Yakut smiled, "and Party organizer for the sovkhoz. You're in luck. I won't turn you in. Anybody else might have taken you to the central farm. Not to turn you in, but because it's forbidden to conceal escaped convicts in your home."

"You're going to take his head to his parents?" the guest asked, moving his tongue with difficulty. "Then they'll find me . . ."

"No, no one will give you away while you are here."

"But . . . I won't be able to stay here forever."

"No, you won't. We'll talk about that later."

They fell silent.

"You . . . do you know anything, about what's happening in the world?"

"In the world it's the same as in the tundra—sometimes a blizzard, sometimes sunshine. They say Stalin's dead."

"Wha-at?" The Russian raised himself on the skin, then fell back weakly, covered his face with his hands and began to weep silently, without tears.

"You're sorry?" The Yakut looked at him in amazement. The narrow eyes flashed evily in his weather-beaten face. "Many of our Yakuts are sorry. But it's understandable for them. They're illiterate, ignorant people, but you . . . surely you're not illiterate? Who are you?"

"N-no, forgive me," the Russian groaned. "There's nothing for me to feel sorry about. That man destroyed me, stole my life."

"Not only *your* life," the Yakut answered thoughtfully. "But now he's dead himself."

"Are you sure?" the Russian turned to face the Yakut. "Perhaps it's a mistake?"

"What mistake! He's dead. As dead as can be. I've already held a meeting at the sovkhoz. It was two weeks before my dog found you."

"Two weeks? I think it was then that I saw the northern lights . . ."

"Yes?" The old man leaned toward him, trying to make out the eyes in their sockets, which were overhung by thick hair. "You have a good memory. The lights were seen on the very day Yakutsk informed us of his death. The lights brought you luck, don't you think?"

"Yes, good luck." He was silent for a while, then added, "And grief too. On that evening I began to eat human flesh."

"You were right." The old man shrugged his shoulders and poured some more liquor into the mugs. "You had no alternative. You couldn't help him at all, but his corpse helped you. And now we can bury his remains. Drink some more, you can drink now, and eat a bit more bread. No meat for the time being, it might make you vomit again. Only broth. Get some sleep. I have to go. My wife will prepare some hot water later, and I'll give you a wash. It's time for you to return to life . . . You lay there more than a month, without coming around. All that's behind you now."

In a few days Vikenty could raise himself on his elbow, to make it easier to watch what was going on in the yarânga. He was wearing fur trousers and a jacket, with the fur next to his skin. It felt strange but gave him great freedom of movement. After the long years of wearing stiff quilted clothing it seemed that his body was constantly filled with a kind of pleasant lassitude . . . He lay for days on end, motionless in his corner, on the bed of reindeer skins. Beside him, on a piece of tin, there was almost always a kerosene lamp burning, and a few books that the family shared with their guest: a Russian-Yakut primer published by the Yakut Ministry of Education; a book, published in the middle of the last century, yellowed with age, written in Russian with old-fashioned spelling and the title page missing; it contained a detailed and thrilling description of the campaigns of Yerofei Khabarov and Semen Dezhnev, who had advanced the possessions of the then mighty Russian empire to the shores of the Pacific; a red book, scuffed but still in one piece—*Biography of Comrade J. Stalin*, Pushkin's *Eugene Onegin*, a *Veterinary Manual for the Treatment of Reindeer*, which the Yakut never used, a *Short Course in the History of the All-Union Communist Party of Bolsheviks* published in 1937 . . . There were a few other books, with the title pages torn out, which had found their way, nobody knew when or how, to this remote region.

When he felt that a little of his strength was returning, he began to read. With the wick turned up a little, he would raise himself on his elbow, prop up the bundle of skins that served as a pillow, and read everything voraciously and without discrimination, suddenly discovering that there were books in the world that he had not read since leaving the Novosibirsk high school, in 1917—apart from the classics of Marxism and Leninism, which he had had to re-read in 1931. At that time, on his return to his beloved Russia after many years at sea, he had been arrested in Vladivostok and had spent two weeks locked up in the Marxism-Leninism reading room in the GPU headquarters, waiting for his fate to be decided.

Now he was delighted, like a child, to be able to open a book, any book at all, and read something about other people and times. Only the biography of Stalin was left aside—he could neither touch it nor throw it away, something held him back, yet sometimes he wanted to glance at that red cover. The presence of the book hypnotized him. Sometimes he could not take his eyes from it, and then he would begin to conjure up the moustached face again, and behind it, in a long line, the many other faces that had passed through his life in the last twenty years.

Reading tired him quickly, and then he would fall asleep. He slept for long periods, whimpering as he dreamed. In the next room they listened to the groans from the corner, but they were not alarmed—the man had survived.

More and more frequently he would feel hungry when he awoke—the nausea had passed. It was difficult to chew meat in his toothless mouth, but he could drink meat broth and even soak in it the dry crusts that the Yakut brought him.

The whole family called him simply "Russ"; he did not know their names either but, to his astonishment, this did not prevent full and friendly mutual understanding between hosts and guest. Sometimes he caught one of them giving him a curious look, or a smile, and he would smile in reply, realizing that it had been years since he had smiled like that.

For days on end the Yakut would be off somewhere in the tundra. Sometimes his wife and son would disappear too. And then Vikenty would be left alone, feeling the fear of loneliness. Once, when the yaranga was deserted and the blizzard was howling outside the hide door, he waited for them for three days, then panicked: straining his withered body he crawled to the hanging covering the entrance to the other half of the yaranga; for a long time he examined the simple furnishings of his hosts' half of the dwelling, then he crawled to the outer door, buried his face in the skin, holding his head in his hands, and lay for several hours, fighting the waves of terror that flooded his weakened spirit. His loneliness, the roar and howl of the wind six inches from his face, on the other side of the skin, and his physical infirmity reduced him to a state of despair; he wanted to see, to feel next to him something, anything, living. So, when the hanging shook, and the shaggy, yellow-white shape of Nord slipped silently into the yaranga, bringing with it the howl of the wind and the cold, he stretched out his hand to the dog, seized its powerful paw, pulled it to him and buried his face in its broad shaggy chest.

Standing over the man, Nord licked his face and hands a few times, then lay down beside him, pressing his heavy, fluffy warm side up against him.

"He thinks you're his prize!" The Yakut smiled at him a few hours later, shaking the snow from himself by the door and looking at the dog and the man lying side by side.

Nord rose sedately to his feet, arched his back, yawned, went up to his master and nuzzled his hand. Vikenty looked at the Yakut in confusion, trying to crawl away, back to his corner.

"You were afraid!" The Yakut sat down on the skin, crossed his legs and looked Vikenty in the eye. "Don't worry, it'll pass. You've come back to us from the dead, you know! They already know about you around here. The Yakuts have never heard of anyone making it here on foot from Kolyma, without reindeer or dogs."

He paused, looking his guest searchingly in the eye, as if undecided about something, then he continued.

"But it's not easy to get over such adventures. You'll have to stay lying down for a long while yet. Now you can crawl out into the snow for five minutes a day. The fresh air will do you good. And you must start to eat more. Only boiled meat, bread, and a little liquor. You've got to realize that after such an experience some of your internal organs may be weakened. Then, when everything's different, you'll have all the medical tests, if you want to live as a man and not an invalid."

"What's put all that into your head? I'm well again!" Vikenty answered firmly.

"Your mind's well again, but not your body. I examined you while you were lying delirious and I know. Do you know what month it is?" He smiled slyly.

Vikenty shook his head, smiling under his beard.

"It's April! There'll be some more snowstorms, but it's warmer. And the sky is blue! Do you hear? The blizzard is over. Put on another skin." He threw Vikenty a bundle. "I'll help you out into the snow."

Vikenty struggled into yet another layer of skin, then fell down exhausted, wiping big beads of sweat from his brow. Taking hold of the edge of the bottom skin, the Yakut deftly dragged him out of the yaranga, knelt behind him, and lifted him by the shoulders.

"It hurts to look!" Vikenty whispered, covering his eyes, which had immediately filled with tears from the bright sun: the endless snowy plain, stretching to the horizon, flashed and sparkled in the bright sunlight, and drops of water from the thawing icicles ran down the sloping wall of the yaranga.

"How blue the sky is!" Vikenty wiped away the tears with his sleeve and lifted his head to the sky, which looked like a huge light-blue tent pitched over the earth, cloudless, only the blue sky above the white plain.

"Yes," the Yakut nodded, "now the sky really is blue for you! It always happens like this in the tundra—and in life, too: gloomy gray sky, snowstorm swirling and roaring, iron-hard frost, and then it all disappears, only the sparkling snow, the icicles, and the blue sky are left."

"How blue! How blue!" whispered his guest again. New tears came into his eyes. But they were tears of another kind.

Soon he could sit up. And he was sitting with a book when the visitors found him, as they came one by one into the yaranga. Vikenty threw aside the book and watched anxiously as some fifteen Yakuts seated themselves along the walls of the yaranga, fixing on him their tanned stone-carved faces. He felt uneasy under the gaze of the fifteen pairs of eyes.

The master of the house sat down between the visitors and Vikenty and placed his hand on Vikenty's knee: "Russ, I've brought all Ivan's family. Ivan whom you ate . . . Some of them speak Russian, some don't. They asked, and I couldn't refuse them. They want to thank you for making it here alive, they want you to visit the grave where Ivan Kotov's head is buried, and they want to hear what happened between you in the tundra. I'll translate. Tell them, Russ, it's important! It's hard for you but you've got to do it. The whole family has come."

Vikenty did not say anything for a few minutes. His face was white and his heart was beating wildly. A feeling of weakness crept over him. He gratefully accepted a cup of liquor from the Yakut, ran his clouded gaze over the faces of the visitors, and began to speak. The fifteen men and women in their identical hide clothing sat before him like the stone idols of the ancient Mongols; they asked no questions, but listened in silence, their intent unblinking eyes fixed on him.

When he had finished his story, in all its detail, there was silence for a few minutes, then one of the visitors said something, getting up from the skins.

"Ivan's father said that he believes you. It's all true. He's glad he has his son's grave, where they buried his head. Since his son's arrest he has hated all Russians. Now he doesn't know which of the Russians are men and which are wolves! You are a man. He expects you to visit him when you're on your feet. You don't need to go to Yakutsk. You can live the rest of your life here in safety." The Yakut finished translating, stood up, and showed his guests from the yaranga. They left behind them a man lying exhausted on the skins in the corner.

The days, weeks, months, passed quickly. Vikenty grew noticeably stronger; he could move about unaided and often went outside the yaranga and sat for hours on a skin, admiring the variegated colors of the summer tundra, which was covered with a green-red carpet of bushes, moss, and bluish patches of lakes, where fish splashed.

When the family was gathered together, he would relate to them for hours on end, through the father, the stories of his own and other people's lives at sea, carefully omitting everything that had happened to him after his return to Russia in 1931. The woman and the boy would listen to him attentively, reclining on the fur-covered floor, then they would go away and the Yakut would begin to tell him in Russian about Yakut life and customs and about events in the other, distant world. Once, during one of these quiet talks, the Yakut told his guest about the "doctors' trial," about Khrushchev, and about Beria's rehabilitation of certain prisoners. "Well, what do you think?" He laughed under his short black moustache, slyly screwing up his eyes at his guest. "Things are happening, eh? Things may be changing! Only none of this has anything to do with you. You must stay here. It's dangerous for you back there."

The Yakut tucked into his reindeer meat in silence, glancing at the Russian, who was rustling the pages of a newspaper.

"It's like another revolution!" Vikenty explained. "Stalin's gone. Maybe the others, too, those . . . I don't know Khrushchev, but I think I can go back." The Yakut stopped chewing and looked at him coldly.

"No, you can't. We didn't bring you back to life just so you could die again . . ."

"No!" Vikenty shook his head stubbornly. "I sense it! Everything is changed there now."

"No!" snapped the Yakut and left the yaranga. He returned after a few days, spoke to his wife about something, and went in to Vikenty.

"Well, I've decided that you may be right. We have a saying that every reindeer knows its path. You know yours. Get ready! The team's waiting. We're going to Ivan's family—three hundred kilometers. Then to Yakutsk."

"A-a . . ." For a moment Vikenty had swallowed his tongue. "But what will you say if they ask you where you've brought me from?"

"I'll say that I've only just found you, patched you up, and brought you there. I'm not afraid! I know Soviet communists. You can trick them like you can any wolf. But where have you been these last months? How should I know? You were hiding somewhere, in an abandoned yaranga. The tundra is large. Nobody's going to do any checking anywhere!"

With a feeling of joy at what lay ahead, and with some regret at what he was leaving in the yaranga, Vikenty dressed himself more warmly, glanced once more at the corner where he had lain for many long months fighting against death and where he had survived, and went out into the snow.

"This is the same sled and team I had when I found you that time," the Yakut said, helping him into the sled. "And my name's Yamar. It's a bad name. Hardly Yakut! But I've managed to live with it. And you will remember me. What's your name?"

"Vikenty. Vikenty Angarov." He offered the Yakut his hand, which was thin as a stick, with the tendons standing out clearly through the yellow skin.

"So we've introduced ourselves!" The old man laughed. "I kept waiting for you to ask me my name, but you never did. Everybody here took a liking to you. Perhaps you'll drop in sometime, when it's all over. But now you've got to go, to the future! I think there's a lot of unpleasantness in store for you, but life is waiting for you out there. Sit down!"

He said something to his wife and son. A minute later, covered with a thick skin, feeling the woman and boy breathing at his sides, and lulled by the motion and the wind, he was being whisked across the snowy plain by the eight-dog team, southward.

Without opening his eyes he had been listening for some time to the conversations of the nurses in the ward, inhaling the odors of medicines together with the aroma of flowers from outside the window.

Then the women's voices stopped and a man's was heard. "Well, how is he, this bearded fellow? Will he be able to travel?"

"No," a woman's voice answered. "He mustn't travel. He grew a lot weaker during the flight from Yakutsk. He shouldn't have been allowed to fly. He should have convalesced in Yakutsk at least another two weeks. According to the medical history we received, he traveled five hundred kilometers on a dog sled before he reached Yakutsk. That's a lot for anyone, let alone someone who's suffered serious malnutrition."

"Yes," the man said, obviously displeased. "But he's got to go before the commission of the Central Committee tomorrow. His case is set for eleven in the morning. He'll need a stretcher. Take good care of him, we don't want him to have a relapse. Then we'd be in trouble!"

"I'll take care of everything, Comrade Senior Physician," the woman's voice echoed after the slam of the door. Then a soft hand rested on his brow. "Well, our dear patient. What a beard you've got! It's time to pull yourself together. You can't just lie around here. You've really been through it! Here's some chicken broth, open your mouth . . ."

Too weak to open his eyes, he parted his lips with effort and felt the savory liquid flow into his throat; he gulped it down and immediately fell into a deep sleep.

He dreamed fleetingly of the shaggy backs of the dogs ahead of the sled, the long stick in Yamar's hand, which had not touched the dogs' backs once throughout the whole long journey, the brief stops to feed the dogs, have a meal and sleep, and then off again. Later . . . the unfamiliar yaranga, crowded with strange people, the big skin on the floor, the pots of boiled reindeer meat, the plates of bread, vodka in cut glasses . . . The noise of conversation and then the sepulchral silence, broken only by the retelling of his story and Yamar's voice . . . He saw the small solitary hill in the tundra, not far from the camp. An ordinary hill, overgrown with moss and surrounded by a shallow swamp. On the top of the hill was a dwarf northern birch, twisted quaintly into the form of a cross. Beneath the roots of the birch lay buried the head of Ivan, his friend, with whom he had shared his terrible journey, from east to west, from slavery to freedom, from death to life.

Then . . . the sled again, drawn by reindeer instead of dogs. Further to the south there was no longer any snow, and the dogs were not strong enough to pull the sled through the mud. And, at last, Yakutsk. Long streets of one- and two-story buildings, tall stone buildings in the center of the town, the inevitable gray and somber edifice that housed the MGB regional office. Yamar's final handshake, some people in military uniforms, footsteps, the odor of medicines . . . Then a long gap in his memory. And another frame—a man with a Yakut face and the epaulets of an MGB captain is sitting on a chair beside the bed. "You can't speak? We won't make you! You've no need to be afraid of us. Unless you've committed some crime since your escape, you're in no danger. The sentence you received is now considered unlawful." The thin lips of the MGB captain with the Yakut face moved quickly, the words, the precious words, sounded unintelligible; he strained to hear, so that he would understand and miss nothing. Then he asked: "But back there, in the camp . . . what happened to them . . . after our escape . . . There was an epidemic . . . perhaps Kotov wouldn't have died if he hadn't come with me."

He saw the captain's brows twitch. The captain shook his head. "No, unfortunately, our Kotov would have died anyway. You got away from there just in time. No one survived! All the huts had to be burned before new people were sent in."

"Are zeks . . . dying there . . . again?" Vikenty asked the man sitting beside him on the chair.

"For the time being, yes." The captain shrugged. "But the camps will soon be abolished. Everything is changing. Try not to die!"

When he opened his eyes again, the captain was no longer sitting on the chair. Then there was a long uncomfortable flight. His head still buzzed with the sound of the engines and he still felt sick from the jolting. He had grown much weaker.

He opened his eyes and saw a sunbeam on the wall, a few empty snow-white cots in the ward, a woman in a white gown standing by the window.

"Nurse!" he called quietly.

"Oh, you've come round!" She turned her round snub-nosed face toward him. "Well, I'm listening, our remarkable patient!"

"Where am I? What's this town?" He stirred in the bed and felt the rustle of the starched pillow case under his head.

"This is a military hospital, at Zagorsk, near Moscow."

"Military?"

"Yes." She blushed slightly. "The hospital of the Ministry for State Security. Here you're absolutely safe!" she joked. "But don't take it into your head to die again. We were really worried about you."

"I'll try!" He tried to smile.

"Now, breakfast." She came toward him with a determined look. "Then get dressed, onto the stretcher and on your way . . ."

He ate obediently the plate of rice gruel with butter and sugar, almost choking on it. Then, half sitting, he allowed her to dress him in a light-blue hospital robe.

"Nurse, will you do me a favor? Somewhere in the woods I lost my wife. And before I put a foot outside this hospital, I want news of me to go to her. You have a pen?"

The woman frowned and silently left the room, returning in a minute with a pencil and a sheet of white paper.

"My dear girl," he began. "I am writing this letter in a hospital and a nurse helps me. I am alive again, but I can only eat and think. I cannot walk. Our troubles in the camp were a trifle compared to what I have come through since. And I survived, this time also, with your help. I thought of you and our son. I wanted to see you both. I wanted to live. Otherwise, I would have died.

"I don't know anything about you and send this news to Medvezhie where I left you, hoping that somebody will get it to you. If I don't get news from you for some time, I will do all in my power to find you. Even from my bed. I will never be happy without you. But if you married a good man or found your happiness otherwise, just respond to me, your old friend, and I will be happy, if you are. I wait for your answer and kiss you both—Vikenty."

The nurse waited for a minute, looking down at the pale face of the man. But he closed his eyes and kept silent, exhausted.

She left and went into the next room, took a stamped envelope from a drawer, returned, and sat at his bed. "Address?" she said.

The patient moved on the bed, and even tried to raise himself on his elbow.

She gently pushed him back.

"Lydia Angarova," he whispered. "The village of Medvezhie, Krasnoyarsk Territory."

"And return?"

"General Delivery, Moscow."

He thought of his elder son, Valery. Where was he living now? Vikenty hadn't heard from him since 1948, the start of his exile. Should he ask the nurse to help? But what could she do? Where could he find out Valery's address? And, besides, for Valery to see him now, still more dead than alive . . . No! He closed his eyes again. The nurse folded the letter, sealed it, and placed it on the table for delivery.

She had to pull him onto the stretcher. Then he felt himself being rolled away from the bed.

The ambulance swished over the asphalt as it sped toward Moscow past the suburban villages and villas. Sometimes he managed to catch a glimpse of the treetops through the window. "Where are they taking me?" The anxious thought pounded in his head, but, like all experienced convicts, he asked no questions, assuming that they would either not answer or lie.

And not until the ambulance had stopped at the entrance and four husky civilians had carried the stretcher out did he see the familiar garden on Nogin Square. That meant the Central Committee of the CPSU. Not the Lubyanka!

The shuffling of feet, the odor of expensive carpets, then everything grew quiet. Through his half-opened lids he saw a long, light room with many windows, in the center of which was a long table covered with a green cloth. Some ten men in civilian clothes were sitting at the table, their eyes fixed on him.

The man at the far end of the table stood up, came over to him, and bent down a little. "Can you stand?"

He shook his head.

So four men approached silently, picked up the stretcher, and placed it on two chairs, right at the end of the table, slightly angled toward the commission. Silence fell. He lay on the stretcher under the gaze of the members of the commission, trying to control the trembling of his hand by clenching his sweating palm, but the nervous shivering would not stop. "Damn you!" he swore under his breath. "Do what you like with me!"

"Will you be able to answer our questions?" he heard, and nodded in reply.

"Your name is Angarov, Vikenty Filippovich?" asked the man at the other end of the table.

"Yes," he answered, barely audibly.

"You returned to the USSR from emigration in 1931?"

"Yes."

"You were arrested?"

"Yes."

"What for? Were you charged?"

"Yes. With suspected espionage."

"How long were you in prison at that time?"

"Two weeks."

"Where?"

"In the Marx . . . Marxism reading room."

"Have you come here to make jokes?"

"No!" He opened his eyes with an effort and saw the stern face of the chairman of the commission and the wry smiles on the other faces.

"You are before the Rehabilitation Commission of the Central Committee of the Party," the chairman continued, calmer now. "Please don't make our work more difficult with your irrelevant jokes. Obviously, life has not joked with you. Please answer!"

"I told you. In the Marxism reading room! That's . . . the truth."

"Why, exactly, in the Marxism reading room?"

"I don't know! Perhaps because it was next to the investigator's office."

"What did you do in the reading room during those two weeks?"

"What do detainees do? I waited . . . for the results of the investigation, and I read. Marx and Lenin."

"Why?"

"There was nothing else to do."

"What conclusions did you come to after all that reading? Do you believe in what you read? Do you believe in the correctness of the cause of building communism in the USSR?"

"I don't know . . . I don't know . . . It's hard for me to judge. I've spent nearly all my time in prison since I returned to the USSR. For me this building work . . . has turned out badly."

"Well, all right, I understand you've had a bit of bad luck. When were you arrested for the second time?"

"In 1936."

"Where?"

"In Archangel."

"Your position?"

"Deputy Head of the Northern Steam Navigation Authority."

"The charges?"

"Spying for Japan."

"Were you a spy?"

"No!"

"Your wife and son?"

"She died, in a camp. My son survived, he's living somewhere, grown up by now."

"Did you sign the court decision?"

"What decision?"

"That you were a spy?"

"I was never a spy."

"You were forced to sign?"

"Yes."

"Did you sign?"

"No."

"How long did your interrogation last?"

"Five days, I think. They fired shots at me, beat me . . ."

He half opened his eyes, gulped for air, and exhaled throatily, at the whole room.

The members of the commission silently exchanged looks.

"My head's spinning," he croaked, "a glass of water!"

"Get the doctor!" snapped the chairman, a short, solidly built man, in a light-gray suit, with red hair hanging down over his forehead.

The door at the back opened; a man in a white gown came in noiselessly and raised a glass containing some kind of pungent liquid to Vikenty's lips. He drank it. The weakness passed. Without speaking, he nodded in reply to the chairman's questioning glance.

"Who beat you?" the chairman of the commission continued.

"The investigator."

"Do you remember his name?"

"Yes, Bydlin."

"And did the investigator Pogodin also beat you?"

"No, he saved me."

"That's interesting!"

"He closed my case and gave me the sentence of ten years' imprisonment to sign. He didn't give any reasons."

"And then?"

"They sent me to prison."

"Bring in the witness!" He heard the chairman's voice.

Two men in civilian clothes entered the room through a side door and stood on either side of the door. A tall, heavy, gray-haired man came in and stopped between them. He had long hands and his fingers bore the scars of many cuts. His fleshy, coarse-featured face was pale. He looked somberly around the room, shuffled his feet, and lowered his head. Vikenty immediately recognized the familiar hateful face and his heart began to jump in his chest, as if it wanted to skip out of the ribcage; he could hardly hear what was being said for the hammering in his temples.

"Your name, witness."

"Bydlin, Yegor Ivanovich."

"Do you know this man, on the stretcher? Lift the stretcher!"

"No, I don't." He shook his head decisively.

"And do you know this man?" The question was directed at Vikenty.

"Yes, it's Bydlin! He beat me!"

"Me?" Bydlin interrupted in amazement. "This is the first time I've set eyes on this man!"

"Citizen Bydlin, you had an official position in 1936?" the chairman asked irritably.

"Yes."

"And what were you doing before that?"

"I worked as a locksmith in a factory."

"Did you obtain the official position yourself or were you invited?"

"I was drafted."

"Did you take part in the interrogation of detainees in 1937?"

"Yes."

"Did you use physical force on them? Did you beat them?"

"Y-yes, but I'm not to blame!"

"Where on their bodies did you beat them?"

"Where? All over!"

"For what purpose?"

"To make them confess."

"Confess what?"

"Well, that they were enemies. I beat our enemies!"

"Why were you sure that you were beating our enemies?"

"They told me, they told us all every day that the whole country was infested . . . by . . . enemies of the people . . . spies! That they were plotting against the Party and Comrade Stalin. I was sure of it! Do you think I would have started beating honest people?"

Silence fell once more. The men at the table said nothing and did not look at one another.

"Citizen Bydlin!" the chairman broke the silence in a hard voice. "Go up to the stretcher. That's right. You don't recognize him?"

"No, I don't."

"Do you remember Captain Angarov, whom you fired at?"

"I . . . I do!" Bydlin turned his drained face to the table, tugging at his lapel with a trembling hand. "But I didn't mean to kill him. I fired as a warning."

"Well, what happened?"

"He still wouldn't sign. He turned out to be stronger than I. Then . . . then I asked my superiors to take me off his case."

Vikenty opened his eyes a little and saw their curious gazes fixed on him.

"But that's not Angarov." Bydlin spread his arms.

"No, you're wrong, that is Captain Angarov. Look him in the eye!"

Vikenty saw the broad face bending over him, the small eyes he had known so well back there, many years ago, burning with hatred and fear. Their eyes met. Bydlin stepped back and turned abruptly to the table. "Is it really? Y-yes, those are his eyes. It's him! Can it really be him?"

He looked, almost in terror, at the thin body on the stretcher, hardly discernible under the blanket.

"Yes, it's him. You may go, witness Bydlin. Issue him a pass." The chairman nodded to someone near the door.

"Captain Angarov." The chairman turned to him when the door had closed behind Bydlin. "We have released Bydlin because we don't think you will exercise your right to have him prosecuted for what happened. Or will you insist?"

"I won't insist. To hell with him, he'll die anyway!" Vikenty whispered.

The chairman nodded. "That's a sensible attitude. It's best to live for the future. But we still have some questions—about the past. How many years were you in the camp?"

"Ten."

"You were released?"

"In 1947."

"Then what?"

"I was harbor master at Riga."

"Well, what happened next?"

"But you know all this! I'm tired. What's the point of it all?"

"Yes, we know. We have to hear it all once more from you. It's necessary for your sake too. Be patient. Why were you sent to Kolyma?"

"A certain Troshkin was at Medvezhie. The scum! A foreman beat his face in. They accused me!"

"Did you beat up Troshkin?"

"No."

"Did you want to?"

"Yes."

"Why didn't you?"

"I was afraid for myself and my family. I was afraid of the law."

"But the foreman wasn't afraid?"

"No, for him the law was unwritten. He was uneducated!"

"Did you agree with the court's decision. Was it correct?"

"No, the decision was rigged, a lie."

"Why didn't you contest it?"

"I couldn't. They sent me off the same day to Vladivostok, to a deportation camp—Pervaya Rechka—and then to Magadan."

"Where did you lose your hand?"

"I cut it off."

"How?"

"With an axe."

"Why? Was it an accident?"

"No, to save my life."

"From whom?"

"From the officers, from the blizzard. That day the whole camp was lost in the forest."

"You knew a blizzard was coming?"

"Yes."

"How? Who told you?"

"No one. I'm an old sailor, I know the weather, the signs."

"Why didn't you tell the officers?"

"I was afraid they would beat me or kill me."

"What could they have killed you for?"

"For nothing. Simply for knowing that a blizzard was on the way."

"What do you intend to do now?"

"Go to sea again, if I survive."

"Do you want to get a visa to sail abroad?"

"Yes."

"You won't stay abroad?"

"No."

"What guarantee can you give?"

"It's too late for me to settle abroad. I will live out my life in my own country. I haven't got long to live. My whole life is here, my lost life, all my graves . . ."

"Do you want to join the Party?"

"Yes."

"Why?"

"To prevent some other bastard taking my place!" he answered viciously, raising himself on his elbow.

"That's well said. But better unsaid." The chairman smiled acidly. "Absolute trust will be placed in you, Comrade Captain Angarov. Comrades, what do you think?"

Vikenty fell back onto the pillow and listened to the muffled whispering at the table.

"There are no objections," the chairman said after a few minutes. "Your case is considered closed. You are rehabilitated, completely. And I ask you—advise you—not to dwell on the past. That might spoil what's left of your life. It's past history. Now you will be taken back to the same hospital. When you are well you will be able to obtain an interview with the minister for the Merchant Marine, Comrade Bakayev. Everything will be decided there. You can ask for your dossier at the KGB reception office, if it interests you."

"Why did you bring me here?" He gave the members of the commission a puzzled look. "Surely you could have reached a decision without me? I haven't told you anything new."

"Yes, you did." The chairman smiled. "We had to make sure that your mind was still intact, that you had retained your memory and way of thinking, and your principles. We do not think you're entirely our man, but you do have principles and a strong will. To the extent necessary, we too are willing to trust such people. And the fact that you didn't try to insist on proceedings against Bydlin shows that you're intelligent and can think logically. You understand what a mess there would be if those who have suffered started using their fists on their former tormentors? Can you imagine how it all might end? The hurricane has passed. It's too late to start waving fists now! Here's the written decree concerning your complete rehabilitation." He stood up, went over to Vikenty and handed him a printed text. "That's all. Good luck! . . . Next!" Vikenty heard, already in the corridor.

"It's really happening!" Vikenty marveled aloud as he sat on a bench in the shady garden of the KGB sanatorium in the Moscow suburb almost a year later and felt the muscles in his arms. "I'm putting on flesh again. It's time I got moving. Nothing but sleeping and eating and no word from Lida. I've had enough of it!"

That same day he managed to slip out of the sanatorium after breakfast. As an exception, he was allowed to keep his things in the ward. His naval uniform, once more with the epaulets of a captain, second rank, had been made to measure and delivered two weeks ago. They had made it a little baggy, thinking that the captain, who was thin as a rail, would probably double in size during the coming months.

He put on the suit. It was like hanging it on a hanger. He sighed and set off for the bus stop. The guard at the gate, who knew everyone by sight, guffawed when he saw the tall, withered figure in the black uniform, which seemed to be blowing about in the wind, like a scarecrow.

He boarded the bus, lay back in his seat, and blissfully closed his eyes. The noise of the wheels and the chatter of the passengers sounded unusually pleasant to him, like the music of life. It was no more than one hundred yards from the bus stop on Nogin Square to the central committee building, but he had to rest on the benches along the way. The duty officer in the reception office, wearing the epaulets of a KGB captain, heard his brief request and glanced sharply at the big face with its taut yellow skin and sunken Mephistophelean eyes. He said sympathetically, "Yes, Comrade Captain, if it's a question of joining or being reinstated in the Party, you need to see Comrade Ponomarev, but that's difficult—he has a lot of visitors. We're making appointments for a month ahead. But I'll try. Wait here."

He had been sitting in a corner, on a green couch, for almost four hours when the captain at last said, "Go on up, third floor, room seven."

With mixed feelings of hostility, hatred, and curiosity he opened the massive, noiseless door. He was confronted with another, exactly the same. He opened it and stepped onto a fluffy reddish carpet, which disappeared off into the distance, toward the far end of the office. And there, as if at the other end of a street, he made out the face of a man sitting at an enormous cloth-covered table, at which stood rows of upholstered chairs. He advanced in silence across the soft carpet, as if on somebody else's legs. He thought the journey would never end.

"Comrade Angarov?" the man at the table said, without getting up or offering his hand. "Sit down." With an almost imperceptible movement of his hand he indicated a chair and Vikenty sat down with relief. He gazed across the table at the shoulders and tense face of a man with smoothly parted dark hair and a rather long nose.

"Excuse me, you're Comrade Ponomarev?" he asked, reddening.

"Yes, I'm Boris Ponomarev." The man nodded, giving his visitor a curious look. "You've come to see me about joining the Party?"

"Yes—that is, I'm not really sure. I had all the testimonials for membership in 1937, just before I was arrested."

Ponomarev grimaced. "They're all lost. Today you won't find your testimonials, or the people who gave them. You must make a new application, if you're ready to."

"Ready?"

"Yes. We don't accept just anyone into the Party. Have you thought it over properly? Membership in the Party involves obligations. It requires integrity, competence, self-sacrifice . . ."

"But Comrade Ponomarev, I've always had all those qualities . . . I've been a communist all my life!"

"Yes?" Ponomarev interrupted, perplexed. He looked away. "But there's the question of Party policy. You have not always followed the general line . . ."

"But my life?" Vikenty flushed, feeling the barrier of hatred between himself and Ponomarev growing, making it difficult for him to think and speak. "Surely you know I haven't done a single thing to harm the Party, though it has persecuted me all my life. I think that entitles me to take my place in the Party. Let the others make room, who haven't suffered what I have!"

"Are you referring to me?" Ponomarev asked icily.

"Not only you, there are plenty of others."

In this wreck of a captain, Ponomarev saw one of those who had been swept into the garbage pits of history by the same purges that had raised him out of those same garbage pits. But there wasn't room at the top for everyone, that was certain. Now the tide had turned and some of the purged had survived and were coming back to Moscow to seek out the ones who had done the murdering and the beating, the ones who had occupied their places in life. Well, this captain was nothing to worry about. He was small fry.

"All right," he said, trying to be conciliatory. "I won't try to prevent your joining the Party. You must work for a year, obtain the testimonials, do everything according to the rules. And what's your attitude toward Nikita Sergeyevich Khrushchev?" With a familiar feeling of triumph he looked at his visitor's confused face, expecting the usual unintelligible reply, one of the many he received every day from his visitors.

"My attitude to Comrade Khrushchev is simple." The captain's voice was firm. "What would your attitude be toward the man who had brought you back into life?"

"But, all the same, you do think you were suppressed without any justification at all?"

"Of course. What justification could there have been?"

"And that Comrade Stalin did all this for his own criminal purposes?"

"Why all these questions?" Vikenty raised his voice, losing his remaining respect for the man. "I don't know whether he had any personal motive, but it was all a crime. Millions of people arrested, beaten, murdered. Communism is good. Is it really impossible to build communism without such experiments?"

He stopped, realizing that he had gone too far. They stared at each other in silence.

"In your interview with the rehabilitation commission you maintained that you had been beaten during your interrogation," Ponomarev said somberly.

"Yes, I was. Don't you believe it?" He watched Ponomarev's gray face with unconcealed anger, realizing that the visit had failed.

"Do you still maintain that people were beaten under our auspices?" Now Ponomarev, in turn, regarded him with open hostility.

"Yes! What am I supposed to say?"

"Not what happened but what your communist conscience tells you to say, if you want to be a communist."

"You mean that according to a communist conscience they didn't beat me?"

"Right! They didn't beat you. It didn't happen." Ponomarev stood up, indicating that the conversation was over.

"Didn't happen?" Vikenty almost choked with rage. "They beat me almost to death! I was lucky. I survived. But how many did not? You should have been thrashed like the others were. Then you'd be singing a different tune. You would never have gotten out! But you were sitting pretty here, enjoying life!"

Vikenty stood up and they leaned forward, like cocks ready to fight, their faces red with rage.

"They let you off too lightly, that's obvious," Ponomarev breathed. "You've understood nothing, learned nothing. I cannot recommend or permit your membership in our Party. Go away and learn some sense!

Then, if you change your opinions . . ."

Vikenty shouted in his face: "Learn sense yourself! You dare to try to teach me! When I was putting up revolutionary posters in Novosibirsk, in 1916, you hadn't been born, hadn't even been thought of! You've built your careers on our backs, you new communists! But your time is coming to an end. I shall live out my life without your Party. You'll have to give me a place in life and some respect. I've survived. You didn't destroy everyone, nor will you. They're only just growing up now, these new ones. They'll be different, they'll see that you all get what's coming to you, sooner or later."

"They really did let you off lightly." Ponomarev said. "It was a waste of time letting you go."

"Are you trying to scare me? Me? Go on! Ring for them to come and arrest me again. Why don't you ring? Or haven't you got the guts?" he shouted into the ashen face of the senior Party official. "If only they would arrest you and take you there and thrash you, even if they gave you only a little of what I got. Then you'd believe that they beat people. Then you'd realize what this kind of communism is."

Ponomarev gestured wearily. "Go away and live your life, but don't bother me anymore. It's pointless. I regret agreeing to see you."

"I know it's pointless! I've wasted my time! But there's nothing to regret!" Vikenty staggered toward the door. "At least you've learned something!"

"Are you trying to tell me what it's all about?" Ponomarev bellowed. "You, who've lost everything through your own folly!"

"My greatest folly," Vikenty shouted from the door, "was to love Russia, to return to my native country, and to want to be an honest man."

He glanced at the pale face at the far end of the office, then went out, slamming the door.

"Really, Comrade!" A middle-aged secretary jumped back in fright from the door, glancing at the few visitors who were waiting to be seen.

"Where's the door here?" Vikenty bellowed at the secretary. The visitors anxiously tucked up their legs, as if the captain was going to pass by them. In the corner hovered the pale-faced KGB captain who had persuaded Ponomarev to see "a likeable comrade, one of those who have suffered."

"This way, Comrade, please!" The woman quickly opened the door.

Vikenty passed through the door and set off straight along the corridor.

"Comrade!" A despairing cry brought him to a halt. "Here," the secretary continued, running after him, "here's your pass. And here's the door. Don't fall down, for heaven's sake!"

Without looking at the woman he slammed the door and hobbled down toward the exit, holding on to the polished brass bannister.

"Where to now?" he wondered in front of the central committee building. With trembling fingers he pushed a cigarette into his mouth and stood striking one match after another until he managed to light it, glancing around with hatred at the passersby. "They're all rushing somewhere. After money, no doubt. The good life! Rushing to join the Party!" He cursed as he walked slowly along in the direction of GUM. Like an automaton, he went into the Slavyansky Bazar restaurant, drank a glass of wine at the bar, and moved on. Although he felt that his legs were giving way, he decided to see it through, and half an hour later he was sitting in the KGB reception office on Kuznetsky Bridge.

"Comrade Angarov, please." A tall colonel wearing gunners' epaulets opened a side door and ushered him in. "Sit down. I've prepared your dossier, as you requested in your application."

He sat down at the other end of the table and buried his nose in some papers. Vikenty sat down on the chair and drew the bulky file toward him. He gazed at it for a long time, unable to make up his mind to open it, then he asked: "Er, Comrade Colonel. This is my dossier?"

"Well, do you think it's mine, then?" The colonel laughed. "It's your dossier, you may be sure!"

"And is everything here, everything that happened?"

"Well, not quite everything, but almost. Go ahead and read it. Don't be afraid."

"May I ask one more thing?" He blushed.

"Yes."

"Are you a member of the KGB?"

"What do you mean, don't I look like one?" The colonel regarded the strange captain in surprise, giving him a broad smile.

"It's not that . . . I don't know. But those epaulets, with the cannon . . ."

"Ah, that's what's confusing you! Yes, I've served all my life in the artillery. I arrived here rather unexpectedly, you might say." He stood up and pushed a silver cigarette box toward Vikenty. "Have a smoke."

Vikenty took a cigarette and lit it, watching the colonel warily.

"You know, there have been a lot of changes here during the past two years," the colonel continued, staring at his visitor. "There are no secrets whatsoever. We have finished one era and started another. I was one of the army officers who arrested Beria. I myself dragged him along the underground corridors to that place from which he has not returned. That was our task. And now here I am, sitting here. Haven't even had time to take off my epaulets! Most of the people here are army officers now."

"And where are the others?"

"The others?" He shrugged evasively. "They've gone their ways. Some have retired, some have other work, and so on . . . To each his own, you know. Go ahead and read, otherwise you won't have enough time to get properly acquainted with your past."

"Thank you," Vikenty said quietly. He gave a more reassured glance in the direction of the KGB colonel with his gunner's epaulets, then opened the file.

He read the yellowed pages, oblivious to his surroundings. His brother Genka—so that was how they killed him! He had killed his interrogator with his fists for trying to torture him. Good lad! They had come running and shot him from the corridor . . . So many papers here! Izakson's secret police report about Kondratyuk, Vikenty's superior in Shanghai, about Angarov's signature on Kondratyuk's sentence. Another paper: conclusions after his arrest in 1931. Not guilty! Character assessment. Competent, capable of occupying the post of People's Commissar of the Merchant Marine. That's what the authorities were disturbed about! A commissar who could not be completely trusted. Bydlin's reports: his request to be released from further interrogation of the prisoner Angarov. More character assessments, records, reports, denunciations. So many denunciations! What fantasies! Ah, here's the data! About his family. His wife, Ekaterina Sergeyevna, buried near Kustanai. That's true! Second wife, Lida . . . remarried, living in Krasnoyarsk, and her address . . . He forced his eyes to keep reading. Elder son, Valentin, married, living in Noginsk in the Moscow suburbs, and his address . . . his foster mother, Anna Ivanovna, died—in Vologda. His parents—dead, buried in Zhitomir . . .

No more on his family. Here's Degtev: demobilized after Khrushchev came to power, now working as a mechanic in an automobile workshop, in Krasnoyarsk. What's this? A letter from Orlov's wife, Nadezhda Alekseyevna, to Beria and a sprawling annotation: "To Abakumov. I can believe it. Leave Degtev in his former post. I forbid his promotion. L. Beria." Aha! Well done, Nadezhda Alekseyevna! She had done her duty to her Orlov. Orlov should see what's happening now!

Investigator Pogodin—now the director of a timber-shipping center near Archangel. Ought to visit that ginger-headed genius, split a couple of bottles of vodka with him, in memory of those five days. Scarface—signed up with his wife for the Kamchatka, the Zaozernaya fishing combine. At least he got out of the camp alive. "I hope he's grateful to me," he thought with pride, as he turned over the pages. Pelageya! A museum piece. Released fully rehabilitated. That means she didn't serve her twenty years. The old girl struck lucky! Her a revolutionary! To hell with all of them!

People's Commissar of the Merchant Marine Rusakov—at last! Died at the beginning of '54. So he wasn't suppressed. Or perhaps he was—it doesn't say. And Sukhov! Dear man! Died in the camp at Kolyma, 1940. And here's Troshkin—he left Medvezhie—for where? God knows. Ought to beat in his filthy mug.

And still more documents. God, so many papers! He gazed dully at the bottomless pile of yellow pages, written over in different hands, different inks, or simply in pencil, typed on all kinds of typewriters, a whole mountain of papers, with dates from 1916 to 1954. It was all there, apart from his interview with Central Committee Secretary Ponomarev, and not a word about the Yakut, Yamar.

"Well, how are you getting on?" he heard, as if in his sleep, and he glanced in bewilderment in the direction of the voice. "It's already eight o'clock." The colonel smiled. "Do you intend to sit here until morning?"

"I'm sorry." Vikenty blushed. "But these things . . . my whole life . . . it's terrible!"

The colonel nodded. "Yes, I know everything. That's why I waited. Captain, you've been sitting in my office for six hours. It's time to get some rest. You won't remember it all anyway. Why should you want to?"

"Ah, why did you allow me to see all this?" Vikenty asked.

"In the first place, you're something of an exception, as a high-ranking worker on the Party schedule. There's a special central committee instruction to familiarize such people with the basic data of their lives—those who suffered . . . Then, all that's over and done with. You won't bring anything back, you won't have your revenge on anyone, you won't do anything to anyone, and you won't learn anything new—you already know it all."

Vikenty nodded forlornly and gazed in confusion at the pile of papers.

"None of this is of any use to you. You've really kept me here six hours for nothing," the colonel said, giving him a weary look. "But here's Orlova's address—I advise you to write it down and pay her a visit. She has always been on your side."

"Why do you think that? She simply respected me."

"Not simply. Not all the documents are here. One or two are missing . . . Will you make it by yourself?" the colonel asked as he showed Vikenty to the door, past the drowsy guard.

"Thank you." He shook the colonel's hand. "I'll make it!"

In the street, he stood for a long time, squeezing in his hand the addresses of Orlova, Lida, and his son Valery. His head was ringing with what he had read. It was as if a film of the last twenty years had been run before his eyes. He came to himself when he noticed passersby casting surprised glances at his strange figure. He started moving, without knowing where he was going, and in half an hour found himself in Korov Street at the Central Post Office. He stood aside, thinking hard of how to approach Lida a second time. He couldn't write a single line. He looked around and fixed his sight on the window "Money Orders," then he reached into his jacket pocket for the advance payment on his rehabilitation. He took a blank, and with a slightly trembling hand, scratched her new address, the figure 2,000, and his name. He gave the money to the girl in the window and left.

"This isn't life, it's purgatory," Vikenty thought wearily when he applied for a pass the next day at the Ministry of Maritime Affairs. A fair-haired girl with painted lips gave him a cursory glance, comparing his face with the photograph in the passport, and handed him the pass to see the minister, Comrade Bakayev.

It was his third visit to this office. One minister, long ago, had told him he would have the job of minister one day; the second had fixed him up with a job in Riga without a visa. Would the third minister tell him something now? They were replaced like gloves.

Still the same table in the same office, and the same gold rings up to the elbow, except that the elbow belonged to a different man. Minister Bakayev strode forward to meet him and offered his hand. "Glad to see you, Comrade Captain. Please sit down."

He went back behind the desk and sat down, staring Angarov in the eye. "He looks you in the eye too, like all his predecessors." Vikenty silently studied the man sitting before him: he was wearing a black uniform with the rings of Director General of the Merchant Marine, the equivalent of vice admiral; his thick red hair was combed straight back; the greenish eyes above the large nose and the prominent chin were intimidating. "So you're sitting here," Vikenty thought, remembering the name Bakayev; he had heard it back in Kolyma. The name had then belonged to one of the directors of the Far-East Section of the Ministry of Water Transport, on whose ships convicts were transported from Nakhodka and Vanino to Kolyma. "When they were shipping me to Magadan in the hold of your *Dzhurma,* you never thought that we would meet like this. Of course you didn't know that I was passing through your domain. But you must have known the name Angarov—when I was a captain and a manager of the Steam Navigation Authority you were still somewhere clambering upwards, toward this office, this chair."

"Well now, Comrade Captain." Bakayev smiled reproachfully. "You didn't restrain yourself in your interview with Comrade Ponomarev! You really overstepped the mark. What was the sense?"

"There is no sense." He nodded, reddening. "But there are feelings! Ponomarev is too young to understand me and my condition. I didn't go to him for favors but to get what belongs by right to a man who has returned from the dead."

"That's true." The Minister smiled politely. "But all the same, Comrade Angarov, it doesn't hurt to be tactful. It's a struggle for survival and power. One must conform to the spirit of the times and adapt oneself. Comrade Ponomarev is an important official of the Party and state. He sees scores of visitors every day, and many of them suffered no less than you, some even more. One must live, don't you agree! The wheel of history! Some are under the wheel, some are in the driver's seat . . . I won't weary you with unnecessary talk, but you must accept the fact that, unless you unconditionally support Party policy, you will not be able to hold the rank of captain . . . I hope that as sailors you and I will find a common language. I would like to see you fully active again. I insisted that the Central Committee issue you with a permanent visa to travel overseas. I am sure that I'm taking no risk . . ."

"I should think not!"

"Yes, yes." The minister pushed over to him a pack of Severnaya Palmira cigarettes, struck a match, puffed out a cloud of smoke, and fixed his attentive gaze on his visitor. "Though that was precisely the trouble. The comrades in the Central Committee are afraid that once abroad you might remember everything and defect. When a seaman or a stoker defects, it's tolerable, but the defection of a captain creates a scandal. I managed to convince the commission that it was precisely what you have endured that would now bind you to this land. And how would you be better off in the West? You can't really think that people in the West will be very interested in your sufferings—they're living their own lives. We will give you money, status, and trust—as much as you want. What do you say, Comrade Angarov?"

"You are not mistaken," Vikenty replied quietly, lowering his head in an effort to hide the unexpected moistness in his eyes. "I'm too late for life in the West. I won't play hide-and-seek with you. You understand my attitude toward communism and toward your Party. But I can say such things only in an interview like this, between ourselves. Of course as a captain, especially one who sails to foreign ports, I will make all the necessary undertakings and will perform my duties conscientiously. I mean both my administrative duties in the running of the ship and my political ones, as the Central Committee requires. I will make full payment for the opportunity to live and work."

"That's sensible." Bakayev nodded, screwing up his eyes in approval. "Neither I nor the comrades in the Central Committee would have believed you if you had spoken differently. We would have thought it all a cunning game. So it's better this way—to talk frankly. I've already called Murmansk. You can obtain the rest of your compensation for the five years since you were forced to leave Riga. It's not much, about forty thousand roubles, but it will help you make a start. We cannot make full restitution of your salary for those years—there simply isn't enough money to go round. Then go to Yalta, to our ministry's sanatorium. After Yalta go straight to Murmansk to Comrade Tsybin, the chief of the Murmansk Steam Navigation Authority. He knows all about your case. You will be given an apartment and, the main thing, a ship—a medium-sized vessel, the factory ship *Alma-Ata*, fourteen thousand tons. At my personal request, once aboard the ship you will immediately take up your membership in the Party, as a candidate, so that you will be able to attend the meetings of the Party organization."

"Look at it philosophically!" He laughed, seeing Angarov's involuntary grimace. "You may not be desperate to become a full member of the Party but you are obliged to become a candidate, otherwise you will have endless trouble managing the crew. We very rarely promote sailors who are not Party members to captain—we're making an exception in your case. Swallow your pride. You'll gradually get used to the situation and look at it more simply. You'll be operating in the Barents Sea, the North Sea, and sometimes the Atlantic, putting in to European ports if necessary. The catch must be made, the production plan must be fulfilled, and there must be no trouble at sea. There will always be five trawlers with the factory ship. That's about all, I think. Turn to me if there are any difficulties. And one more request—forget everything and don't worry about anything. The past will not return. Live quietly, don't look back. And . . . you haven't lost your knowledge of the sea during the years you've been roaming about on land?"

"Me!" The unfeigned exclamation brought a smile to the minister's face.

"I'm sorry if I've offended you!" He stood up and came out from behind the desk. "I take my question back. Happy sailing, Captain!"

"Thank you, Comrade Bakayev, thank you for everything, I didn't expect it," he muttered, shaking the minister's hand.

"What's the Barents Sea with its storms to him!" Bakayev gazed pensively at the door through which the captain had disappeared. "To have sailed through such a storm! As long as he doesn't get into any more political trouble. If he does, they won't listen to me anymore in the Central Committee."

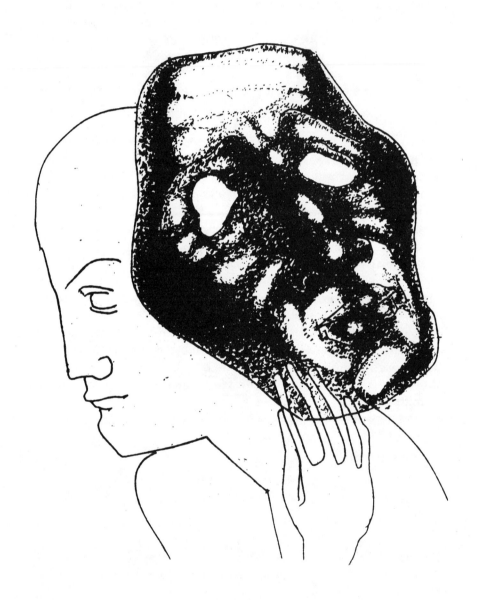

14

BLUE SKY

When he had received his money Vikenty went into the Central Post Office and stood in a corner, watching the noisy crowd. He thought, "What am I to do with the money? How can I use so much? Send it again to Lida? No, I sent it once. I must wait for her response. Who can I give it to? My son Valery? Yes, I must go there. Right now!"

A half-hour later he emerged from Izmailovo subway station, got into a taxi, and gestured to the driver, "Noginsk!"

The driver turned his startled face to him. "Captain, do you want to wait for another passenger? It's five roubles one way. Can you afford it?"

"Yes! And more!" Vikenty almost banged him on the shoulder. "Let's get going!"

Scenting money, the driver stepped on the gas. The gray Volga slipped quickly through the outskirts of Moscow, came out onto the main Moscow-Shatura highway, and sped ahead. The wind was howling past the car and making it pitch a little. The cars they overtook drifted back one after the other; the speedometer showed 130 kilometers an hour.

A half-hour later he pushed a crisp ten-rouble note into the driver's hand and nodded in reply to his almost rapturous look. Carrying the black bag with the presents, he set off along the road, reading the numbers of the houses. The pink, two-storied houses stood in an even row along one side of the road; on the other side a dense wood came right down to the ditch. In the distance he could see the masts of a radio station and a power station from which the high-tension lines stretched away into the wood.

A few minutes later he was sitting at a table in a spacious room, furnished plainly and without taste, its one big window covered by a white curtain. A two-year-old boy was sitting at the table, his large gray eyes fixed on the grizzled, one-handed captain.

"I'll be right there, Comrade Captain." A woman's voice carried from the kitchen, then the smiling face of a young woman appeared for a moment in the doorway. She was fair-haired, with simple features, and was wearing a green checked apron over her dress. "I'll be right there, I'm just preparing dinner."

He sat in silence, resting his head on his hand, and gazed at the boy, the simple furnishings, the woman hurrying to and from the table.

She covered the whole table with plates of cold meat, boiled potatoes, pickled cucumbers and tomatoes, and produced an opened bottle of vodka and a glass. Then she sat down across the table, smiled at the strange visitor, and said, "Have a drink, Comrade Captain! My husband will be back soon. He works quite close, at the substation. He's an engineer."

"This is your son?" he asked, his heart aching as he looked at his first grandchild.

"Yes." She smoothed the boy's red curls. "His father named him Vikeshka, after his grandfather."

"Ah." He coughed. "Is your husband's name Valery?"

"Yes," she said warily. "How do you know?"

He smiled mysteriously. "And where do you work?"

"I'm a hairdresser, in a men's salon, here in Noginsk." She gave him a wide, winning smile. "Come down there, I'll give you the latest styling! I thought you'd just come on some official business, but you even know my husband's name. Are you a relative of my Valery?"

"Yes, I am."

"Oh?" She looked up in surprise. "But he never told me he had any relatives . . . He only said that his father had died somewhere in Siberia."

"Why died?" he asked, trying to smile.

"Valery says he waited ten years until his father came back. Then his father disappeared again. He was arrested, probably, in Stalin's time. Not one letter all those years. So he decided that this time he had died. It wasn't difficult to die there, was it? So many people never came back."

"What's your name?" He leaned toward her over the table.

"Tonya!" She recoiled.

"Tonya . . . Tonyechka, did you know Anna Ivanovna?"

"Anna . . . Ivanovna?" She stood up, her hands at her throat. "You knew her too? You . . . oh forgive me! I had no idea. I didn't recognize you! You're not a bit like your photo. You're quite, quite different. Vikenty Filippovich!" She stepped toward him, but stopped, hesitating. Then she buried herself trustingly in his arms, pressing her face against his chest.

"So you knew her?" He gently squeezed her fragile body against his own, then held her away and kissed her cheek. "When did she die?" He sat down on his chair and smiled at her tenderly.

"Yes, I knew her." Tonya stood by the table, embarrassed by her tears; she straightened her hair and looked joyfully at the captain. "I went to the same school as Valery, in Vologda. Then we lost touch somehow, but met again in nineteen-fifty. I was at her funeral. She was like a mother to Valery . . . " She picked up the boy, not sure what to do next. "This is your granddad!"

"Hullo, little fellow!" Vikenty stretched out his arm and took the sturdy body. The boy looked at him warily, then immediately felt at ease and poked his finger into Vikenty's sleeve.

"Yes, I'm your granddad." He squeezed the boy against his cheek. Tonya went to the window and turned away, holding her handkerchief to her eyes. "I'm your daddy's father. And these rings mean that I'm a captain, in the merchant marine. And here's your father."

He slowly lowered the boy to the floor and raised his eyes to the man standing in the doorway, a little shorter than himself, but with his eyes. He was wearing blue overalls, and boots, and had deep creases on his forehead and at the corners of his mouth. Only his eyes looked young and firm.

"Are you . . . father?" Valery looked at him almost with terror. "You didn't die? You're alive? Not a single word all these years . . . Almost all my life . . . "

"Valery! My son!" Vikenty stood by the edge of the table gripping the back of the chair. "You must forgive me everything. I've lived a bad life. But I'm not to blame . . . I'm glad that you're a man, that you have a family, such a nice wife, Tonya . . . ."

She stepped quickly to her husband and took his hand.

As if waking from a trance, Valery stepped forward, embraced his father, without even giving him a chance to lift his arms, kissed him on both cheeks, then turned away. Vikenty stood with his head lowered, feeling a burning sense of outrage against his fate, against everyone.

"Well, father, don't just stand there!" Valery took him by the shoulders, sat him at the table, and winked at his wife. She poured some vodka into the glass, put out two more glasses, and sat down next to her husband, looking at him with eyes filled with love.

"Don't be angry, father." Valery stared at the table, holding his glass in his hand. "It's hard for me. I'd almost forgotten you. Although I've remembered you all my life. Until the day I die I'll never forget your bristly cheek, from when we were in Archangel, before you were arrested. And then there were only memories of you. Except for one short encounter. So you've survived! I envy you your strength. I don't think I would have managed it! When we saw each other in forty-seven you promised to show me my mother's grave . . . "

"Yes." Vikenty sat hunched up, aged, his face tired, avoiding the eyes of his son and his daughter-in-law. "I'll show you her grave. But not just yet. Tomorrow I'm going to Yalta. I've got to get back on my feet. I've survived but I'm sick. There's something wrong with my liver, apart from everything else. But I'm going to try to live the rest of my life standing up. I don't like lying down . . . Then I'm going to Murmansk, as captain of a big trawler. Then I'll take some leave. We'll go to Kustanai together. I'll show you her grave. She was young and beautiful once. It was . . . we had a beautiful life together . . . But now there's your life, yours and Tonya's. Here, I've brought you some things." He raised his moist eyes to them. "It'll help you, while you're getting set up."

He stood up, placed his bag on the chair, took out a package wrapped in newspaper and laid it on the table. Valery and Tonya looked at the package in silence, waiting to hear what this tall, bony man with the hard eyes would say next.

"Here, Valery, Tonya." He looked at them hopefully. "Here is twenty thousand roubles."

"What are you talking about?" she said. "All that money? For us! Where did you get it, Vikenty Filippovich? We can't . . . "

"Be quiet, Tonya!" Valery interrupted her, still avoiding his father's eyes. "It's a lot, Father, we're not used . . . and anyway, where did you get so much, and why? You need money yourself."

"A lot? Where did I get it? I need money?" He stood in the middle of the room, his face flushed with emotion. "You think that's a lot? But do you know how much money I would have earned if I hadn't spent those fifteen damned years behind the wire, if I'd lived like a human being, like other people? Do you know how much money I would have earned? No, you don't! But they know!" He motioned with his head, toward the ceiling. "And they gave me this money, these kopecks, as part of what they owed me. And I couldn't help you all these years because I was outside the world. You were young, only just married, I guessed you were beginning your life on the floor, without a bed, beginning with wooden spoons and plates, and I couldn't help you. I haven't got a life of my own. I've lost everything. I have no one but you. And I've nowhere to put this money. Why do I need it? What can I do with it? Or don't you want to know me? You want me to go away?"

He threw the package on the floor, covered his face with his one hand and stood, as if on deck, his legs wide apart, swaying, breathing throatily.

Tonya was weeping, her face buried in the table, holding her head in her hands. Valery laid his hand on his father's shoulder. "I'm sorry. You know, this is the first time in my life as a man that I've really met you. And all that money! And your past! We're still afraid of it all. Don't be angry. We'll need time . . . You can see yourself that it's hard for us to make ends meet, living from one pay day to the next. But we're gradually getting on our feet. We need money . . . we'll take it, with thanks. You can have our smaller bedroom. Vikeshka will sleep with us. And they're promising to give our neighbor a separate apartment. Then it'll be much easier. Sit down." He tugged him by the sleeve. "Forgive us. Let's have a drink!"

"Yes, I'll have a drink." Vikenty raised his wet, reddened eyes to them. "I understand you. But do you understand me? The young can't understand the old. And happiness can't understand misery!"

Driven by a light breeze, the greenish-blue, foamless waves rolled gently onto the sloping beach, where the large pebbles sparkled in the sunshine. The water flowed over the small rocks and the tanned bodies of the vacationers. Directly above the beach towered a cliff, on which trees could be seen, and the white wall of a restaurant. Sounds of conversation there carried to the beach. If you walked along the golden sand, picking your way through the wooden deckchairs and the bodies of the vacationers, you would come to Yalta, the jewel of the Black Sea. The white and green town, with its black lines of cypresses, spread like wings of a firebird along the bay and up the mountainsides, drowning in the hot summer air, saturated with the aroma of gardens, mountains, and sea.

Vikenty turned onto his back and blissfully offered his wet face to the sun. The salt water nibbled at his body, which was steaming in the fierce rays of the sun. A white triangular sail flashed in the distance.

> "A lonely sail stands out in the sea's blue mist,
>> What is it seeking in this distant country?
> What has it left in its native land?" *

He recalled the poem; he could never remember the poet's name, but the poem had stayed with him all his life.

It was the last day of his vacation. For a whole month nothing but the sea, the sun, endless breakfasts and dinners, even come-hither looks from women. They disregarded his mangled left arm for the sake of his tanned and well-shaped body. But he kept to himself and avoided making acquaintances. For then he would have had to talk and he wanted to be quiet, not to think about anything, to wash away everything that his heart and his body had absorbed throughout his life, of which little now remained. So he lay for a whole month at the water's edge, listening to the noise of the breakers, gazing into the blue distance, which had so attracted him in his youth. During that month he sent a second letter to Lida, telling her he wanted to see her and asking her to come to Moscow, with her husband if she wished. He had asked her to leave a message for him at the Central Post Office in Moscow, saying when and how they should meet. Today he would find if she had replied.

That afternoon he took a taxi to Simferopol, then an airplane for Moscow. A brief postcard was waiting for him at General Delivery at the Central Post Office: "My dear! Vik! So glad! Expecting you. Hotel Moscow, room 102. Love, your Lida."

Holding this precious postcard and smiling at the passersby, he hurried along Kirov Street, then across Dzerzhindky Square, down toward the hotel.

Out of breath, he almost ran along the deep, green hotel carpet. He reached the door, knocked, turned the handle without waiting for an an-

*From Lermontov's "The Sail."

swer, and went into the room. An elderly black-haired man in a green robe was sitting on the bed holding a newspaper. By a table stood a middle-aged woman in an elegant light-brown suit, her hair drawn back tightly into a knot, and with Lida's gentle gray eyes. It was she, only her figure was a little fuller, and there were more lines under her eyes. But the eyes themselves were the same: attentive, frank, kind, the same eyes that had looked at him throughout the years of their married life in the camp.

For a moment he stood motionless, his eyes fixed on her, not knowing what to do or what to say. Lida was holding the hand of a boy of about ten. She released it, stepped toward him, wrapped her arms around him, and was still, her nose buried in his neck. He held her to him, smoothing her hair with his right hand.

Vikenty almost crushed the slim body, remembering the woman who had shared his room in the camp and their love, his parting from his son, and from Lida lying insensible in the rain—after the court had passed sentence, in the village of Medvezhie.

Finally, he looked at the flushed face of the man on the bed and said in embarrassment, "I'm sorry, this is my wife!"

"Yes, of course." The man turned red as a lobster and threw the newspaper onto the floor. "But she's my wife too!"

Abruptly, Lida stepped away and took his hand. Looking at her husband she said, "Vsevolod, it's him! My Vikenty! Let me introduce you. Angarov—my first husband and my friend, and this is Vsevolod Mikhailovich Kunitsyn, my husband."

They shook hands, watching her all the time, as if expecting further instructions about what to do and say.

"Kiss your father!" She pushed Tolik up to Angarov. The boy stared anxiously at the strange man.

"Tolik! My son!" he whispered, kissing the boy's face and looking into his eyes. "You've forgotten me. That doesn't matter. You're a good boy." He lowered him to the floor and looked gratefully at Lida and Kunitsyn.

"Well, men!" She smiled at them radiantly. "Let's go, to the restaurant! We've got a lot to talk about. Vsevolod, get dressed! We'll wait for you in the restaurant, on the fifteenth floor. Let's go!"

Kunitsyn glanced anxiously at the door and began to get dressed. Lida dragged Tolik along, holding him tightly by the hand, while with her other hand she took Vikenty by the elbow, gazing into his face with happy eyes.

In the spacious sparkling restaurant she chose a table near the window, sat Tolik down, and pulled Vikenty after her.

"Where are you going?" he asked, at a loss.

"Onto the balcony!" She pulled him out onto the chilly balcony, slammed the door behind her with her foot and flung her arms around his neck. She covered his face with kisses, whispering through her tears, "My dear one, my best one, my camp friend! Those years together, our room—do you remember? Baked potatoes! Do you remember Riga? Do you remember Medvezhie? Our hut and the sleeping platform, and the stream? It was a whole lifetime for me. A hard and beautiful life. I waited years for you. I went to Krasnoyarsk, I wrote to you, I looked for you, and I waited. But I couldn't get any information about you. I thought I would never see you again. I kept our son and I kept you in my heart, and I kept your manuscripts. Do you remember, how you used to write at night, hiding it from Troshkin? I've brought them. You can take them with you today."

She stopped, embarrassed, and looked him straight in the eye, as if to answer his silent question. "You know, Vik, your money was like a bolt from the blue. Not a word for years and then, all of a sudden . . . "

"But my letter from the hospital?"

"Letter?"

"Yes, a nurse wrote it for me and mailed it to Medvezhie."

She shook her head in silence.

"The pigs!" he said. "Either the nurse never sent it or those blockheads in the village preferred not to bother themselves with our ruined life."

"But I received your lettter from the Black Sea. You knew my address. How?"

"How?" He smiled evasively. "From the best house in Moscow."

She looked bewildered, but kept silent. And then her eyes suddenly filled with tears. She was looking at his arm, where it ended at his wrist.

"Ah, my dear woman!" He kissed her on her wet eyelids and caressed her with his right palm, holding her against him with the stump of his left arm. "Forgive me. What could I have done? That's how life went, away, downhill! . . . I lost my hand in order to survive. I was lucky. And are you happy?"

"Yes! No! I mean, yes, he's a good man. But how could anyone in the world replace you! Come on, they're waiting for us. We'll talk at the table." She pushed the door, without even a glance at the view of Moscow by night, sparkling with a million lights.

Vsevolod Mikhailovich could hardly help smiling, as he watched his wife and her former husband hurrying toward the table.

"Hold your plate, Tolya." He turned his adopted son toward him. "I'll give you some meat." He busily served some roast meat from the big china dish onto the plates, avoiding their happy, embarrassed faces.

"Friends!" Vikenty raised his glass of vodka. "I ask you to drink, to drain your glasses! We have good reason. You, Vsevolod Mikhailovich, drink! All I seem to do these days is meet people and drink! I want to drink to my wife, to Lida, to your wife, to this marvelous woman. You two have been lucky. But I thank you for taking my place with her and with my son. It's bad for a woman to live alone in the world. And to Tolik—may he never experience what we did!"

After the third glass their faces brightened. For the first time that evening, Kunitsyn too began to talk.

"I'm an engineer, you know, a geologist," he said abruptly, leaning forward over his plate. "I'm mostly away every summer, lost in the taiga and tundra. Prospecting. But in winter I take it easy. They gave me a week's leave on account of your arrival and Lida's trip . . . But what do you intend to do?" His anxiety showed in his voice and expression.

Lida said nothing, not looking at them.

"I'm going to sea, from Murmansk," Vikenty answered quietly, then turned to her. "But what about Troshkin? Did you ever see him again?"

"I did!" Her face turned to stone. "On the street in Krasnoyarsk. He ran away from me. I asked Vsevolod to beat his face in, but he doesn't want to."

Kunitsyn gave an embarrassed smile.

"It doesn't matter." Vikenty nodded to her. "I'll be in Krasnoyarsk soon, after my first voyage. He'll get what's coming to him. But what about Svetlana and Pashka Zubov?"

"They really helped me!" She turned pale and lowered her eyes. "They stayed with me a whole month after your arrest, didn't leave the house for a moment. I didn't want to go on living then, you see . . . "

They fell silent.

"How quickly life passes!" She raised her head and looked him in the eye. "We've already been here three days. Waiting for you. He has to get back to work. We're leaving tonight. Will you see us off?"

He nodded without speaking and gave his son a long, yearning look.

Two hours later they were standing on the platform at Yaroslavl Station by the door of the sleeping car of the Yenisei express.

Kunitsyn carried the bags into the train in silence and then came back out and stood facing Angarov. "Say goodbye to your son. I wish you success in life!" He held out his hand. "I'll be glad to see you out our way."

"Thank you!" Vikenty shook his hand, avoiding his eyes, and then Kunitsyn boarded the train again and he hugged Tolya. "You'll do what your mother tells you?"

"I always do!" the boy answered, staring wide-eyed at the mysterious captain, who had appeared so unexpectedly in his life and was now disappearing just as quickly.

"Do you love your daddy?" Vikenty asked, gazing after Vsevolod Mikhailovich.

"Yes, I do." Tolik clung to him, his arms around his neck, and looked into his face.

"Who bought you this gray coat?"

"My dad." The boy reddened and looked hesitatingly up at the train window. "He buys me things but I never ask him."

Vikenty's heart tightened with pity for the boy and for himself. Always somebody else bought things for his sons. "Do you remember a small village in the woods where you lived before you went to Krasnoyarsk?"

"Yes." The boy nodded. "I remember a house, woods, river."

"And who lived in this house?"

"There was an old woman," the boy said, after a long silence.

Let it be so. At least he did not remember the arrest. It was better for him. "Did your mother tell you that you had another father? I am your first father."

"Yes." The boy hardly moved his pale lips. "Mother said. Will you come visit us? Will you come back to me? Where are you going now?"

"I will come back, Tolya, my dear son. You love your mother and your second father. He's a good man. I am a sea captain. I'm going to the North and to the sea. Then I will come back and bring you a big present, and I will write to you and you will write to me."

"Good." The boy smiled, squeezing his sleeve with both hands.

"Off you go!" He lowered his son to the ground. "Your father's waiting for you, and mummy's just coming. And remember me, the old captain. I'll sail down to visit you!"

"Good!" Tolik waved to him from the top of the steps, glanced once more at his face and disappeared.

"My love!" He pressed her face to him. "Goodbye, live and wait, we'll meet again. Be happy. My address is General Delivery, Murmansk."

"Yes. Have a good voyage! I'll look forward to our meeting." She kissed him, oblivious to the people crowding around them, turned and went into the car.

"Another meeting over!" he thought sadly. "Ah, my Lida! Now you belong to somebody else." He glanced at his watch: 9 P.M. Still early. Now what? Should he visit Orlova? Yes, every day was precious.

He strode off, his arms thrust into the pockets of his raincoat, right across the center of the city, in the direction of Kutuzovsky Prospect. Before resuming his voyage into the past he wanted to breathe, to be, in the noise of the street.

He came out onto the Sadovoye ring road. He stopped for a minute on Vosstaniye Square opposite the elegant American Embassy building. "So you're still there, dear warriors against communism?" he whispered aloud. "Do you eat on time? Do you play golf? But you know nothing about what's happening here or why! Well, well! Let the calf catch the wolf! And those celebrities, the representatives of the Red Cross, who innocently murdered ten zeks in the snow at Kolyma simply by going there. Are they here too? Are they making cocktails or are they already back in the States, making money? Go ahead, live, digest your tasty lunches. But you can't turn your backs on our suffering. Because our suffering is not just Russian suffering, it's ours and everyone's. You don't understand that now, but one day you will, when its too late." He cursed, then glanced around: a man in a gray raincoat and cap was standing at a bus stop and watching him closely. Vikenty gave a strained smile and moved on along the dark sidewalk, avoiding the people coming toward him and grinning despite himself at the avalanche of cars rushing toward him on the right side of the highway, toward the Three Stations.

At Smolensk Square he turned right, onto the bridge, without even a glance at the tall building that housed the Ministry of Foreign Affairs. Beyond the bridge, on the right, floated the Ukraina Hotel, looking just like an Egyptian pyramid. Fifteen minutes later he came out of the elevator on the fifteenth floor of the massive building, holding the slip of paper with the address in his hand. He knocked, not noticing the tiny bell-knob. He waited, gazing around the landing, which was painted pale brown and was sparklingly clean. A fluffy carpet covered the whole area. Mats of various colors lay outside each of the four massive doors, which were lined with either black or yellow leather.

The door opened. A gray-haired man of medium height stood in the dimly lit passage, examining the unexpected guest with puzzled eyes. The broad blue stripes of a general showed up on his trousers; the collar of his uniform jacket was unfastened, the big star of an air force major-general gleaming dully on the gold epaulets. His jutting jaw, compressed lips, narrowed eyes, and short gray crew cut gave him the appearance of an ex-boxer.

"Er, excuse me." Vikenty gave the man an embarrassed smile. "Perhaps I've mistaken the address? I'm looking for Orlova, Nadezhda Alekseyevna . . . "

"You're not mistaken." The general opened the door wider, but his expression did not change. "Come in and wait here. I'll call her."

He motioned Vikenty to a chair near a lacquered magazine table and a full-length mirror, then went away. There was a white telephone on the table. The walls and ceiling were papered, and the floor was covered with pale carpets, creating an atmosphere of comfort and quiet.

He did not hear when a side door opened silently and a good-looking woman in her thirties came into the hall. She was dressed in an expensive blue robe, tied at the waist with a gold ribbon. She had a wide blue ribbon in her long golden hair, which flowed down over her shoulders. She wore fluffy white slippers on her unstockinged feet. She stood to one side, her attractive face with its dimpled chin turned toward the guest. She raised her lightly penciled brows. Amazement and joy showed in her eyes.

Feeling her gaze upon him, he got up from the chair. Color rushed to his face. The general gave his wife and the guest a careful look, then went into the other room.

For a few moments they gazed into each other's eyes.

"You! You've come?" She started, as if waking from a trance, stepped toward him and offered her hand. He pressed his lips to her soft white fingers, which smelled of expensive perfume. He released her hand and stared expectantly into her eyes. "Ach!" She gestured with her hand, stepped closer, and pulled him to her. Winding her arms around his neck, she kissed him full on the lips, then stepped away and threw open the door into the spacious, richly furnished living room.

"Come in, Citizen Technical Chief, Vikenty Filippovich, Comrade Captain! You're like the Flying Dutchman—you live forever, unsinkable! Come in! Oh, I'm going to have a real drink today! Sasha!" she called cheerfully. "Come on out, there's no reason to hide. He's one of us!"

The general emerged from a third door, which was covered by a curtain, and shook hands. "Aleksandr Matveyevich Makhotin—pleased to meet you!"

"And I'm very pleased to see you," the guest answered with feeling as he squeezed the general's hand. "Angarov, Vikenty Filippovich."

"That's quite a grip you've got there!" Makhotin wriggled his fingers to loosen them after the handshake.

"That's because I've only got one hand," Vikenty said with a laugh. "The strength of both hands has remained in one."

"Have something to drink!" Makhotin went over to a long, oval, black-laquered table, from which the edges of a thick, beige knitted cloth hung almost to the floor. The curtain covering the doors and windows, the carpets, the luxurious couch, the Riga-work cabinet, the two chandeliers with their myriad glass icicles. It was all rich, simple, in good taste.

"Sit down!" She pulled them both by the sleeve and almost forced them onto the chairs.

"Sasha, you don't need telling. While I set the table . . ."

"I don't need telling!" The general laughed and took a bottle of Armenian brandy and three glasses from the cabinet. He placed them on the table, together with a pack of imported cigarettes. "I have a very clever wife—she understands the mind of the male."

He filled the glasses and turned his heavy face to his guest. "How, if it's not a secret, did you find our address?"

"In the KGB reception office on Kuznetsky Bridge." Vikenty looked Makhotin straight in the eye.

A shadow crossed Makhotin's face. "At the KGB?" he asked, leaning back in his chair and giving his guest a hostile look. "But how can I be of help to you?"

"No, no, Aleksandr Matveyevich." Vikenty shook his head wearily. "It's not that. They let me see my dossier. It has all the addresses—of everyone I've known all these years. I was the technical chief in the camp that Orlov—Aleksandr Andreyevich—commanded. Now, after fifteen years behind the wire, I've received my rehabilitation. Tomorrow I'm going to Murmansk, to take command of a ship. This month has been one visit after another—I'm re-establishing contact with people I had lost."

"I see!" The general laughed in embarrassment. "Then I apologize. I thought it was something else. Did you know Orlov long?" He turned his head toward the kitchen, from which they could hear the sound of crockery. Nadezhda Alekseyevna almost ran into the room and placed on the table a deep dish, made of green crystal, almost overflowing with black pressed caviar, from which two silver spoons projected.

"You don't live badly!" Vikenty could not help smiling as he watched her pour from a cloth bag, straight onto the table, a whole pile of smoked, oily Caspian roach.

"No, we don't, Captain dear." She bent down to his face. "We were always aristocrats and we haven't given up our position."

She went out again, leaving the fragrance of her perfume behind.

"Yes, a long time," Vikenty answered, salivating at the sight of the spread, the like of which he had not seen for many years. "He died in my arms. Did you know him?"

"I should say I did!" A shadow of grief flitted over the general's face. "We served in neighboring divisions in the First World War. He was a lieutenant-colonel and I was just a lieutenant. We almost lived the same life. In the Civil War we fought against the Whites, against our former friends and comrades, against our own class . . . Then he joined the MVD forces and I went into the air force—a bit further away from politics. To tell you the truth, although I've been in the Party all my life, I'm not overly fond of Marxism or Leninism or communism or the Party. Or Stalin, who's an insignificant figure in history. He was simply carried up to the surface by the current . . . Yes, you eat up!" He leaned forward and pushed the whole pile of roach over to Vikenty. He broke one open himself, revealing the layer of red caviar and the succulent salted flesh.

"You do live well!" Vikenty laughed and ate some roach with a sip of brandy. "And look, the spoons are sticking up out of the caviar like masts."

"Not a bad image." Makhotin laughed. "Very vivid. That's my Nadezhda, she's always stirring things up. She can tell good from bad but she's always saying 'These new peasant-princesses shovel down their caviar with table spoons, and we'll do the same. We must keep up!' We don't use the stores, we get everything from the warehouse—delivered to the apartment. If they don't have something at the warehouse, we import it from abroad. So we live quite well—and you can't say that of the rest of them."

Nadezhda Alekseyevna came back and placed on the table plates of meat pies, jellied sterlet, thinly sliced cold salmon, mushrooms in sour cream, a decorated earthenware pot of plain boiled potato, from which steam was rising, thinly sliced herring with spring onions, three plates with cutlets a la Kiev, and several bottles of beer.

"I'm sorry." She glanced joyfully at the men's flushed faces. "Your visit was unexpected, and the ice-box was almost empty. I just put a few things together quickly. Vikenty Filippovich, don't think badly of us because of this modest spread."

She sat down and, with a sly smile, pulled a bottle of Moskovskaya vodka from underneath the table. "This is our vodka, our savior! I'm going to drink vodka, you can please yourselves." Her eyes grew serious. "This evening is in memory of the past. It was dark and cruel but it's our Russian past, when vodka and potatoes adorned our lives."

Frowning, the men each drained a half glass of vodka and began to eat, serving themselves from each of the many plates in turn, spilling sauce onto the tablecloth.

Vikenty broke the silence. "Tell me, Aleksandr Matveyevich, if it's not a secret, how did things turn out for you in the old days?"

"It's very simple." Makhotin wiped his lips with a napkin and lit a cigarette. "Before the war I was already a squadron commander, an instructor—I taught aviation at a school for pilots, just outside Moscow. It shames me to think of those planes, flying bookshelves, they were, and that organization—it was all such a mess . . . I was arrested in nineteen thirty-eight, for telling an anecdote. I can't even remember what it was about. My heart ached for our army, mounted on their horses, with their sabres, while in the west Hitler was preparing his panzer armies. Hitler, you know, knew how to fight a war . . . Yes, and I was sitting behind bars on the Pechora River—I was lucky!"

He paused. Nadezhda Alekseyevna's mood had changed to sadness. She was listening, not looking at the men, thinking her own thoughts. Vikenty waited in silence.

"Did they beat you after you were arrested?" the general asked.

"Yes. And shot at me. But I surfaced."

"Many of our men didn't surface," Makhotin said, shaking his head sadly. "So many experienced pilots died in the camps. So many were shot! Our places were filled by army men—sergeants! In the first months of the war, the German aces shot them down as if it was target practice. So many men died for nothing, until it dawned on Stalin to release the officers who were still alive from the camps . . . So I was lucky. I was in prison for three years, all told. The war got me out. I was wounded a couple of times, in Eastern Prussia. By the end of the war I was commanding a division. And now I work at staff headquarters, in one of the departments . . ."

"At staff headquarters!" Angarov looked at him with respect. "You've come a long way. What's the set-up like there?"

"Complicated!" The general laughed quietly. "Those who've had experience of the camps, and those who've got some brains anyway, who value Russian honor and blood—they're working for something new, for de-Stalinization, but there are plenty of others trying to slow things down—they dream of Stalin and hate Khrushchev. There are two camps, in fact, at staff headquarters and throughout the army: the Stalinists and their opponents. Of course the future is ours, but the way will be difficult and long. We're now doing all we can to ensure that at least the army will take orders only from the Party and to prevent the KGB from ever again coming under the control of one man. The people in the KGB organs really took a beating after Stalin's death. But of course the guilt for their crimes rests not so much with the executives themselves as with our political system. The best thing would have been never to have made this revolution, not to have permitted the establishment of Soviet power. But now it's too late. It's no use putting up your fists when the fight's over."

"I went off to sea after the revolution." Vikenty looked guiltily at his hosts. "I didn't return to Russia until nineteen thirty-one. I don't know what happened here or how."

"But I know very well." The general poured a half glass of vodka down his throat, grimaced, and shoved a piece of roach into his mouth.

"Let's talk about ourselves for a bit!" Nadezhda Alekseyevna laid her hand on her husband's shoulder. "Do you remember, Vikenty Filippovich, the day my Orlov died? I flew off to Moscow that very same day. I lost my head completely. I spent one day in Moscow and went straight back to Krasnoyarsk and buried Aleksandr Andreyevich in the town cemetery. His grave's there in a corner, with an iron fence. There's a headstone on the grave, with a star, just as for a soldier . . . And then back to Moscow again. You can't imagine what it was like here then. The war was at its height. But Beria received me straightaway. And do you know he proposed to me? I was in tears telling him about Orlov and Degtev, and he talked to me about bed. That loathsome, slobbery creature! 'Get Degtev!' I shouted in his face. 'Destroy him! I'll do anything you want!' 'No,' he said, and laughed, 'I can't destroy him. He may be a fool but he's a faithful servant, and it's wartime too—my power is limited for the moment, I'm taking a big risk. But I'll block his career, for your sake . . .' Then the telephone rang, summoning him to Stalin—just in time! If you could have seen his face. He forgot about me immediately."

"Would you really have yielded to him?" Makhotin glanced at his wife with interest.

"To achieve something? Yes, of course!" she exploded. "There have been plenty of examples in history when women saved people or brought about changes by sacrificing their bodies. You men would sell your souls for the sake of your careers. You don't sell your bodies simply because there's no demand for them. The only reason you're always reproaching women for immorality is because it helps you cover up your own sins. Look Sasha!" She stood up and stared him in the eye. "You were a friend of my Orlov. Your wife died of hunger in the siege of Leningrad, and I found you through the personnel office at staff headquarters. I simply wanted to complain, to seek help and sympathy, like a twig lost in the ocean. I didn't love you then, I lived by the memory of my Orlov. You proposed to me at our second meeting, when you were wounded and flew back from the front. I accepted and became your wife. At the time it was policy; love came later. I did the right thing, but to begin with, it was just policy. When Orlov died I lost all I had. But I got that 'all' back. I know this society. I have no other. And I want to live!"

She paused. Then, calmer, and embarrassed at the frankness of her outburst in front of the two men, she looked affectionately at Angarov. "And you, Vikenty Filippovich, I liked you as a human being and as a man, even in the camp. I thought about you when I returned to Moscow after the funeral, but what could I do. I realized that I didn't have the connections to get you released. I couldn't do anything to help. But I was sure that you would find your way out sooner or later. You're strong. Orlov told me a lot about you. And then you disappeared completely. For years it was impossible to find out where you were, where they had hidden you. That's how bad things had become at the MGB before Stalin died. Well, I'm glad that you're here. Drink your vodka!" She leaned across and with a trembling hand poured vodka from the green bottle into the glasses. Aleksandr Matveyevich grimaced and stared into his glass. He felt uncomfortable. Nadya had had a drop too much.

"Stop it, Sasha!" She came up behind him, wrapped her arms around his shoulders, and pressed her face against his short gray hair. She smiled across his head at Vikenty. "You see, I can read my husband's thoughts at a distance. He's ashamed of me today. But surely I taught you society manners, my general!" She shook him as hard as she could.

"All right, I give in!" He slapped her small, firm palm. "You're my commander."

Makhotin was thoroughly drunk and kept giving his wife looks of delight and desire. Vikenty sat in his chair, blissfully happy, eagerly taking in every word, every detail, of the furnishings and crockery and silver, and of the lives of these two people who had managed to resist and to preserve themselves at the top of the social ladder. What an enormous difference between Katya and Lida and this Nadya, a boisterous woman who had grown up in the midst of the new Soviet elite! And perhaps she was right. What else could the weak do but give way to the strong? But wherein lay the strength of the strong? In moral degeneracy?

"More vodka!" Although scarcely able to keep her feet, Nadya refilled the glasses, smiling artfully at the two men, who were completely drunk and were having trouble staying upright in their chairs. "Eat, my generals!"

She drank down another shot of caviar into her mouth, then suddenly she gripped the tablecloth, dropped her face straight onto the table, and began to sob, her whole body shaking.

Makhotin rose unsteadily to his feet. He gripped the back of his chair with one hand and with the other tried to pull his wife away from the table. Then he pushed hard against her shoulders and shifted her back onto the chair.

"Are you . . . strong?" she mumbled, gazing up at her husband with a tear-stained face. "Are you strong too?" She turned to Vikenty, who was sitting as if in a dream, fighting against the vodka roaring in his head. "You're all so strong! You're both noblemen, aren't you? Noblemen? And me too! We're all birds of a feather. We all lost Russia! Why did it happen? Why did you let it happen, eh? You're poor politicians! I know politics but I'm a weak . . . woman. You don't like communists? But they're stronger than you, yes, yes! Forgive me, I'm drunk! How my heart aches! What a vile life!"

"Nadya, really!" Makhotin sobered a little. He stood next to her, looking in confusion now at his drunken wife, now at his guest.

"What-at, Nadya?" She tried to stand, then sat down again. "I've been Nadya . . . all my life. A bad woman. Dissolute. I . . . I simply want to live . . . But I'm surrounded by death all the time."

Catching Makhotin's glance, Vikenty stood up decisively. He almost fell down, then gripped the edge of the table and moved toward Nadya. Together they took her by the arms and laid her on the couch.

"Thank you. I'm sorry, Vikenty . . . Filippovich," she whispered, covering her eyes with her hand. "I'm drunk . . . I love vodka! I'm a Russian peasant and my heart aches. Ach, you're weak, you good people . . . I'm going to sleep . . ."

Makhotin fetched a big gray shawl and threw it over his wife. Then the two men returned to the table. Vikenty poured out more vodka and fixed his inebriated but steady gaze on Makhotin.

"She says we're weak people, Comrade General."

"Yes, weak!" The general threw his jacket over the back of the chair and sat in his thin white shirt. "Once we had lost everything, once they had swept us aside in the struggle for power, we were weak."

The general tipped some more vodka straight down his throat and fixed Vikenty with a somber gaze.

"Well, we two were lucky anyway, my dear Comrade Captain! But it's really all nonsense! She's a clever one, my Nadezhda. I've never seen a cleverer woman! I love her as a wife and as a daughter, or as you will. And I'm not even jealous of Orlov. His portrait's over there, on the wall . . . You wanted to ask me something else, but you won't say what."

Vikenty said nothing and laid his head on his arms. The general squinted at the black sleeves with the gold rings.

"And do you like Khrushchev?" He laughed at the captain's wary look. "I like him! Not just because he released you and tens of millions like you from prison. But because he's shaken up the whole country, the whole world. After Stalin he took our unhappy people in his peasant's hand, his iron paw and . . ."

"I agree!" Vikenty almost shouted. "Because if it hadn't been for him, I wouldn't be sitting here now!"

"Yes, but that's subjective. There's also the fate of the nation. A peasant like him was just what was needed, but he won't be sitting in that seat for very long."

"Why not?"

"He's got a lot of enemies. He's upset the economic interests of the whole privileged class that served Stalin. There are many who won't forgive Nikita for what he has done."

"Are you thinking of that already?" Vikenty looked at him in fear.

"Yes! Rubbish!" Makhotin waved his hand vaguely. "I know him and all the rest of them. He's flesh of the flesh of Stalinism. With one hand he destroys the vestiges of Stalinism, with the other he establishes his own personality cult. You understand!" He leaned across the table toward Vikenty. "It all happens quite naturally. He can't do anything different. But we have ahead of us a whole era in which there'll be a return to normal life after the past forty years of darkness."

"I'm sorry, Aleksandr Matveyevich, but didn't you ever think of emigrating? I mean back then, in the old times?"

"I did! Who didn't think about it? But we were swept along by events. And I didn't trust the West much either. And later, after the revolution, I stayed in the army—for good. I knew what it was all about then. You know, Vikenty Filippovich, we Russians are sentimental by nature. That's why we lost to all these economists and Marxists. They were more firmly grounded in reality than we were! Everything that we of the old ruling class did and everything that the West did for us—it was all stupidity and mistakes! It brought the Bolsheviks to power. It was like a game of chess with three main players: the Whites—the emigration; the Reds—the victors; and the people—on whose backs it was all taking place. All the players got their desserts. The Reds all died at Stalin's hands; the Whites emigrated and vanished into the economic belly of the West. And the people . . . well, our people, as always, suffered most of all. Tens of millions! A fifth of the population sacrificed!"

"Does that mean, Aleksandr Matveyevich, that the Russian emigration suffered least of all?" Vikenty looked the general in the eye, completely sobered by the conversation, which had seized at his heart.

"It does." Makhotin smiled, glancing quickly at the shapely blue figure of his wife sleeping on the blue couch. "Of course, it's no sweet life for a Russian abroad, with his innate sentimentality. But it's better than dying in a camp, even though they can't escape the blame for the loss of Russia to the communists. Although I'm not sure that all of them over there understand that. Do you want to sleep?" His guest was leaning back in his chair, his eyes closed.

Vikenty shook himself. "No, it's just that all the visiting and talking these past few weeks has tired me a little. It's terrible! I feel as if I'm walking along a beach after a storm and it's covered with the wreckage of ships and people dying, and every one of them is telling me about the storm and the sinking of his own ship. I'm tired, I don't mind telling you. I ought to leave for Murmansk soon. I haven't been to sea for almost seventeen years. Well . . ."

"I understand!" Makhotin nodded and poured vodka into the glasses. "But you're very strong all the same—you can certainly drink!"

"It's almost morning," Vikenty said as he struggled out from behind the table.

"Where are you off to?" the general asked in surprise. "You should get some sleep. We have three rooms."

"Ah, no." Vikenty shook his head stubbornly. "Please excuse me. I'm grateful, of course, Aleksandr Matveyevich, especially for the meal and your hospitality, and for our talk . . . But now I have one more visit to make, while it's still dark and there are no people about."

"You . . . have you . . . have you had too much?" The general gazed anxiously at his guest. "You are still going to visit someone? Tonight?"

"Yes, tonight!" He strode decisively into the passage, took his raincoat from the hanger, and pulled it on. "I've been waiting for this meeting almost all my life. I'm talking about Stalin. I want to visit his grave and spit on it." He swayed and gripped the door handle.

"Just a minute!" Makhotin went back into the living room. He caught up with Vikenty on the staircase. "I'll help you, I have a car. And then I'll take you to the airport. I'll get you a flight straightaway."

Vikenty agreed without saying anything.

They had reached the courtyard, which was covered over with leafy treetops and shut in on all four sides by multi-story apartment buildings. Makhotin got into the ancient Moskvich standing by the entrance and opened the door for Vikenty. They drove in silence across predawn Moscow. The dark, sleeping houses looked onto the empty streets with their hundreds of silent windows.

"Just like Pompeii!" the general muttered.

Vikenty nodded.

"Where to? Where shall I stop?"

"There, near GUM. Don't you get out." He climbed out of the car at the corner, opposite St. Basil's Cathedral, and set off across the empty square toward the mausoleum.

"Amazing fellow!" Makhotin thought. He watched from the car as the tall black figure walked toward the Kremlin wall. His regular steps on the cobblestones echoed all around Red Square. In the distance, near the Museum of the Revolution, he could see a few couples. At the entrance to the mausoleum, like two statues, he could make out the dark shapes of the guards. Almost hidden behind the firs, two men in gray raincoats and caps were sitting on a bench right under the wall. They were paying close attention to the car that had stopped across the square and to the man striding toward the mausoleum.

A few minutes later two other men stopped near the car; one of them bent down to the window and touched the brim of his hat. "Excuse me, Citizen, may I see your papers?"

Makhotin nodded and offered the man his red general's identity book.

"I'm sorry!" The man stepped back and saluted again. "But, Comrade General, this is unusual. What are you doing here? And why aren't you in uniform?"

"Not in uniform?" Makhotin answered coldly but politely. "Because it's the middle of the night and I'm not at work. I'm waiting here because I gave a lift to a sailor acquaintance of mine who's leaving in the morning for Murmansk, to join his ship, and who wants to pay his respects at the mausoleum of Vladimir Ilich."

"I see," the man said. "Well, in that case, I beg your pardon." The two men went away.

Meanwhile Vikenty had crossed the square and had stopped near the mausoleum. He stood for a minute, his head on one side, watching the stone figures of the guards. He remembered his visit to this place in '47, after he had left the camp, and his brief conversation with the two MGB men. Stalin had still been alive then, and the sword of Damocles had been hanging over Angarov. Now all the roles were changed. His legs were trembling. As he had crossed the square, alone, with nothing but the sound of his own footsteps, he had been imagining that he was going to the scaffold. Yet it seemed to him also that he was traveling the path he had dreamed about—to see the remains of the man on whom he had not been able to spit while he was living. But what was the sense in spitting on his remains?

He clenched his moist palm and compressed his lips. His head was roaring after the seven hours of drinking. He went up, toward the wall, and stood in front of the mausoleum. As if turned to stone, but swaying on his feet, he gazed at the huge marble coffin. Fear gripped his heart. "What am I doing?" He tried to pull himself together. "I've lost my nerve in front of the idol! It's only stone and inside there's just a dead body. The worms will have it! Just as the worms have eaten my Katya. What, Soso, did you want to be immortal like your teacher? And they buried you near him? It's true you didn't leave instructions in your will that you were to be laid to rest beside him. You died very modestly, Soso. Why did you ever leave Georgia? Do you know what you did on earth? Have you counted up those souls, their bodies, the oceans of blood and tears? All my life, all the time you were torturing me, I dreamed of spitting on your grave. I'm standing here, over your bones. I turned out to be stronger than you!"

As he stood by the memorial, leaning forward, tears rolled from his eyes, tears of suppressed rage, of hatred, of pity for the others and for himself. He wept at the hopelessness of his dream—he was too late!

"We ought to get him away from there," whispered one of the men in gray, behind a fir tree. "He might have something in his pockets."

"Wait," his companion whispered, holding his pistol ready. "There's plenty of time. Look, he's taken his hands out of his pockets."

Vikenty removed his right hand from the pocket of his black raincoat and pressed it to his face. He stood motionless for several minutes, then turned away and sat down on a bench, wiping his eyes with his sleeve. Then he bent double, buried his face on his knees, and took his head in his hand and the stump of his arm. His shoulders shook.

One of the men nudged the other in the side. "Do you know something, he's crying. Crying at the mausoleum! What a people! Didn't they take enough of a beating!"

They put away their guns and stared through the dawn twilight, trying to make out his face. After a minute the black figure rose and, with head lowered, made its way slowly across the square, toward GUM, where the little Moskvich was standing at the corner.

The car door swung open for him. Stumbling on the cobblestones like a drunk, Vikenty got in, collapsed on the rear seat, and closed his eyes.

"Did you spit on him?" The general broke the silence, staring straight ahead through the windshield.

"No!"

Makhotin said nothing.

"I couldn't. It's only a corpse behind the wall. And I couldn't. For the first time in my life I couldn't do what I wanted to do, something easy . . ."

"Oh, no, it's not easy," Makhotin sighed as he switched on the ignition. "It would be easy for a weak person to spit, even on himself. But it's hard for a strong person to spit on somebody's remains. It would be a sign of weakness."

"You may be right," Vikenty muttered. "Damn! Even dead he was inaccessible to me."

"He was accessible to you all his life, because you understood him. Well, let's go or else they'll be back and cause trouble. I'll get you to the airport now. Have you many things?"

"What things?" Vikenty calmly spread his hand. "I travel light. They're all in this bag. Are you going to get some sleep after the airport? You're tired. I'm sorry for ruining your night."

"Ruining it?" The general smiled as he drove off toward the Moscow River, on the way to Vnukovo. "It's been a marvelous night. Pushkin would have been envious! Not to mention my colleagues. It's a pity you didn't say goodbye to Nadya."

"I'll be in Moscow again. I'll drop by."

"I hope so. I'll see you off, rush home, get into my uniform and go straight off to headquarters. I have a Party meeting at eleven."

"A Party meeting? How can you?"

"You know what they say, my dear Vikenty Filippovich? If you want to live, you bend with the wind. And you'll crawl through the eye of a needle in order to live. I'm even the Party organizer in my department!"

"I'll be damned!" Vikenty said, almost with delight. "You're to be envied. And the minister had to persuade me just to become a candidate . . ."

"I'll tell you the truth: they're just nursing you along. If I weren't Party organizer, somebody else would be. He'd be sitting on my neck and pushing his despicable policies behind a screen of fine talk. Then it would be harder for me to bear. There are many people like me, very many: communists, yes—in form, but Russians at heart; educated, experienced people, dedicated people. And Russia's future belongs to us. We are the only force that is really changing this monstrous system. It can't be changed from outside, from abroad. People outside simply don't understand what they're dealing with. But we know and we are on the inside, at the heart of things. And we will succeed. So that blood will never again be shed. So that Russia will never go hungry. So that Russians will be able to travel freely throughout the world and not have to sit behind the fence. The time is coming, my dear Captain."

He turned sharply to the right, onto Leninsky Prospect, and accelerated. The city was already awakening. In the distance, solitary pedestrians were hurrying along the sidewalks.

"I'm very glad to have met you," Vikenty said from the rear seat in a contented sleepy voice. The car sped along the highway, which was hemmed in on both sides by the forest. "This night has been special for me. I've never heard such talk from anyone. It means more to me than spitting on his grave."

"I didn't think you would spit. You need to hit a living enemy, not a dead one. And you did hit him, you and the others like you. Obliquely. He knew about the millions like you. And it didn't help to prolong his life. . . . The next turning's Vnukovo. I'll get you a ticket in ten minutes. You'll be in Murmansk in two or three hours. And as you sailors say, the wind's set fair."

"I've been traveling around offices for a month." Vikenty smiled wearily to himself as he gazed out of the huge window that took up the whole of the wall in the spacious office of Tsybin, the head of the Murmansk fishing fleet. All offices were different in their shape, color, furnishings, but they had something in common. What was it? The occupant, who always regarded his visitor with eyes that were condescending-hostile, friendly-tired, inquiring-indifferent. Ponomarev had been condescending-hostile! Even the occupant of such an office as this had no right to greet any visitor with just one expression. A combination of any two constituted the minimum of administrative tact, without which no occupant of an office could remain for the prescribed period.

Vikenty glanced at Tsybin, who was talking with somebody on the telephone. He was short and fair-haired, his face tanned by wind and salt water. And the black uniform suited him. But his build was somehow unusual in a native of the White Sea region.

The office was oval-shaped; the greenish carpet resembled the color of sea water; the walls were covered with huge maps—Europe, the world, the Arctic, the USSR, a detailed map of the Northern Basin and the Murmansk harbor waters. This map had tiny models of the ships of the fishing fleet from Novaya Zemlya to the Bay of Biscay. Outside the window the day was gray and rainy; squalls of rain lashed against the glass. The town beyond the window looked strange to him, because he had flown in only two hours earlier, and yet he felt at home. He had grown accustomed to the north. There was something familiar, something of home in the cold rain, in the wet disheveled town, the small hills with the tiny houses squeezed along the sides of the bay, in the dozens of boats of all sizes moored at the piers or standing in the roadstead, flying the flags of countries from all over the world. Somewhere among these boats, the large factory ship, *Alma Ata,* was awaiting him—his new home. The floating fish-factory carried a crew of a hundred and about five hundred workers, of whom some four hundred were women. A complicated collective!

"I'm sorry, Comrade Captain." He replaced the receiver and turned his very pale blue eyes on his visitor. "They give me no rest. It's the fishing season. Big business! But there's no need to tell you that. You had just as much bother in Archangel. Yes," he added, seeing his visitor's face darken, "I understand! You will forgive me, but we sailors are straightforward people and we must understand each other. This is my point: you'll go to sea, you'll get over the past, you'll get tired, other things will come up; perhaps you may even want to join the head office as my deputy."

"Thank you, Kuzma Stepanovich." Vikenty smiled despite himself at the directness of his colleague and new chief. "But I think this time my career will be limited to the captain's bridge. If I have to abandon it, I'll go ashore for good."

Tsybin smiled. "I'm giving you my biggest factory. I commanded it for six years before they dragged me into this office. It's a good ship, although it's old. You'll make up your own mind about it. We've made everything ready for your arrival. You'll get the keys of your apartment in the officers' building from administration and supply, one floor down. It's even been furnished. They called me just now from the harbor master's office. You sail at three in the afternoon. The captain of the *Alma-Ata* is waiting for you so that he can hand over the ship. He's being transferred to the Odessa Steam Navigation Authority, in warmer parts. And you'll get one or two other things in the first department of the authority—

they'll explain it all to you. I hope to see you soon!"

Tsybin came out from behind the desk with a friendly smile and showed his visitor to the door.

Next door, in the first department, Vikenty signed the necessary forms and received a revolver, a code book, and some foreign currency in a small strong box—dollars and pounds. He descended the broad wooden staircase, which was darkened with age, glanced gratefully at the windows of the fishing fleet authority, and climbed into the waiting official car.

Unlike Archangel, the streets here were not made of wood but were paved with stone and sometimes even asphalted. And there were more stone houses; geography made a difference.

At the gates he showed his pass and entered the harbor area, enjoying the odors of salted fish, water, tackle . . . On the waterfront the hulls of the ships rose up as black walls, and above them stretched the goose necks of the cranes, moving ceaselessly between hold and pier, loading or unloading boxes, bales, machinery.

He strode the harbor, jumping over coils of rope, walking around stacks of boxes ready for loading, piles of metal, machinery, avoiding the people scurrying in all directions, the trucks and trolleys; he heard the good-natured cursing of the stevedores and the shouts of "haul away" as he hurried along. It was as if he was trying to make up in a few minutes the lost seventeen years.

He went up the main gangway and stepped on board his *Alma-Ata*. He nodded to the seaman on watch at the gangway, climbed up to the spar deck, and knocked on the door of the captain's cabin.

The captain was a stout, elderly man with dark eyes and a gentle look: well-fed and tranquil. Somewhere in the depths of his heart, Vikenty felt a stab of pain for the past; this man was one of those who had not spent their years in prison, but who had been at sea, serving the regime and their own interests. They greeted each other drily. The cabin was well appointed with carpets, polished furniture screwed down to the deck, and pictures on the bulkheads. The tables were covered with papers, documents, receipts.

"Shall we begin, Comrade Angarov?" The captain sat down at the table and laid his plump hand on a pile of papers. "There's a lot to do—we might not be finished before you sail."

"Thank you, Comrade Sklovsky," Vikenty answered, gazing through the big round bull's-eye at the forward deck. "Let's not waste time. I've already prepared a paper—read it." He passed a white sheet of paper to the captain. "If you've no objection, we'll sign it and that will be that. I don't want to start digging around in these papers."

Sklovsky gave the new captain a puzzled look and read aloud: "Deed of transfer and acceptance. It is hereby confirmed that this day, seventeen October, nineteen fifty-four, I, I.S. Sklovsky, captain of the factory ship *Alma-Ata,* handed over my vessel to Captain V.F. Angarov in full sea-going order, having on board the quantities of water, fuel, and food prescribed for the forthcoming voyage, and equipment and packaging for the factory. I also confirm that the vessel is fully manned in accordance with the manning-table and the qualifications of the officers and men are sufficient to ensure the successful completion of the voyage. It is also confirmed hereby that a detailed examination of the papers was not carried out, since the vessel was about to sail. Handed over by Captain Sklovsky, accepted by Captain Angarov. Port of Murmansk, seventeen October, nineteen fifty-four."

"It's odd!" Sklovsky turned the white paper over in his hands. "I've been going to sea for many years now, but I've never met with anything like this before. All the papers should be checked carefully, so that there won't be any claims, so that I won't be held responsible . . . ."

"Yes." Angarov nodded, restraining his hostility with an effort. "Some other time. I hope that this document states the true position. Or are there any serious discrepancies?"

"What do you mean?" Sklovsky flushed. "What do you take me for? I'll report all this to the authority!"

"What will you report?" He turned abruptly to face Sklovsky. "There have already been enough reports about me in the past twenty years. There is no need for you to join that dirty company. If everything in this paper is true, let's sign it and say goodbye. I need every minute."

"All right. But if we don't check and something goes wrong, you'll be the one to suffer." Sklovsky shrugged, scrawled his signature, pulled on a leather coat and a cap with the crab emblem, and made for the door without saying goodbye.

"Comrade Sklovsky!" Vikenty was standing in the middle of the cabin. "We're still sailors. A drink! There's no need to lose your temper. We all have our own way of doing things."

"Yes . . ." Sklovsky gave a confused smile and flushed, then sat down irresolutely on the edge of the bunk. "I'm not against . . ."

"Please!" Angarov took an opened bottle of brandy from the table and poured out two glasses. "Here, Comrade Captain, let's drink to our sailors' code and to each other's success!"

Sklovsky drank the brandy, stood up without a word, gave the new occupant of the cabin a quick astonished look, and went out, closing the door behind him.

Angarov found the crew list, glanced through it and picked up the telephone. "Is that the first mate? Please come to my cabin."

"How do you do, Yevgeny Ivanovich," he said a minute later, greeting a tall, solidly built young officer. "Sit down. I have a few requests to make of you. Please take all these papers and sort them out—get the second and third mates to help you if necessary—and tell me whether they correspond with this deed of transfer and acceptance."

"But Vikenty Filippovich . . ." the first mate began, reddening slightly.

"How do you know my name?"

"From . . . people . . . I found out at the authority. How did you know mine?"

"I looked at the crew list. It's simpler."

They both laughed.

"The thing is, Comrade Captain," the first mate said seriously, "most of these papers I've never seen before. Captain Sklovsky used to take care of such matters himself."

Angarov nodded. "I understand. I'll give you three days to get it done. How are the preparations for the voyage coming along? We sail in two hours. The men? The customs inspection? Have the authorities been requested to complete the formalities for sailing?"

"Yes, it's all done, more or less," the first mate answered.

"Why 'more or less'?" Angarov was sitting at the table, watching the first mate just as a school principal might regard a senior student who didn't yet know his capabilities and duties.

"Well, you see . . ." He shrugged. "I've never done anything on my own accord, without Sklovsky telling me. It was always 'what if you do something wrong?'"

"It can't be helped. We all have our own ways. Prepare the vessel for sailing, completely. Don't do it all yourself—let all the officers help. You're the master of the ship! You'll take charge of casting off and putting to sea yourself."

"Me?" The first mate stood up, unable to conceal his amazement.

"Yes. Now please excuse me, I'm tired," Angarov answered drily.

From the bridge, the crowd that had come to see the ship sail showed up as a black mass. A drizzly rain was falling as the main gangway was removed. A brass band was playing on the pier, but the sound of the music was quickly drowned in the gusts of wind. Other vessels were moored ahead and astern of the *Alma-Ata* and a force-5 wind was blowing from the beam. Angarov was standing right at the end of the bridge; he was wearing fur-lined black oilskins with the hood pulled up over the cap with the crab emblem. He was watching the first mate, who was pacing nervously to and fro from the wheelhouse to the end of the bridge, waiting for the order to cast off.

"Go ahead, Yevgeny Ivanovich!" Angarov gestured to him.

The first mate picked up the loud hailer, and his voice sounded over the pier. "On the tug: take the lines! Aft: cast off breast, cast off stern line! Leave the spring!"

Somewhere in the stern a winch began to rumble, hauling in the manila hawsers with which the ship had been moored to the bollards on the pier. Held by the bow lines and the spring line on the stern, the ship began to move out, stern first, the steel cable stretched taut like a violin string from the stern to the tug. The water foamed in a raging stream from under the tug's screw.

The band struck up again, louder this time; the people in the crowd on the pier shouted, wept, waved their hands and handkerchiefs. Each of them had a dear one or a friend who was going away to sea on a long trip. And each member of the crew was being seen off by someone on the pier. Everyone except the captain.

The ship had swung out, its stern toward the bay and its bow almost at right angles to the pier.

"Cast off forward!" The first mate ordered, with greater assurance now. He went to the wheelhouse and took hold of the handle of the siren. The long, hollow, farewell blast of the siren echoed over the bay. Short blasts from the vessels standing in the harbor rang out in reply. The crowd on the quay was quickly dispersing. The tug cast off the lines, hooted farewell, and returned to harbor at full speed.

"Half ahead!" The first mate, trying hard not to smile, pushed forward the lever of the ship's telegraph and went over to the captain, who was standing motionless. "I didn't do anything wrong, Comrade Captain?"

"You're the first mate," Angarov answered quietly. "You're not entitled to do any of these things wrong. You cast off correctly—no mistakes!"

They fell silent. The harbor and the vessels in the roadstead had been left behind. The ship had come out into the open sea. A lead-gray sky hung over the water. An east wind, force-7, was driving a heavy swell topped with whitecaps toward the west. Pitching gently, the factory ship was sailing on a course of 330°, north westward, toward the Norwegian coast.

The two men stood at the starboard end of the bridge: the young navigation officer in a black parka and the old captain in his black oilskins.

"Full ahead!" the captain said quietly. The mate moved the handle of the telegraph. The ship shuddered slightly and picked up speed, leaving an even stream of foam astern. To port, the rocky coastline of the Kolsky Peninsula floated past through the shroud of rain and mist.

"The wind's making me cry!" The captain glanced at the mate and quickly wiped away a tear with his sleeve.

"Not me!" the mate gave his new chief a curious look.

"That's because our eyes are different," the captain answered, half joking. "For example, tell me what color the sky is just now?"

"What kind of question is that, Vikenty Filippovich?" The mate was puzzled. "It's gray, rainy."

"It is for you," the captain said quietly, "but for me it's blue."

"I don't understand. Is it some kind of joke, Comrade Captain?"

"In your place I wouldn't understand the joke either. This sky appears blue only to people with my sight. I have three-dimensional sight."

"I've never heard of such a thing." The mate looked at the captain in disbelief.

"People have such sight who can see vertically, many years ahead and into the past."

"Do you suppose that I could ever have such sight?"

"You could. Anyone can. But I hope to God you never do!"

They both fell silent, listening to the whistle of the wind and the rhythmical shudder of the deck.

GLOSSARY

Bironovshchina: The oppressive regime of E.I. Biron, a German nobleman and favorite of the Russian Empress Anna Ioannovna (reigned 1730–40).

Budenny: Commander of the Soviet cavalry, famous for his role in the Civil War and for his large moustache.

Cheka: Abbreviation of the All-Russian Extraordinary Commission for the Suppression of Counter-Revolution, Sabotage and Speculation, the police force established by the Bolsheviks in 1917.

CPSU: The Communist Party of the Soviet Union.

Duma: The Russian parliament before the October Revolution of 1917.

Four Portraits: Of Marx, Engels, Lenin, and Stalin.

GPU: Glavnoye Politicheskoye Upravleniye, the Chief Political Administration, successor of the Cheka.

Gulag: The Central Camps Authority.

GUM: State Department Store in Moscow, biggest in the Soviet Union.

KGB: Committee for State Security; replaced MGB in the Khrushchev era.

Kharcho: A Caucasian soup, made with spices, lamb, and rice.

Kolkhoz: A collective farm, more independent than the sovkhoz, or state farm.

Komsomol: Young Communist League, for those aged fourteen to twenty-six.

Kontra: Abbreviation of Kontrrevolyutsioner, or counter-revolutionary.

Kraslag: The Krasnoyarsk Camps Authority, a division of the Gulag.

Kuzbass: The second largest coal basin in the U.S.S.R. (in southwestern Siberia).

Lubyanka: Moscow headquarters of the Soviet secret police.

MGB: Ministry for State Security, the Soviet political police during the later years of the Stalin era.

Muzhik: A peasant; also prison slang applied to those who break with the thieves' tradition by working and to others outside the thieves' elite.

MVD: Ministry of Internal Affairs, the arm of the Soviet police that handles non-political crimes.

Narzan: Famous Caucasian mineral water.

NKVD: People's Commissariat for International Affairs; Soviet police force prior to World War II; during the war it was divided into the MGB and MVD.

Oprichnina: Ivan the Terrible's secret police.

Pioneers: The Communist League for children aged nine to fourteen.

Putilov Plant: A heavy machine factory in Petrograd (later Leningrad) and center of workers who supported the Bolshevik Revolution.

Red Tabs: Slang for NKVD troops, who wore red epaulets.

Sovkhoz: State farm.

Taganka: A Moscow neighborhood.

Taiga: The Siberian forest.

Three Knights: Vasnetsov's well-known painting of three heroes of Russian folklore: Ilya Muromets, Dobrynya Nikitich, and Olesha Popovich.

Troikas: Three-member security police tribunals during Stalin's purges.

Vertinsky: Russian emigré singer.

The author, Victor Muravin, belongs to the first generation of Russians to have been brought up entirely under Stalinism. A native of Vladivostok, he spent nine years as a seaman in the Soviet Pacific and Arctic. Denied a visa to sail abroad, he gave up the sea, working first as a stevedore and later as a teacher of English and of American studies. He became an associate professor and head of his department at a Siberian college and published two widely used textbooks of English.

Muravin was forced to abandon his country for political reasons. He sought but was refused asylum at two foreign embassies, which resulted in a lengthy interrogation by the KGB. Granted an exit visa in the early seventies, as a kind of exile, he came to the United States, where he now works as a translator while waiting to return to sea.

The illustrator, Ernst Neizvestny, is one of the Soviet Union's foremost visual artists. Best known in the West for his confrontation with Nikita Khrushchev over the validity of abstract art, Neizvestny emigrated to America in 1976 after finding it increasingly difficult to pursue his artistic goals in his own country. He now lives and works in New York City.